HOLLIDAY

AN ONI PRESS PUBLICATION

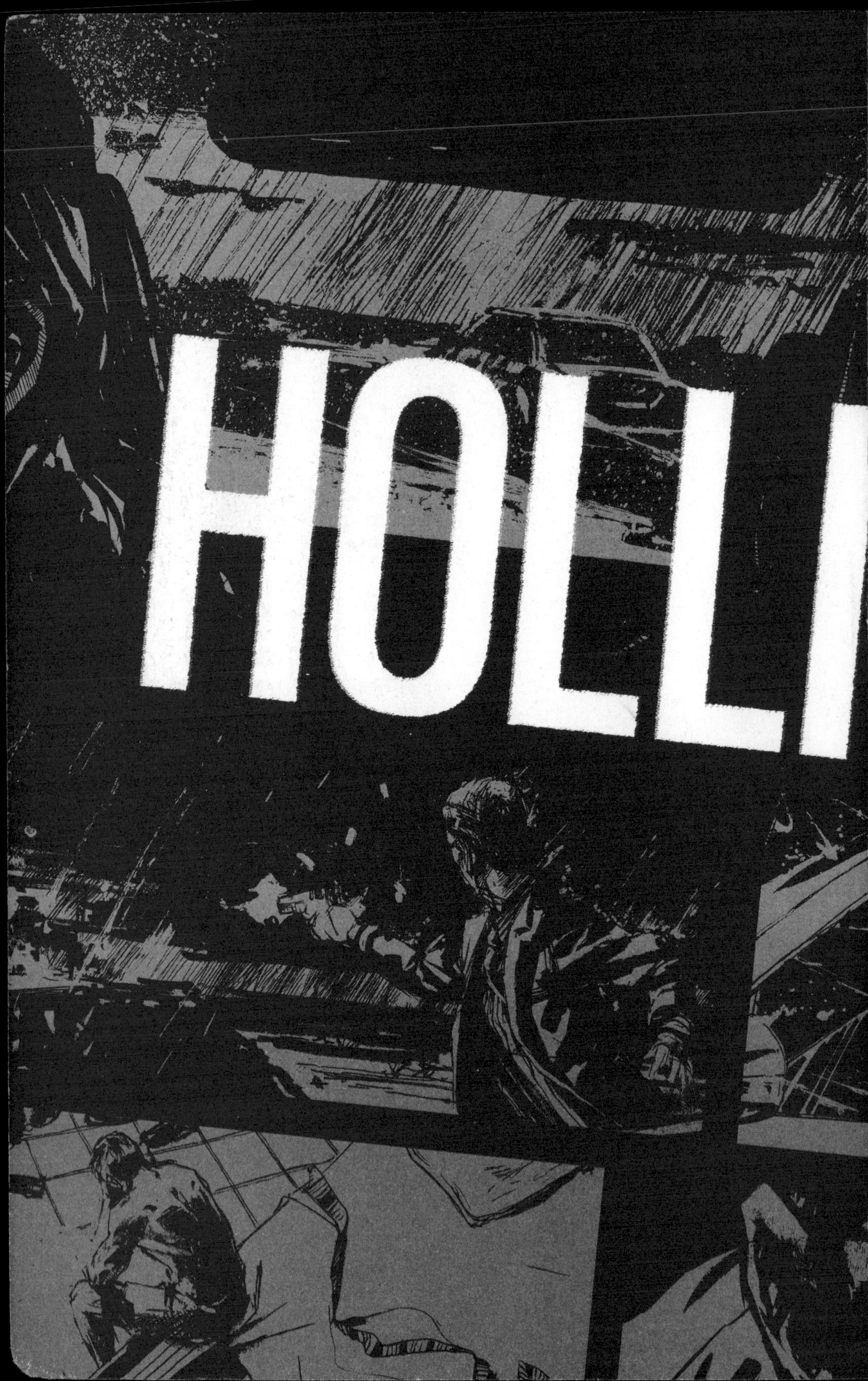
HOLLI

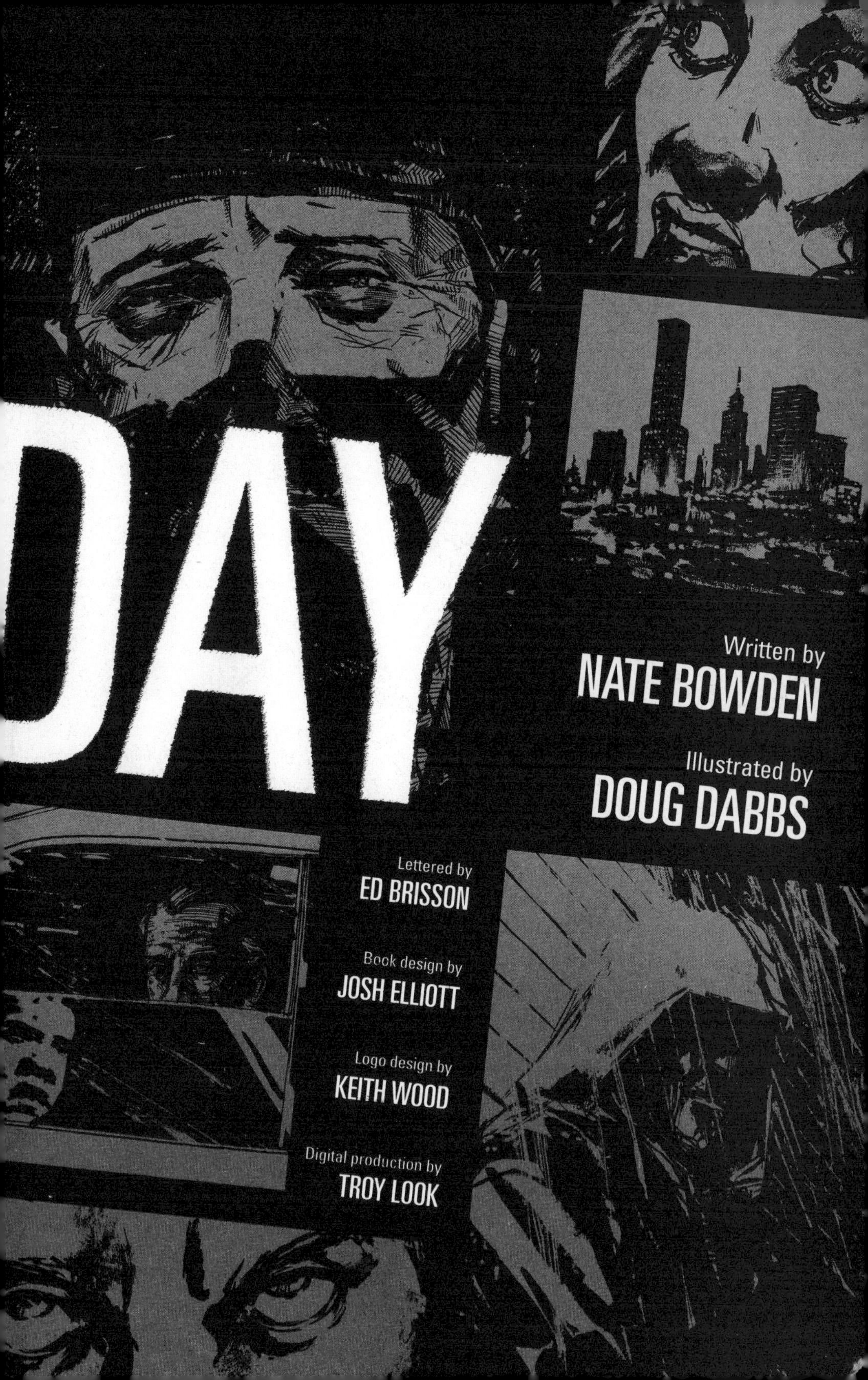

DAY

Written by
NATE BOWDEN

Illustrated by
DOUG DABBS

Lettered by
ED BRISSON

Book design by
JOSH ELLIOTT

Logo design by
KEITH WOOD

Digital production by
TROY LOOK

Published by Oni Press, Inc.
Joe Nozemack, publisher
James Lucas Jones, editor in chief
Cory Casoni, marketing director
Keith Wood, art director
George Rohac, operations director
Jill Beaton, editor
Charlie Chu, editor
Troy Look, digital prepress lead

ONI PRESS, INC.
1305 SE Martin Luther King Jr. Blvd.
Suite A
Portland, OR 97214
USA

www.onipress.com

10 9 8 7 6 5 4 3 2 1

PRINTED IN U.S.A.

First Edition: May 2012
ISBN: 978-1-934964-65-1

Library of Congress Control Number: 2012930367

Although obviously re-imagined for
the modern era, Holliday is true to the
events leading up to October of 1881
and after. Doc is often characterized
as the faithful sidekick to Wyatt
Earp and while the climax certainly
revolves around the lawman, what's
fascinated me is just how much of a
catalyst Holliday was to history. I've
attempted to capture truth in lieu of
sensationalism and let that history
provide the drama.

–NATE BOWDEN

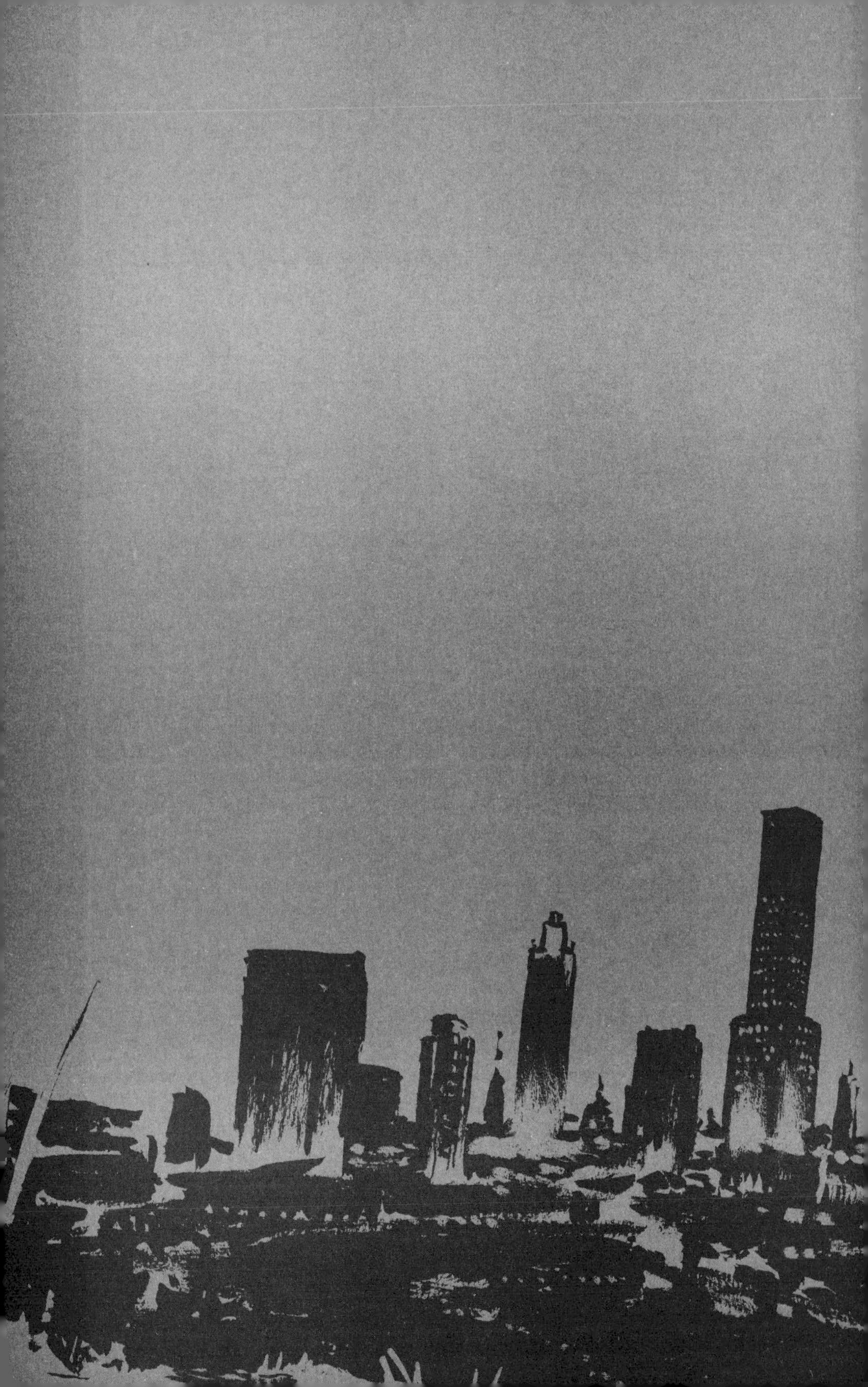

Savannah College of Art and Design

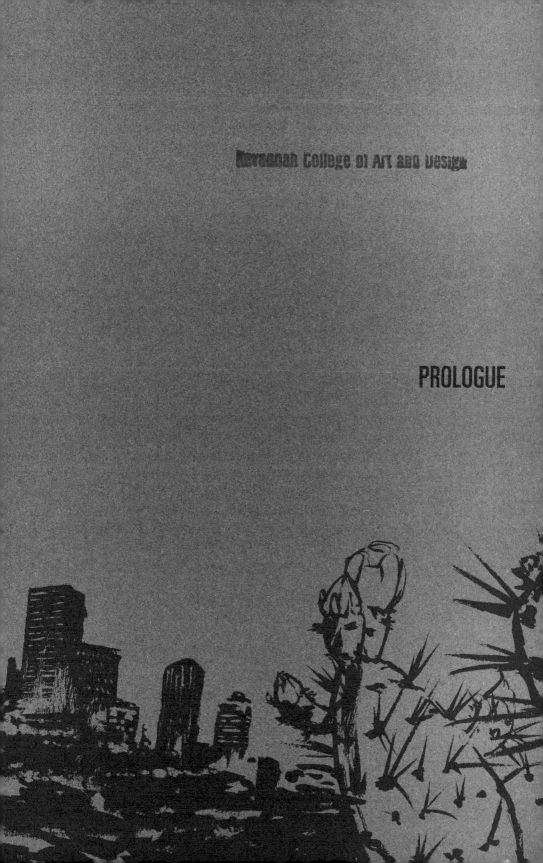

PROLOGUE

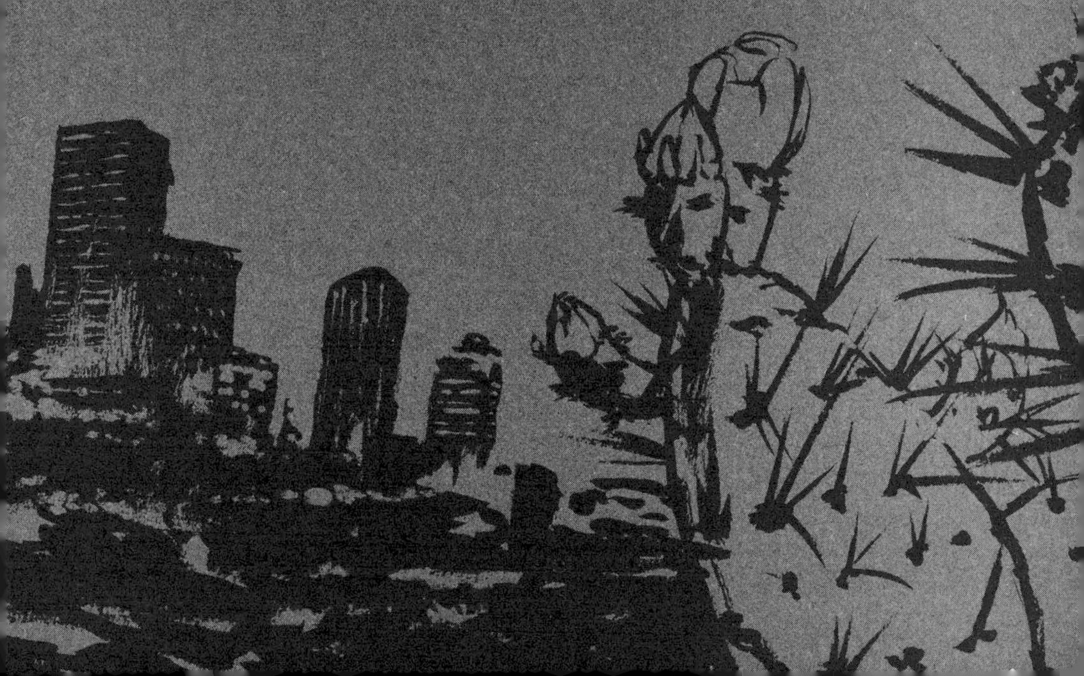

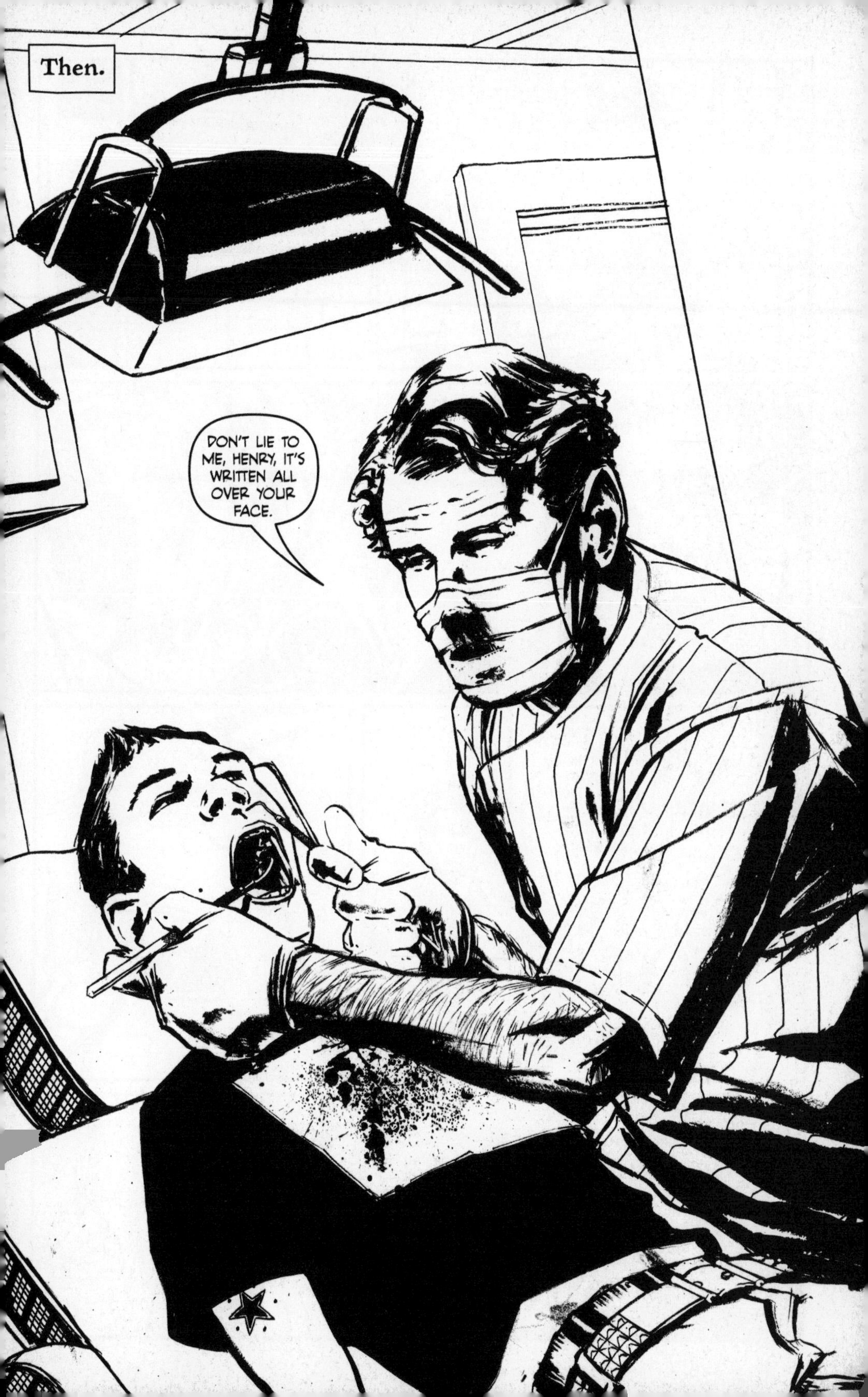
Then.
DON'T LIE TO ME, HENRY, IT'S WRITTEN ALL OVER YOUR FACE.

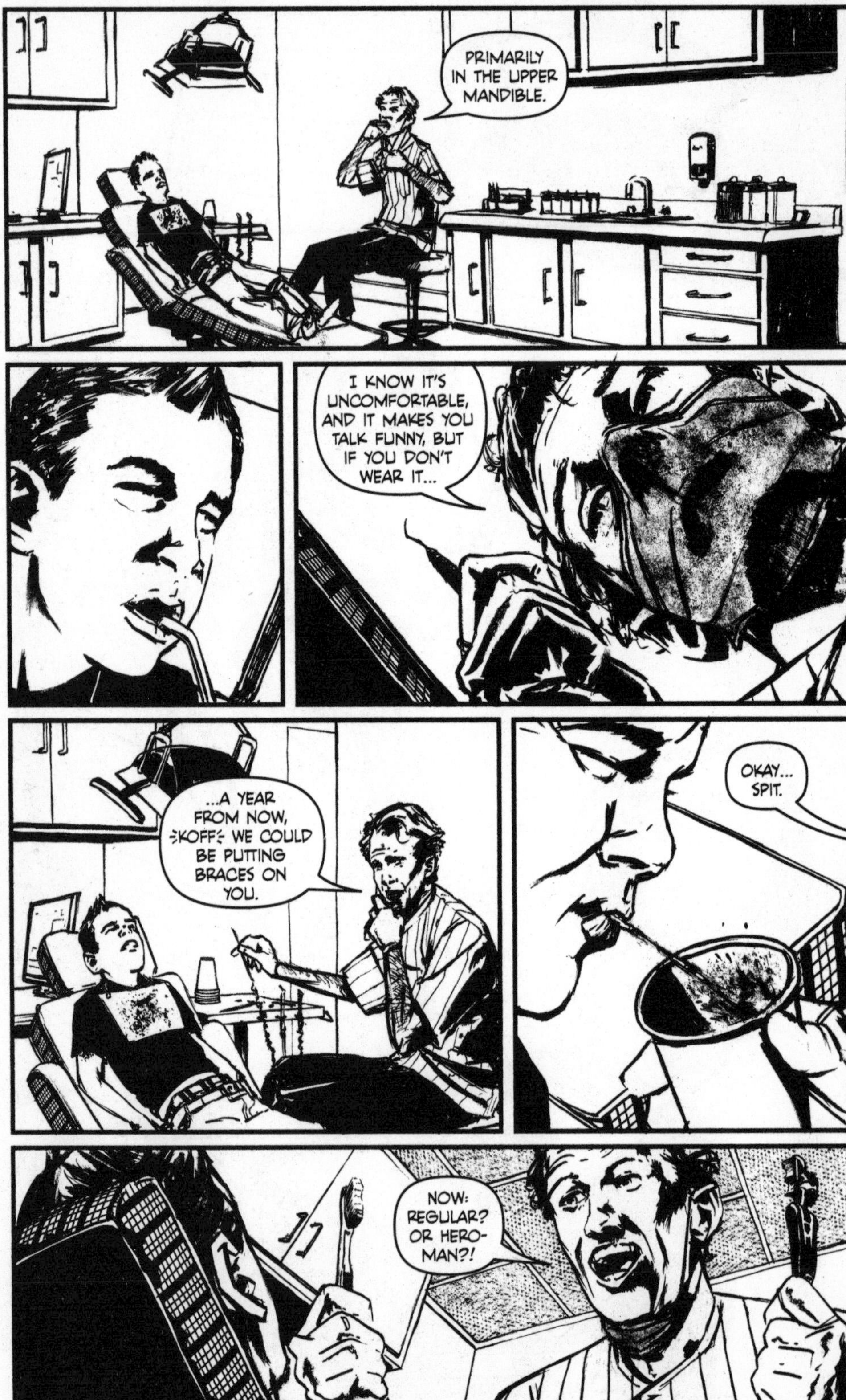
PRIMARILY IN THE UPPER MANDIBLE.
I KNOW IT'S UNCOMFORTABLE, AND IT MAKES YOU TALK FUNNY, BUT IF YOU DON'T WEAR IT...
...A YEAR FROM NOW, ⁼KOFF⁼ WE COULD BE PUTTING BRACES ON YOU.
OKAY... SPIT.
NOW: REGULAR? OR HERO-MAN?!

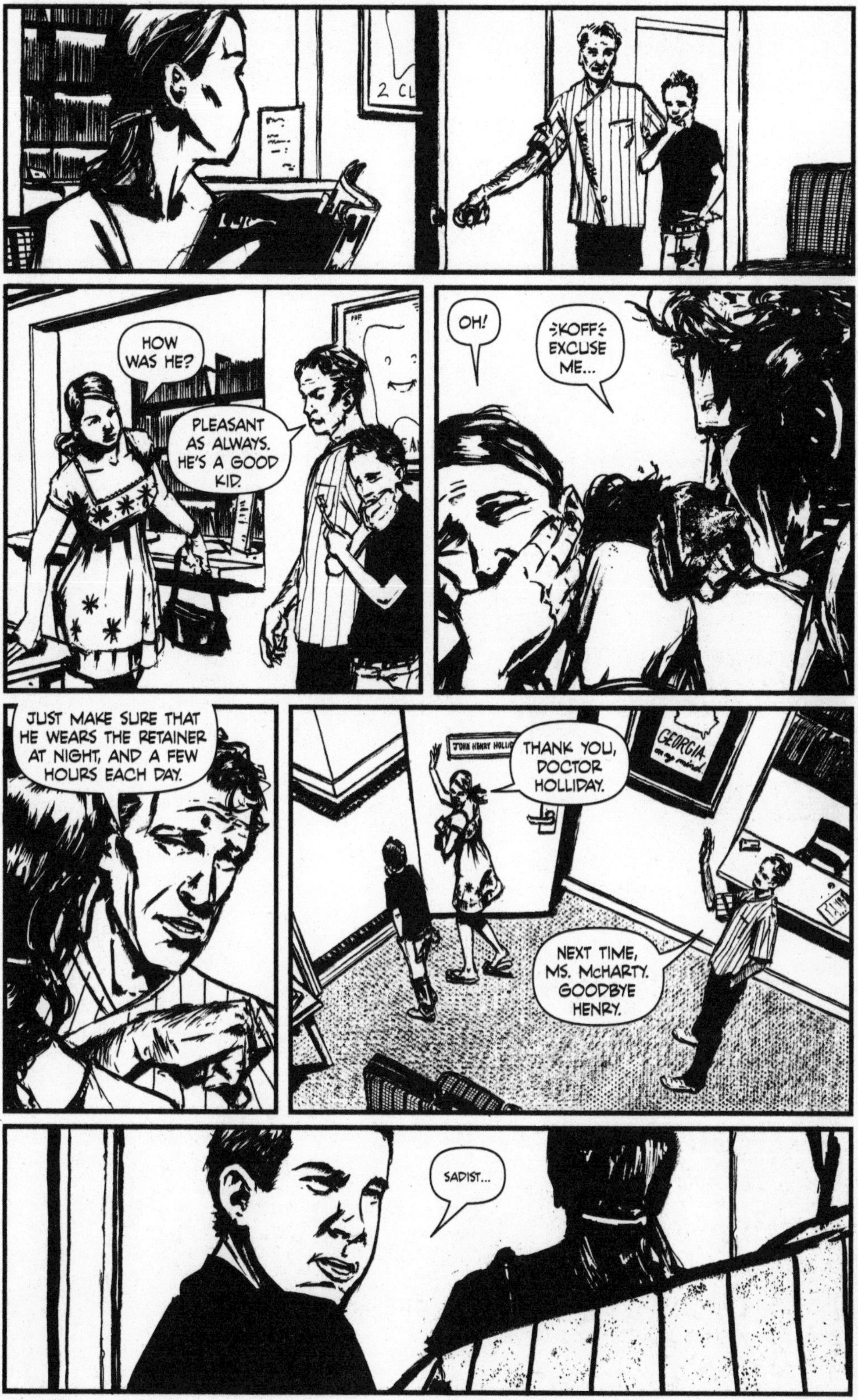
HOW WAS HE?
PLEASANT AS ALWAYS. HE'S A GOOD KID.
OH!
KOFF EXCUSE ME...
JUST MAKE SURE THAT HE WEARS THE RETAINER AT NIGHT, AND A FEW HOURS EACH DAY.
JOHN HENRY HOLLID
GEORGIA
THANK YOU, DOCTOR HOLLIDAY.
NEXT TIME, MS. McHARTY. GOODBYE HENRY.
SADIST...

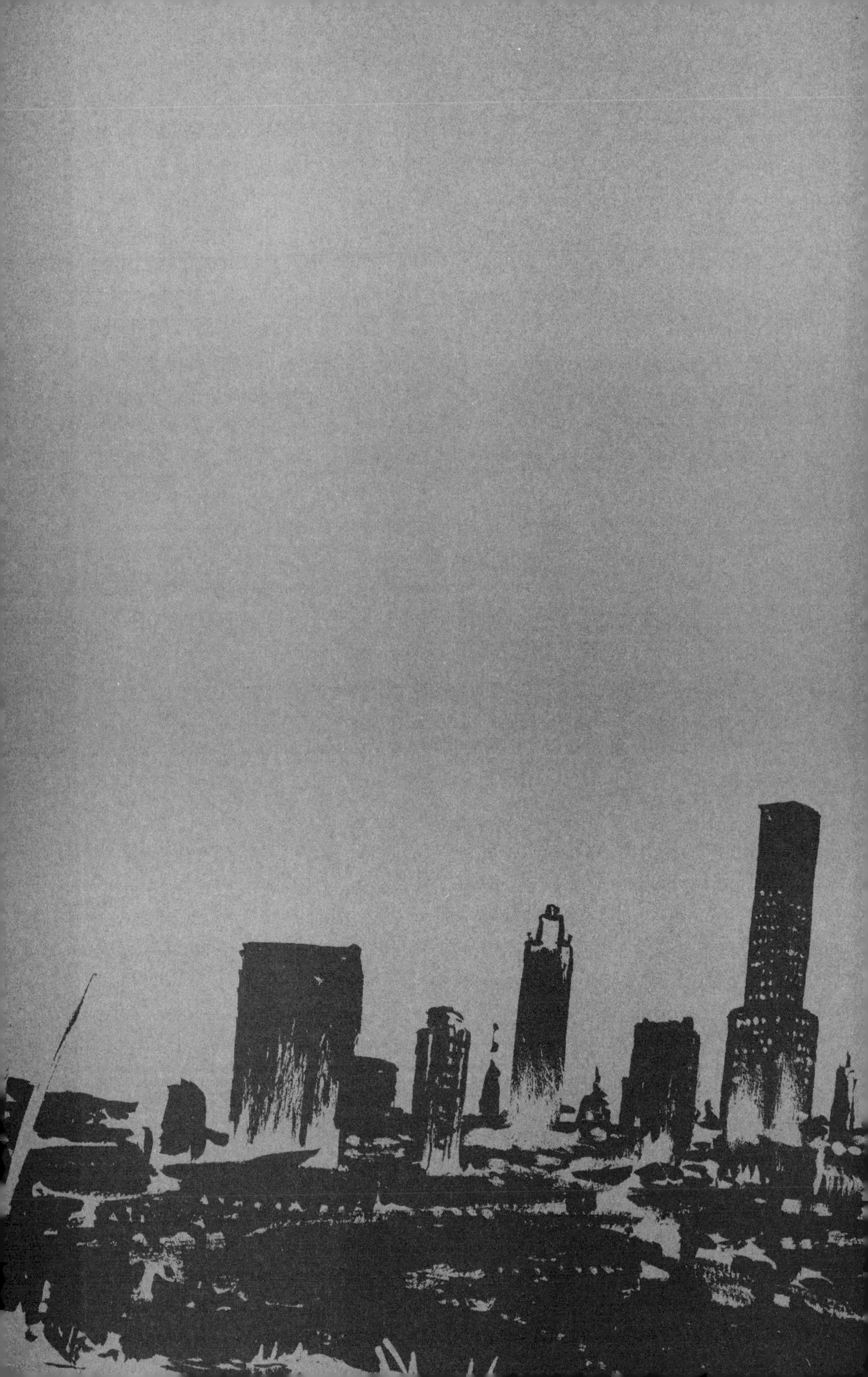

CHAPTER ONE

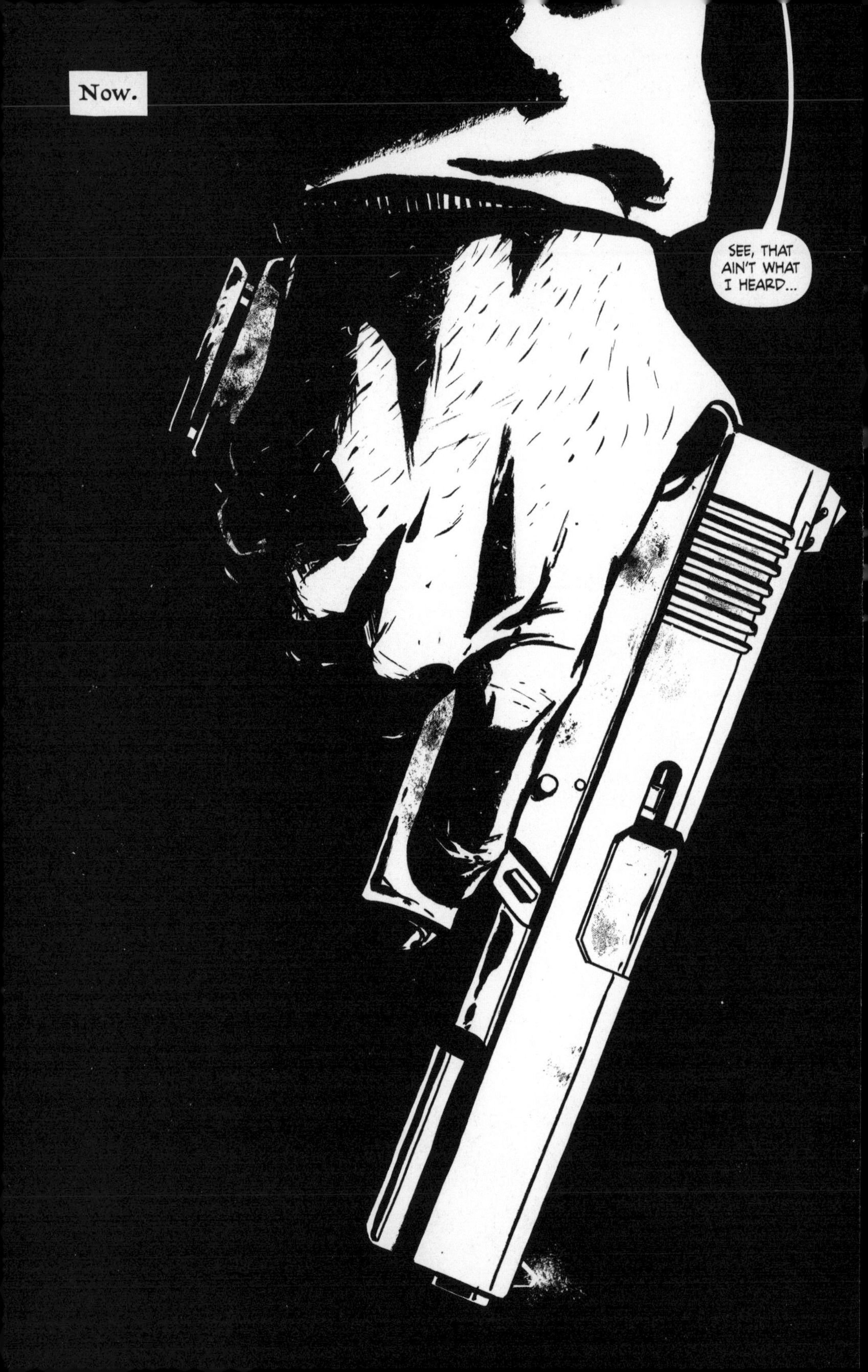
Now.
SEE, THAT AIN'T WHAT I HEARD...

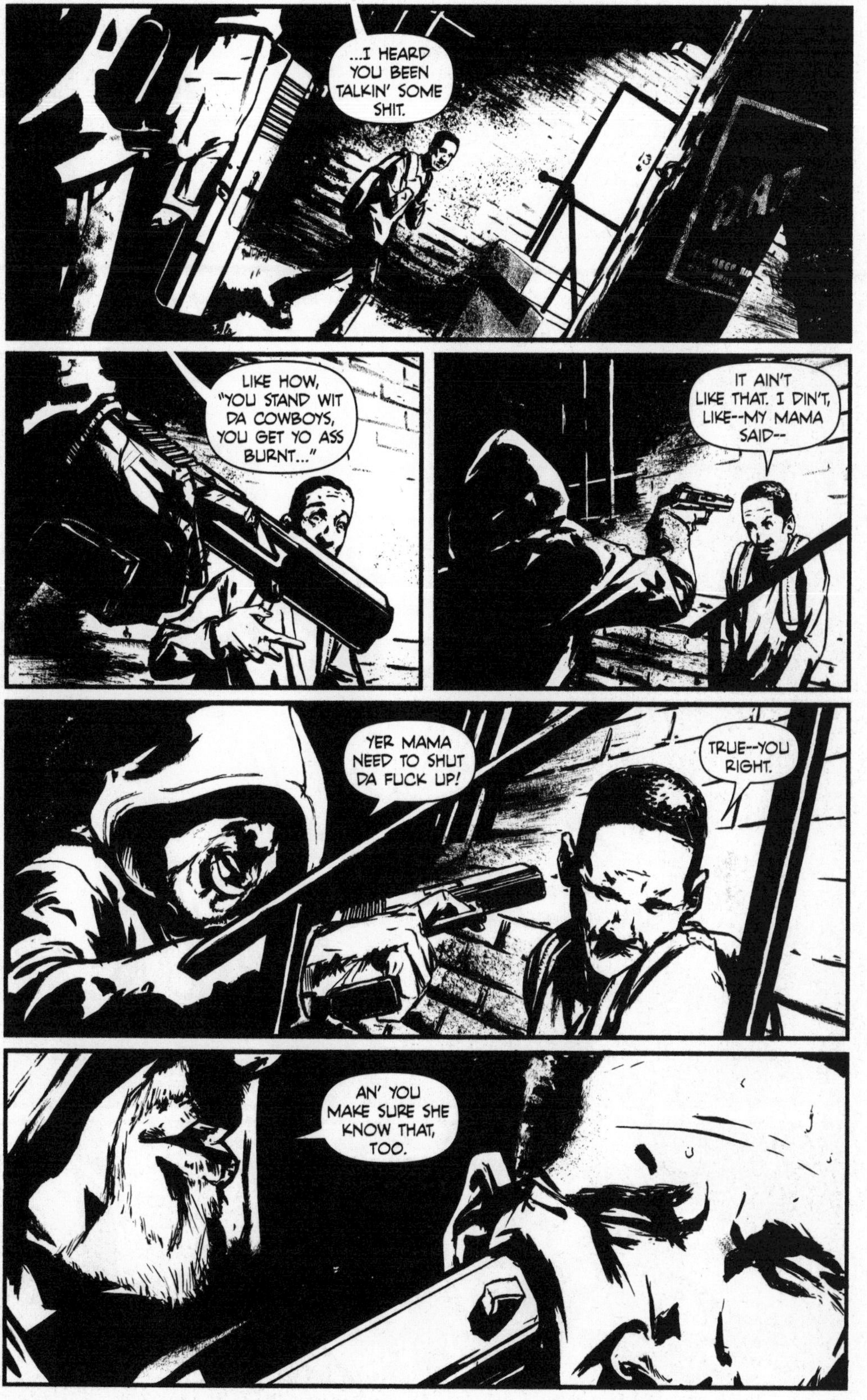
...I HEARD YOU BEEN TALKIN' SOME SHIT.
LIKE HOW, "YOU STAND WIT DA COWBOYS, YOU GET YO ASS BURNT..."
IT AIN'T LIKE THAT. I DIN'T, LIKE--MY MAMA SAID--
YER MAMA NEED TO SHUT DA FUCK UP!
TRUE--YOU RIGHT.
AN' YOU MAKE SURE SHE KNOW THAT, TOO.

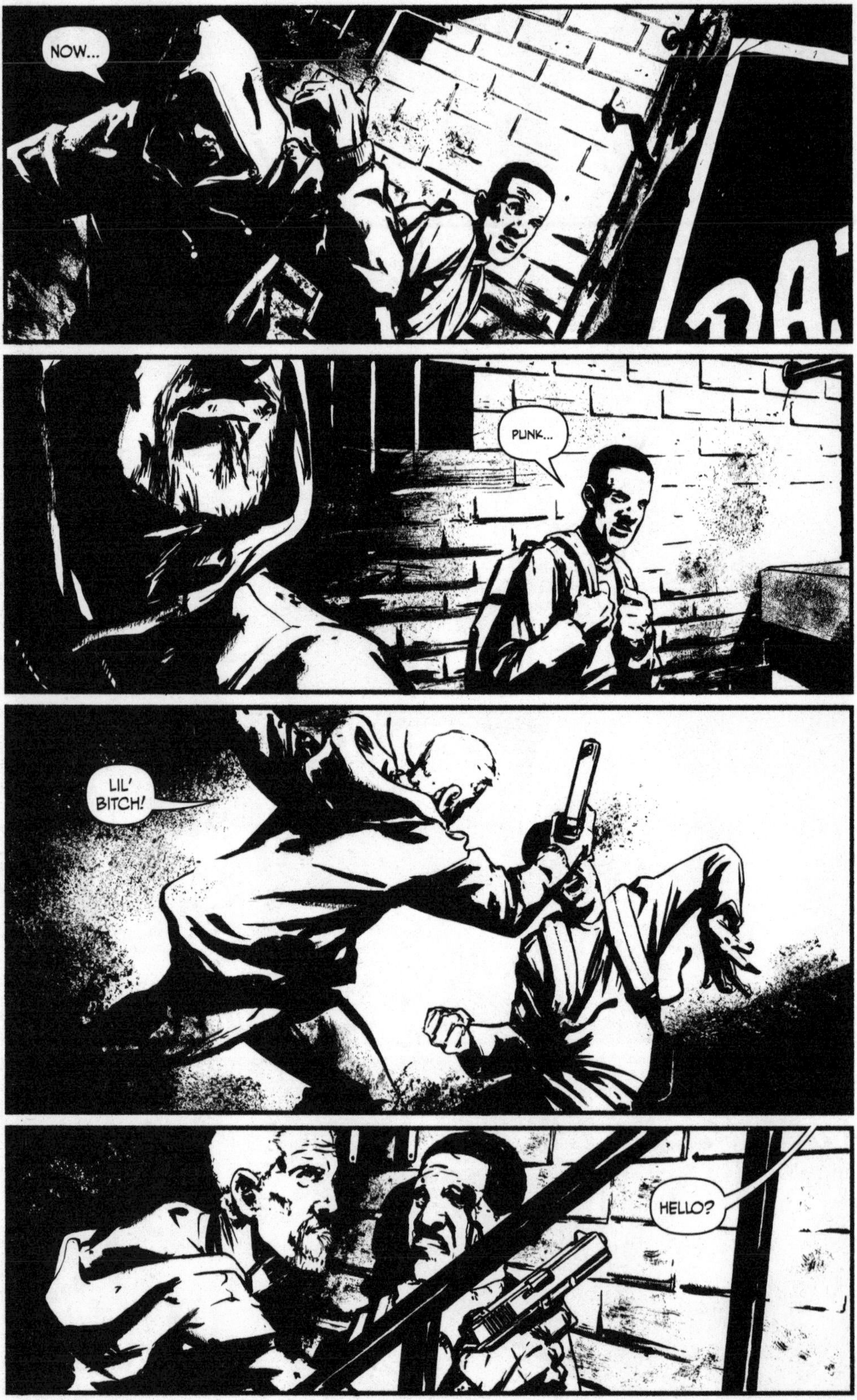
NOW...
PUNK...
LIL' BITCH!
HELLO?

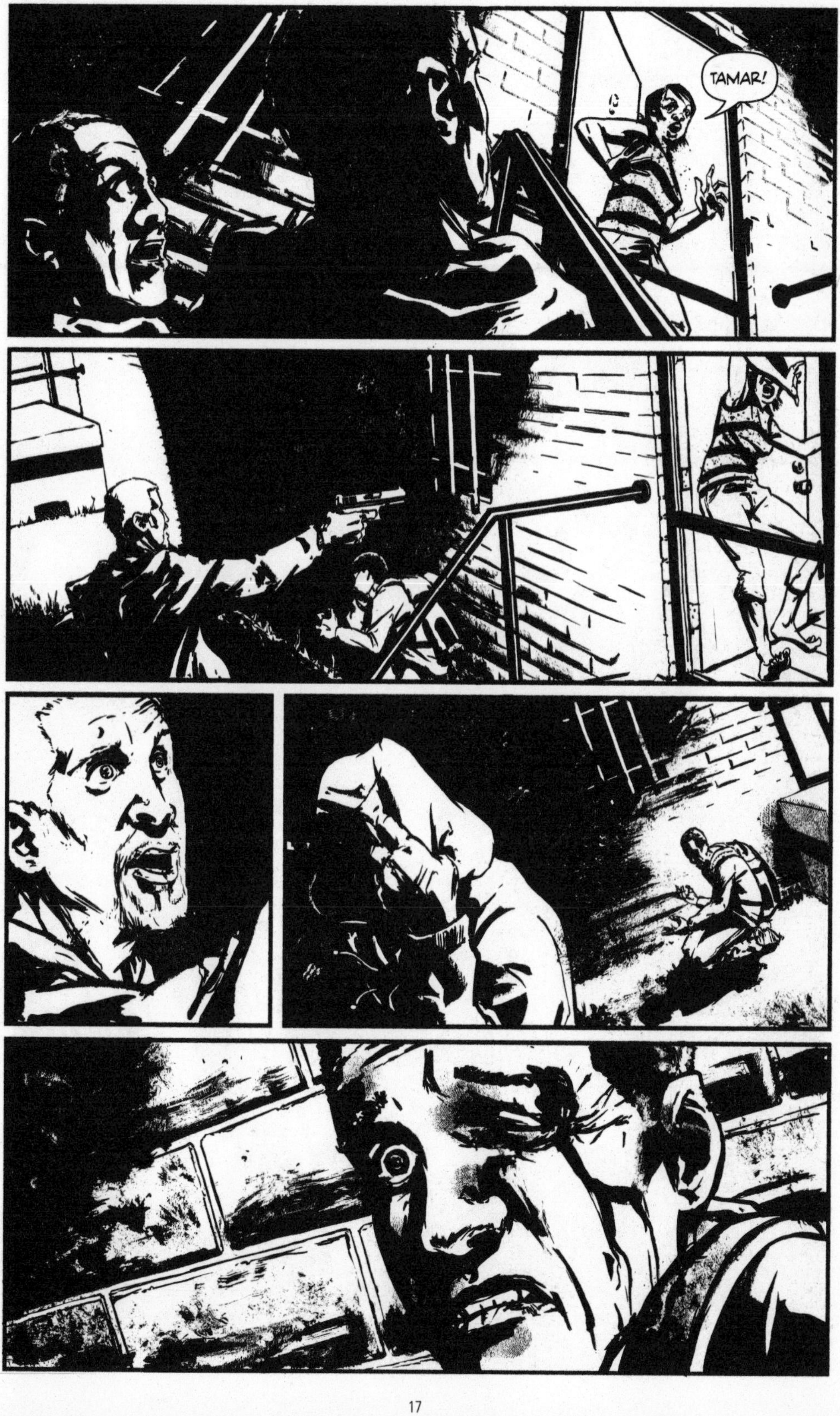
TAMAR!

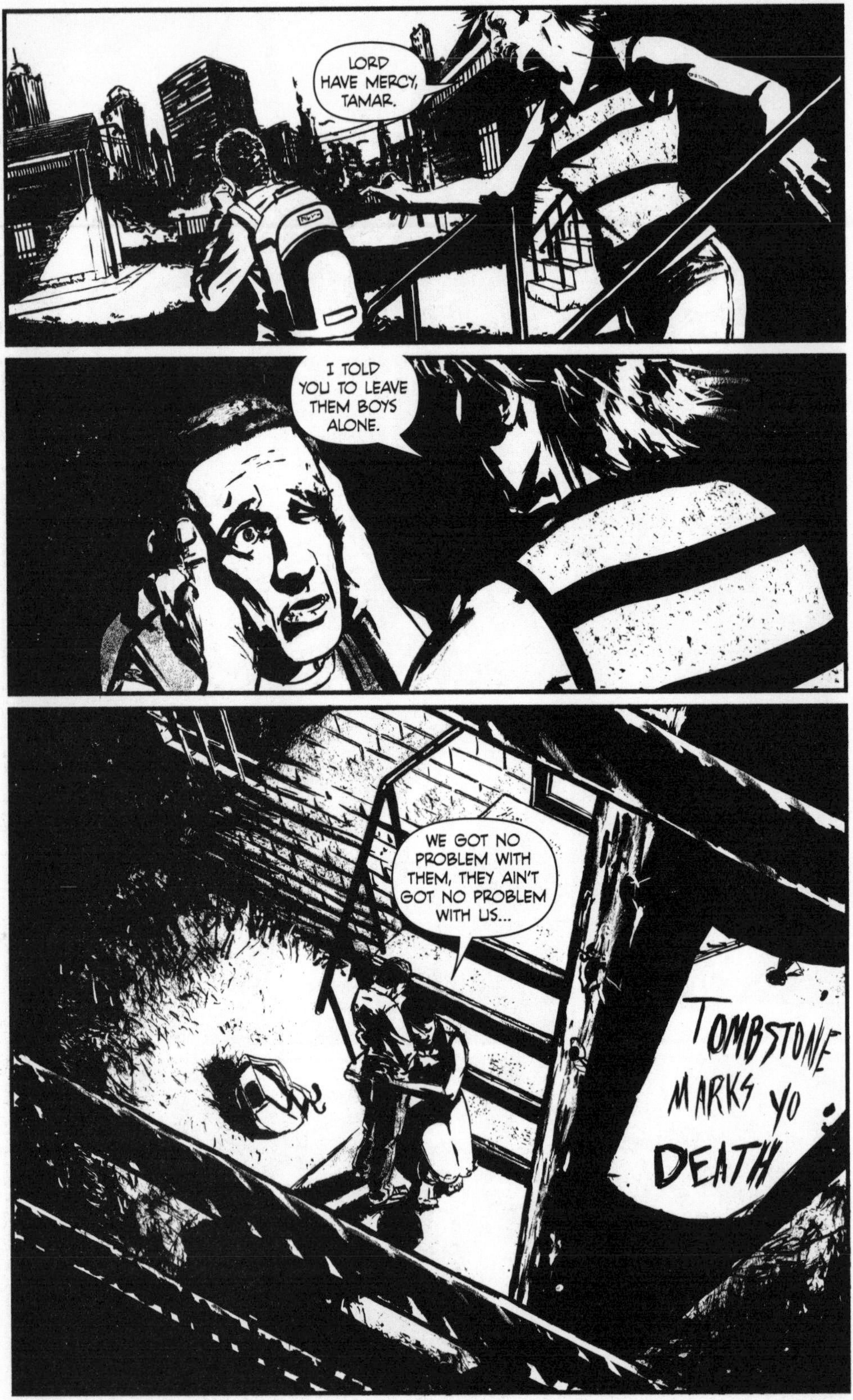
LORD HAVE MERCY, TAMAR.
I TOLD YOU TO LEAVE THEM BOYS ALONE.
WE GOT NO PROBLEM WITH THEM, THEY AIN'T GOT NO PROBLEM WITH US...
TOMBSTONE MARKS YO DEATH

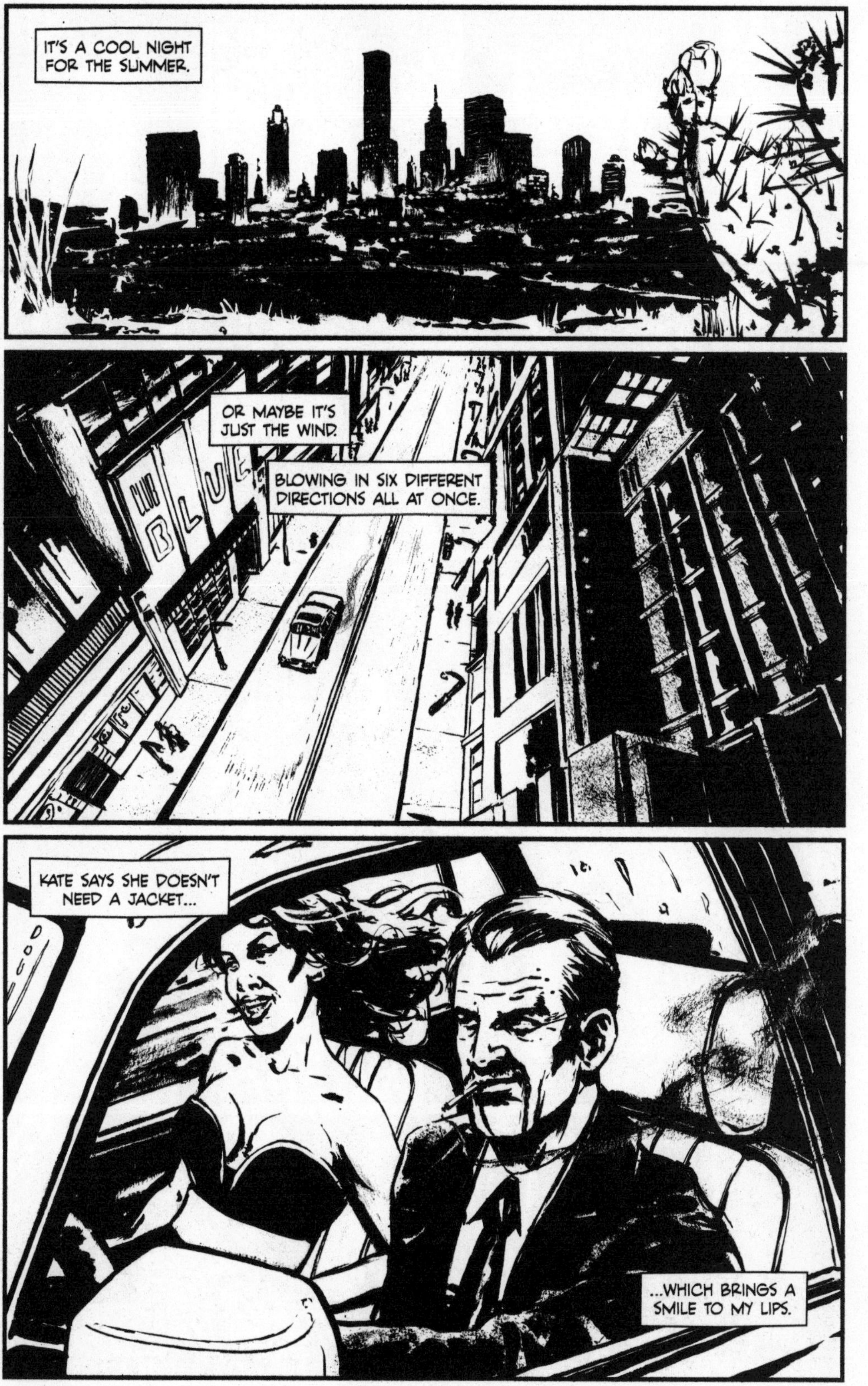
IT'S A COOL NIGHT FOR THE SUMMER.
OR MAYBE IT'S JUST THE WIND.
BLOWING IN SIX DIFFERENT DIRECTIONS ALL AT ONCE.
KATE SAYS SHE DOESN'T NEED A JACKET...
...WHICH BRINGS A SMILE TO MY LIPS.

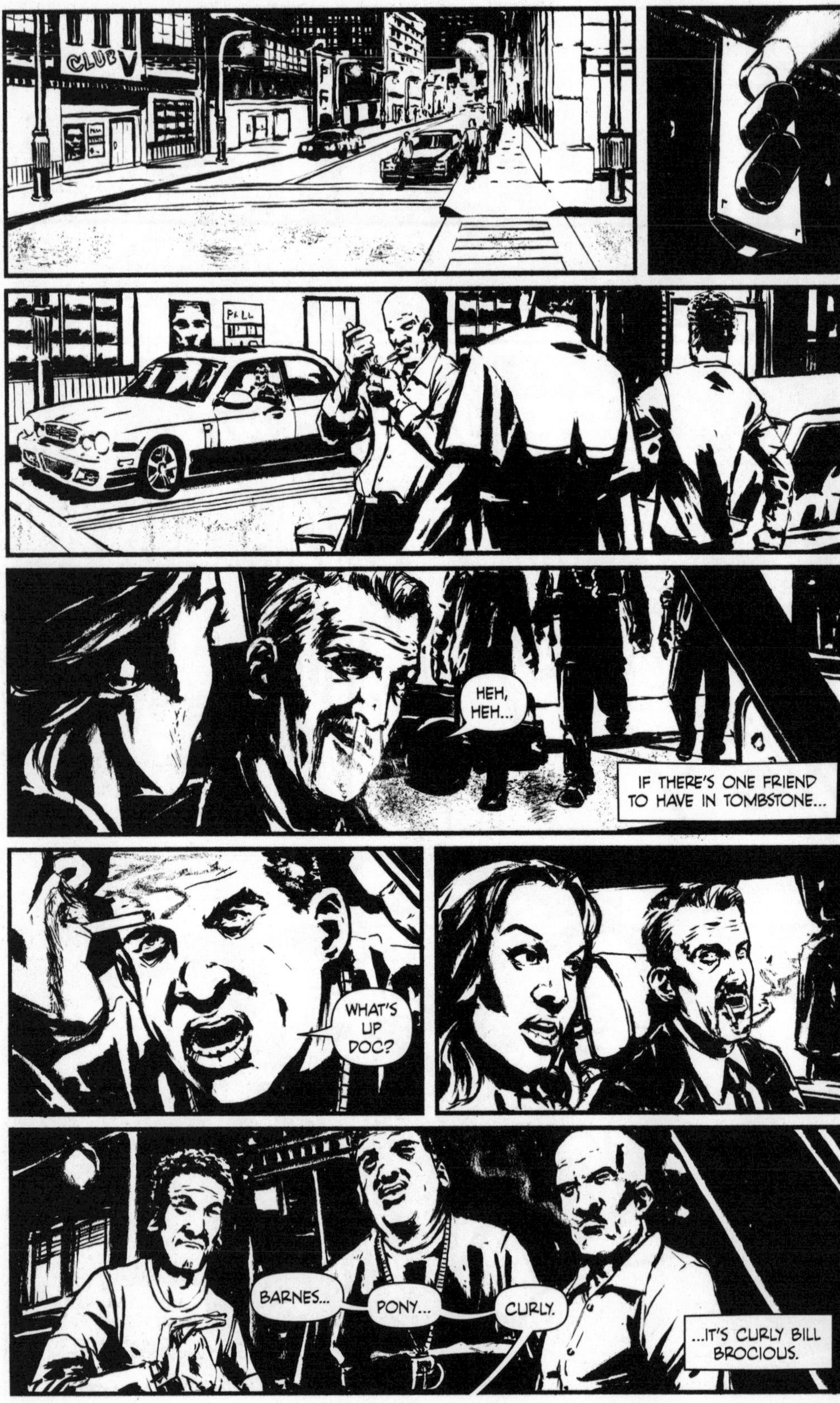
CLUB V
HEH, HEH...
IF THERE'S ONE FRIEND TO HAVE IN TOMBSTONE...
WHAT'S UP DOC?
BARNES...
PONY...
CURLY.
...IT'S CURLY BILL BROCIOUS.

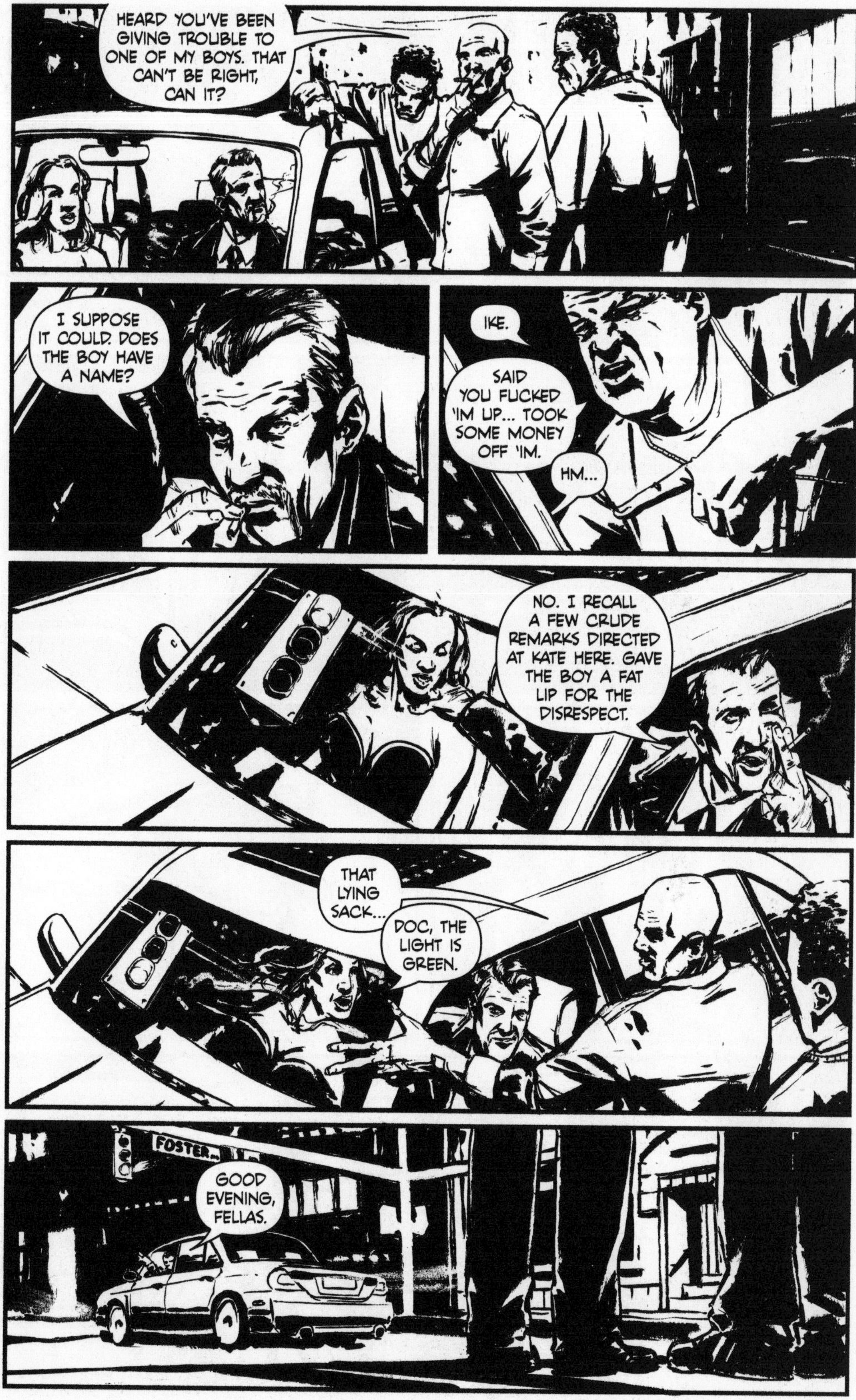
HEARD YOU'VE BEEN GIVING TROUBLE TO ONE OF MY BOYS. THAT CAN'T BE RIGHT, CAN IT?
I SUPPOSE IT COULD. DOES THE BOY HAVE A NAME?
IKE.
SAID YOU FUCKED 'IM UP... TOOK SOME MONEY OFF 'IM.
HM...
NO. I RECALL A FEW CRUDE REMARKS DIRECTED AT KATE HERE. GAVE THE BOY A FAT LIP FOR THE DISRESPECT.
THAT LYING SACK...
DOC, THE LIGHT IS GREEN.
FOSTER
GOOD EVENING, FELLAS.

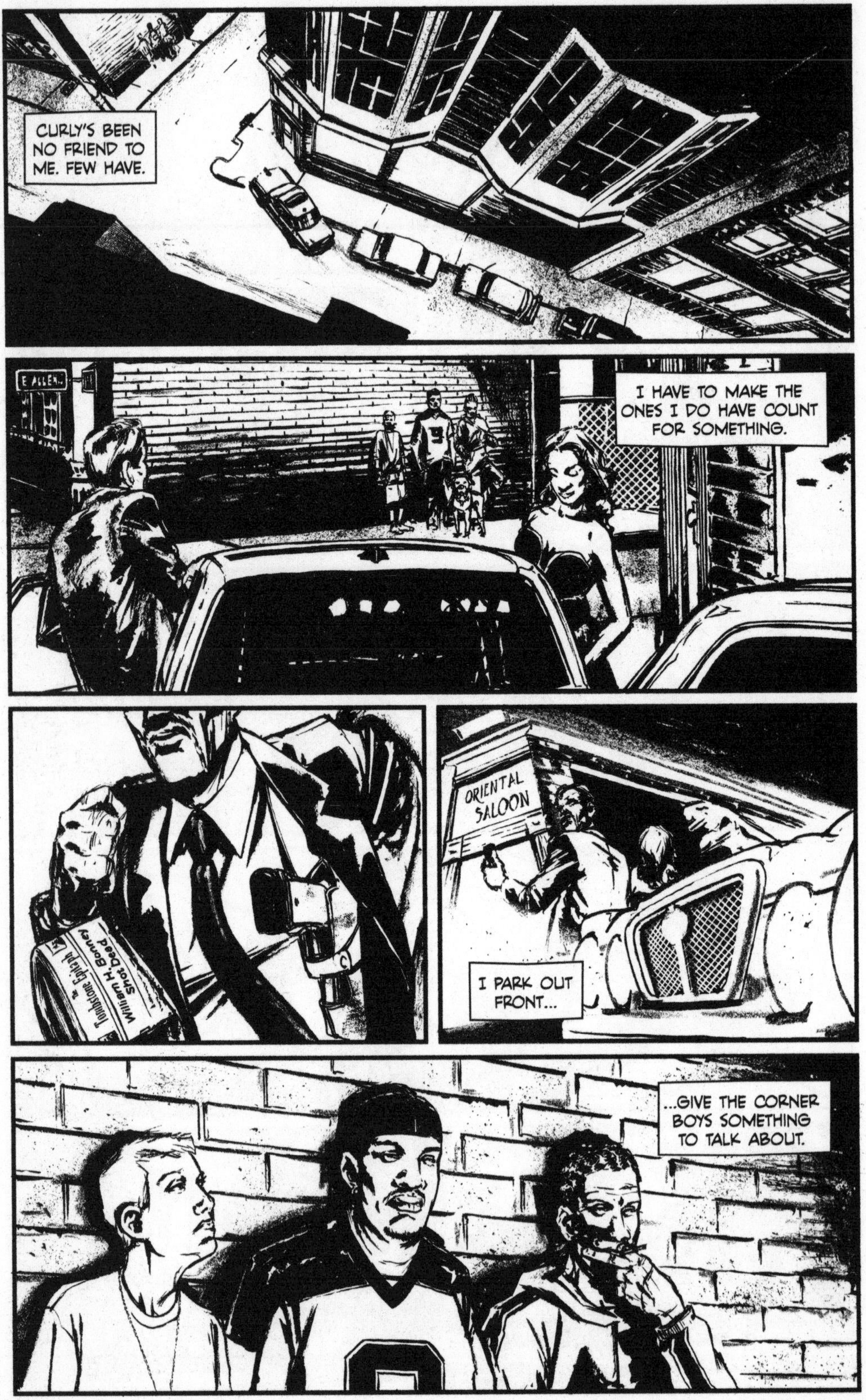
CURLY'S BEEN NO FRIEND TO ME. FEW HAVE.
I HAVE TO MAKE THE ONES I DO HAVE COUNT FOR SOMETHING.
Tombstone Epitaph
William H. Bonney Shot Dead
ORIENTAL SALOON
I PARK OUT FRONT...
...GIVE THE CORNER BOYS SOMETHING TO TALK ABOUT.

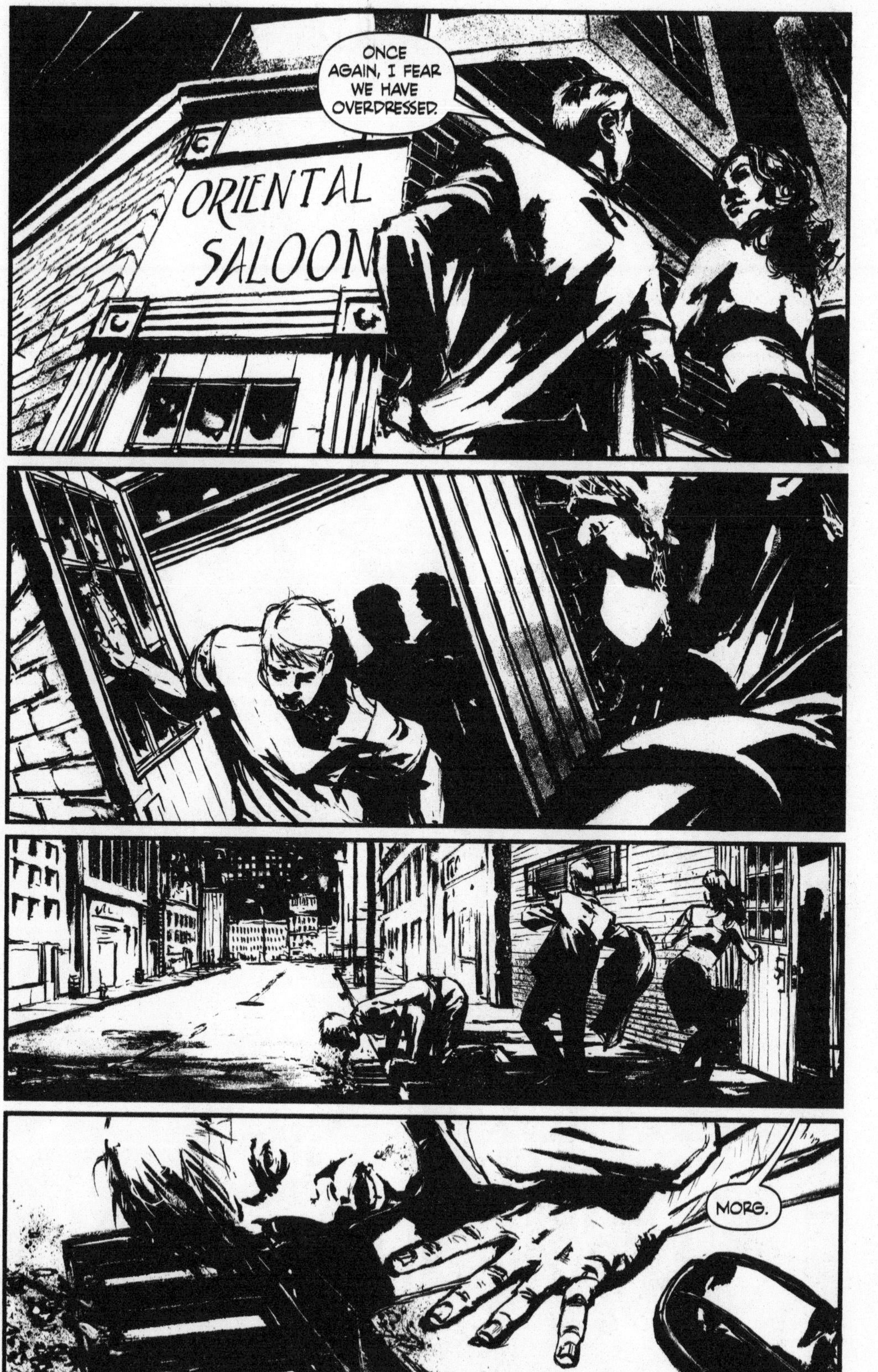
ONCE AGAIN, I FEAR WE HAVE OVERDRESSED.
ORIENTAL SALOON
MORG.

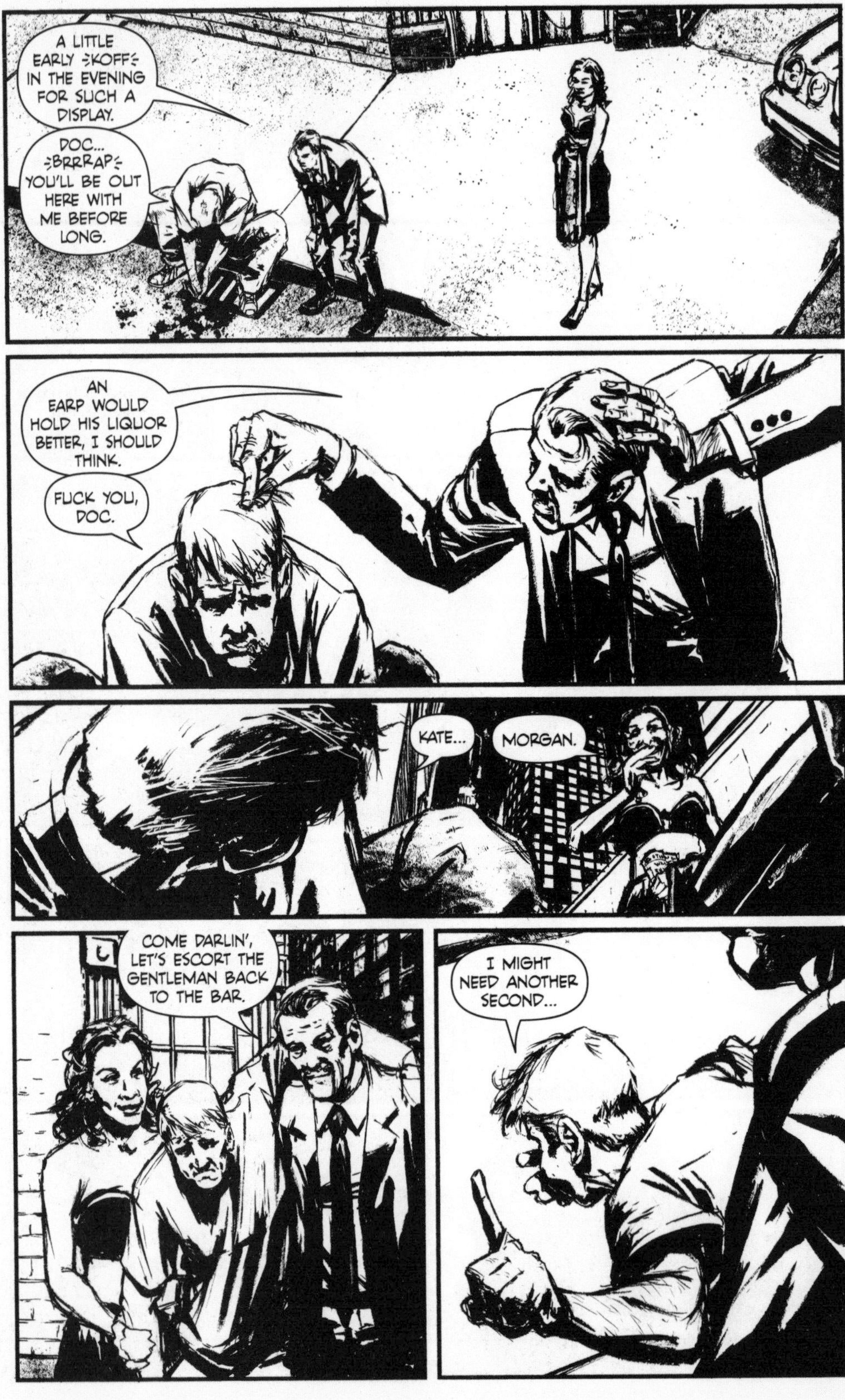
A LITTLE EARLY ⁼KOFF⁼ IN THE EVENING FOR SUCH A DISPLAY.
DOC... ⁼BRRRAP⁼ YOU'LL BE OUT HERE WITH ME BEFORE LONG.
AN EARP WOULD HOLD HIS LIQUOR BETTER, I SHOULD THINK.
FUCK YOU, DOC.
KATE...
MORGAN.
COME DARLIN', LET'S ESCORT THE GENTLEMAN BACK TO THE BAR.
I MIGHT NEED ANOTHER SECOND...

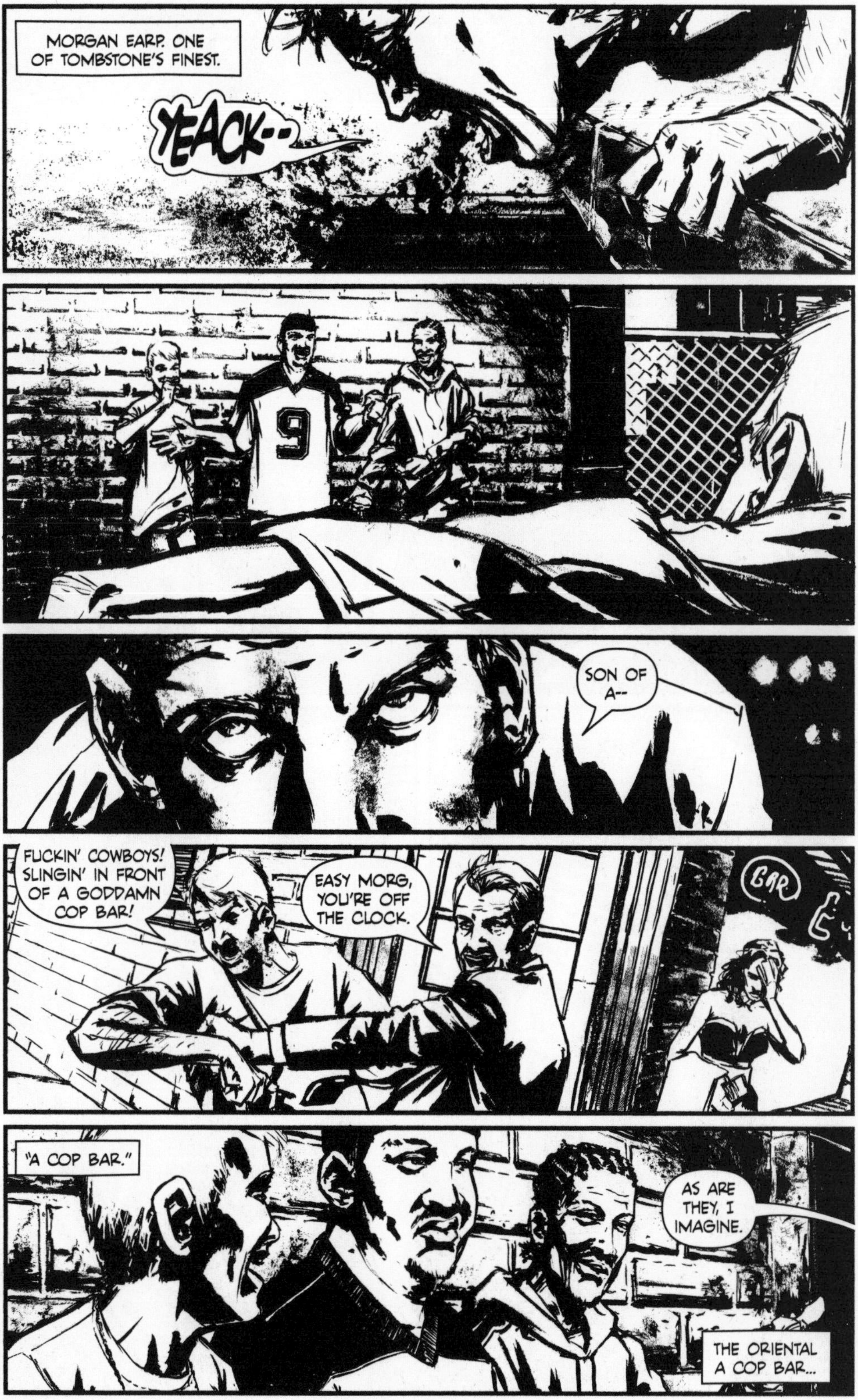
MORGAN EARP. ONE OF TOMBSTONE'S FINEST.
YEACK--
SON OF A--
FUCKIN' COWBOYS! SLINGIN' IN FRONT OF A GODDAMN COP BAR!
EASY MORG, YOU'RE OFF THE CLOCK.
BAR
"A COP BAR."
AS ARE THEY, I IMAGINE.
THE ORIENTAL A COP BAR...

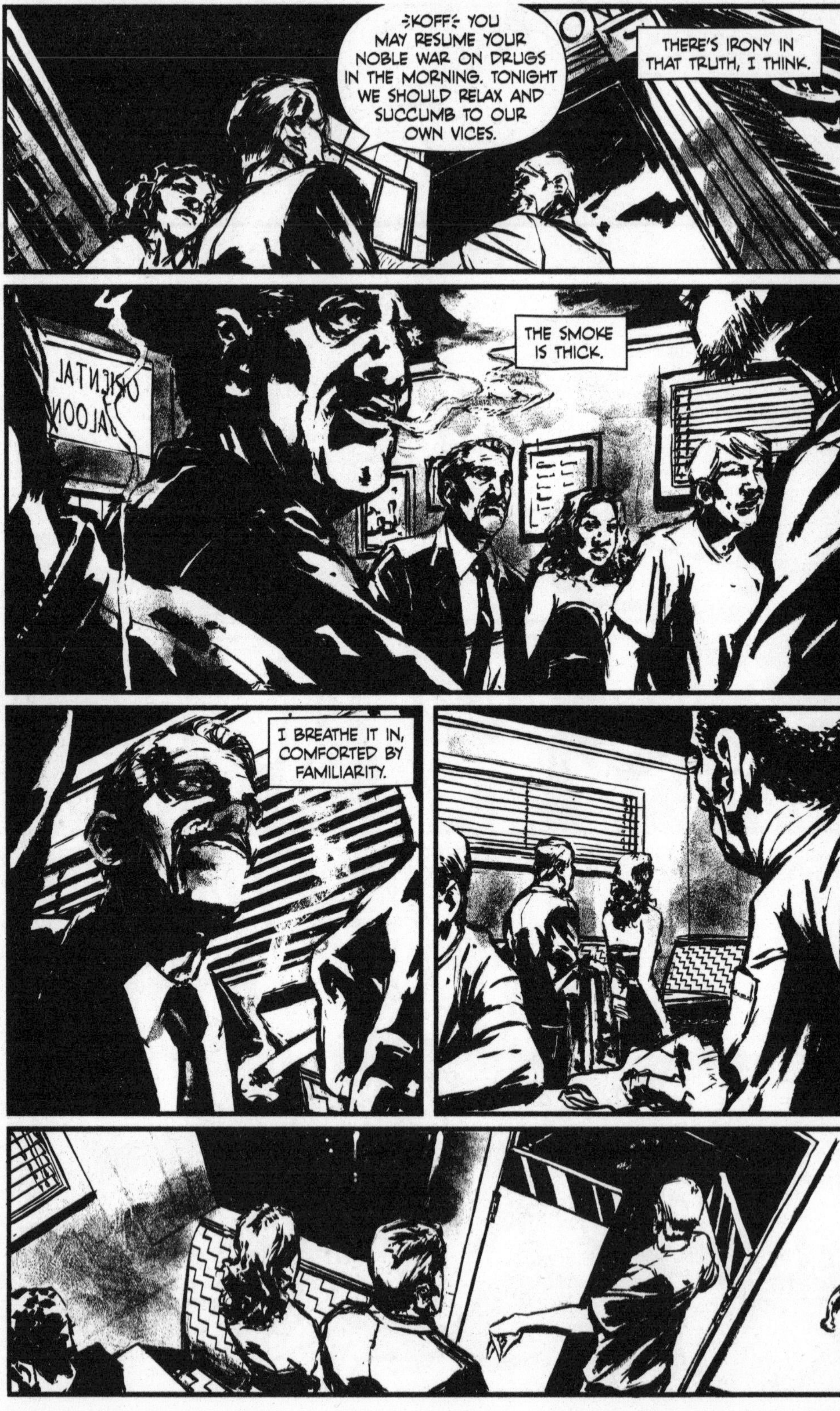
KOFF YOU MAY RESUME YOUR NOBLE WAR ON DRUGS IN THE MORNING. TONIGHT WE SHOULD RELAX AND SUCCUMB TO OUR OWN VICES.
THERE'S IRONY IN THAT TRUTH, I THINK.
THE SMOKE IS THICK.
I BREATHE IT IN, COMFORTED BY FAMILIARITY.

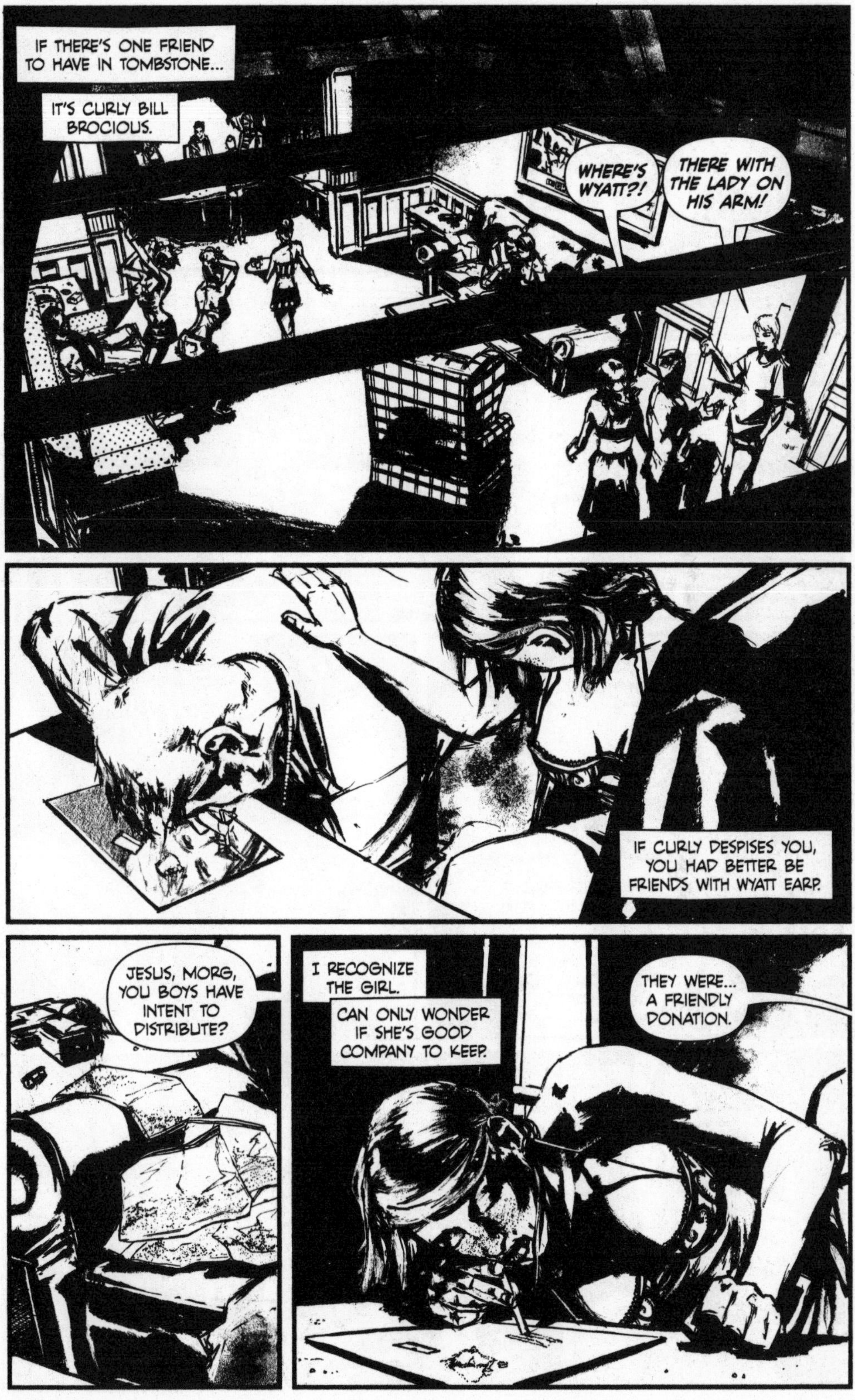
IF THERE'S ONE FRIEND TO HAVE IN TOMBSTONE...
IT'S CURLY BILL BROCIOUS.
WHERE'S WYATT?!
THERE WITH THE LADY ON HIS ARM!
IF CURLY DESPISES YOU, YOU HAD BETTER BE FRIENDS WITH WYATT EARP.
JESUS, MORG, YOU BOYS HAVE INTENT TO DISTRIBUTE?
I RECOGNIZE THE GIRL.
CAN ONLY WONDER IF SHE'S GOOD COMPANY TO KEEP.
THEY WERE... A FRIENDLY DONATION.

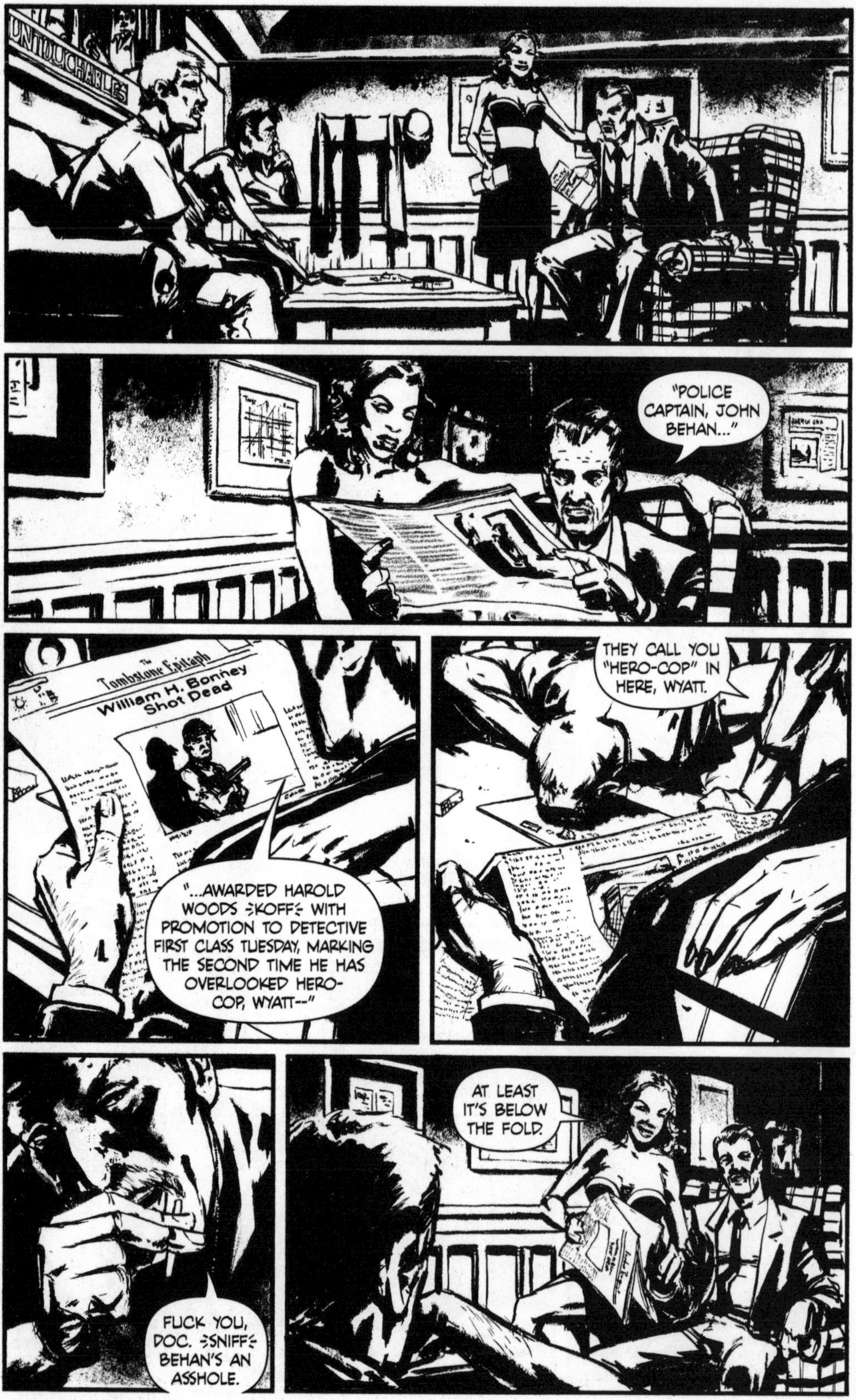
UNTOUCHABLES
"POLICE CAPTAIN, JOHN BEHAN..."
The Tombstone Epitaph
William H. Bonney Shot Dead
"...AWARDED HAROLD WOODS ⸗KOFF⸗ WITH PROMOTION TO DETECTIVE FIRST CLASS TUESDAY, MARKING THE SECOND TIME HE HAS OVERLOOKED HERO-COP, WYATT--"
THEY CALL YOU "HERO-COP" IN HERE, WYATT.
FUCK YOU, DOC. ⸗SNIFF⸗ BEHAN'S AN ASSHOLE.
AT LEAST IT'S BELOW THE FOLD.

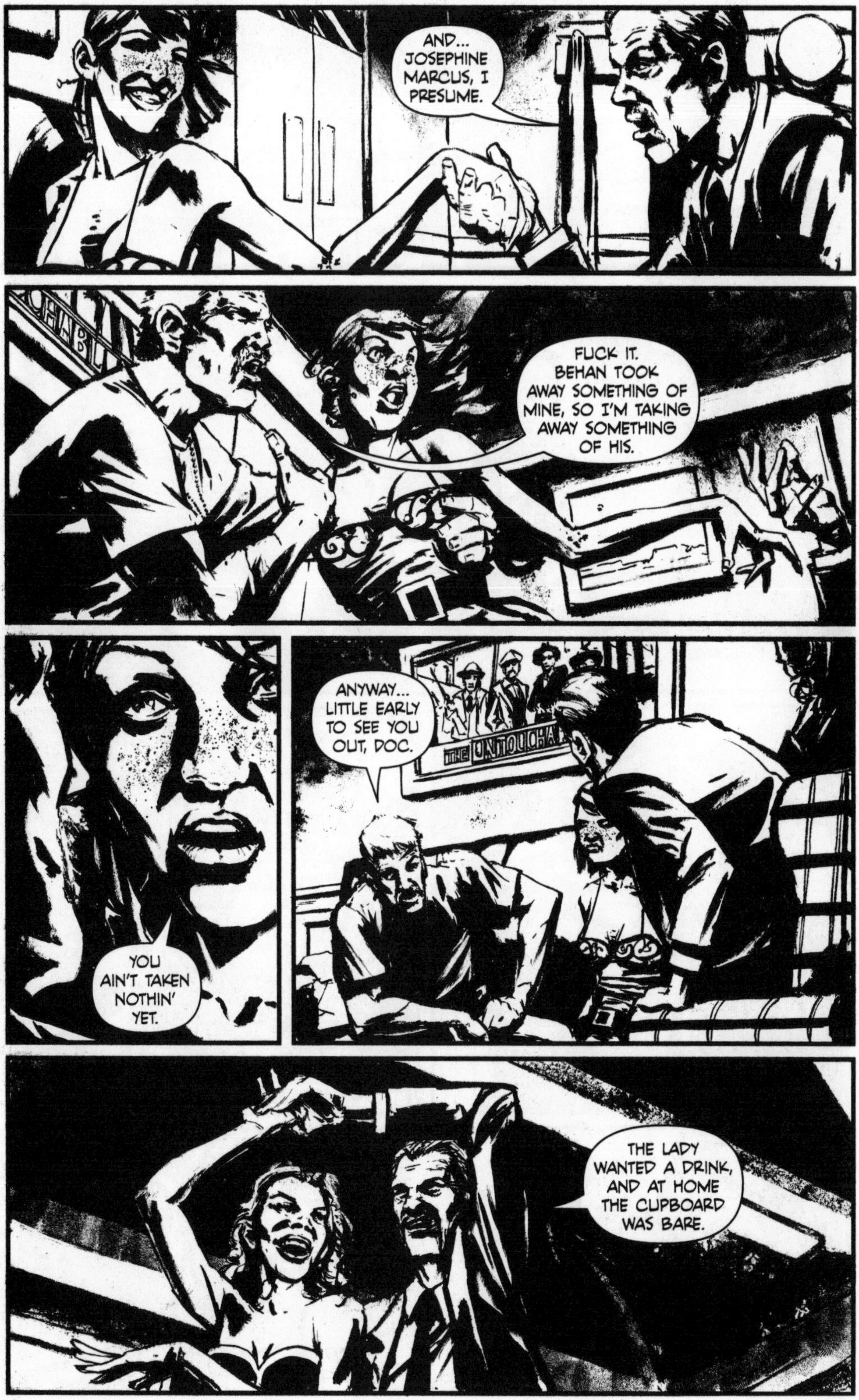
AND... JOSEPHINE MARCUS, I PRESUME.
FUCK IT. BEHAN TOOK AWAY SOMETHING OF MINE, SO I'M TAKING AWAY SOMETHING OF HIS.
YOU AIN'T TAKEN NOTHIN' YET.
ANYWAY... LITTLE EARLY TO SEE YOU OUT, DOC.
THE UNTOUCHA
THE LADY WANTED A DRINK, AND AT HOME THE CUPBOARD WAS BARE.

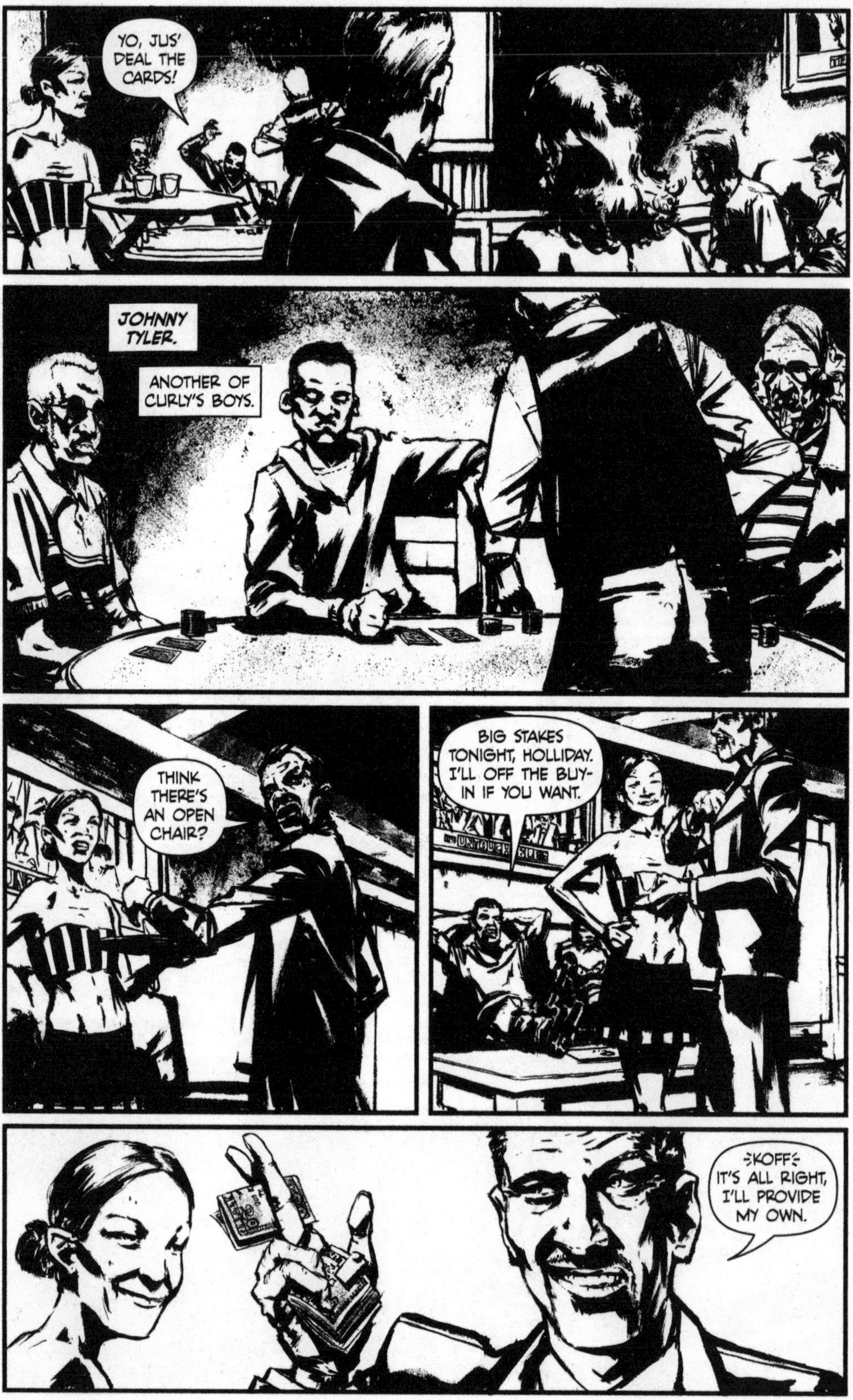
YO, JUS' DEAL THE CARDS!
JOHNNY TYLER.
ANOTHER OF CURLY'S BOYS.
THINK THERE'S AN OPEN CHAIR?
BIG STAKES TONIGHT, HOLLIDAY. I'LL OFF THE BUY-IN IF YOU WANT.
UNTOUCHABLES
KOFF IT'S ALL RIGHT, I'LL PROVIDE MY OWN.

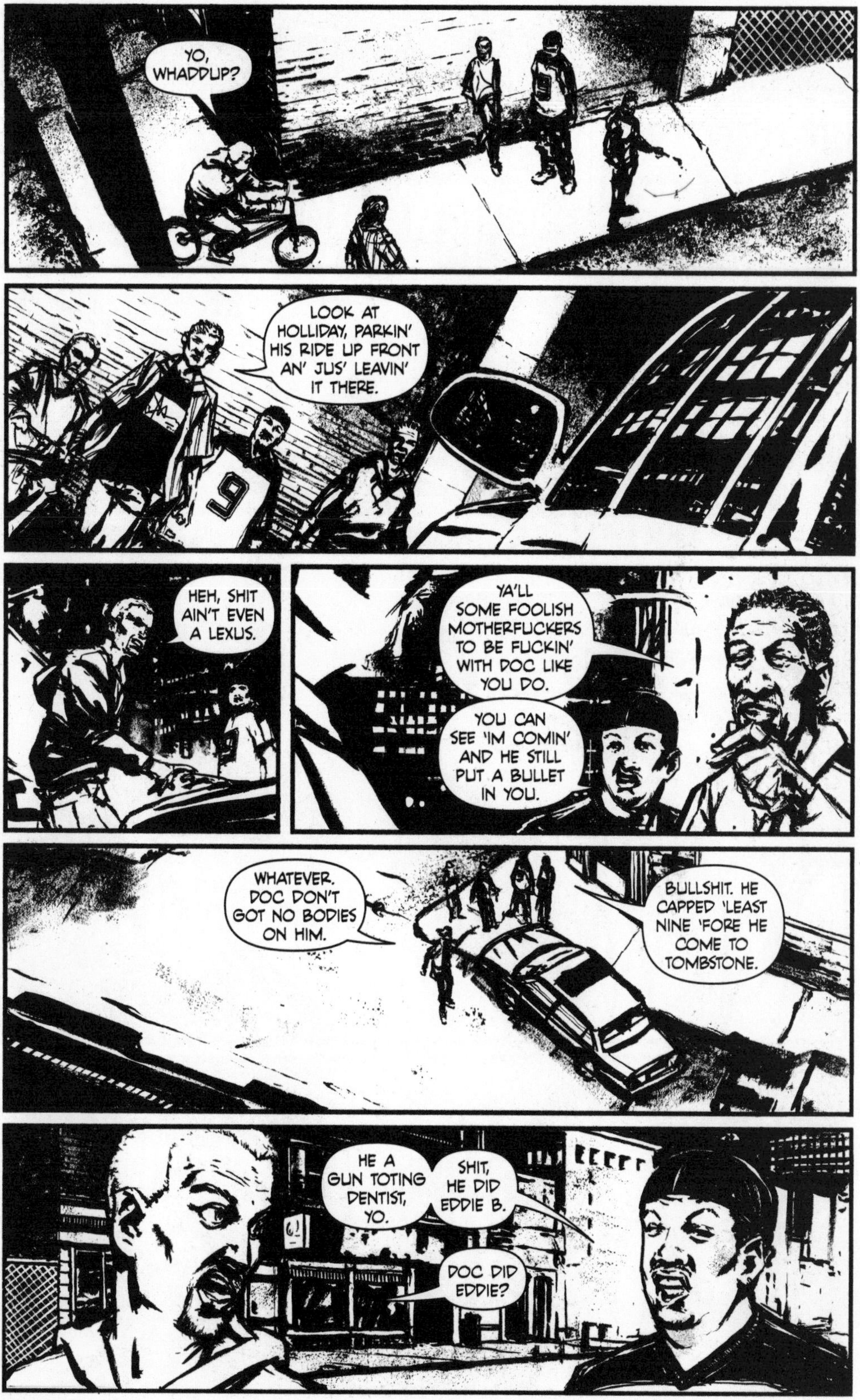
YO, WHADDUP?
LOOK AT HOLLIDAY, PARKIN' HIS RIDE UP FRONT AN' JUS' LEAVIN' IT THERE.
HEH, SHIT AIN'T EVEN A LEXUS.
YA'LL SOME FOOLISH MOTHERFUCKERS TO BE FUCKIN' WITH DOC LIKE YOU DO.
YOU CAN SEE 'IM COMIN' AND HE STILL PUT A BULLET IN YOU.
WHATEVER. DOC DON'T GOT NO BODIES ON HIM.
BULLSHIT. HE CAPPED 'LEAST NINE 'FORE HE COME TO TOMBSTONE.
HE A GUN TOTING DENTIST, YO.
SHIT, HE DID EDDIE B.
DOC DID EDDIE?

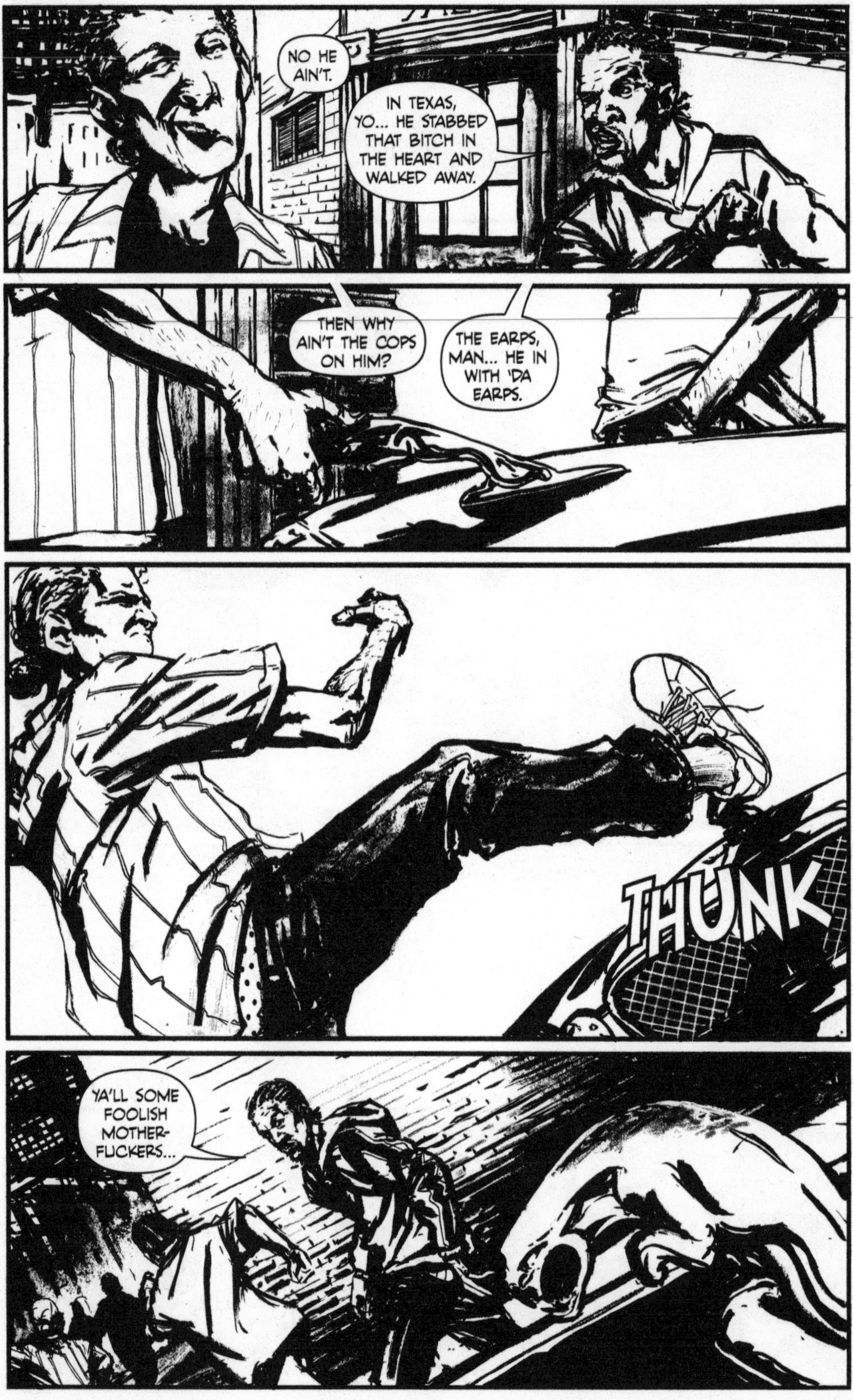
NO HE AIN'T.
IN TEXAS, YO... HE STABBED THAT BITCH IN THE HEART AND WALKED AWAY.
THEN WHY AIN'T THE COPS ON HIM?
THE EARPS, MAN... HE IN WITH 'DA EARPS.
THUNK
YA'LL SOME FOOLISH MOTHER-FUCKERS...

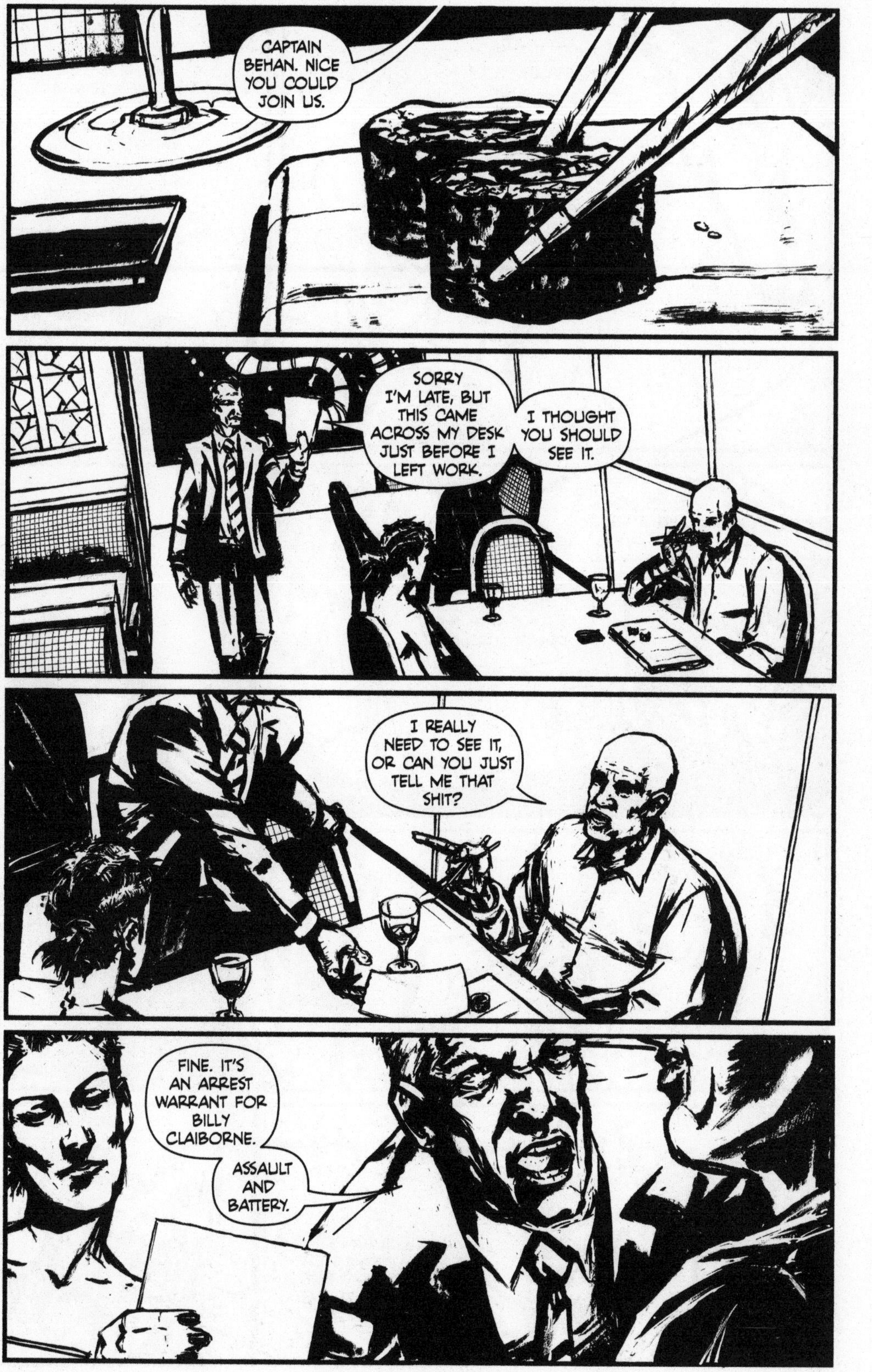
CAPTAIN BEHAN. NICE YOU COULD JOIN US.
SORRY I'M LATE, BUT THIS CAME ACROSS MY DESK JUST BEFORE I LEFT WORK.
I THOUGHT YOU SHOULD SEE IT.
I REALLY NEED TO SEE IT, OR CAN YOU JUST TELL ME THAT SHIT?
FINE. IT'S AN ARREST WARRANT FOR BILLY CLAIBORNE.
ASSAULT AND BATTERY.

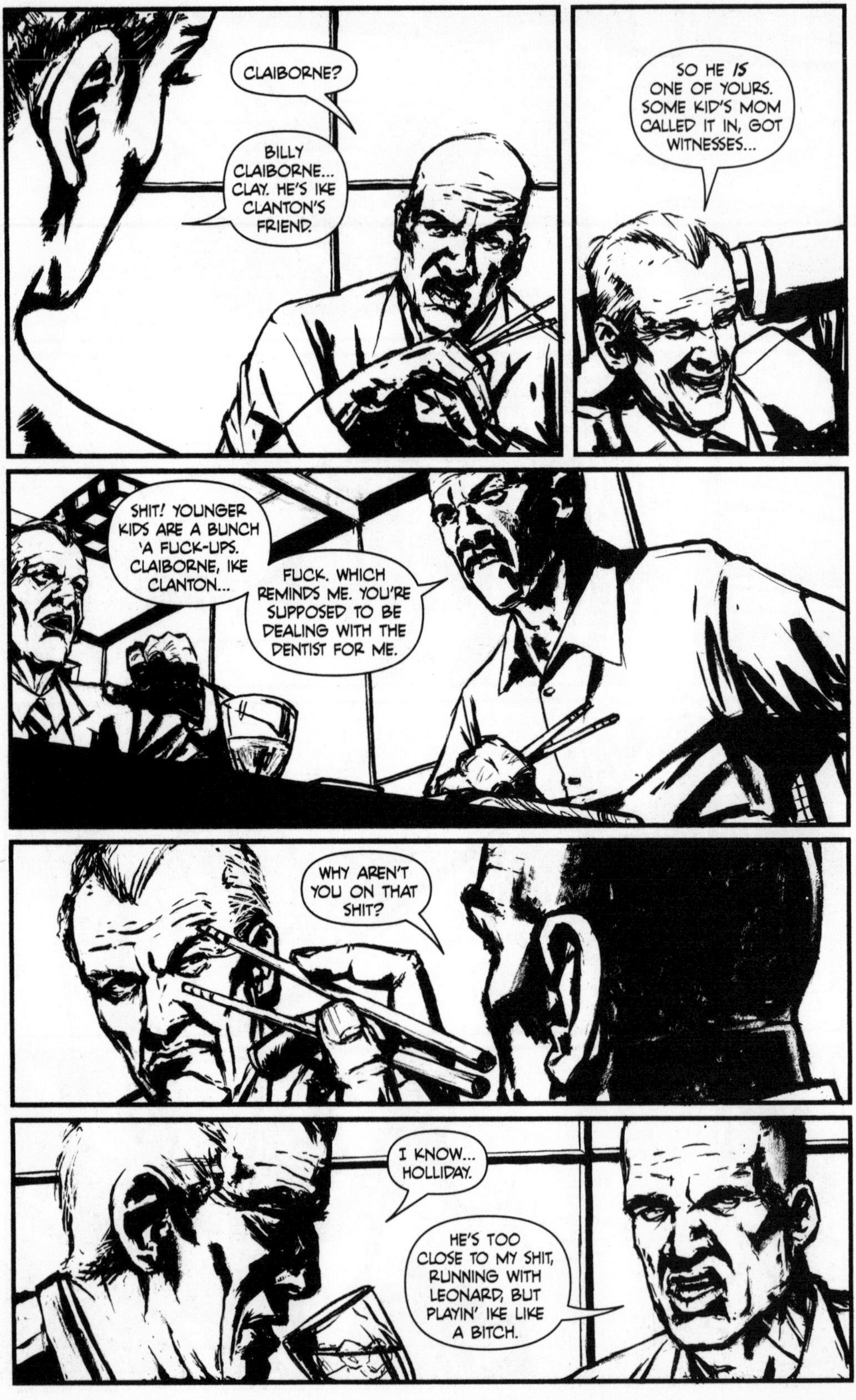
CLAIBORNE?
BILLY CLAIBORNE... CLAY. HE'S IKE CLANTON'S FRIEND.
SO HE *IS* ONE OF YOURS. SOME KID'S MOM CALLED IT IN, GOT WITNESSES...
SHIT! YOUNGER KIDS ARE A BUNCH 'A FUCK-UPS. CLAIBORNE, IKE CLANTON...
FUCK. WHICH REMINDS ME. YOU'RE SUPPOSED TO BE DEALING WITH THE DENTIST FOR ME.
WHY AREN'T YOU ON THAT SHIT?
I KNOW... HOLLIDAY.
HE'S TOO CLOSE TO MY SHIT, RUNNING WITH LEONARD, BUT PLAYIN' IKE LIKE A BITCH.

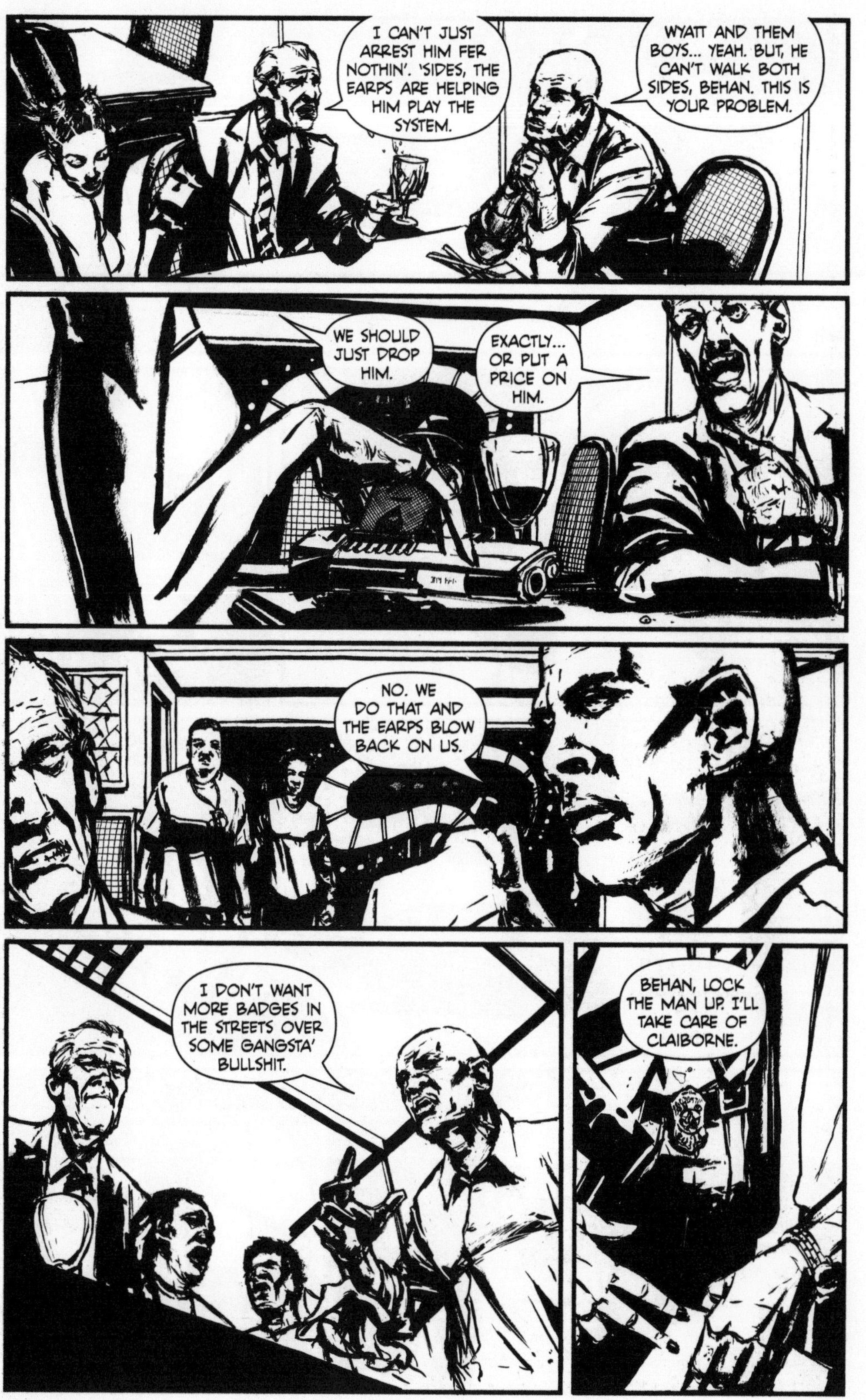
I CAN'T JUST ARREST HIM FER NOTHIN'. 'SIDES, THE EARPS ARE HELPING HIM PLAY THE SYSTEM.
WYATT AND THEM BOYS... YEAH. BUT, HE CAN'T WALK BOTH SIDES, BEHAN. THIS IS YOUR PROBLEM.
WE SHOULD JUST DROP HIM.
EXACTLY... OR PUT A PRICE ON HIM.
NO. WE DO THAT AND THE EARPS BLOW BACK ON US.
I DON'T WANT MORE BADGES IN THE STREETS OVER SOME GANGSTA' BULLSHIT.
BEHAN, LOCK THE MAN UP. I'LL TAKE CARE OF CLAIBORNE.

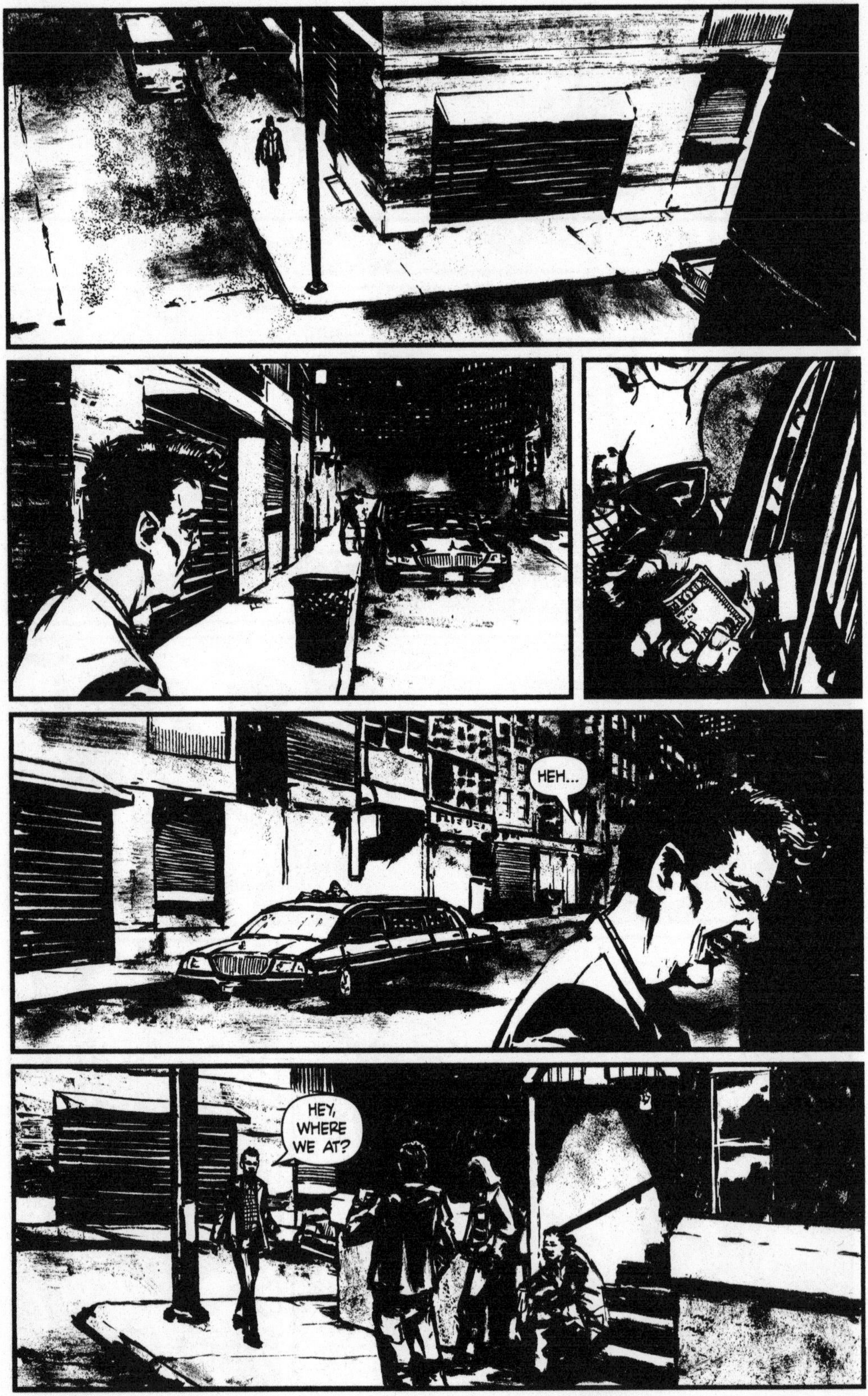
HEH...
HEY, WHERE WE AT?

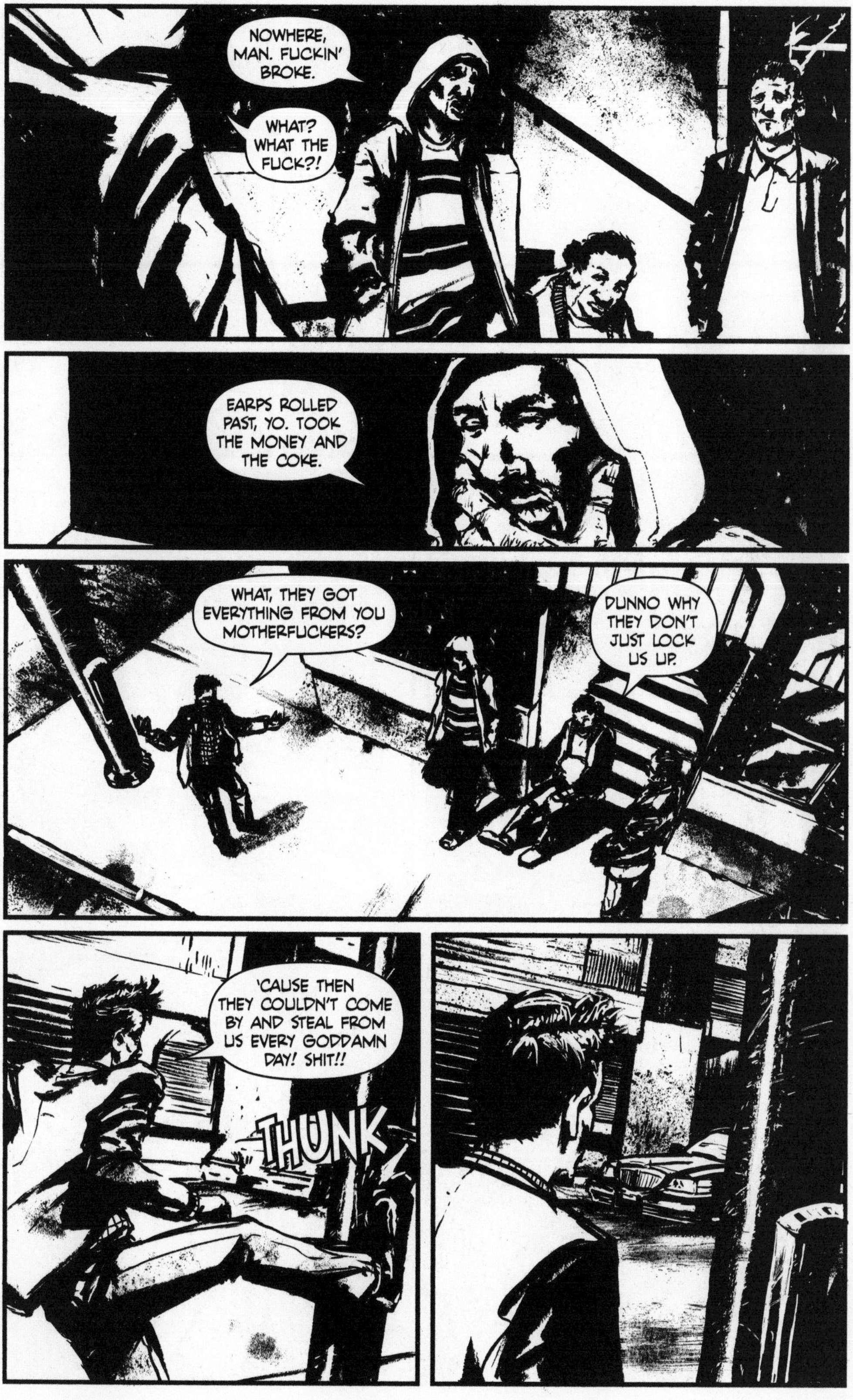
NOWHERE, MAN. FUCKIN' BROKE.
WHAT? WHAT THE FUCK?!
EARPS ROLLED PAST, YO. TOOK THE MONEY AND THE COKE.
WHAT, THEY GOT EVERYTHING FROM YOU MOTHERFUCKERS?
DUNNO WHY THEY DON'T JUST LOCK US UP.
'CAUSE THEN THEY COULDN'T COME BY AND STEAL FROM US EVERY GODDAMN DAY! SHIT!!
THUNK

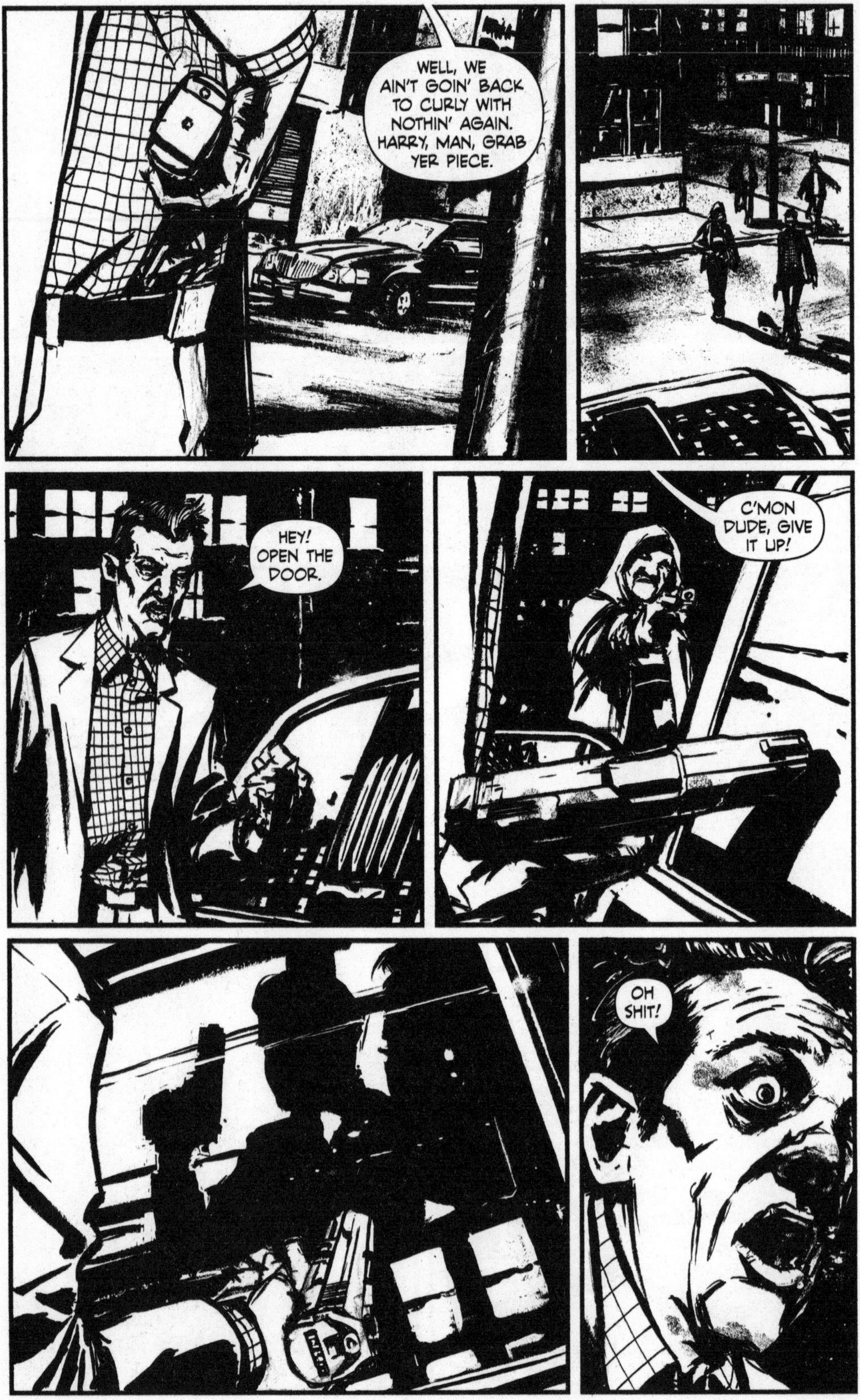
WELL, WE AIN'T GOIN' BACK TO CURLY WITH NOTHIN' AGAIN. HARRY, MAN, GRAB YER PIECE.
HEY! OPEN THE DOOR.
C'MON DUDE, GIVE IT UP!
OH SHIT!

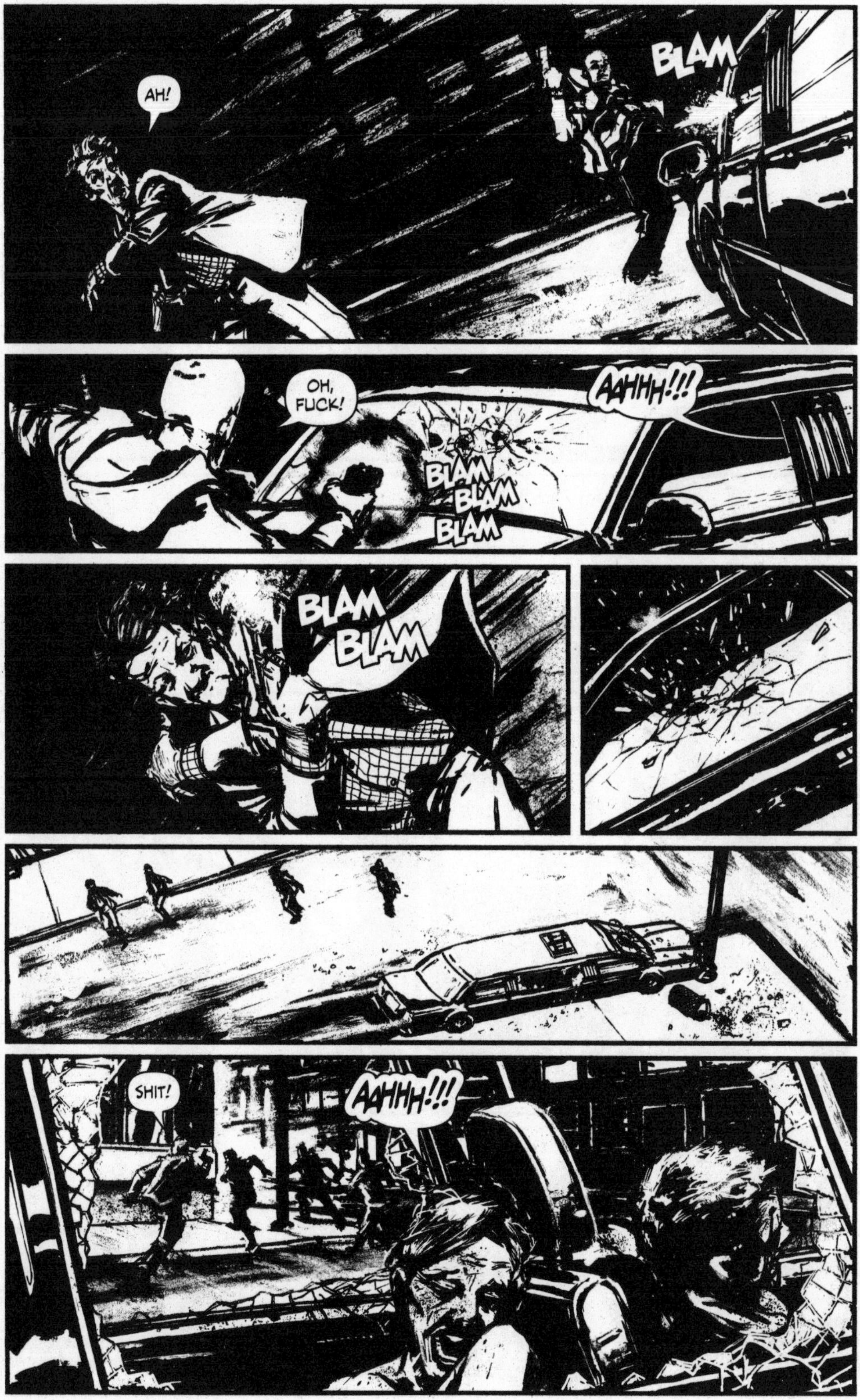
AH!
BLAM
OH, FUCK!
AAHHH!!!
BLAM
BLAM
BLAM
BLAM
BLAM
SHIT!
AAHHH!!!

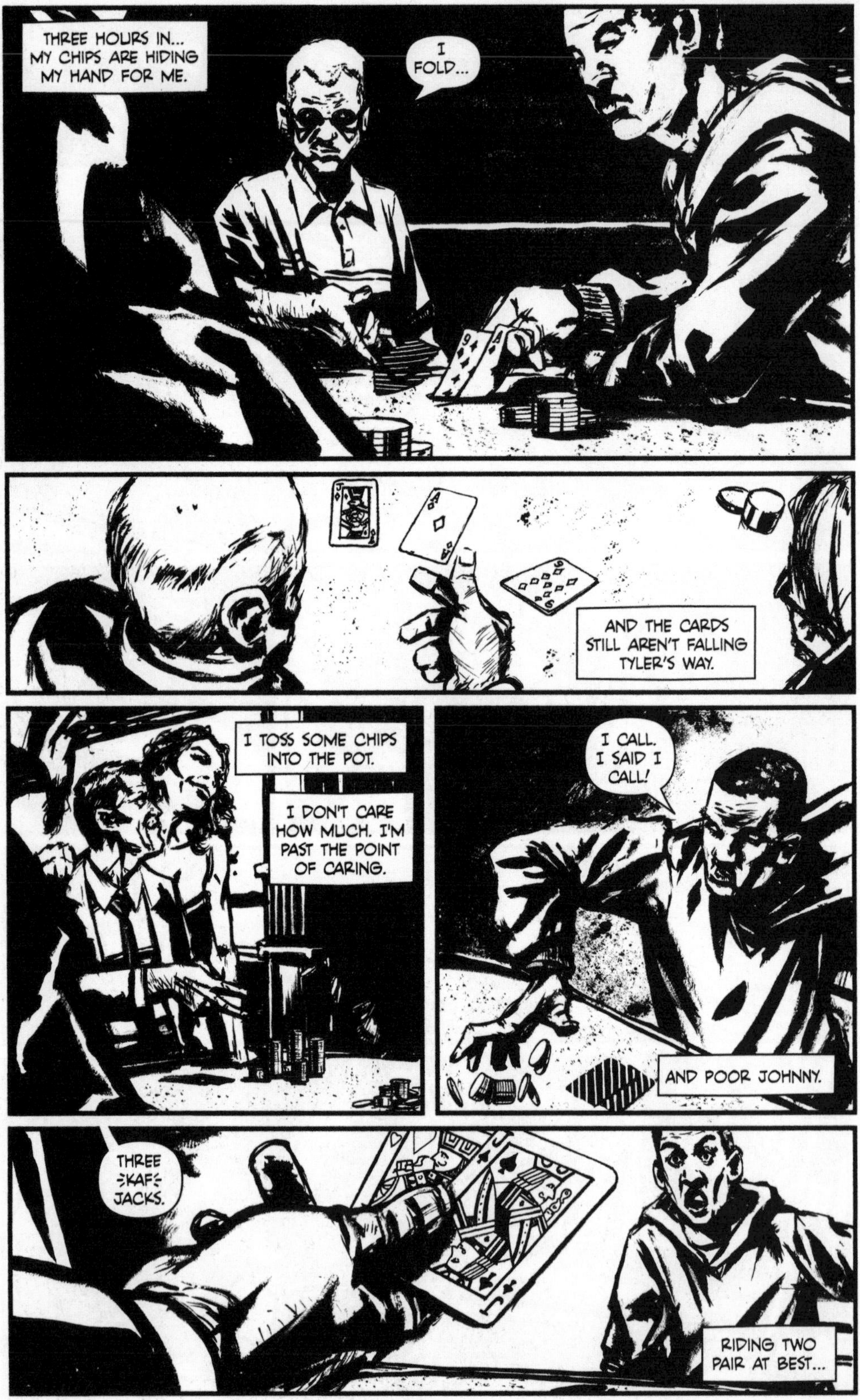
THREE HOURS IN... MY CHIPS ARE HIDING MY HAND FOR ME.
I FOLD...
AND THE CARDS STILL AREN'T FALLING TYLER'S WAY.
I TOSS SOME CHIPS INTO THE POT.
I DON'T CARE HOW MUCH. I'M PAST THE POINT OF CARING.
I CALL. I SAID I CALL!
AND POOR JOHNNY.
THREE KAF JACKS.
RIDING TWO PAIR AT BEST...

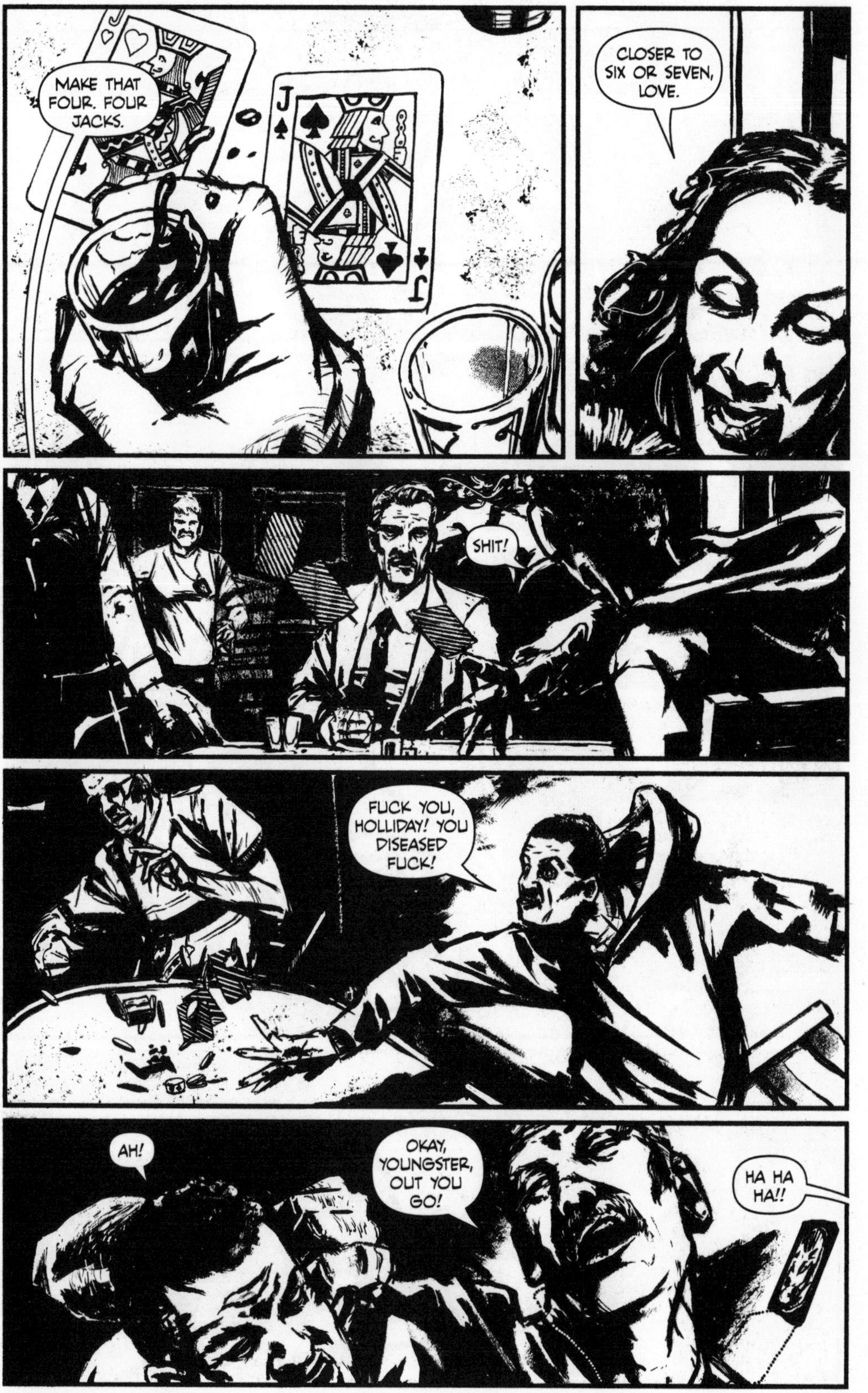
MAKE THAT FOUR. FOUR JACKS.
CLOSER TO SIX OR SEVEN, LOVE.
SHIT!
FUCK YOU, HOLLIDAY! YOU DISEASED FUCK!
AH!
OKAY, YOUNGSTER, OUT YOU GO!
HA HA HA!!

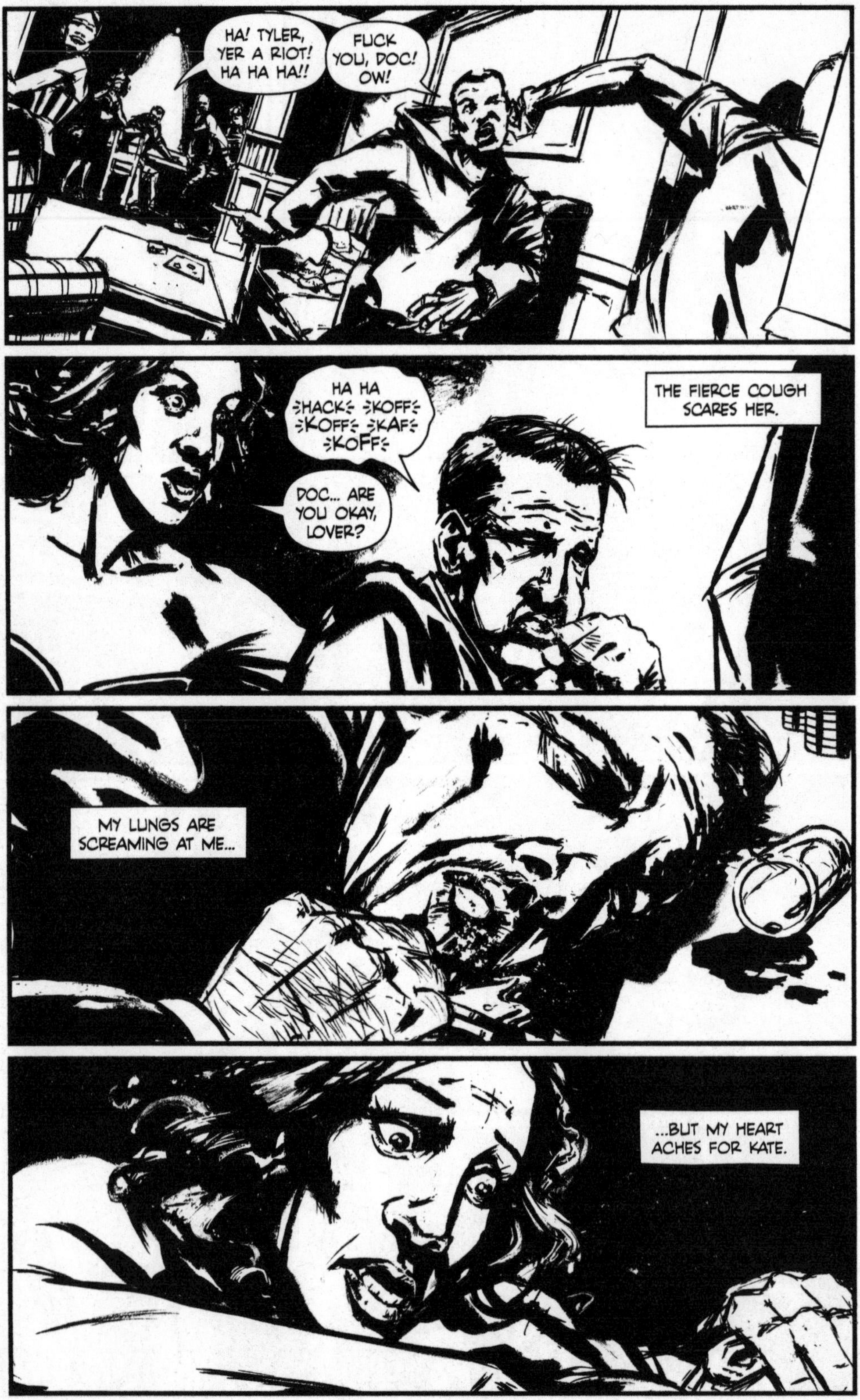
HA! TYLER, YER A RIOT! HA HA HA!!
FUCK YOU, DOC! OW!
HA HA -HACK- -KOFF- -KOFF- -KAF- -KOFF-
THE FIERCE COUGH SCARES HER.
DOC... ARE YOU OKAY, LOVER?
MY LUNGS ARE SCREAMING AT ME...
...BUT MY HEART ACHES FOR KATE.

CHAPTER TWO

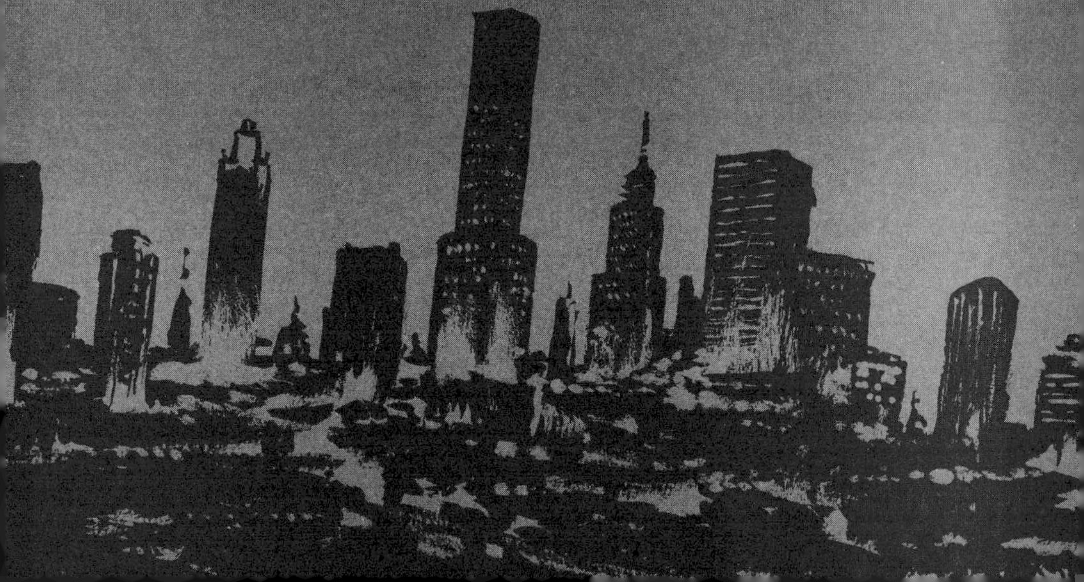

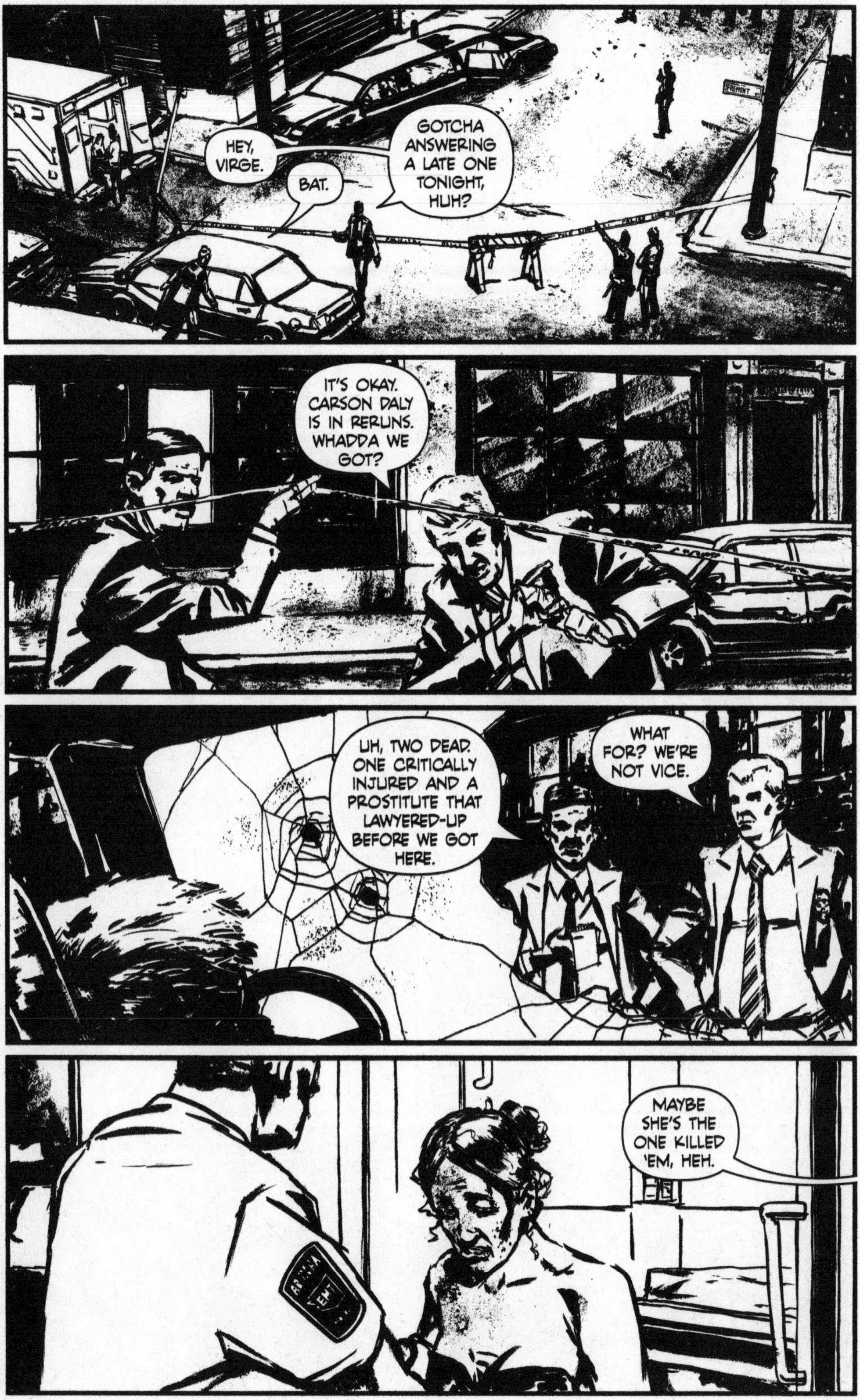
HEY, VIRGE.
BAT.
GOTCHA ANSWERING A LATE ONE TONIGHT, HUH?
FREMONT ST
IT'S OKAY. CARSON DALY IS IN RERUNS. WHADDA WE GOT?
UH, TWO DEAD. ONE CRITICALLY INJURED AND A PROSTITUTE THAT LAWYERED-UP BEFORE WE GOT HERE.
WHAT FOR? WE'RE NOT VICE.
MAYBE SHE'S THE ONE KILLED 'EM, HEH.
EMS

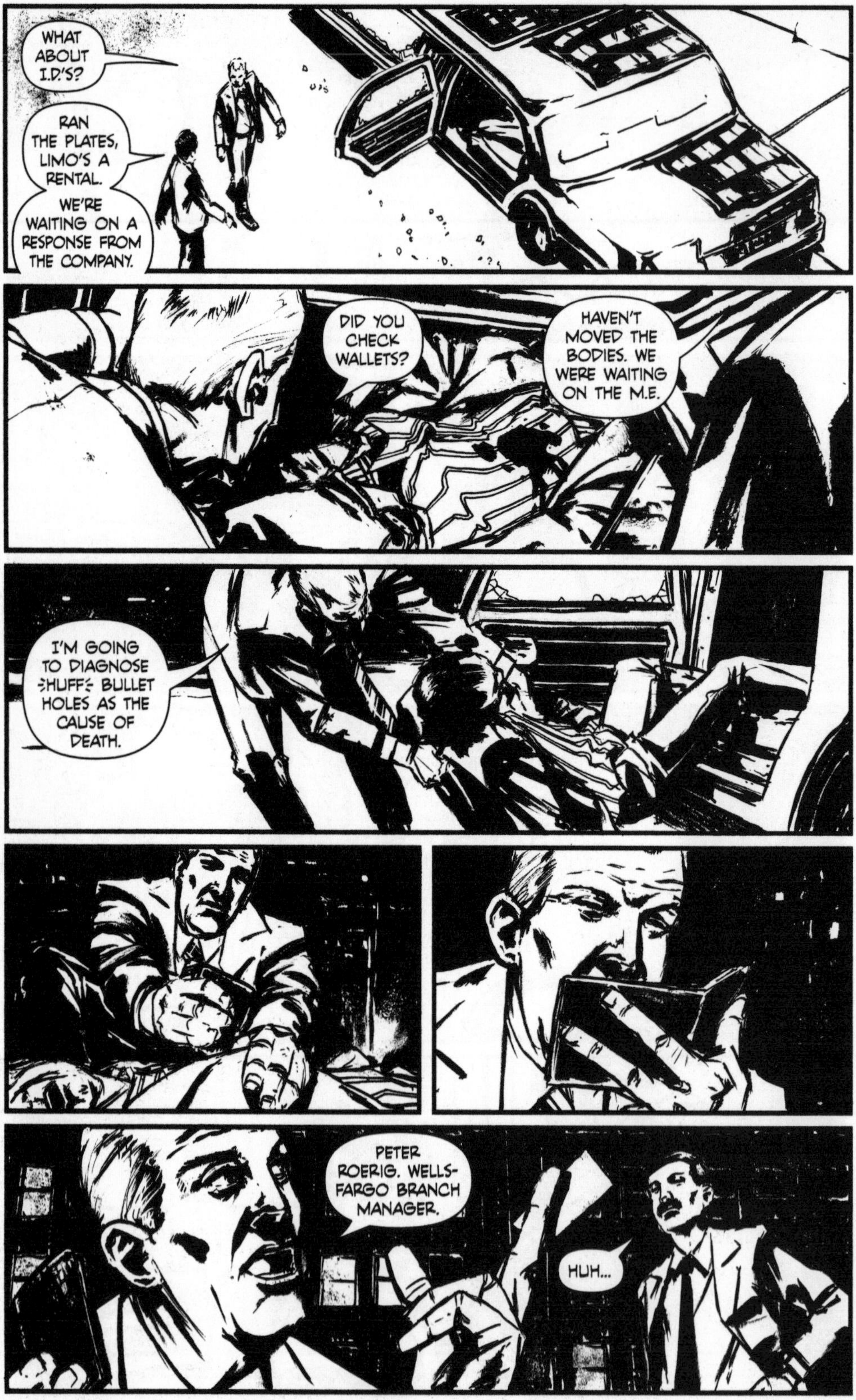
WHAT ABOUT I.D.'S?
RAN THE PLATES, LIMO'S A RENTAL.
WE'RE WAITING ON A RESPONSE FROM THE COMPANY.
DID YOU CHECK WALLETS?
HAVEN'T MOVED THE BODIES. WE WERE WAITING ON THE M.E.
I'M GOING TO DIAGNOSE -HUFF- BULLET HOLES AS THE CAUSE OF DEATH.
PETER ROERIG. WELLS-FARGO BRANCH MANAGER.
HUH...

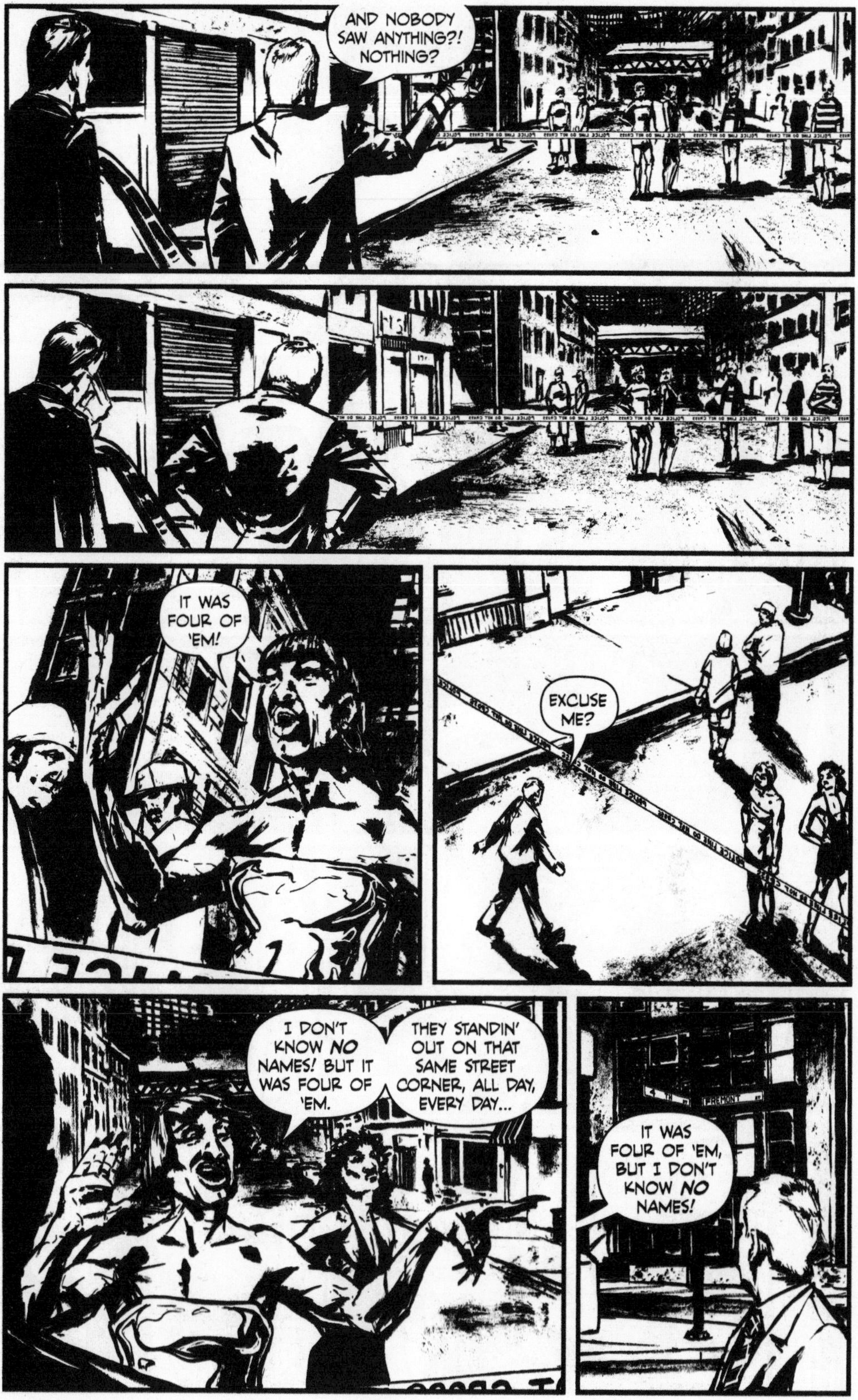
AND NOBODY SAW ANYTHING?! NOTHING?
IT WAS FOUR OF 'EM!
EXCUSE ME?
I DON'T KNOW *NO* NAMES! BUT IT WAS FOUR OF 'EM.
THEY STANDIN' OUT ON THAT SAME STREET CORNER, ALL DAY, EVERY DAY...
IT WAS FOUR OF 'EM, BUT I DON'T KNOW *NO* NAMES!

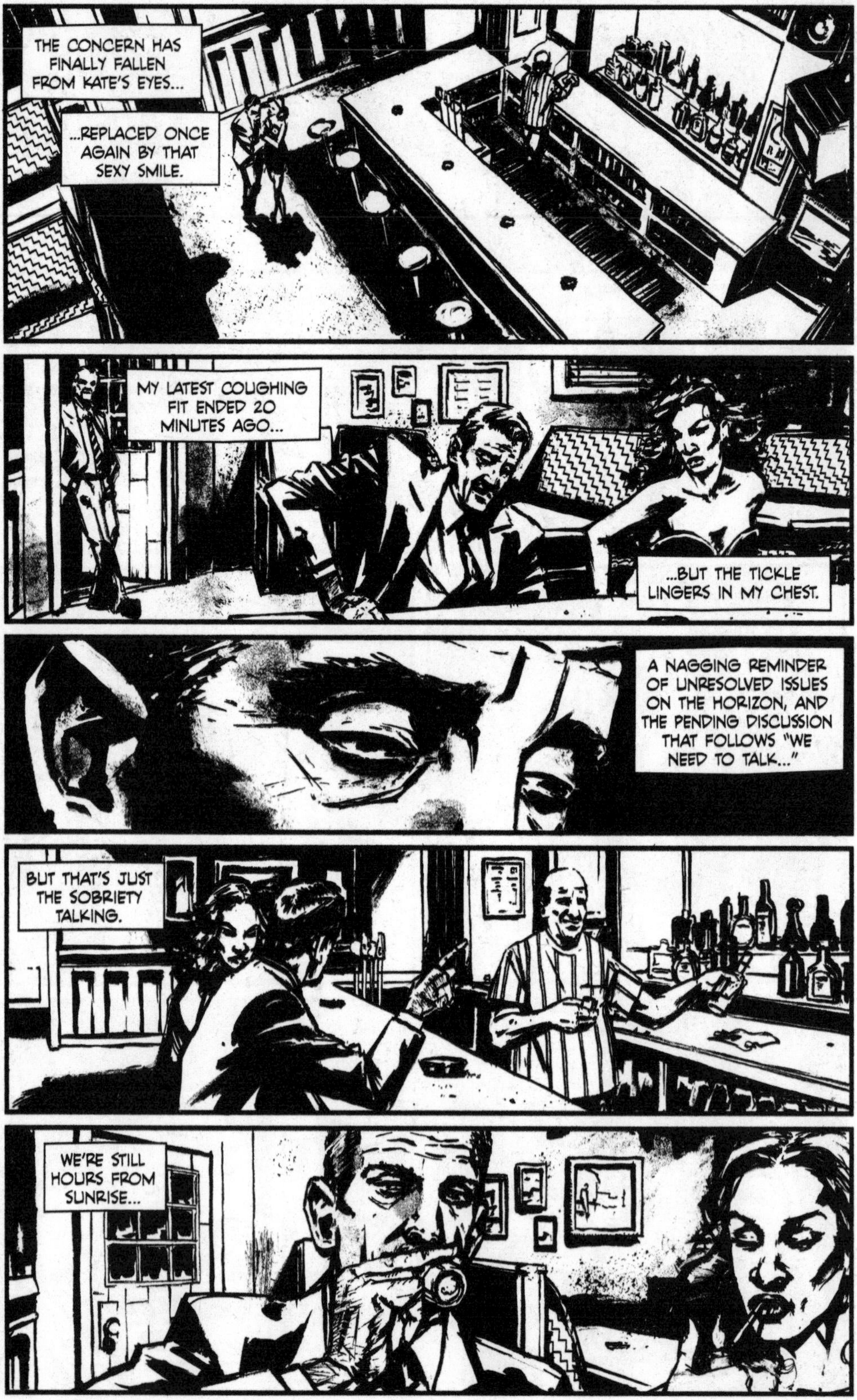
THE CONCERN HAS FINALLY FALLEN FROM KATE'S EYES...
...REPLACED ONCE AGAIN BY THAT SEXY SMILE.
MY LATEST COUGHING FIT ENDED 20 MINUTES AGO...
...BUT THE TICKLE LINGERS IN MY CHEST.
A NAGGING REMINDER OF UNRESOLVED ISSUES ON THE HORIZON, AND THE PENDING DISCUSSION THAT FOLLOWS "WE NEED TO TALK..."
BUT THAT'S JUST THE SOBRIETY TALKING.
WE'RE STILL HOURS FROM SUNRISE...

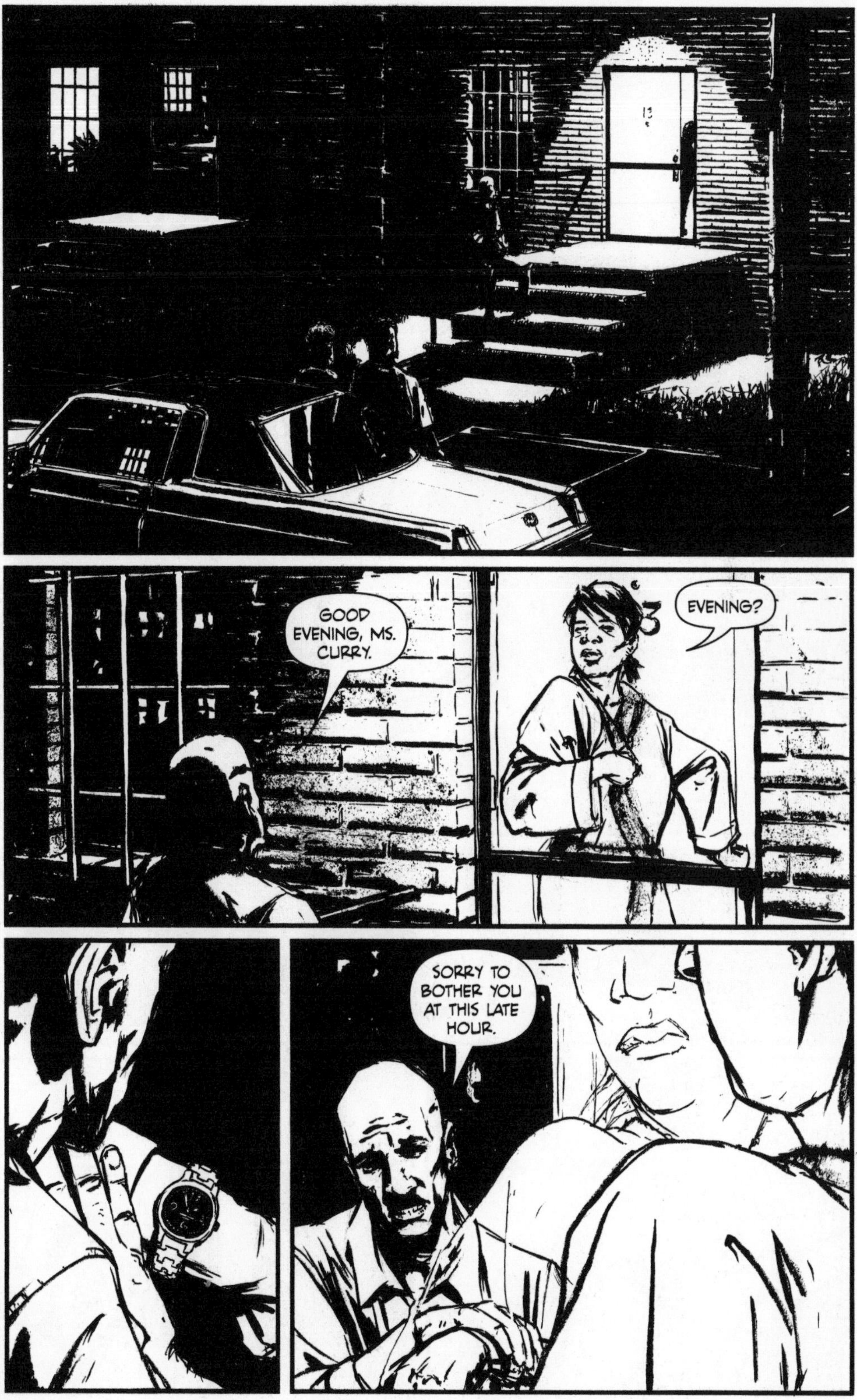
GOOD EVENING, MS. CURRY.
EVENING?
SORRY TO BOTHER YOU AT THIS LATE HOUR.

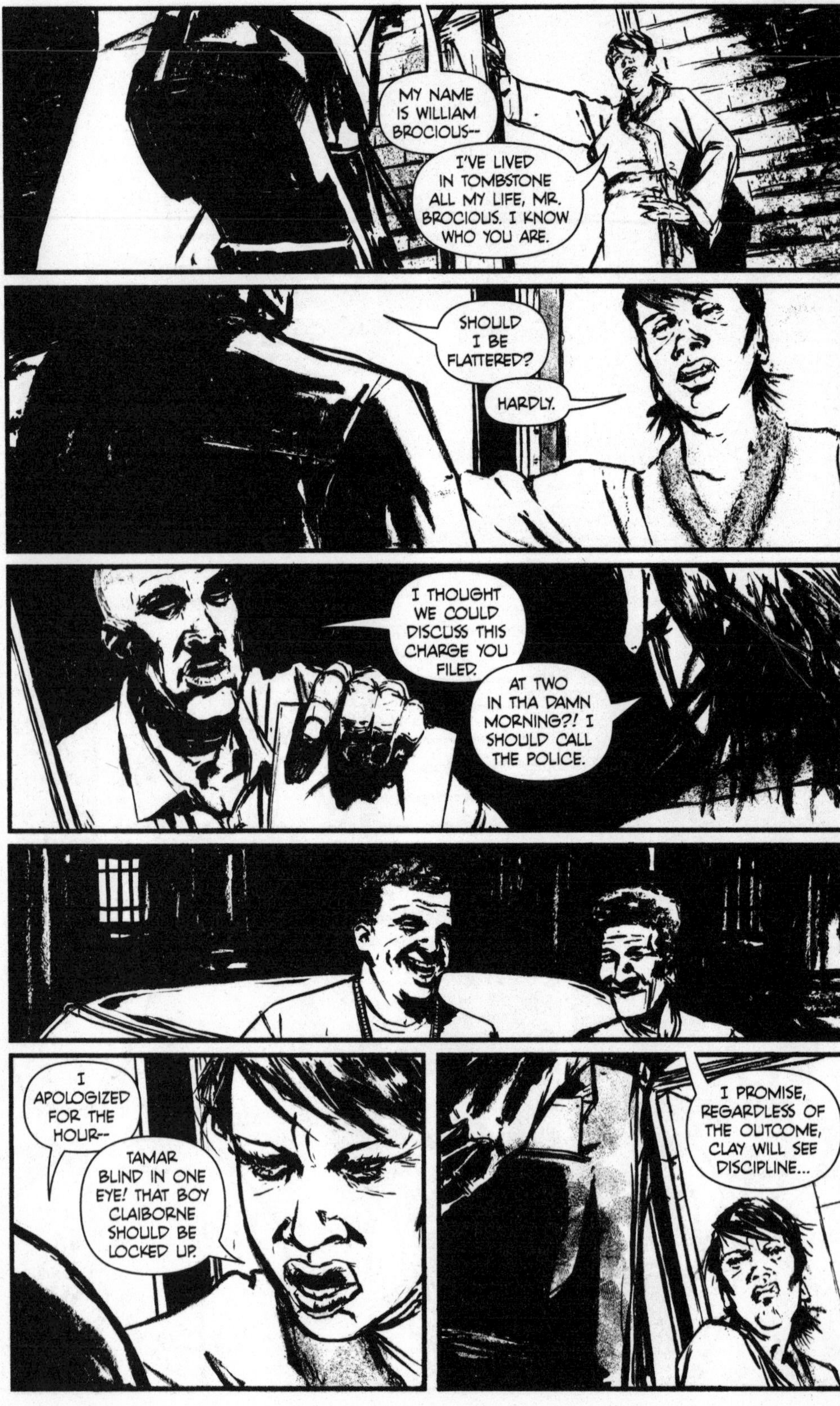
MY NAME IS WILLIAM BROCIOUS--
I'VE LIVED IN TOMBSTONE ALL MY LIFE, MR. BROCIOUS. I KNOW WHO YOU ARE.
SHOULD I BE FLATTERED?
HARDLY.
I THOUGHT WE COULD DISCUSS THIS CHARGE YOU FILED.
AT TWO IN THA DAMN MORNING?! I SHOULD CALL THE POLICE.
I APOLOGIZED FOR THE HOUR--
TAMAR BLIND IN ONE EYE! THAT BOY CLAIBORNE SHOULD BE LOCKED UP.
I PROMISE, REGARDLESS OF THE OUTCOME, CLAY WILL SEE DISCIPLINE...

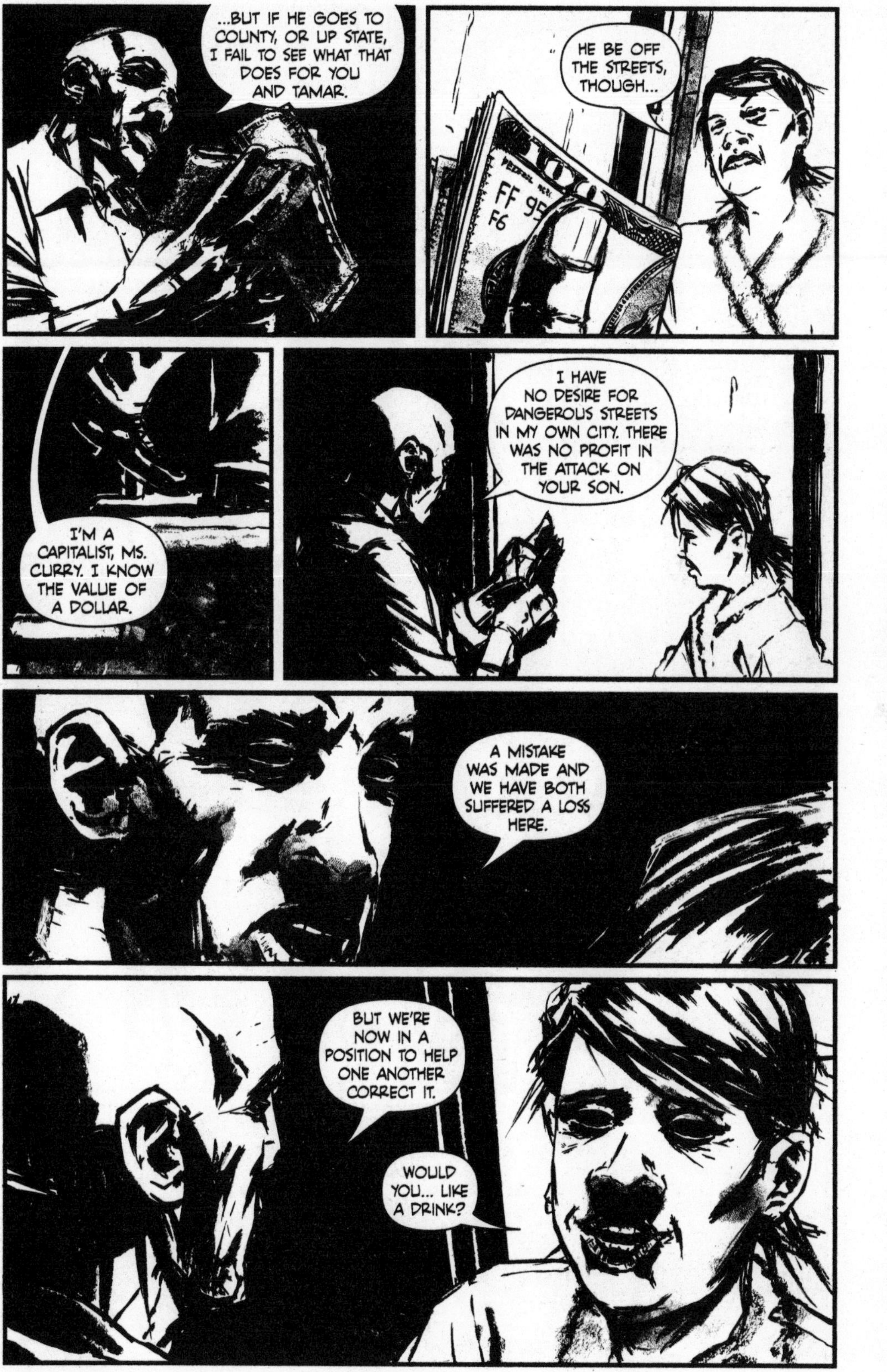
...BUT IF HE GOES TO COUNTY, OR UP STATE, I FAIL TO SEE WHAT THAT DOES FOR YOU AND TAMAR.
HE BE OFF THE STREETS, THOUGH...
I'M A CAPITALIST, MS. CURRY. I KNOW THE VALUE OF A DOLLAR.
I HAVE NO DESIRE FOR DANGEROUS STREETS IN MY OWN CITY. THERE WAS NO PROFIT IN THE ATTACK ON YOUR SON.
A MISTAKE WAS MADE AND WE HAVE BOTH SUFFERED A LOSS HERE.
BUT WE'RE NOW IN A POSITION TO HELP ONE ANOTHER CORRECT IT.
WOULD YOU... LIKE A DRINK?

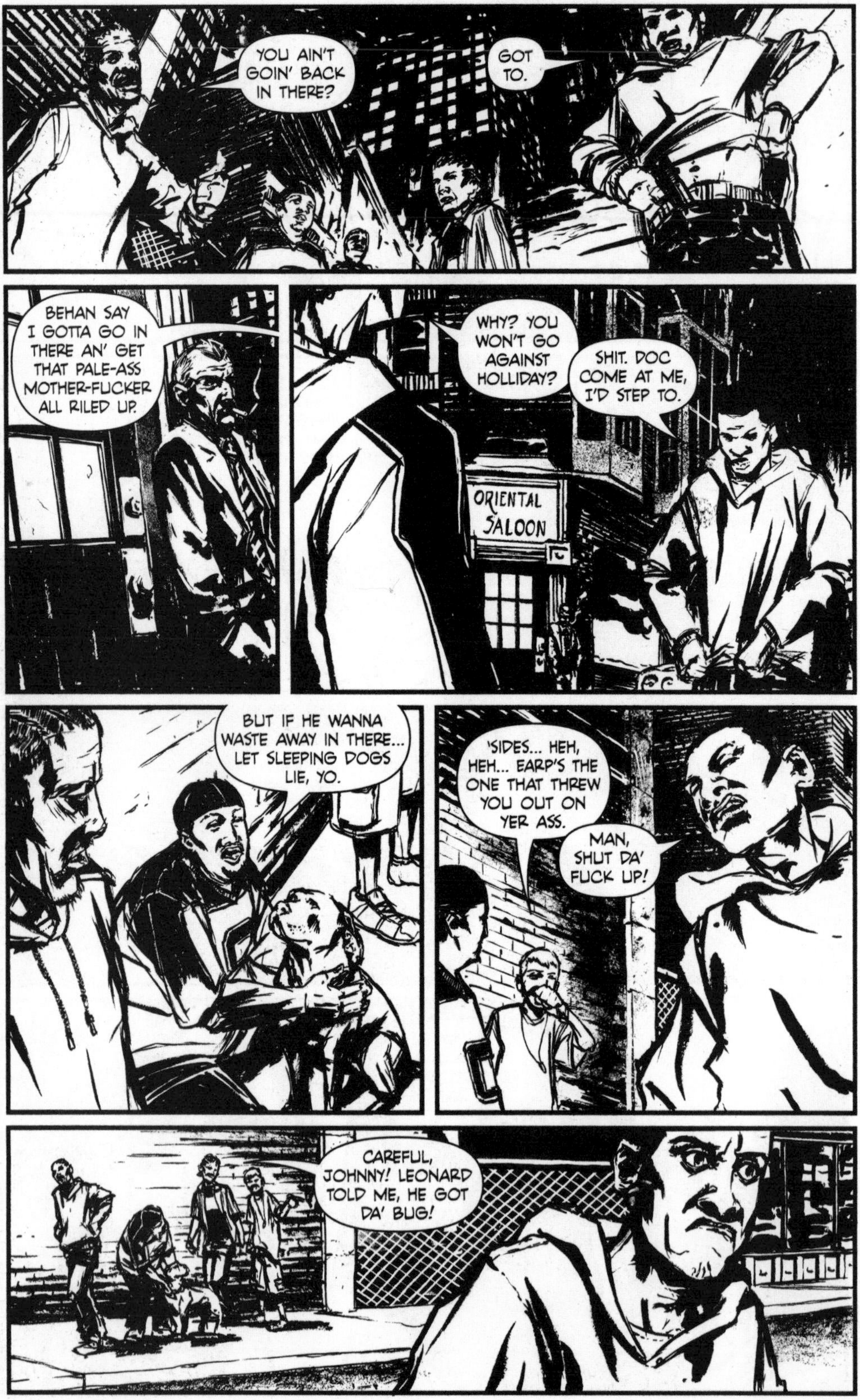
YOU AIN'T GOIN' BACK IN THERE?
GOT TO.
BEHAN SAY I GOTTA GO IN THERE AN' GET THAT PALE-ASS MOTHER-FUCKER ALL RILED UP.
WHY? YOU WON'T GO AGAINST HOLLIDAY?
SHIT. DOC COME AT ME, I'D STEP TO.
ORIENTAL SALOON
BUT IF HE WANNA WASTE AWAY IN THERE... LET SLEEPING DOGS LIE, YO.
'SIDES... HEH, HEH... EARP'S THE ONE THAT THREW YOU OUT ON YER ASS.
MAN, SHUT DA' FUCK UP!
CAREFUL, JOHNNY! LEONARD TOLD ME, HE GOT DA' BUG!

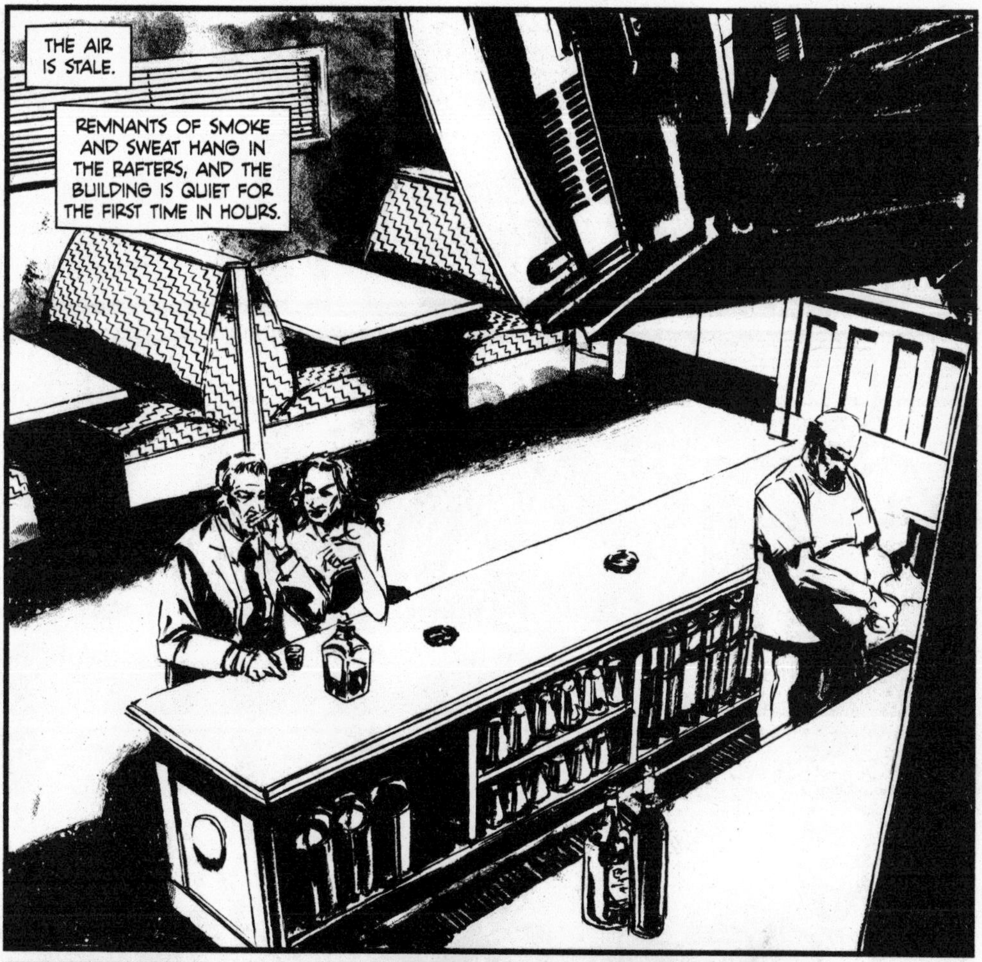
THE AIR IS STALE.
REMNANTS OF SMOKE AND SWEAT HANG IN THE RAFTERS, AND THE BUILDING IS QUIET FOR THE FIRST TIME IN HOURS.

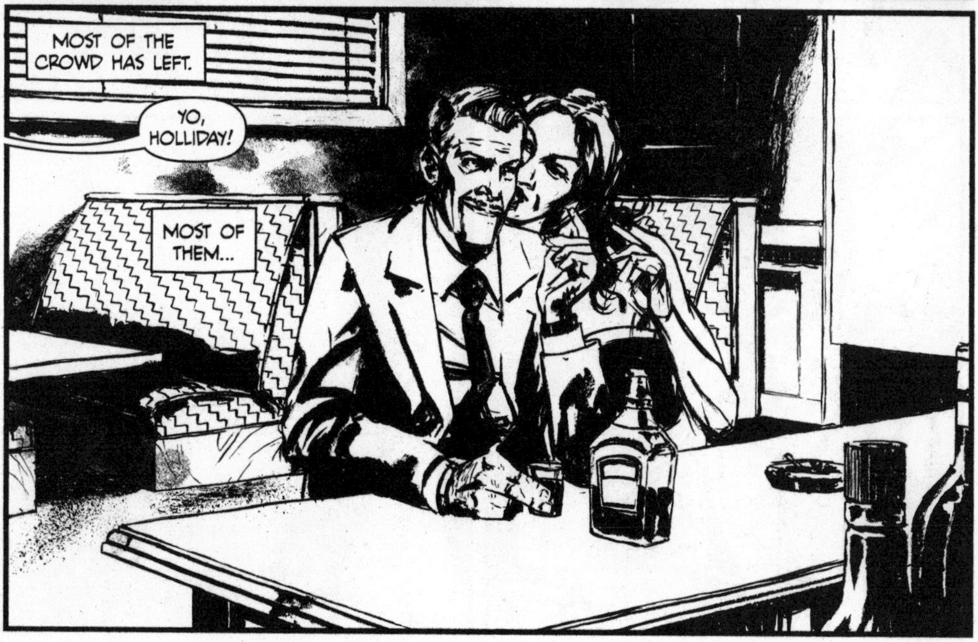
MOST OF THE CROWD HAS LEFT.
YO, HOLLIDAY!
MOST OF THEM...

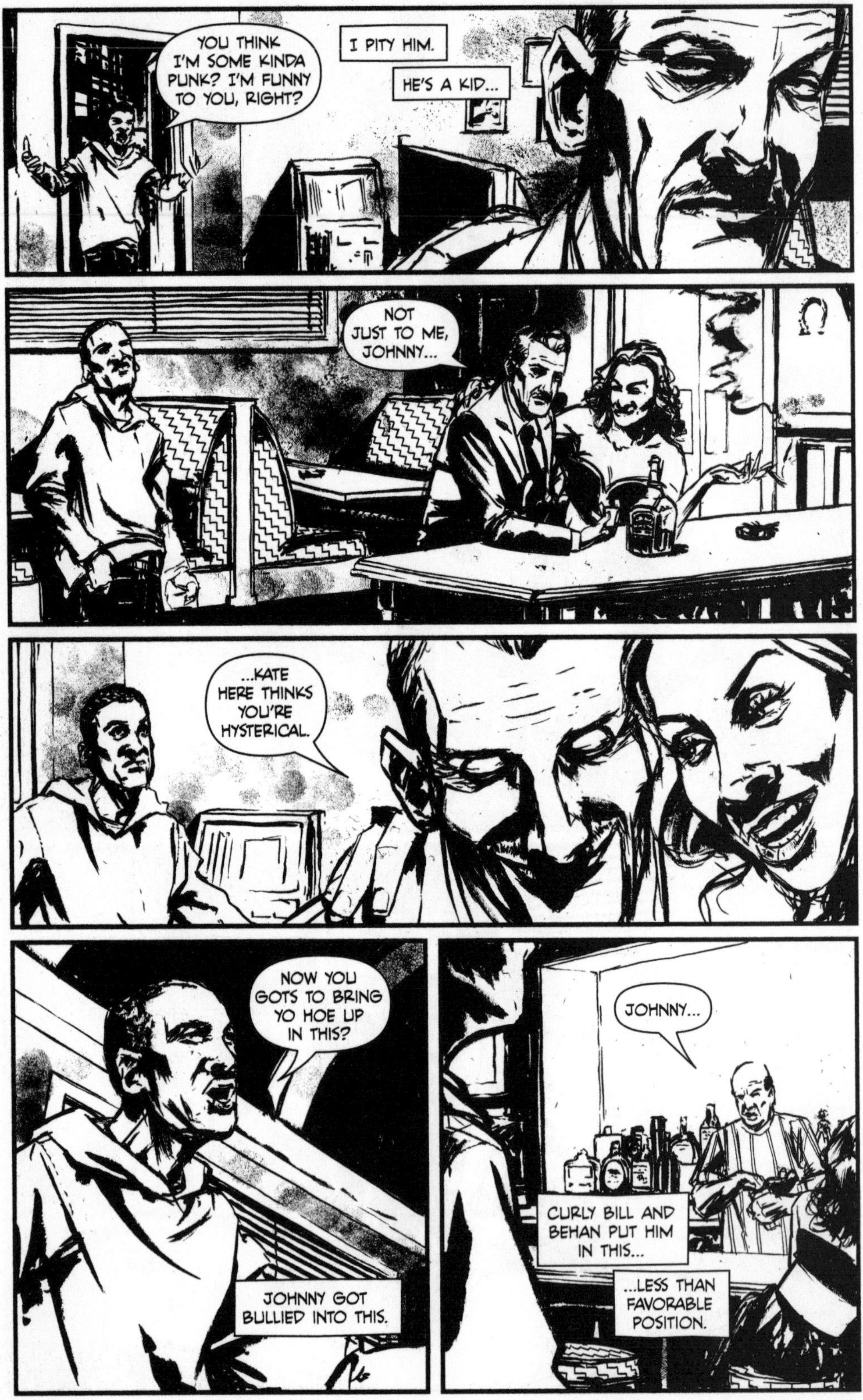
YOU THINK I'M SOME KINDA PUNK? I'M FUNNY TO YOU, RIGHT?
I PITY HIM.
HE'S A KID...
NOT JUST TO ME, JOHNNY...
...KATE HERE THINKS YOU'RE HYSTERICAL.
NOW YOU GOTS TO BRING YO HOE UP IN THIS?
JOHNNY GOT BULLIED INTO THIS.
JOHNNY...
CURLY BILL AND BEHAN PUT HIM IN THIS...
...LESS THAN FAVORABLE POSITION.

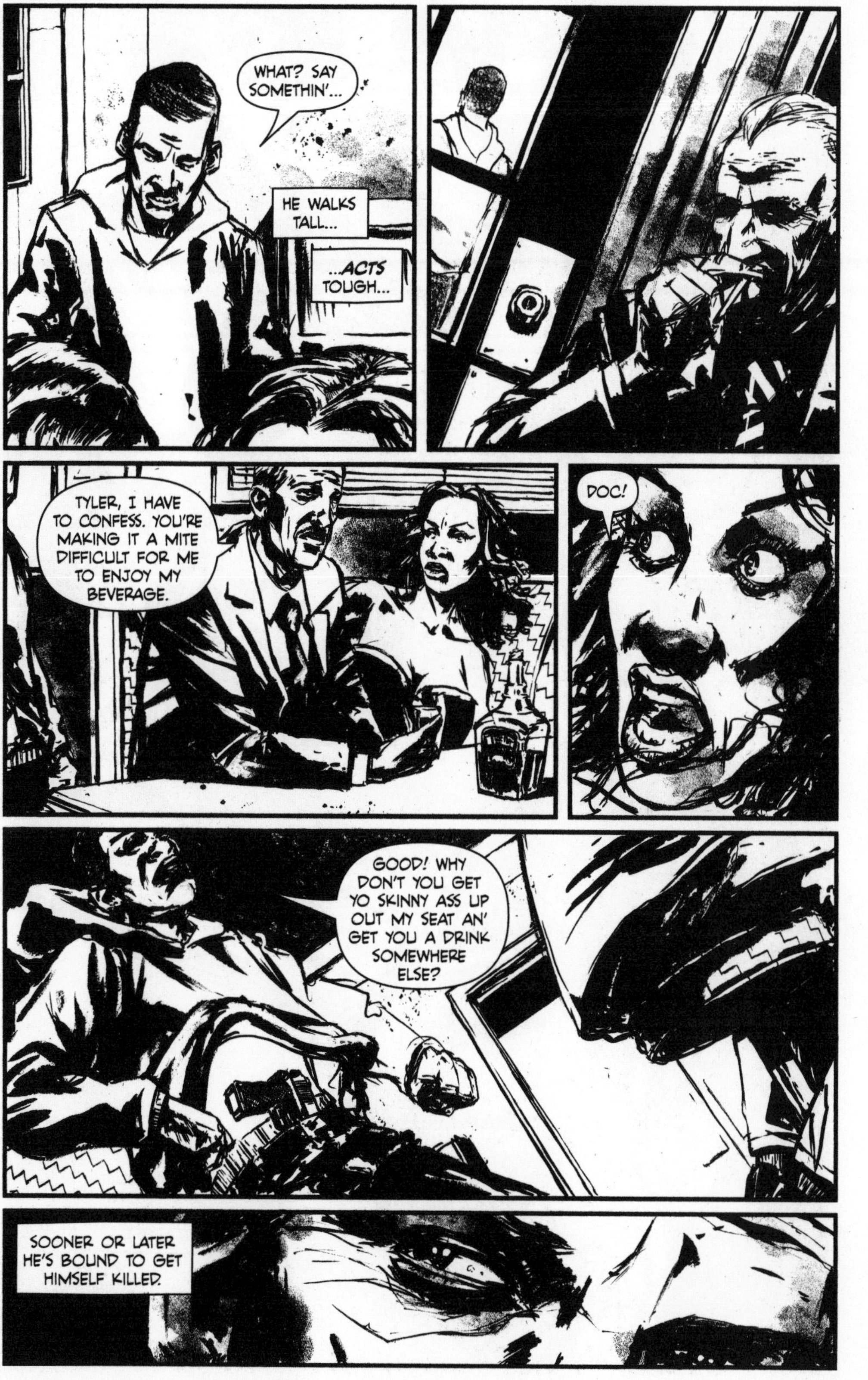
WHAT? SAY SOMETHIN'...
HE WALKS TALL...
...ACTS TOUGH...
TYLER, I HAVE TO CONFESS. YOU'RE MAKING IT A MITE DIFFICULT FOR ME TO ENJOY MY BEVERAGE.
DOC!
GOOD! WHY DON'T YOU GET YO SKINNY ASS UP OUT MY SEAT AN' GET YOU A DRINK SOMEWHERE ELSE?
SOONER OR LATER HE'S BOUND TO GET HIMSELF KILLED.

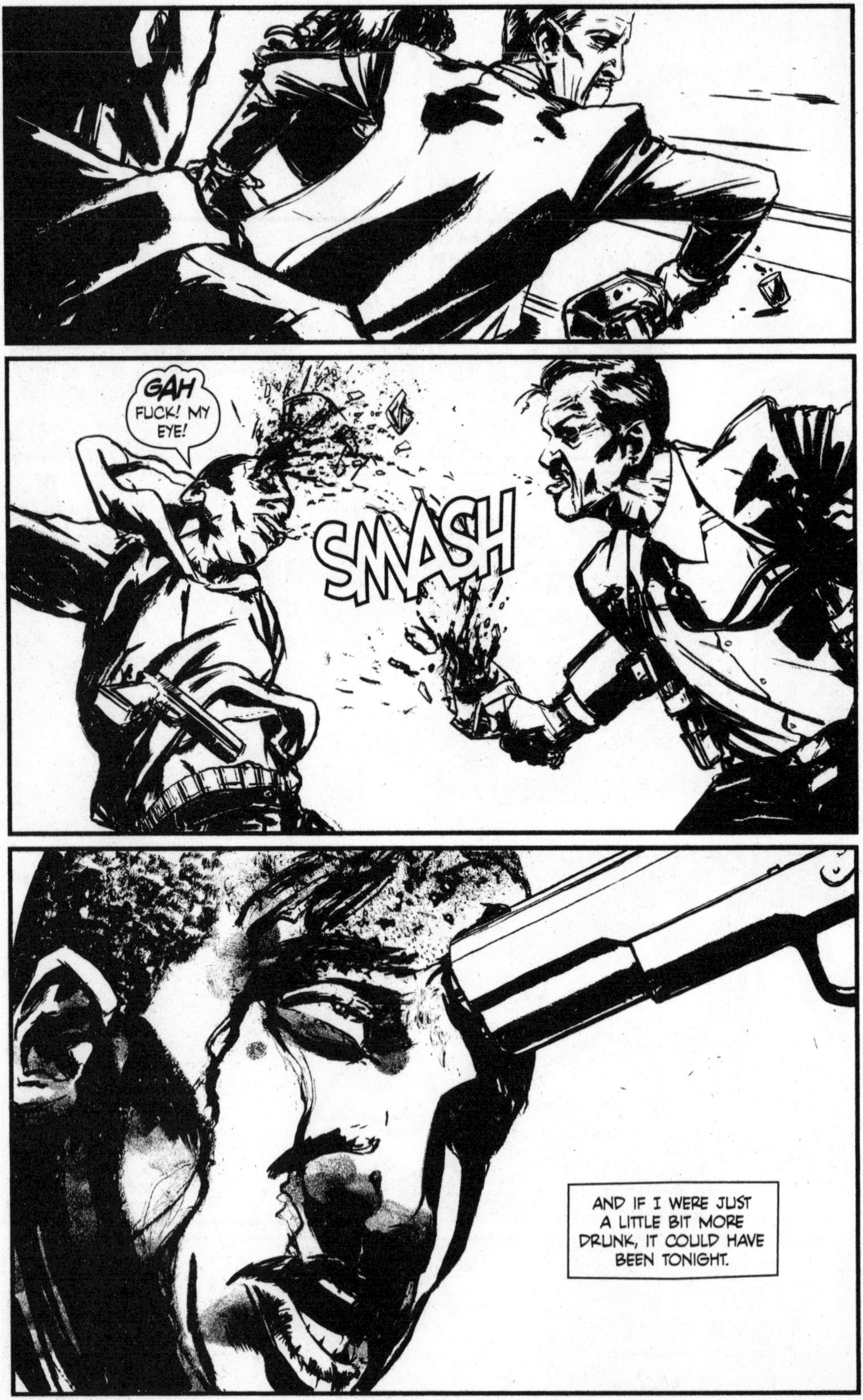
GAH FUCK! MY EYE!
SMASH
AND IF I WERE JUST A LITTLE BIT MORE DRUNK, IT COULD HAVE BEEN TONIGHT.

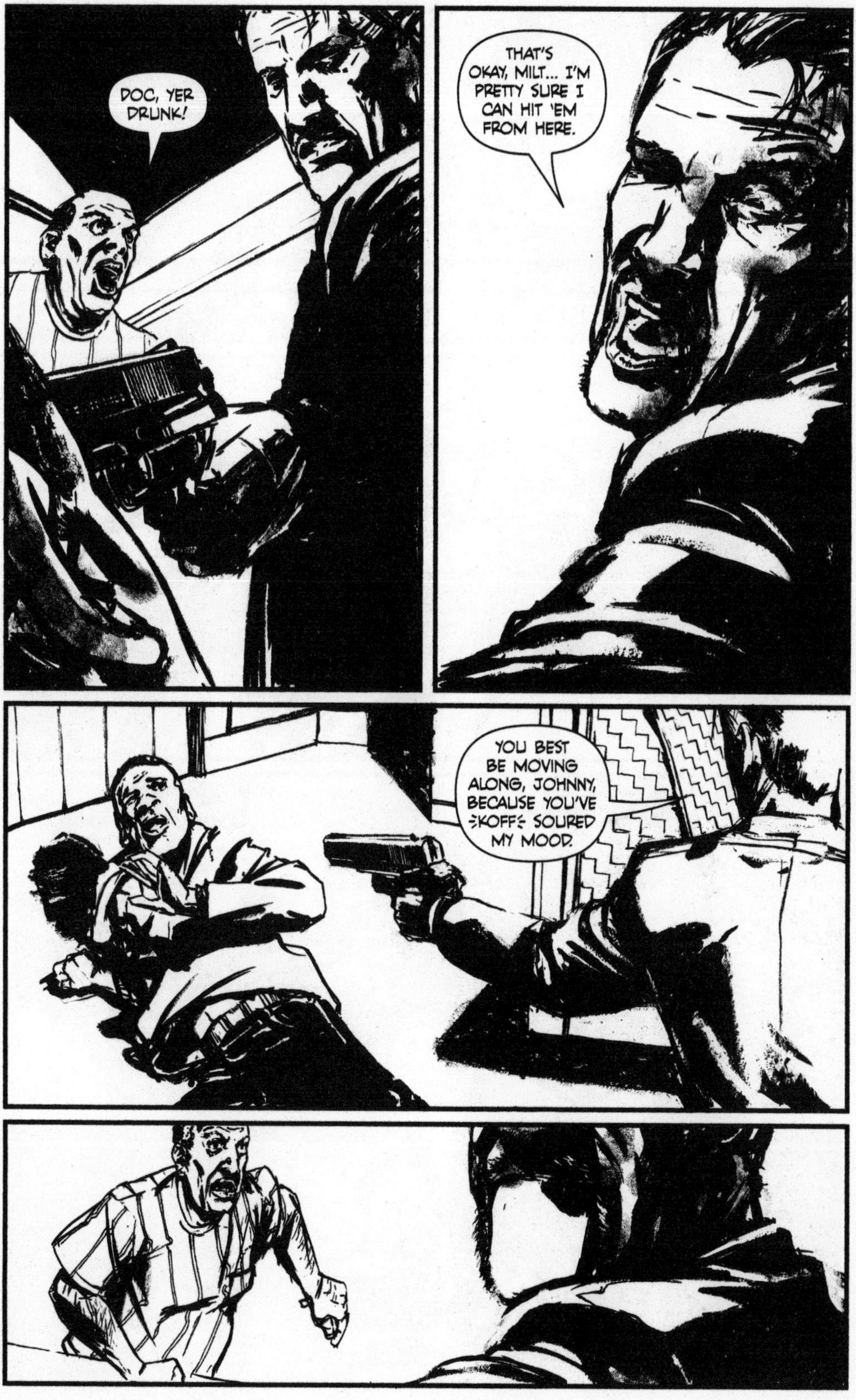
DOC, YER DRUNK!
THAT'S OKAY, MILT... I'M PRETTY SURE I CAN HIT 'EM FROM HERE.
YOU BEST BE MOVING ALONG, JOHNNY, BECAUSE YOU'VE -KOFF- SOURED MY MOOD.

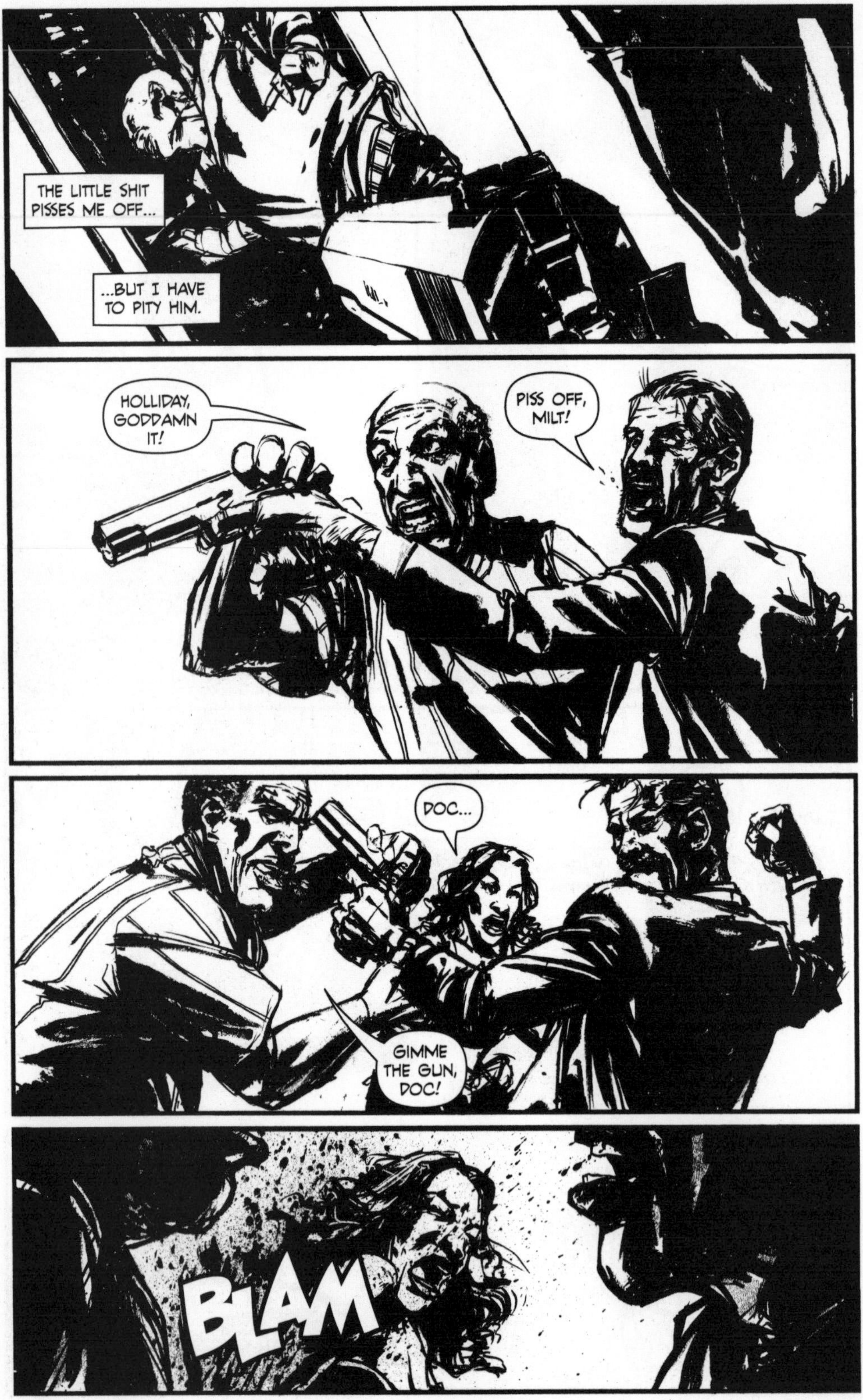
THE LITTLE SHIT PISSES ME OFF...
...BUT I HAVE TO PITY HIM.
HOLLIDAY, GODDAMN IT!
PISS OFF, MILT!
DOC...
GIMME THE GUN, DOC!
BLAM

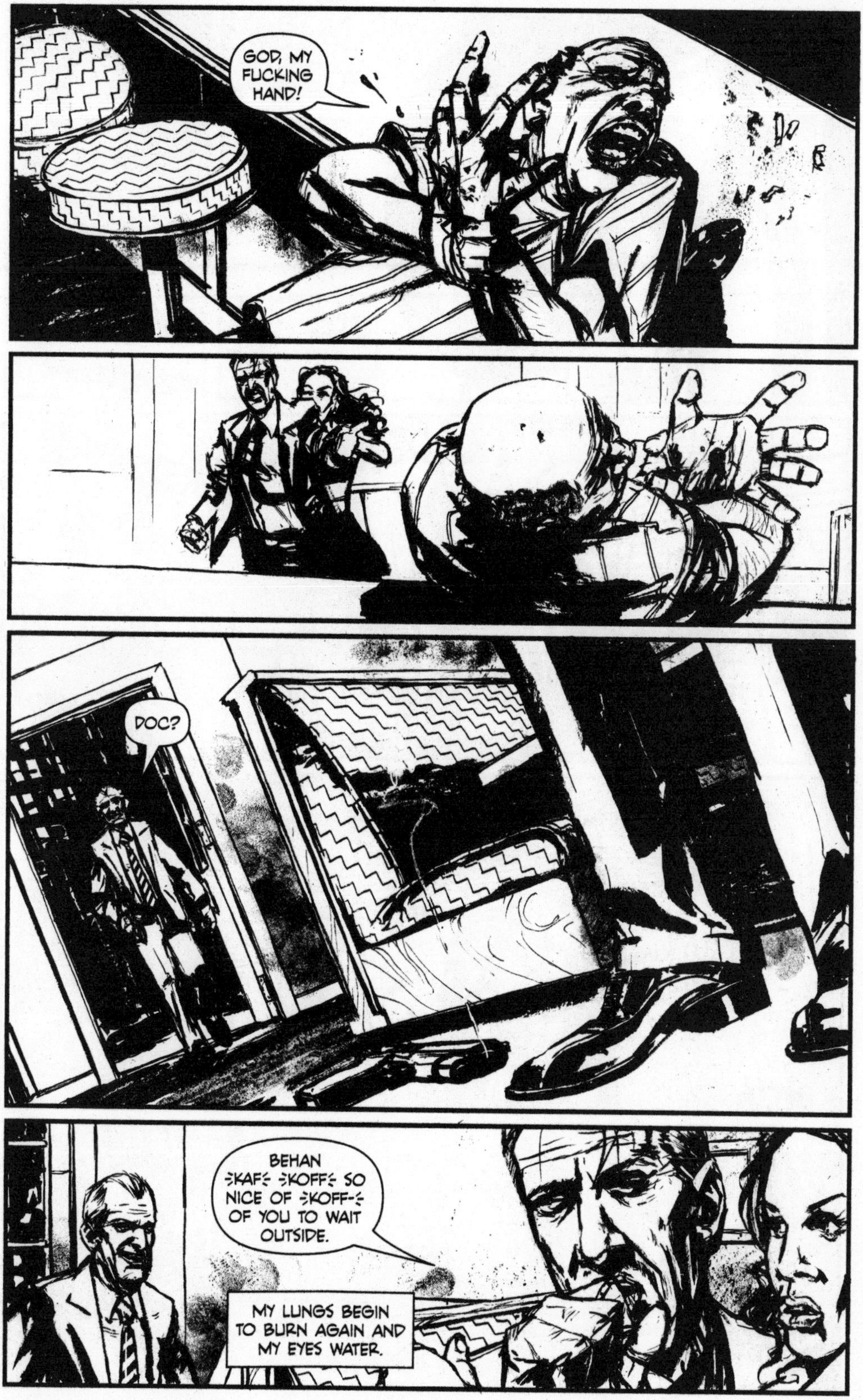
GOD, MY FUCKING HAND!
DOC?
BEHAN ⸗KAF⸗ ⸗KOFF⸗ SO NICE OF ⸗KOFF⸗ OF YOU TO WAIT OUTSIDE.
MY LUNGS BEGIN TO BURN AGAIN AND MY EYES WATER.

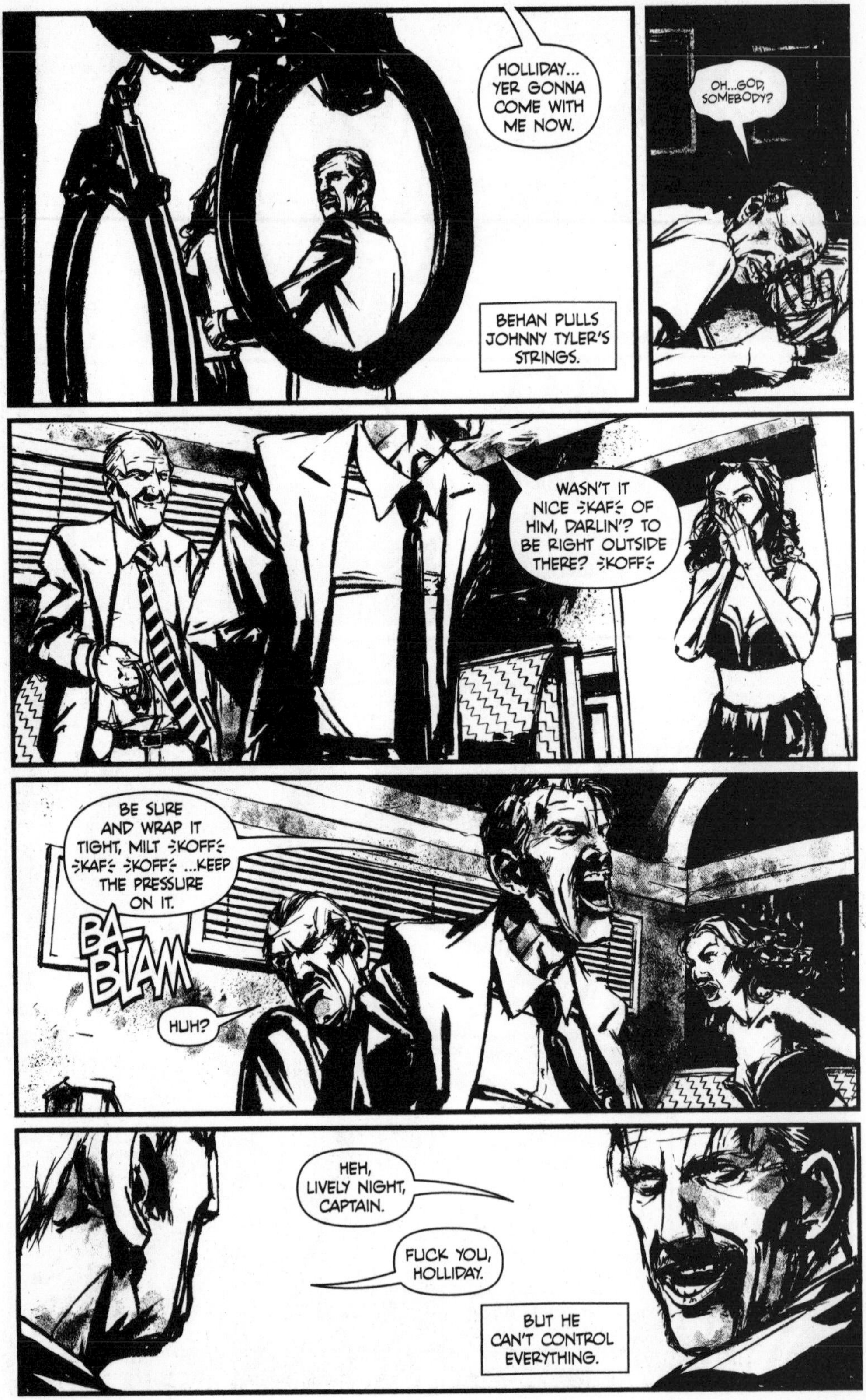
HOLLIDAY... YER GONNA COME WITH ME NOW.
BEHAN PULLS JOHNNY TYLER'S STRINGS.
OH...GOD, SOMEBODY?
WASN'T IT NICE =KAF= OF HIM, DARLIN'? TO BE RIGHT OUTSIDE THERE? =KOFF=
BE SURE AND WRAP IT TIGHT, MILT =KOFF= =KAF= =KOFF= ...KEEP THE PRESSURE ON IT.
BA BLAM
HUH?
HEH, LIVELY NIGHT, CAPTAIN.
FUCK YOU, HOLLIDAY.
BUT HE CAN'T CONTROL EVERYTHING.

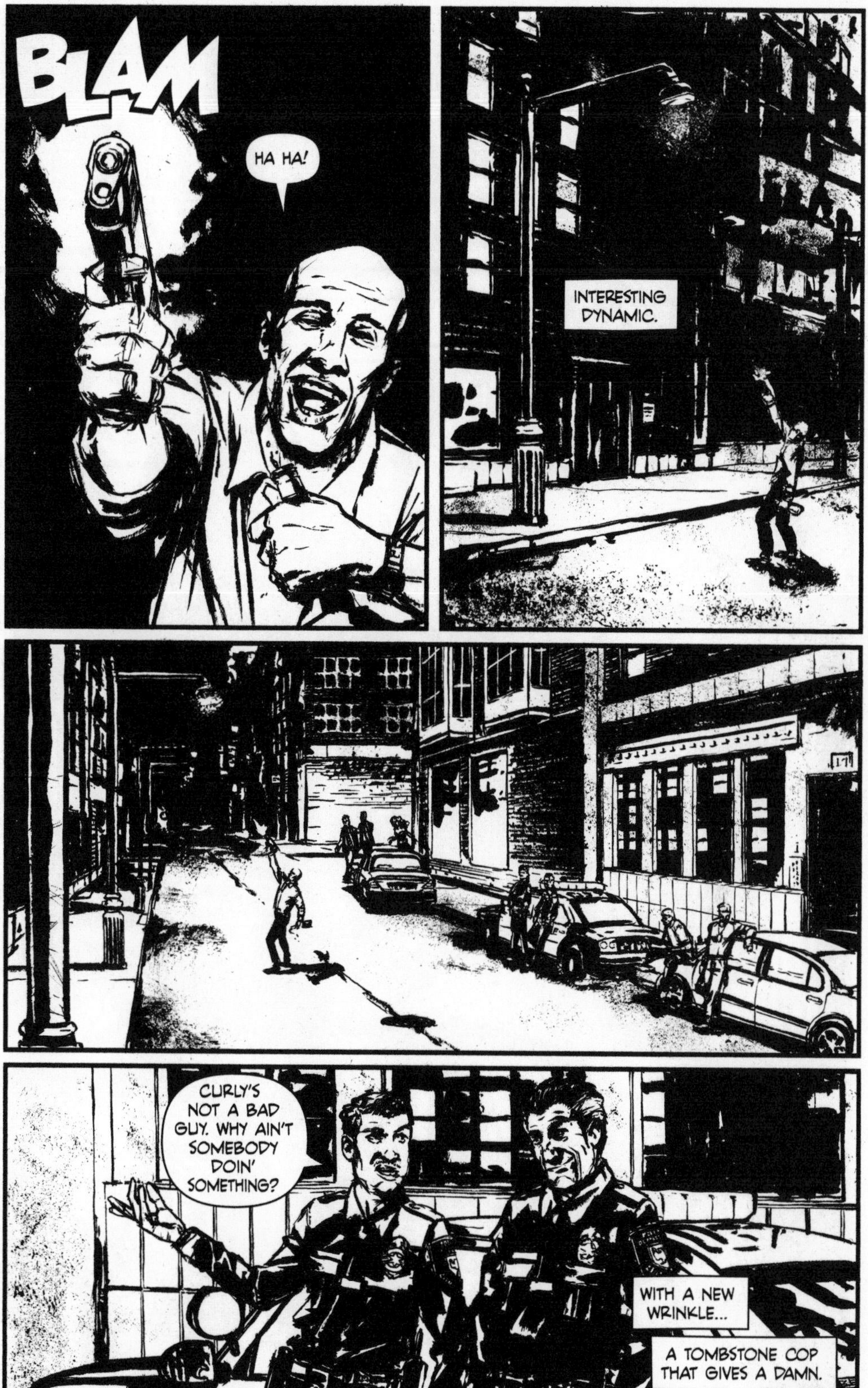
BLAM
HA HA!
INTERESTING DYNAMIC.
CURLY'S NOT A BAD GUY. WHY AIN'T SOMEBODY DOIN' SOMETHING?
WITH A NEW WRINKLE...
A TOMBSTONE COP THAT GIVES A DAMN.

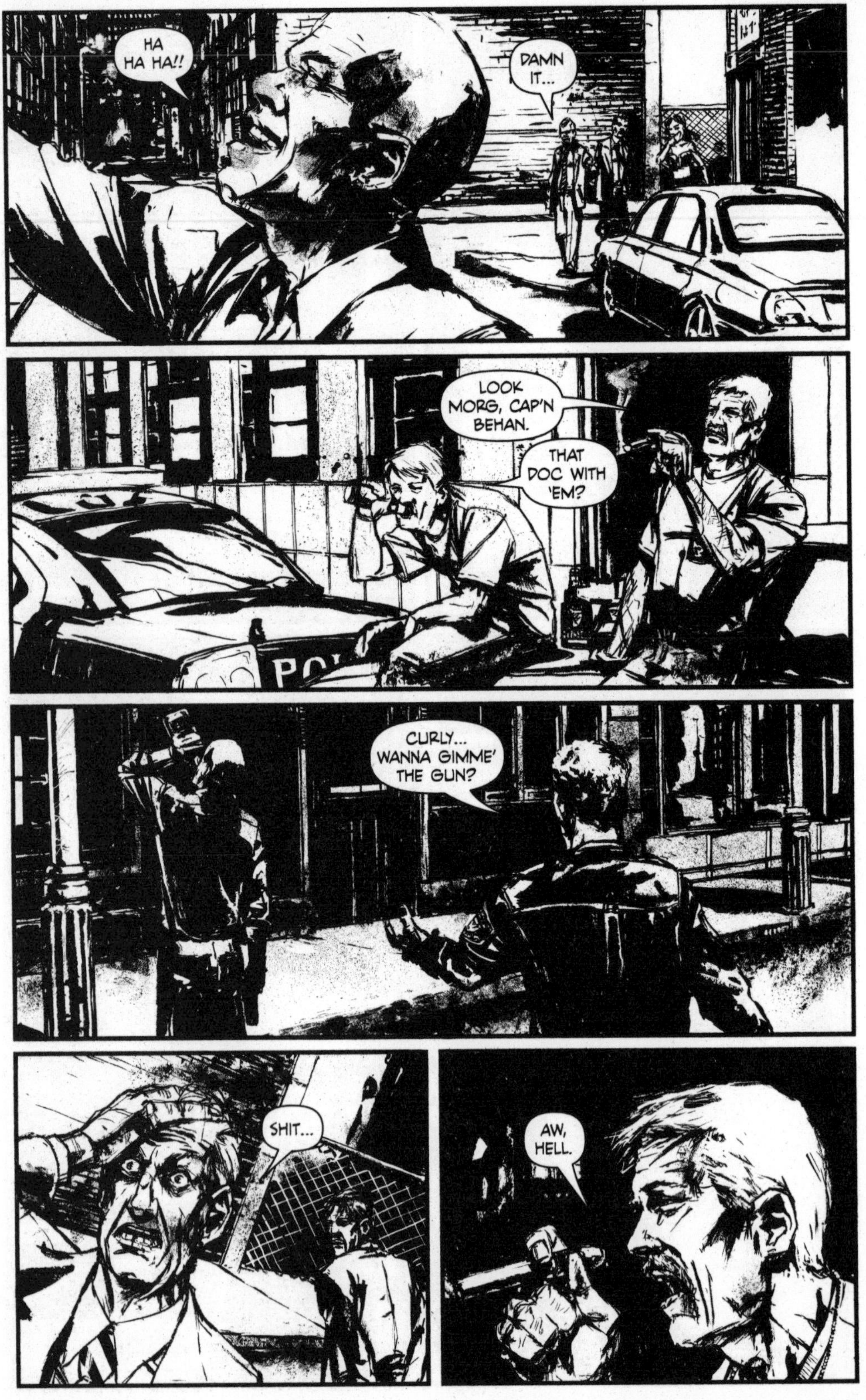
HA HA HA!!
DAMN IT...
LOOK MORG, CAP'N BEHAN.
THAT DOC WITH 'EM?
POL
CURLY... WANNA GIMME' THE GUN?
SHIT...
AW, HELL.

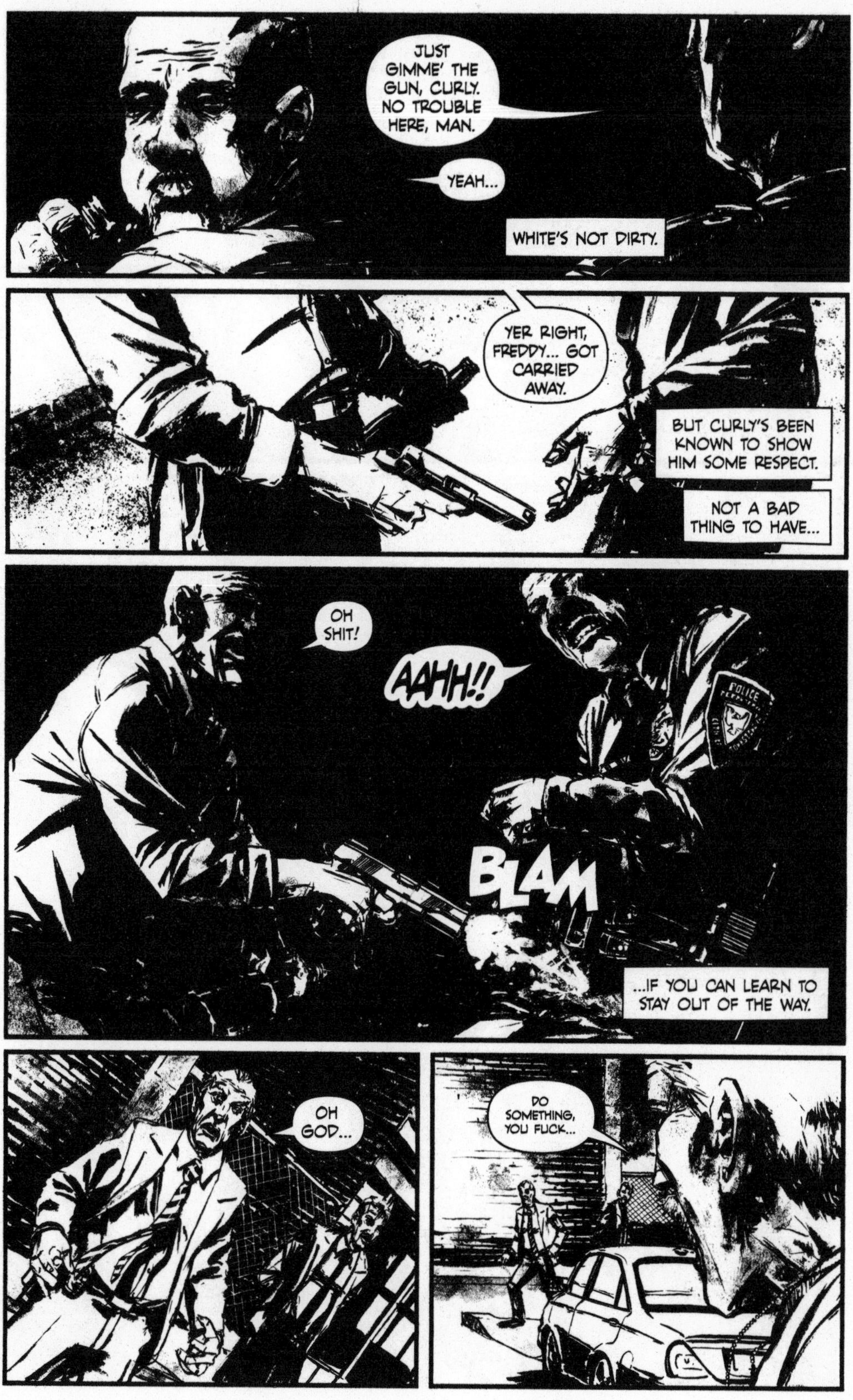
JUST GIMME' THE GUN, CURLY. NO TROUBLE HERE, MAN.
YEAH...
WHITE'S NOT DIRTY.
YER RIGHT, FREDDY... GOT CARRIED AWAY.
BUT CURLY'S BEEN KNOWN TO SHOW HIM SOME RESPECT.
NOT A BAD THING TO HAVE...
OH SHIT!
AAHH!!
BLAM
...IF YOU CAN LEARN TO STAY OUT OF THE WAY.
OH GOD...
DO SOMETHING, YOU FUCK...

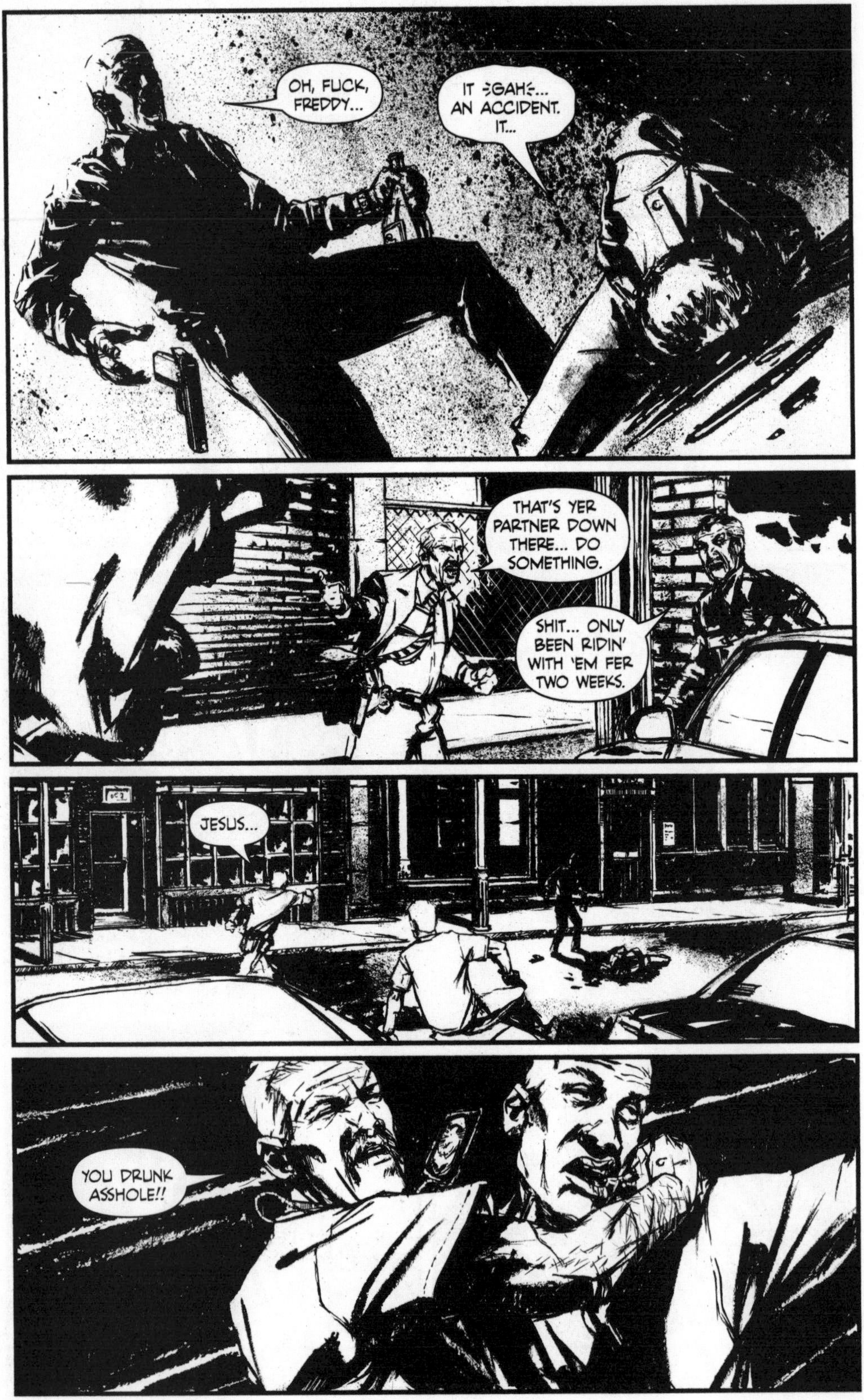
OH, FUCK, FREDDY...
IT GAH... AN ACCIDENT. IT...
THAT'S YER PARTNER DOWN THERE... DO SOMETHING.
SHIT... ONLY BEEN RIDIN' WITH 'EM FER TWO WEEKS.
JESUS...
YOU DRUNK ASSHOLE!!

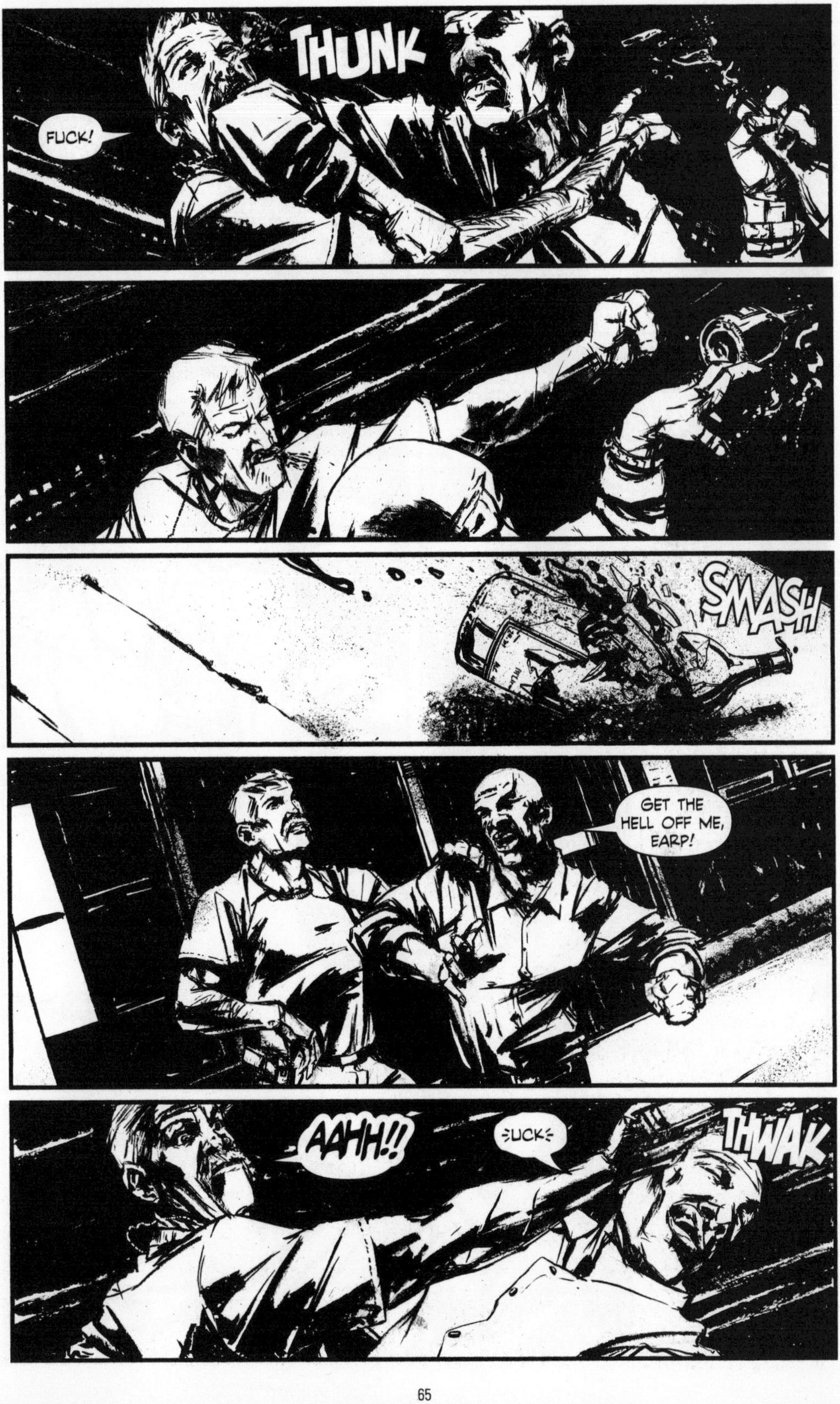
THUNK
FUCK!
SMASH
GET THE HELL OFF ME, EARP!
AAHH!!
UCK
THWAK

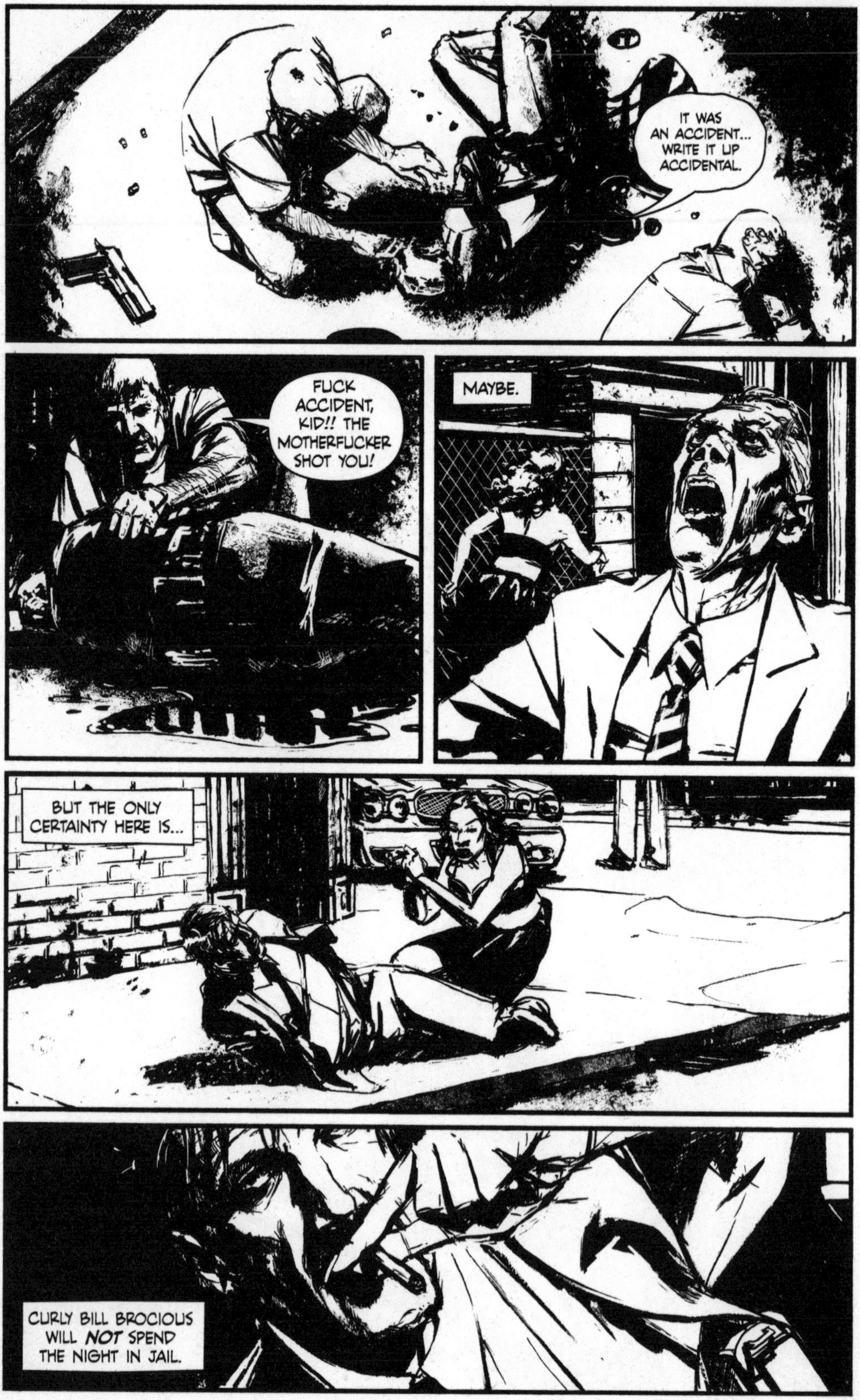
IT WAS AN ACCIDENT... WRITE IT UP ACCIDENTAL.
FUCK ACCIDENT, KID!! THE MOTHERFUCKER SHOT YOU!
MAYBE.
BUT THE ONLY CERTAINTY HERE IS...
CURLY BILL BROCIOUS WILL *NOT* SPEND THE NIGHT IN JAIL.

CHAPTER THREE

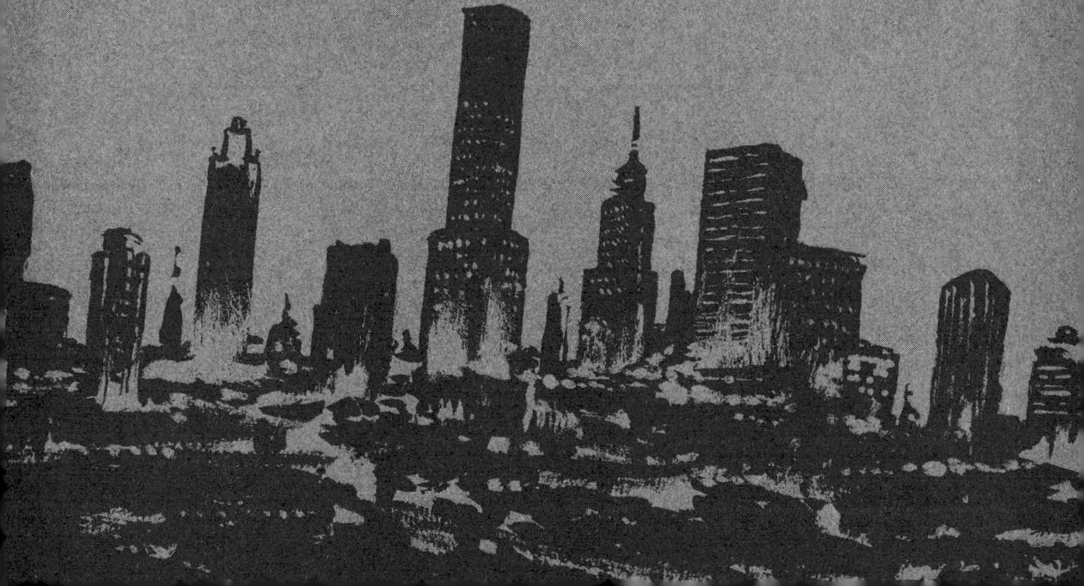

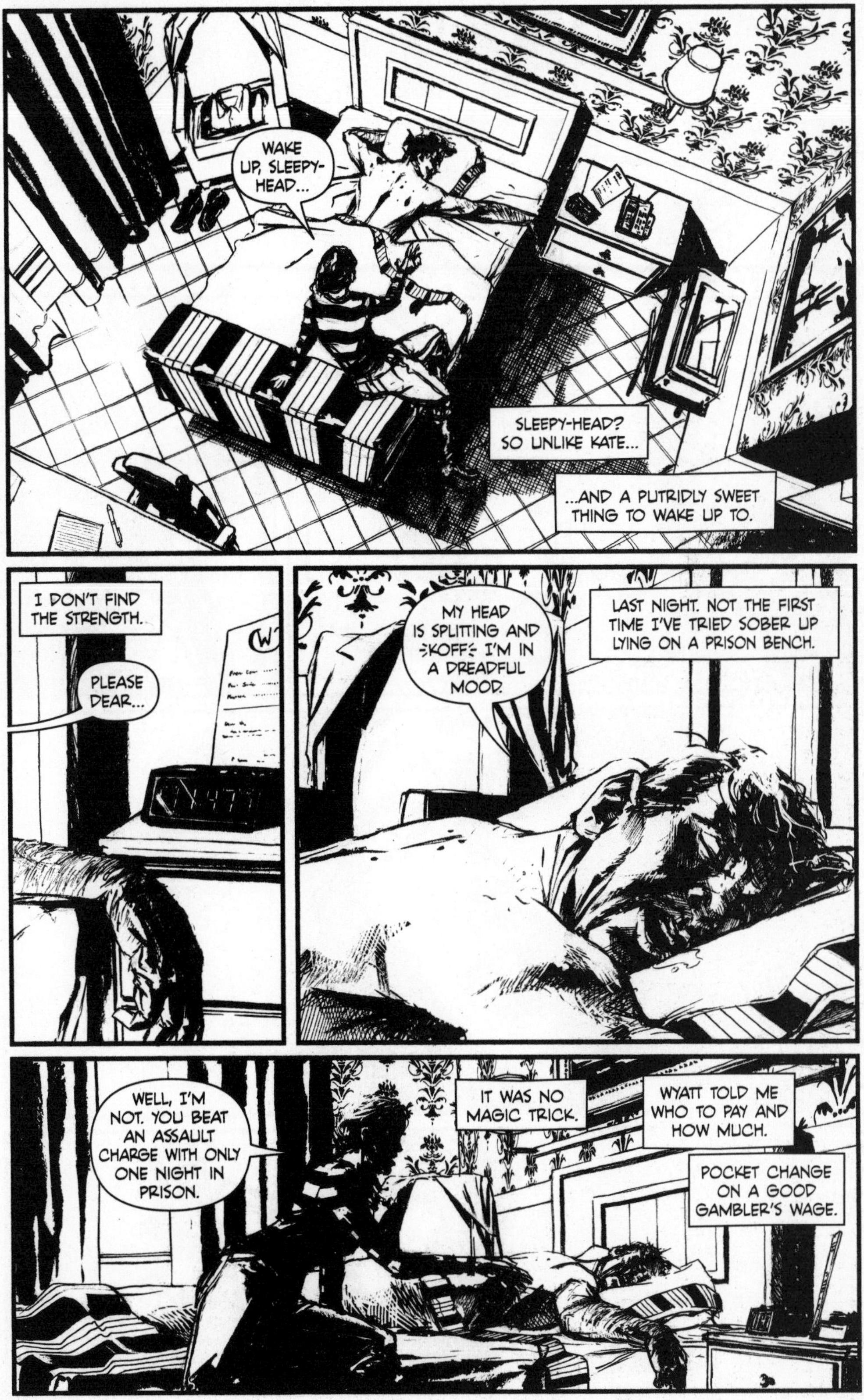
WAKE UP, SLEEPY-HEAD...
SLEEPY-HEAD? SO UNLIKE KATE...
...AND A PUTRIDLY SWEET THING TO WAKE UP TO.
I DON'T FIND THE STRENGTH.
PLEASE DEAR...
MY HEAD IS SPLITTING AND *KOFF* I'M IN A DREADFUL MOOD.
LAST NIGHT. NOT THE FIRST TIME I'VE TRIED SOBER UP LYING ON A PRISON BENCH.
WELL, I'M NOT. YOU BEAT AN ASSAULT CHARGE WITH ONLY ONE NIGHT IN PRISON.
IT WAS NO MAGIC TRICK.
WYATT TOLD ME WHO TO PAY AND HOW MUCH.
POCKET CHANGE ON A GOOD GAMBLER'S WAGE.

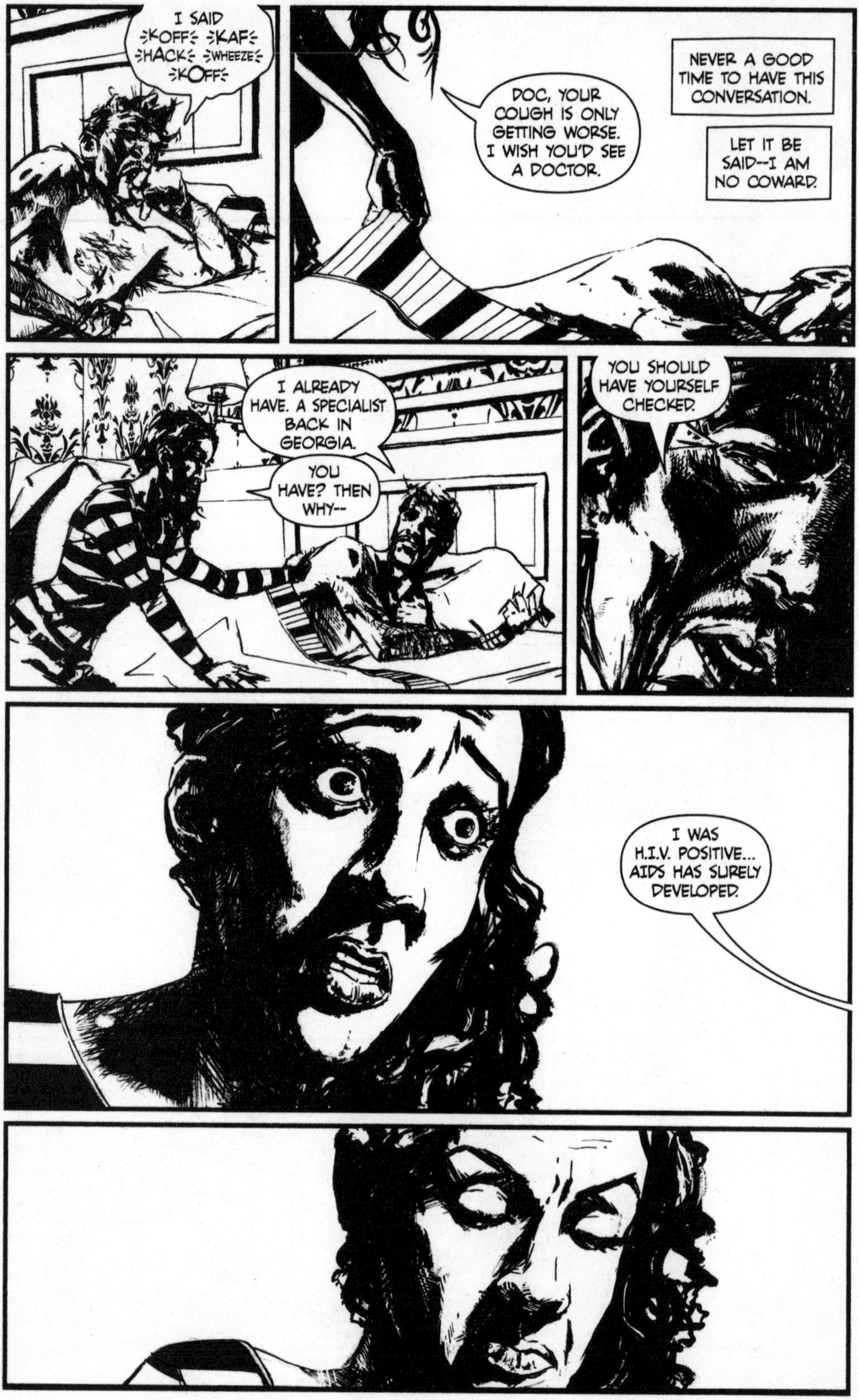
I SAID
KOFF KAF HACK WHEEZE KOFF
DOC, YOUR COUGH IS ONLY GETTING WORSE. I WISH YOU'D SEE A DOCTOR.
NEVER A GOOD TIME TO HAVE THIS CONVERSATION.
LET IT BE SAID--I AM NO COWARD.
I ALREADY HAVE. A SPECIALIST BACK IN GEORGIA.
YOU HAVE? THEN WHY--
YOU SHOULD HAVE YOURSELF CHECKED.
I WAS H.I.V. POSITIVE... AIDS HAS SURELY DEVELOPED.

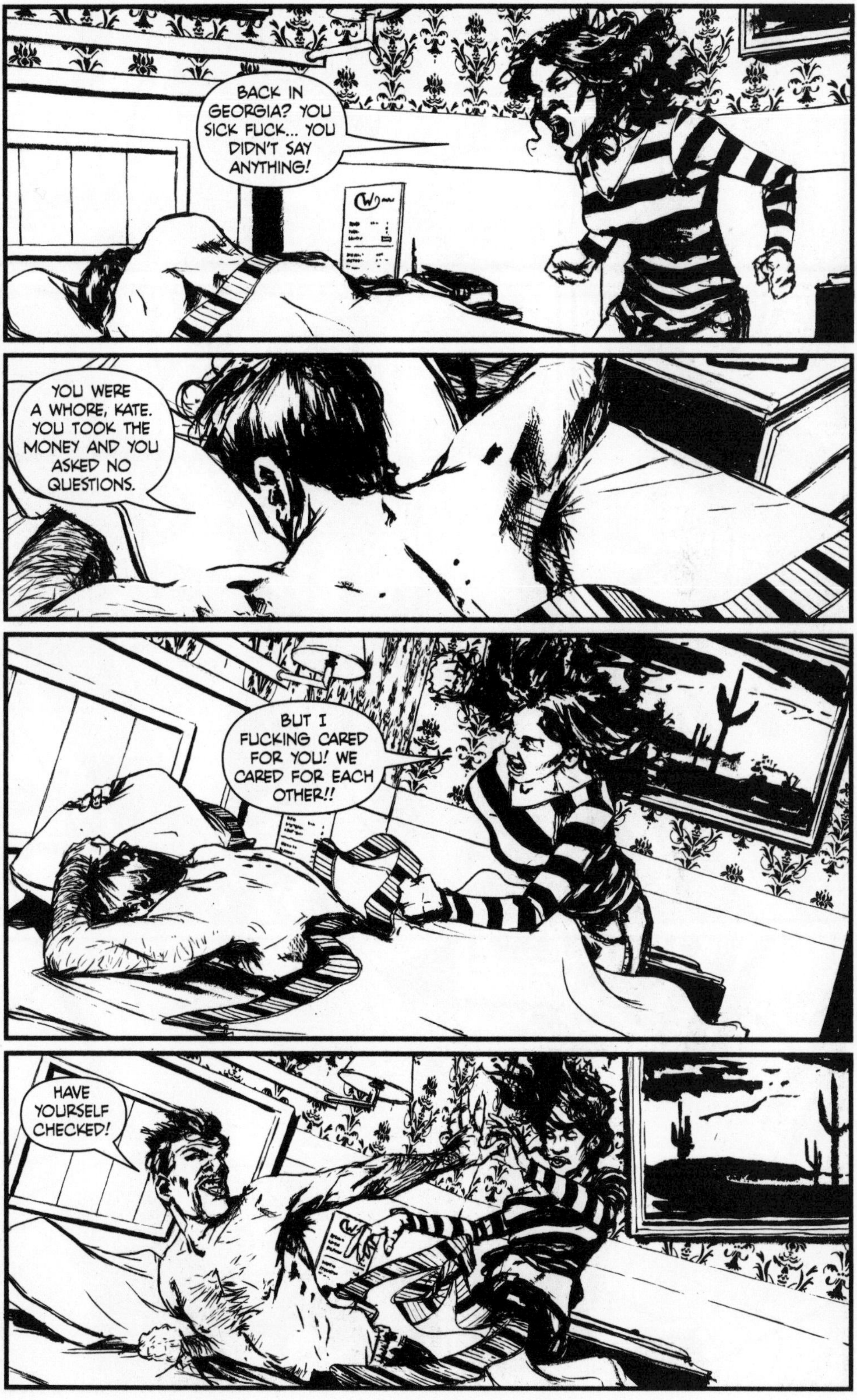
BACK IN GEORGIA? YOU SICK FUCK... YOU DIDN'T SAY ANYTHING!
YOU WERE A WHORE, KATE. YOU TOOK THE MONEY AND YOU ASKED NO QUESTIONS.
BUT I FUCKING CARED FOR YOU! WE CARED FOR EACH OTHER!!
HAVE YOURSELF CHECKED!

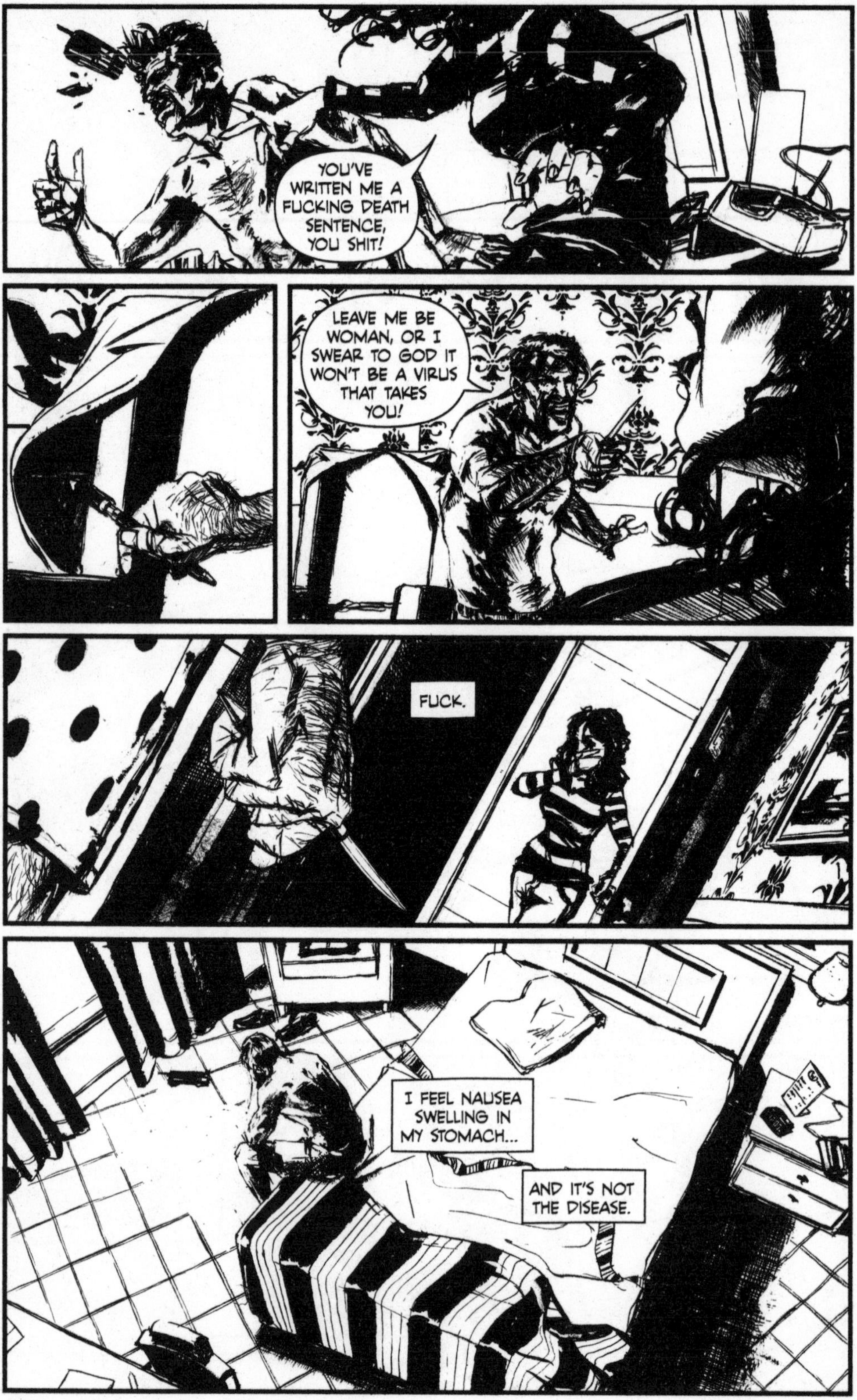
YOU'VE WRITTEN ME A FUCKING DEATH SENTENCE, YOU SHIT!
LEAVE ME BE WOMAN, OR I SWEAR TO GOD IT WON'T BE A VIRUS THAT TAKES YOU!
FUCK.
I FEEL NAUSEA SWELLING IN MY STOMACH...
AND IT'S NOT THE DISEASE.

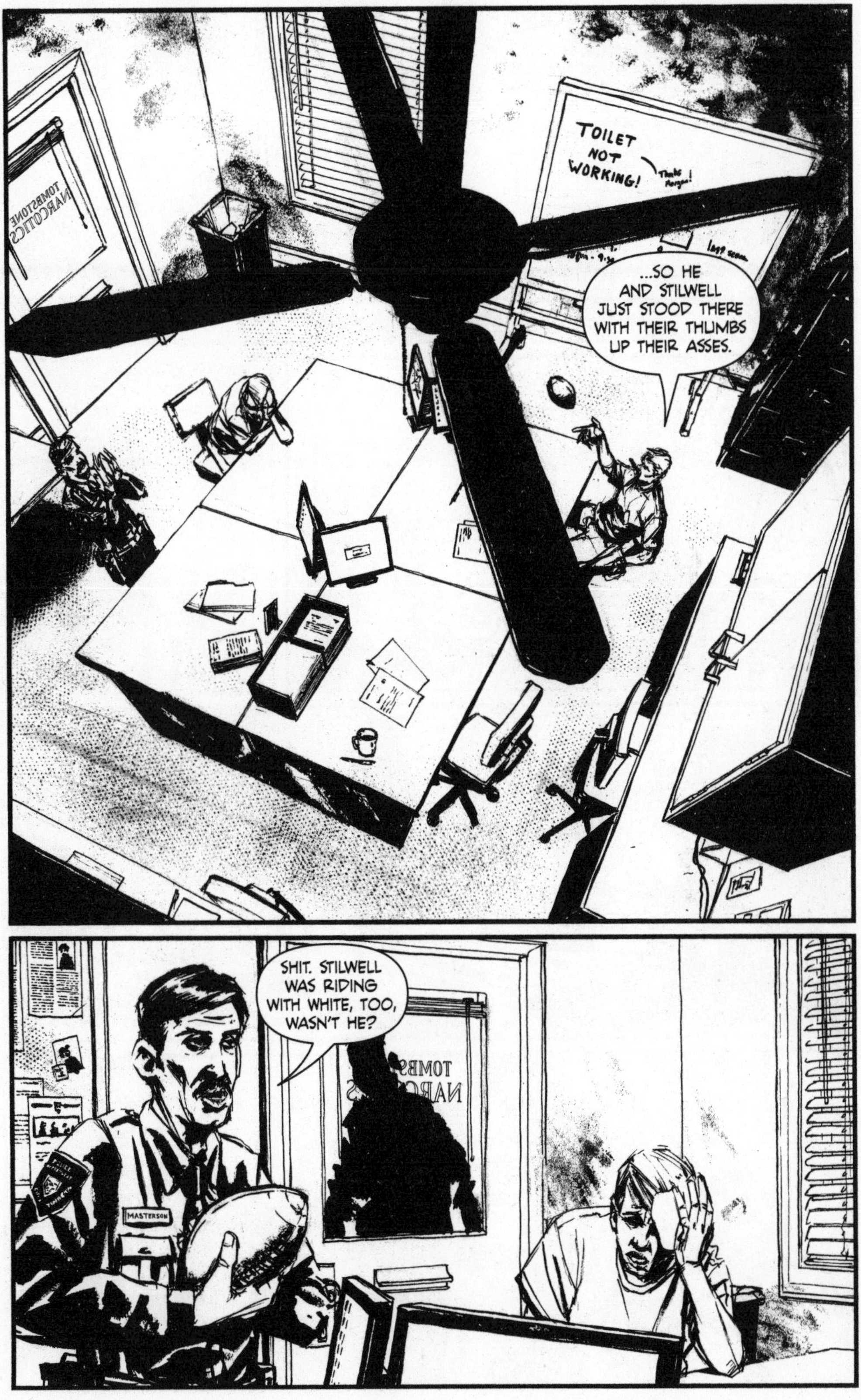
TOILET NOT WORKING!
...SO HE AND STILWELL JUST STOOD THERE WITH THEIR THUMBS UP THEIR ASSES.
SHIT. STILWELL WAS RIDING WITH WHITE, TOO, WASN'T HE?
MASTERSON

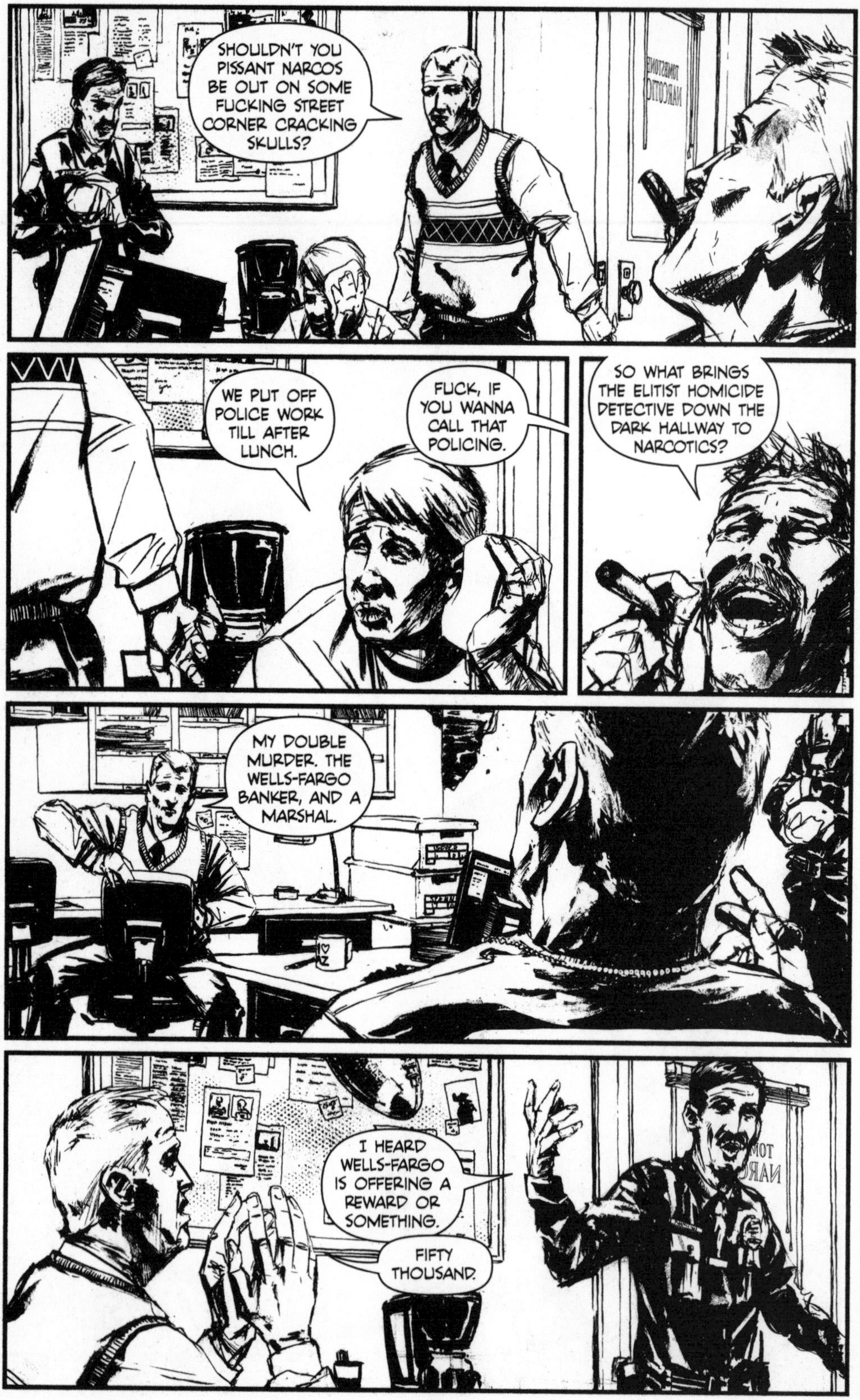
SHOULDN'T YOU PISSANT NARCOS BE OUT ON SOME FUCKING STREET CORNER CRACKING SKULLS?
TOMBSTONE NARCOTICS
WE PUT OFF POLICE WORK TILL AFTER LUNCH.
FUCK, IF YOU WANNA CALL THAT POLICING.
SO WHAT BRINGS THE ELITIST HOMICIDE DETECTIVE DOWN THE DARK HALLWAY TO NARCOTICS?
MY DOUBLE MURDER. THE WELLS-FARGO BANKER, AND A MARSHAL.
I HEARD WELLS-FARGO IS OFFERING A REWARD OR SOMETHING.
FIFTY THOUSAND.

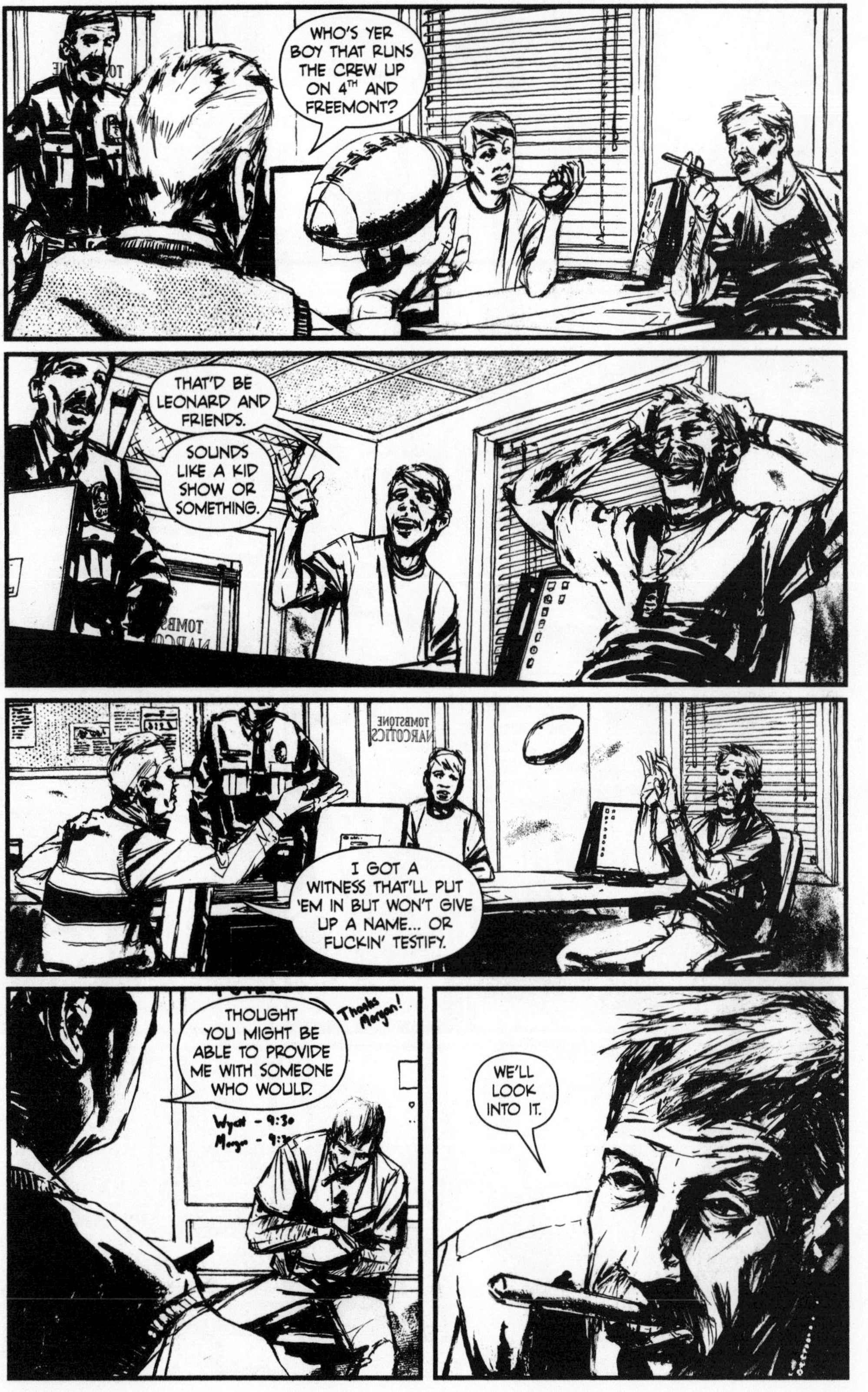
WHO'S YER BOY THAT RUNS THE CREW UP ON 4TH AND FREEMONT?
THAT'D BE LEONARD AND FRIENDS.
SOUNDS LIKE A KID SHOW OR SOMETHING.
I GOT A WITNESS THAT'LL PUT 'EM IN BUT WON'T GIVE UP A NAME... OR FUCKIN' TESTIFY.
THOUGHT YOU MIGHT BE ABLE TO PROVIDE ME WITH SOMEONE WHO WOULD.
Thanks Morgan!
Wyatt - 9:30
WE'LL LOOK INTO IT.

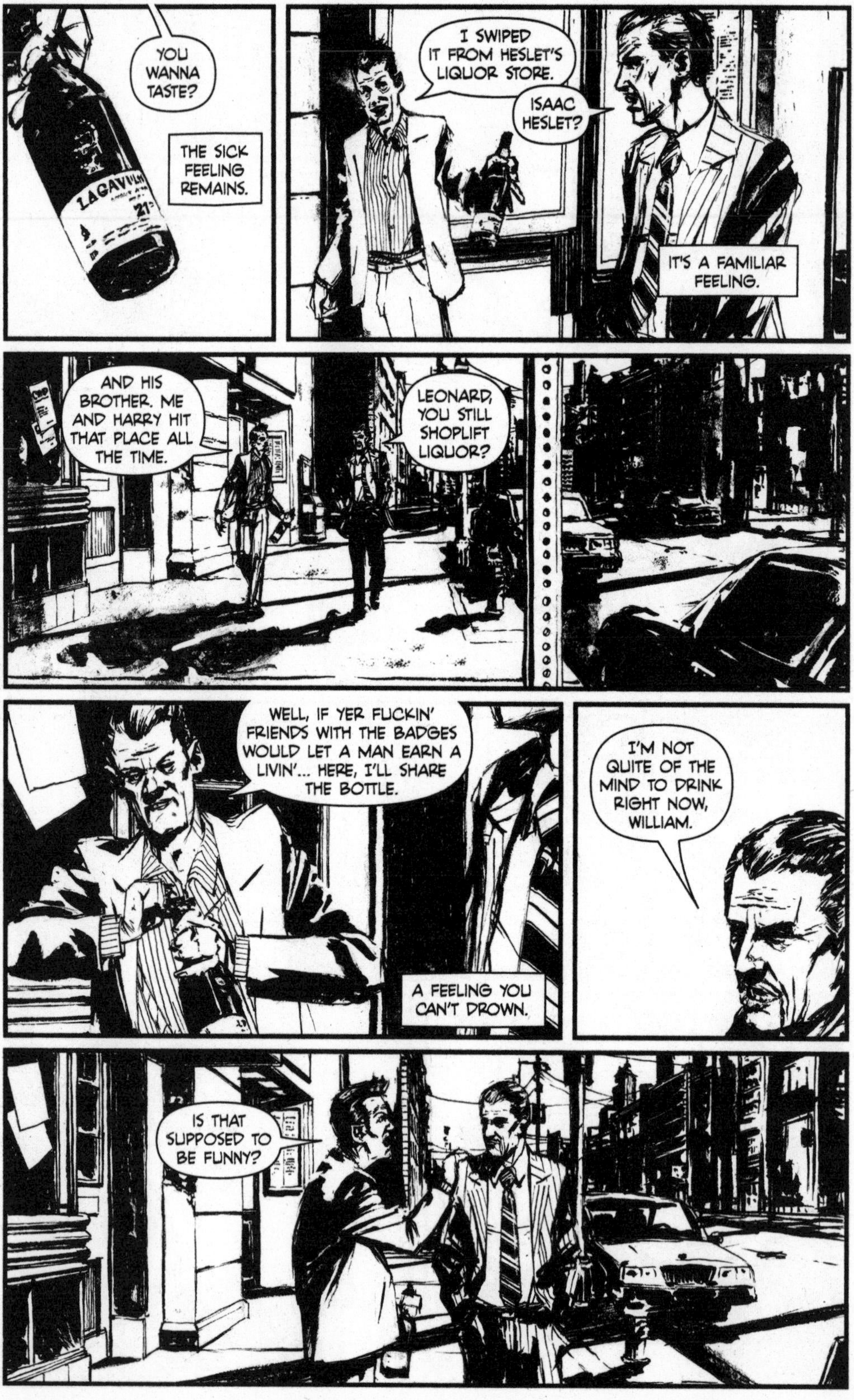
YOU WANNA TASTE?
THE SICK FEELING REMAINS.
I SWIPED IT FROM HESLET'S LIQUOR STORE.
ISAAC HESLET?
IT'S A FAMILIAR FEELING.
AND HIS BROTHER. ME AND HARRY HIT THAT PLACE ALL THE TIME.
LEONARD, YOU STILL SHOPLIFT LIQUOR?
WELL, IF YER FUCKIN' FRIENDS WITH THE BADGES WOULD LET A MAN EARN A LIVIN'... HERE, I'LL SHARE THE BOTTLE.
A FEELING YOU CAN'T DROWN.
I'M NOT QUITE OF THE MIND TO DRINK RIGHT NOW, WILLIAM.
IS THAT SUPPOSED TO BE FUNNY?

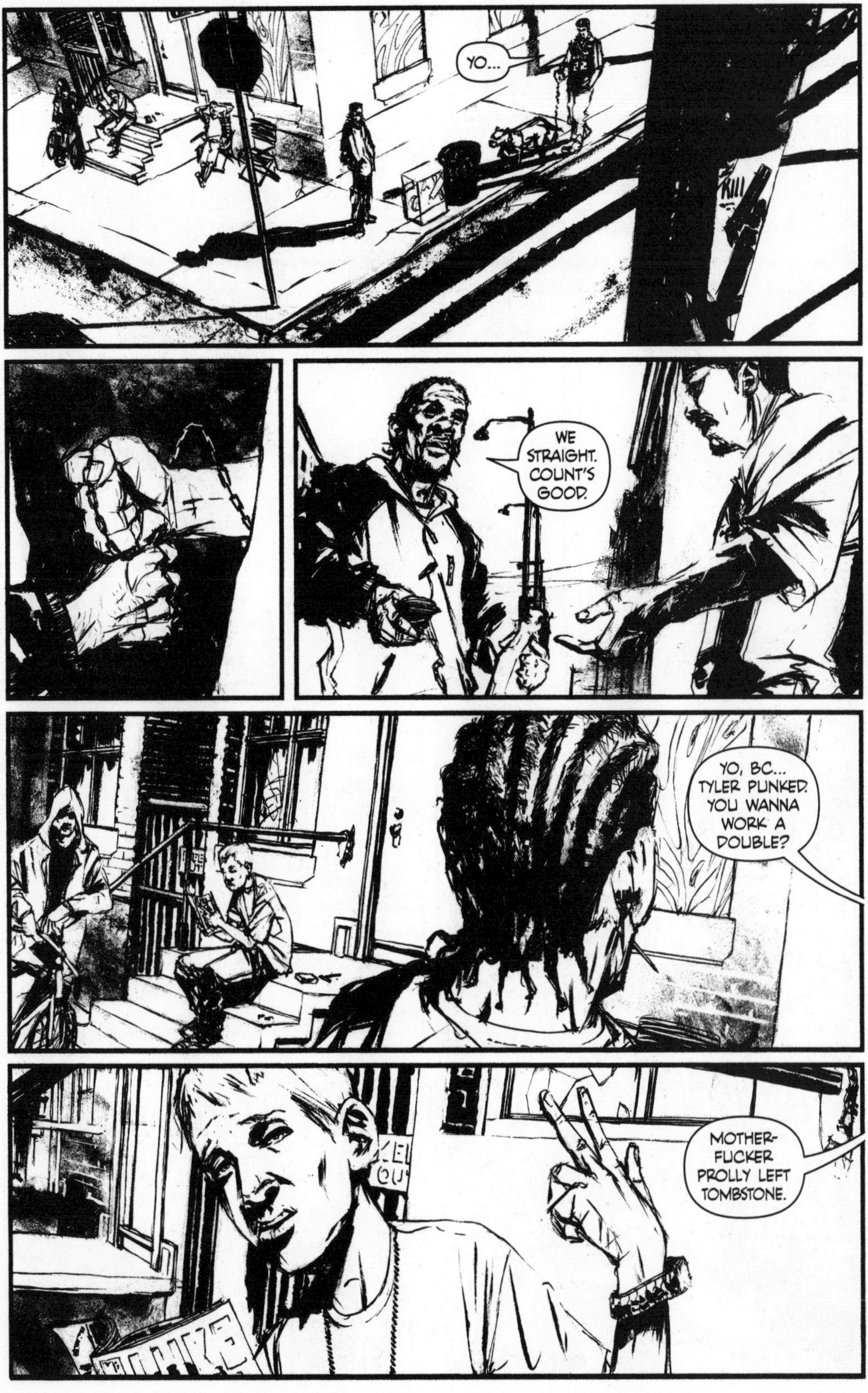
YO...
WE STRAIGHT. COUNT'S GOOD.
YO, BC... TYLER PUNKED. YOU WANNA WORK A DOUBLE?
MOTHER-FUCKER PROLLY LEFT TOMBSTONE.

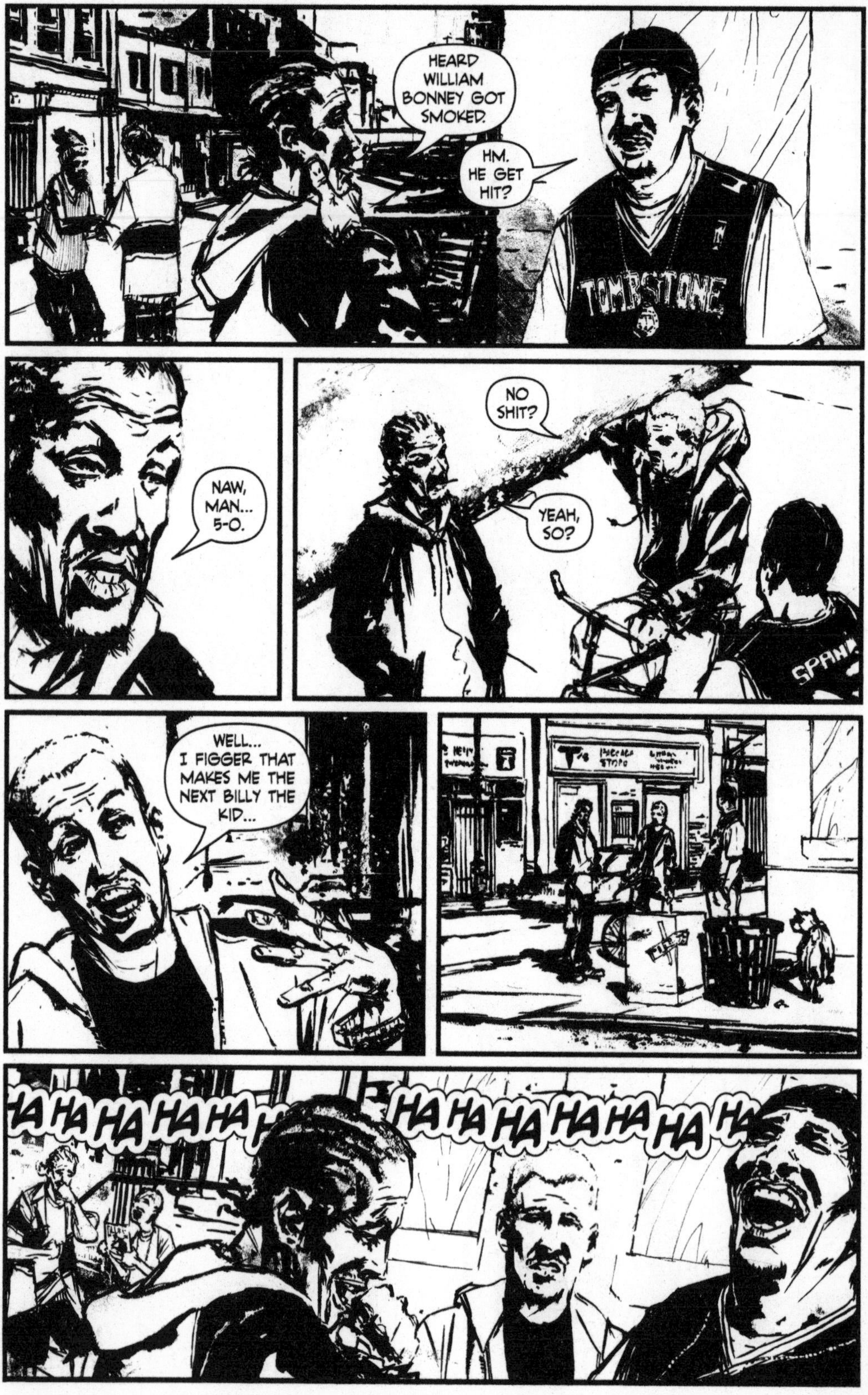
HEARD WILLIAM BONNEY GOT SMOKED.
HM. HE GET HIT?
TOMBSTONE
NAW, MAN... 5-O.
NO SHIT?
YEAH, SO?
WELL... I FIGGER THAT MAKES ME THE NEXT BILLY THE KID...
HA HA HA HA HA
HA HA HA HA HA HA HA HA

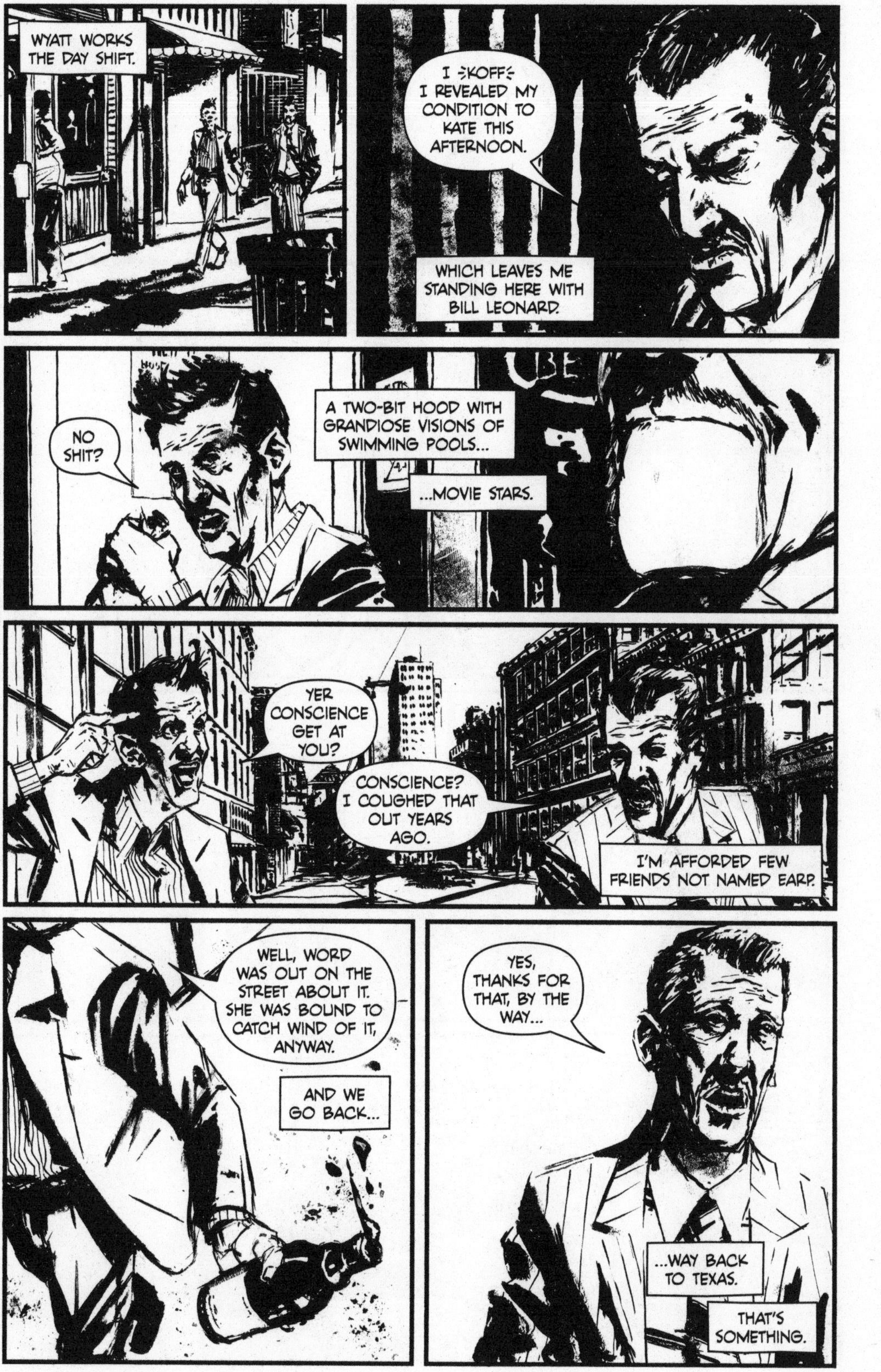
WYATT WORKS THE DAY SHIFT.
I =KOFF= I REVEALED MY CONDITION TO KATE THIS AFTERNOON.
WHICH LEAVES ME STANDING HERE WITH BILL LEONARD.
NO SHIT?
A TWO-BIT HOOD WITH GRANDIOSE VISIONS OF SWIMMING POOLS...
...MOVIE STARS.
YER CONSCIENCE GET AT YOU?
CONSCIENCE? I COUGHED THAT OUT YEARS AGO.
I'M AFFORDED FEW FRIENDS NOT NAMED EARP.
WELL, WORD WAS OUT ON THE STREET ABOUT IT. SHE WAS BOUND TO CATCH WIND OF IT, ANYWAY.
AND WE GO BACK...
YES, THANKS FOR THAT, BY THE WAY...
...WAY BACK TO TEXAS.
THAT'S SOMETHING.

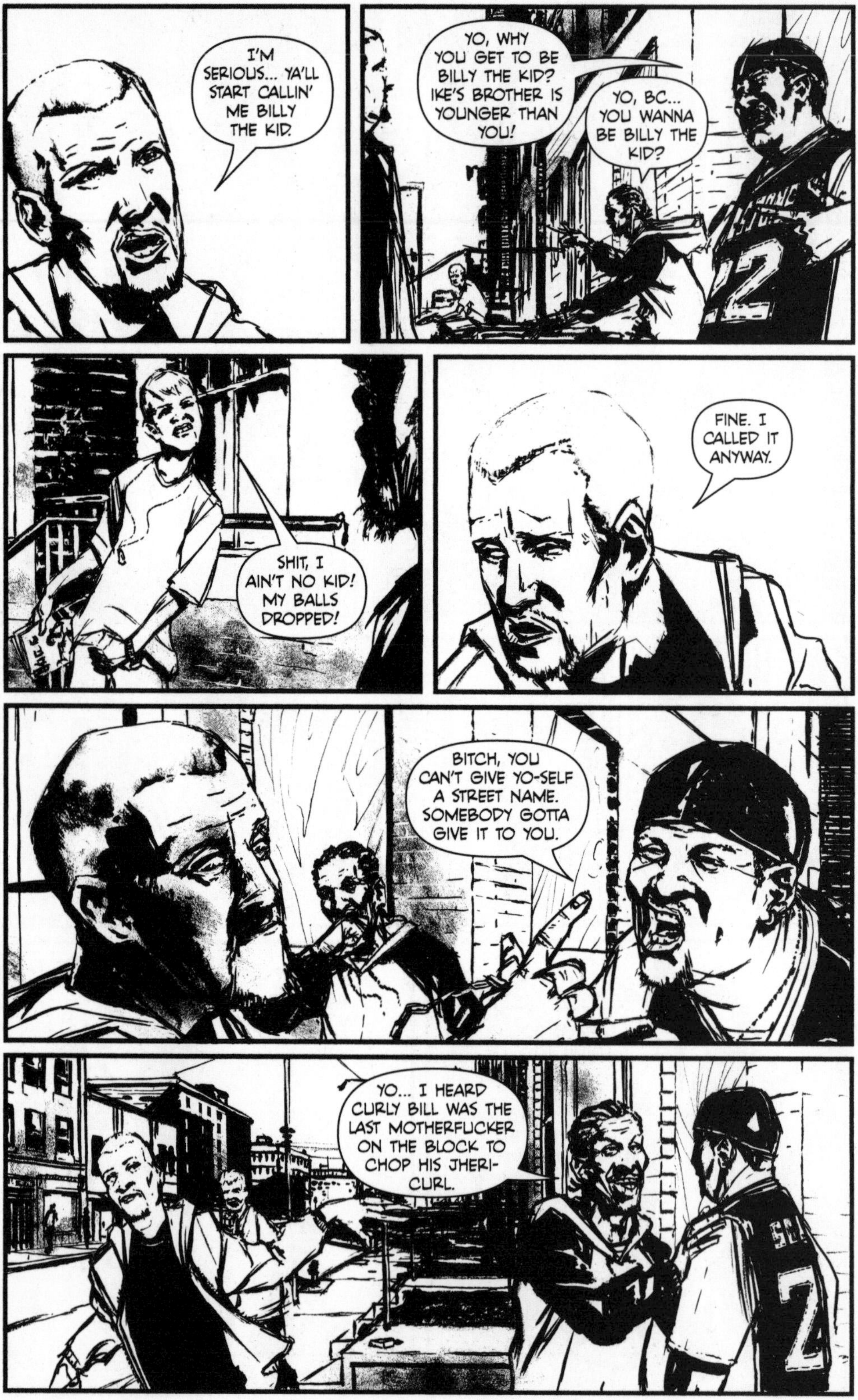
I'M SERIOUS... YA'LL START CALLIN' ME BILLY THE KID.
YO, WHY YOU GET TO BE BILLY THE KID? IKE'S BROTHER IS YOUNGER THAN YOU!
YO, BC... YOU WANNA BE BILLY THE KID?
SHIT, I AIN'T NO KID! MY BALLS DROPPED!
FINE. I CALLED IT ANYWAY.
BITCH, YOU CAN'T GIVE YO-SELF A STREET NAME. SOMEBODY GOTTA GIVE IT TO YOU.
YO... I HEARD CURLY BILL WAS THE LAST MOTHERFUCKER ON THE BLOCK TO CHOP HIS JHERI-CURL.

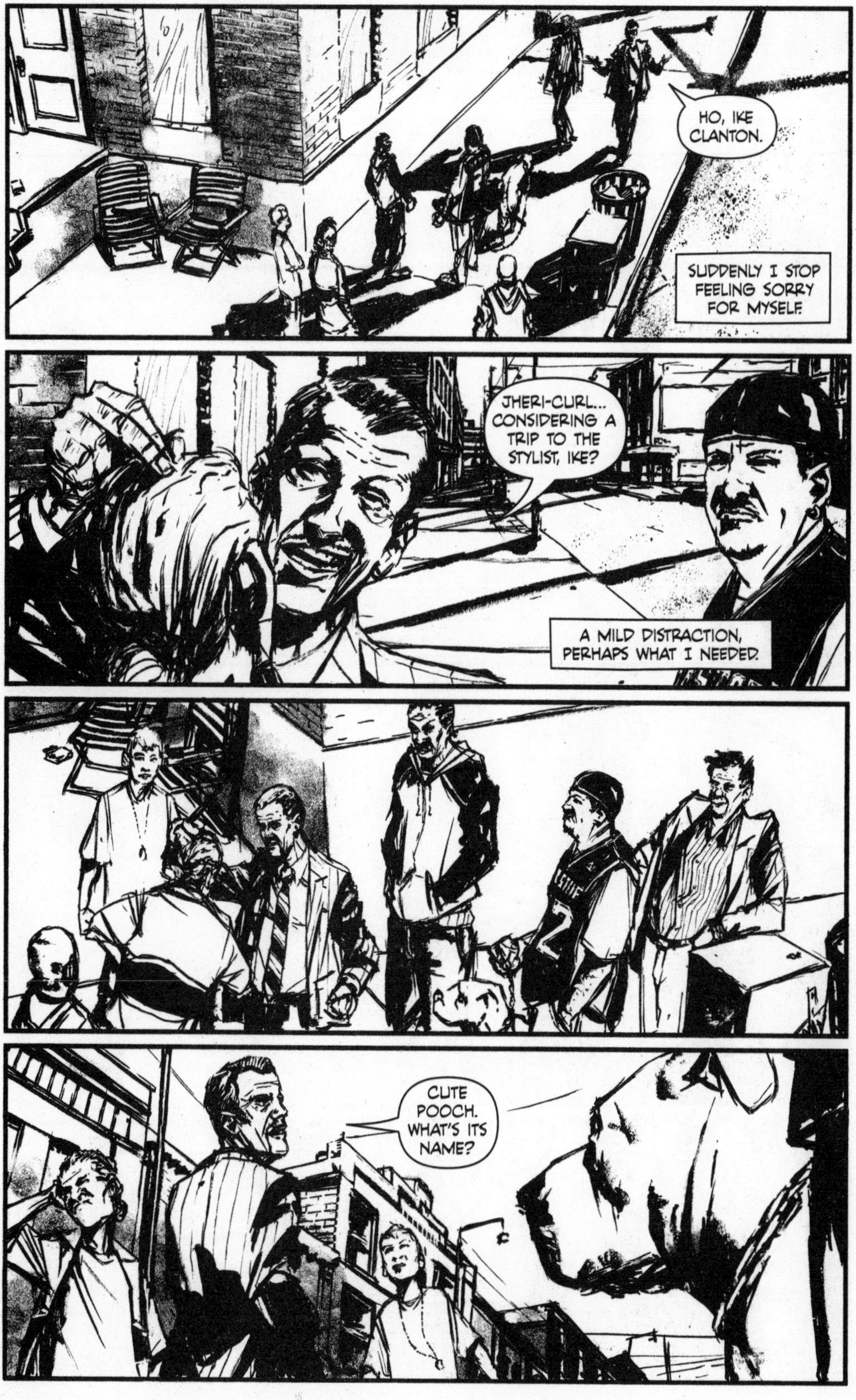
HO, IKE CLANTON.
SUDDENLY I STOP FEELING SORRY FOR MYSELF.
JHERI-CURL... CONSIDERING A TRIP TO THE STYLIST, IKE?
A MILD DISTRACTION, PERHAPS WHAT I NEEDED.
CUTE POOCH. WHAT'S ITS NAME?

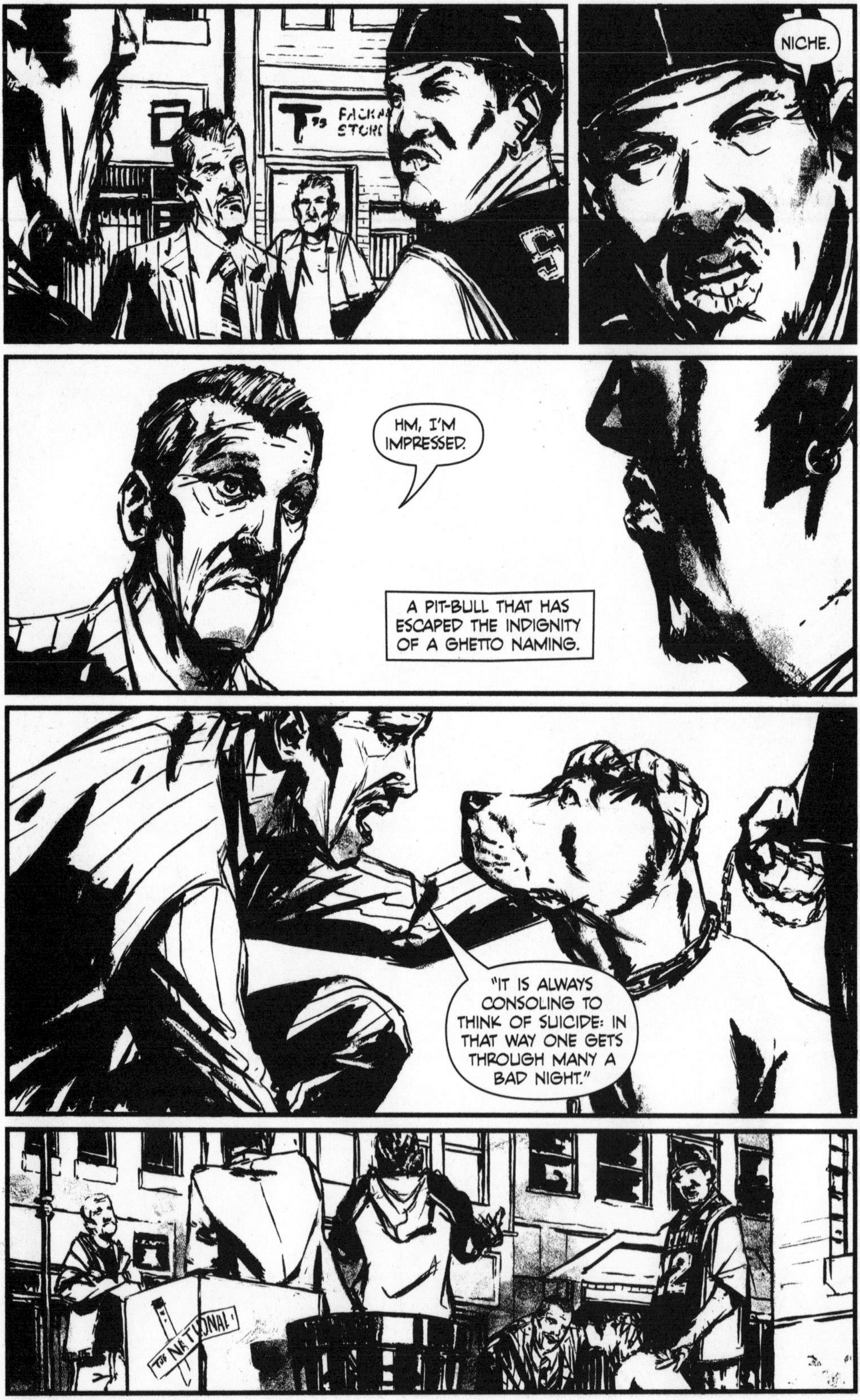
NICHE.
HM, I'M IMPRESSED.
A PIT-BULL THAT HAS ESCAPED THE INDIGNITY OF A GHETTO NAMING.
"IT IS ALWAYS CONSOLING TO THINK OF SUICIDE: IN THAT WAY ONE GETS THROUGH MANY A BAD NIGHT."

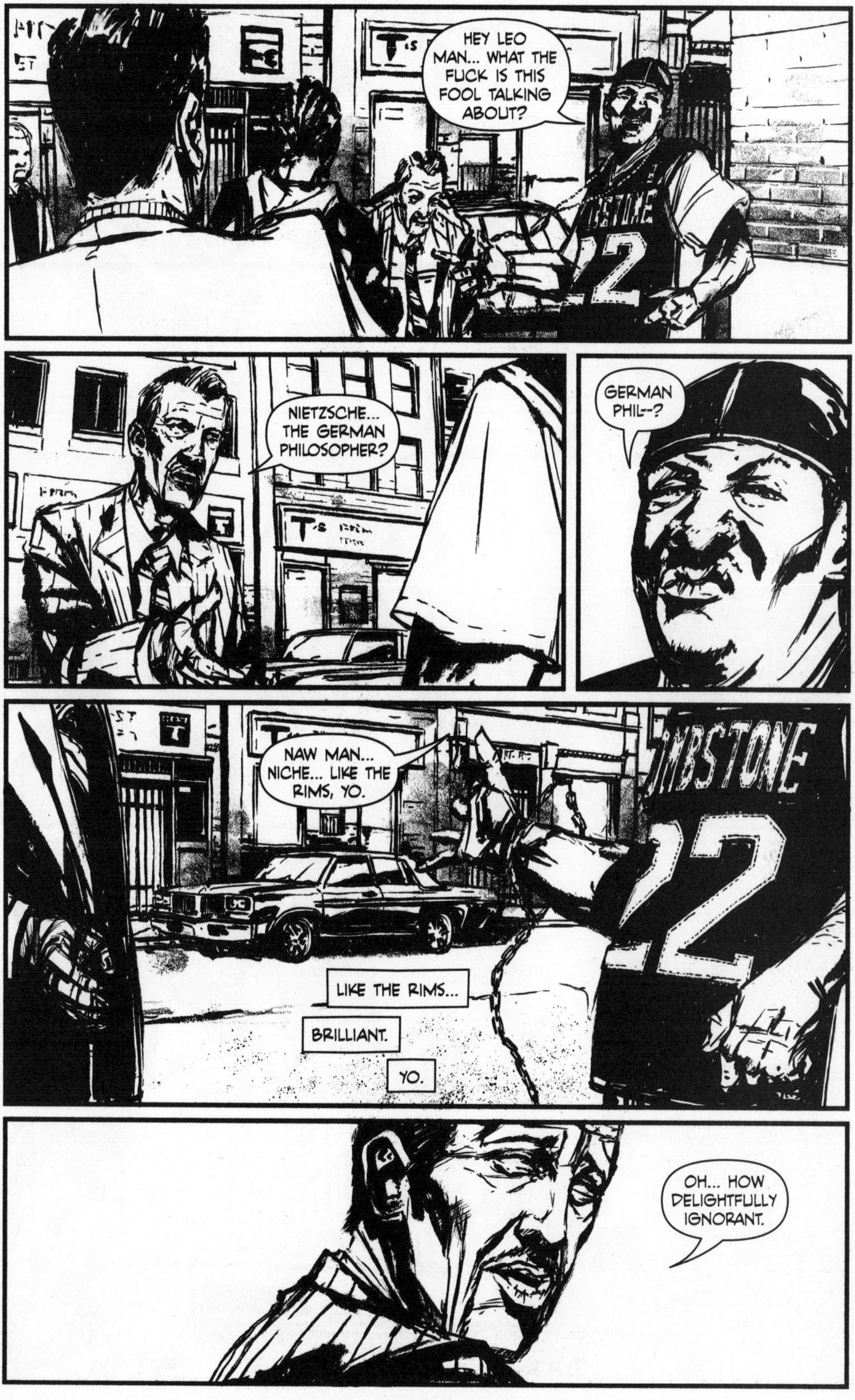
HEY LEO MAN... WHAT THE FUCK IS THIS FOOL TALKING ABOUT?
NIETZSCHE... THE GERMAN PHILOSOPHER?
GERMAN PHIL--?
NAW MAN... NICHE... LIKE THE RIMS, YO.
LIKE THE RIMS...
BRILLIANT.
YO.
OH... HOW DELIGHTFULLY IGNORANT.

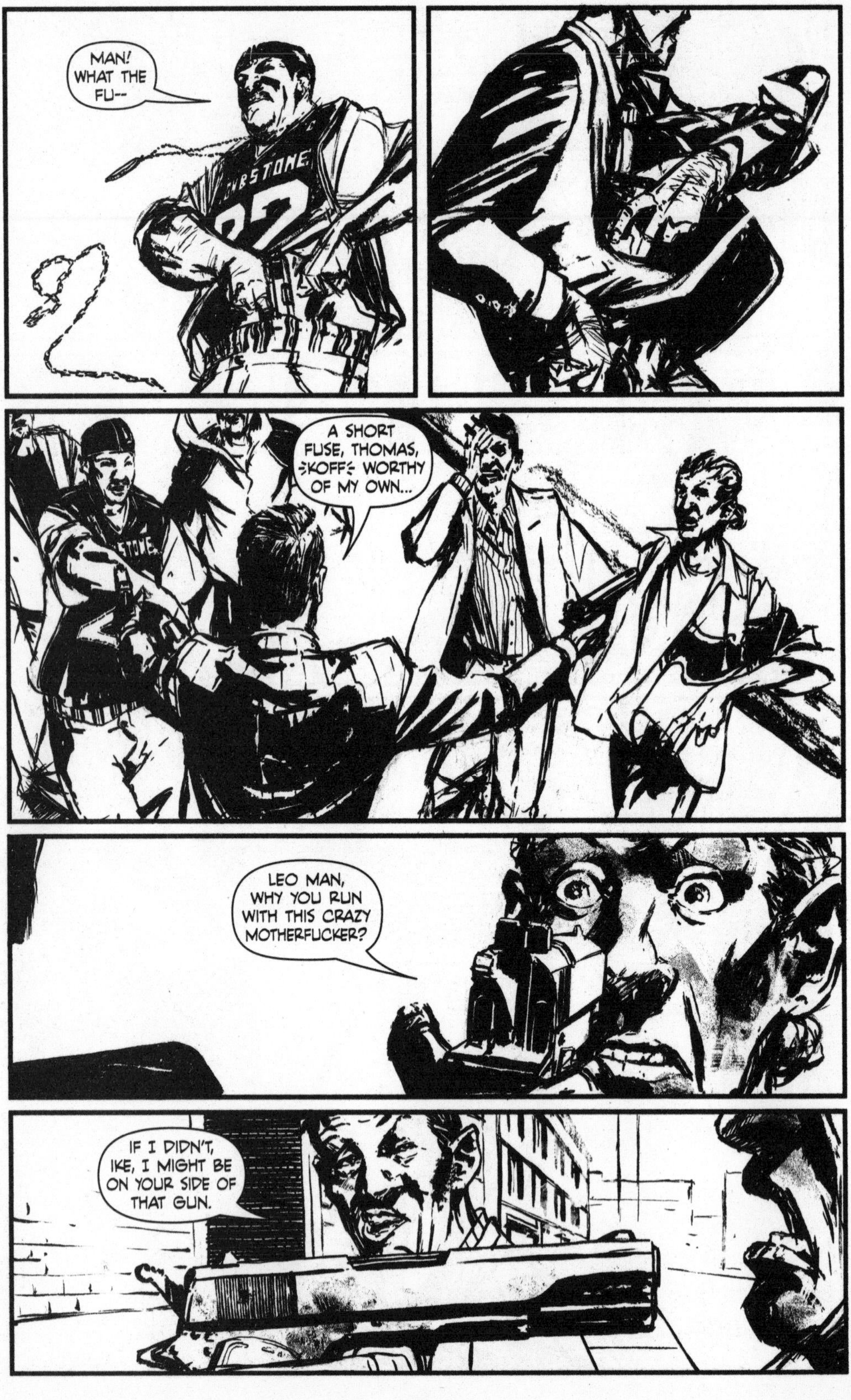
MAN! WHAT THE FU--
A SHORT FUSE, THOMAS, KOFF WORTHY OF MY OWN...
LEO MAN, WHY YOU RUN WITH THIS CRAZY MOTHERFUCKER?
IF I DIDN'T, IKE, I MIGHT BE ON YOUR SIDE OF THAT GUN.

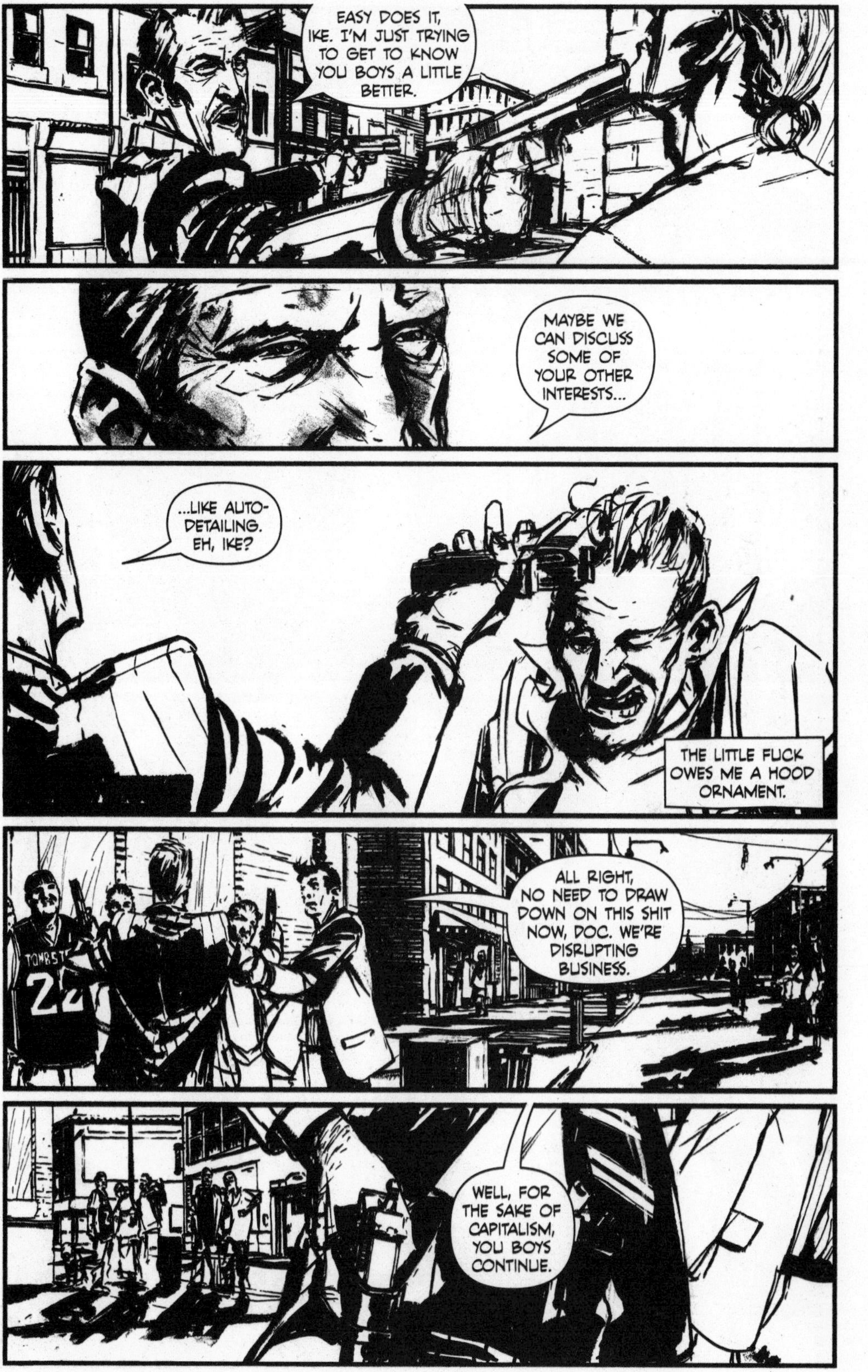
EASY DOES IT, IKE. I'M JUST TRYING TO GET TO KNOW YOU BOYS A LITTLE BETTER.
MAYBE WE CAN DISCUSS SOME OF YOUR OTHER INTERESTS...
...LIKE AUTO-DETAILING. EH, IKE?
THE LITTLE FUCK OWES ME A HOOD ORNAMENT.
ALL RIGHT, NO NEED TO DRAW DOWN ON THIS SHIT NOW, DOC. WE'RE DISRUPTING BUSINESS.
WELL, FOR THE SAKE OF CAPITALISM, YOU BOYS CONTINUE.

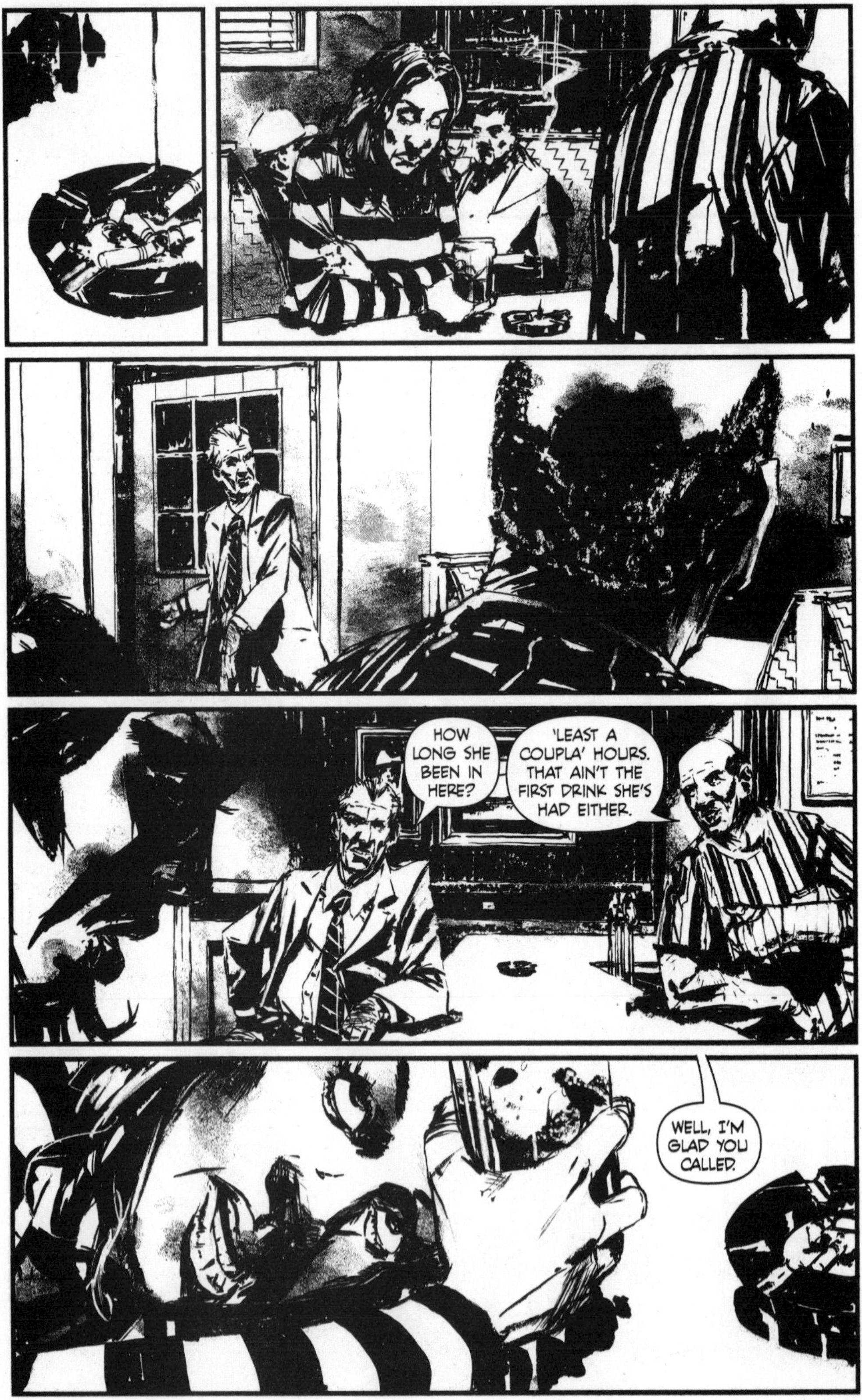
HOW LONG SHE BEEN IN HERE?
'LEAST A COUPLA' HOURS. THAT AIN'T THE FIRST DRINK SHE'S HAD EITHER.
WELL, I'M GLAD YOU CALLED.

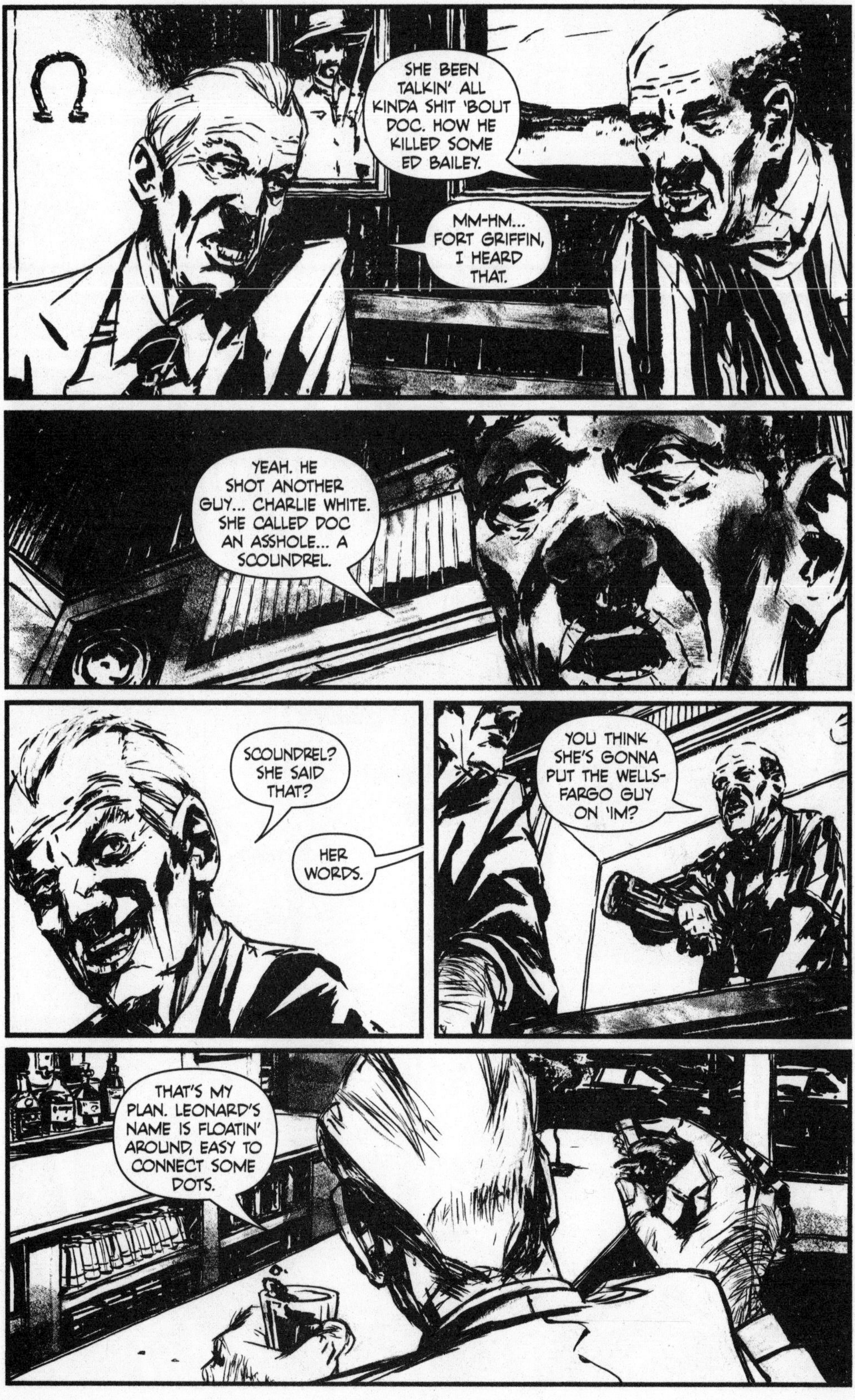
SHE BEEN TALKIN' ALL KINDA SHIT 'BOUT DOC. HOW HE KILLED SOME ED BAILEY.
MM-HM... FORT GRIFFIN, I HEARD THAT.
YEAH. HE SHOT ANOTHER GUY... CHARLIE WHITE. SHE CALLED DOC AN ASSHOLE... A SCOUNDREL.
SCOUNDREL? SHE SAID THAT?
HER WORDS.
YOU THINK SHE'S GONNA PUT THE WELLS-FARGO GUY ON 'IM?
THAT'S MY PLAN. LEONARD'S NAME IS FLOATIN' AROUND, EASY TO CONNECT SOME DOTS.

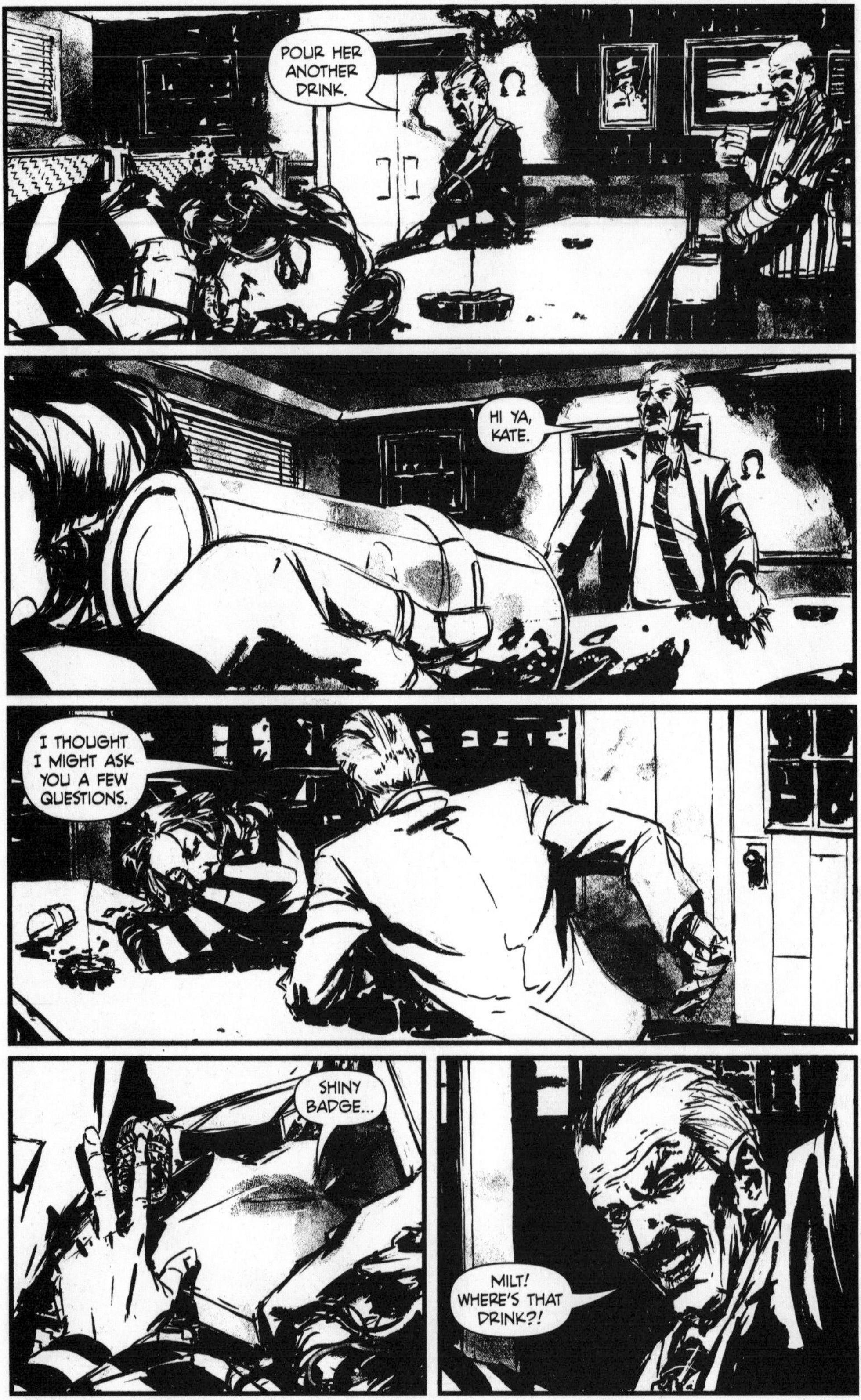
POUR HER ANOTHER DRINK.
HI YA, KATE.
I THOUGHT I MIGHT ASK YOU A FEW QUESTIONS.
SHINY BADGE...
MILT! WHERE'S THAT DRINK?!

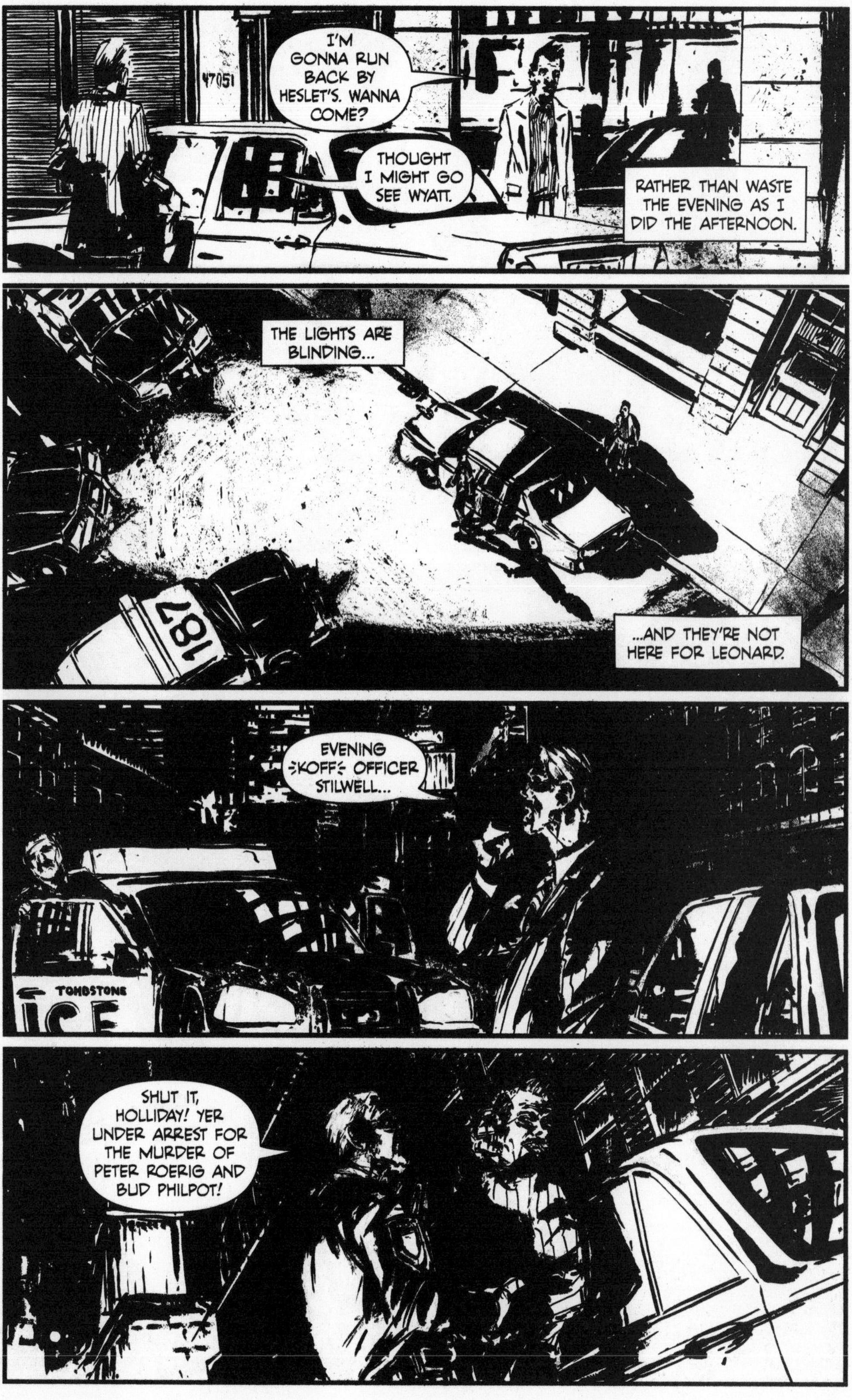
47051
I'M GONNA RUN BACK BY HESLET'S. WANNA COME?
THOUGHT I MIGHT GO SEE WYATT.
RATHER THAN WASTE THE EVENING AS I DID THE AFTERNOON.
THE LIGHTS ARE BLINDING...
187
...AND THEY'RE NOT HERE FOR LEONARD.
EVENING ≈KOFF≈ OFFICER STILWELL...
TOMBSTONE
ICE
SHUT IT, HOLLIDAY! YER UNDER ARREST FOR THE MURDER OF PETER ROERIG AND BUD PHILPOT!

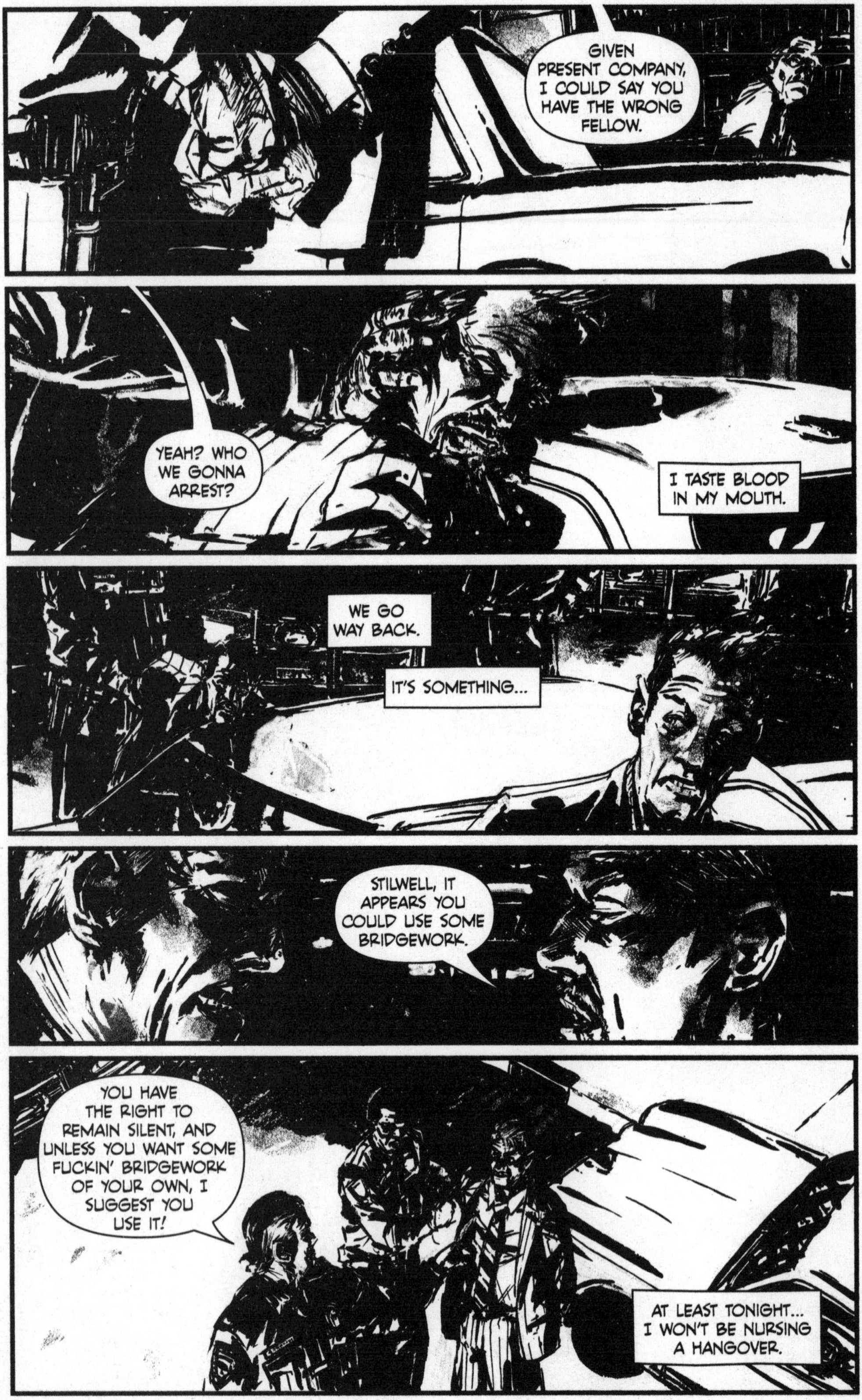
GIVEN PRESENT COMPANY, I COULD SAY YOU HAVE THE WRONG FELLOW.
YEAH? WHO WE GONNA ARREST?
I TASTE BLOOD IN MY MOUTH.
WE GO WAY BACK.
IT'S SOMETHING...
STILWELL, IT APPEARS YOU COULD USE SOME BRIDGEWORK.
YOU HAVE THE RIGHT TO REMAIN SILENT, AND UNLESS YOU WANT SOME FUCKIN' BRIDGEWORK OF YOUR OWN, I SUGGEST YOU USE IT!
AT LEAST TONIGHT... I WON'T BE NURSING A HANGOVER.

CHAPTER FOUR

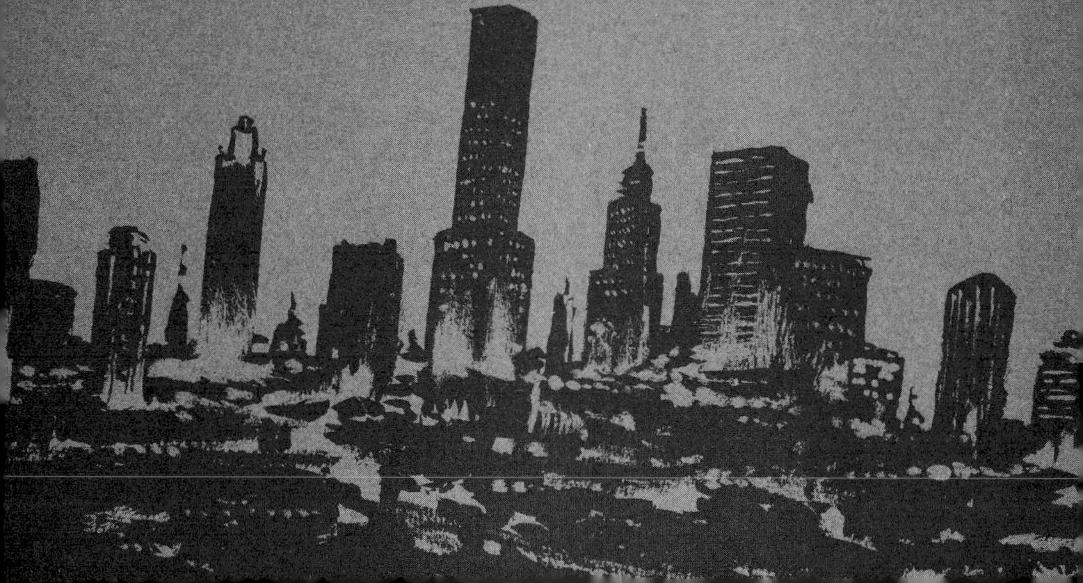

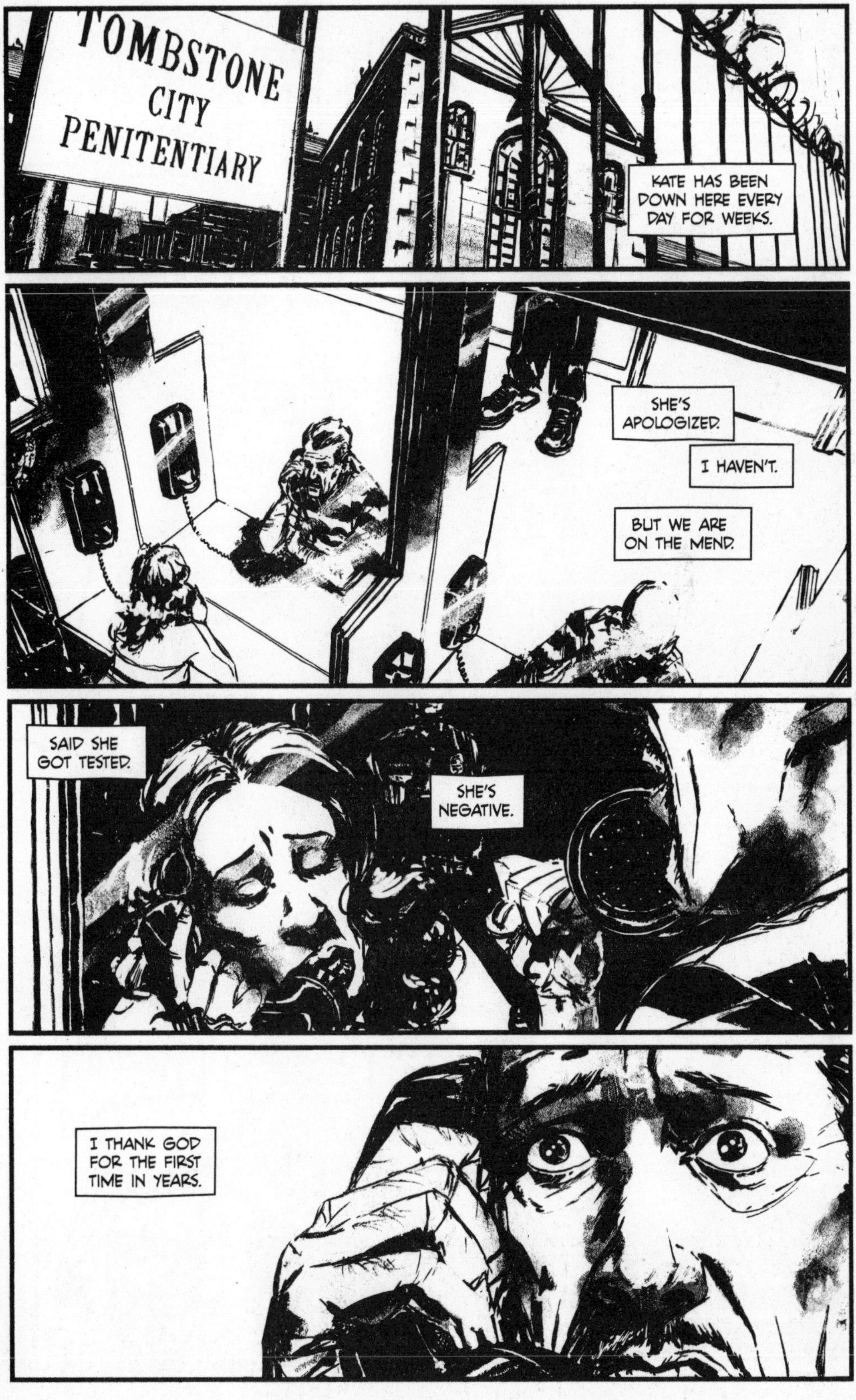
TOMBSTONE
CITY
PENITENTIARY
KATE HAS BEEN DOWN HERE EVERY DAY FOR WEEKS.
SHE'S APOLOGIZED.
I HAVEN'T.
BUT WE ARE ON THE MEND.
SAID SHE GOT TESTED.
SHE'S NEGATIVE.
I THANK GOD FOR THE FIRST TIME IN YEARS.

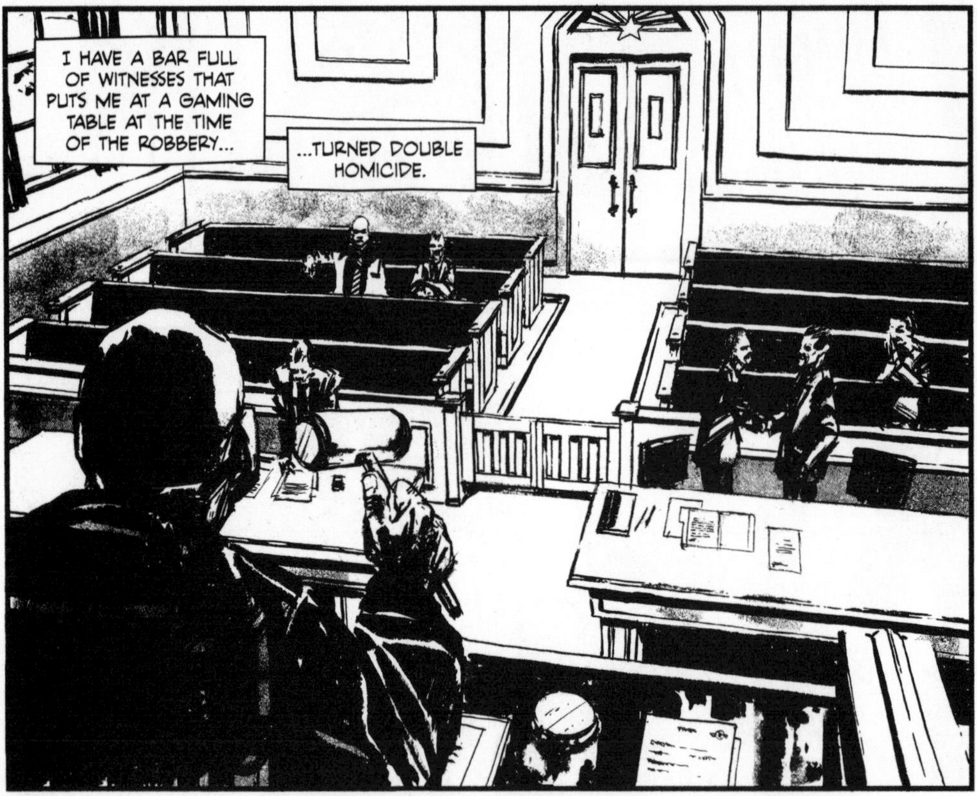
I HAVE A BAR FULL OF WITNESSES THAT PUTS ME AT A GAMING TABLE AT THE TIME OF THE ROBBERY...
...TURNED DOUBLE HOMICIDE.

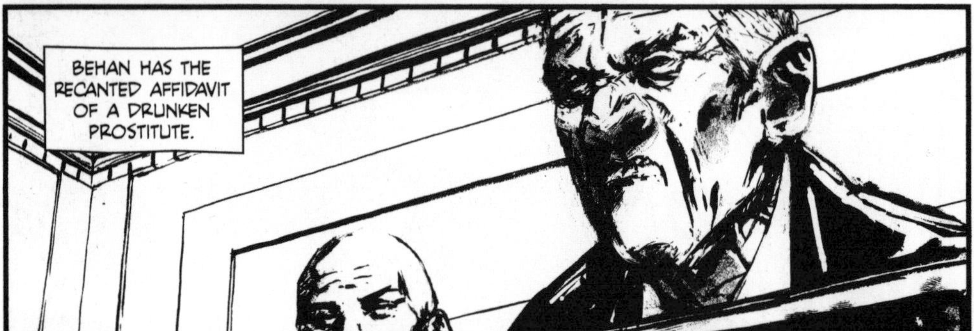
BEHAN HAS THE RECANTED AFFIDAVIT OF A DRUNKEN PROSTITUTE.

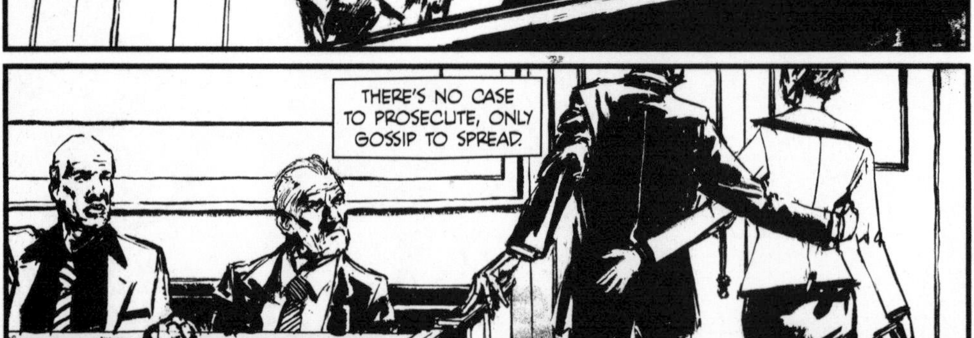
THERE'S NO CASE TO PROSECUTE, ONLY GOSSIP TO SPREAD.

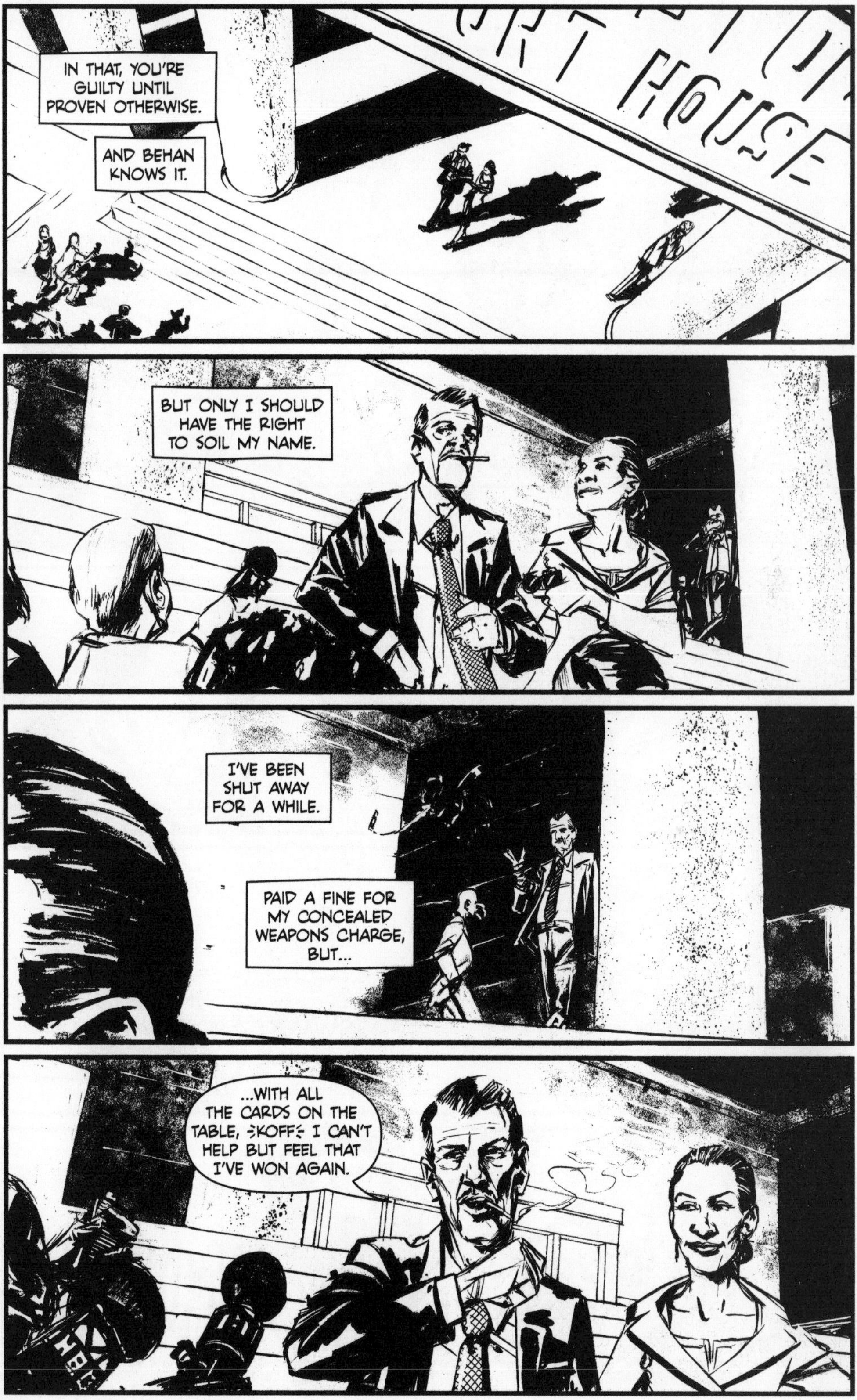
IN THAT, YOU'RE GUILTY UNTIL PROVEN OTHERWISE.
AND BEHAN KNOWS IT.
HOUSE
BUT ONLY I SHOULD HAVE THE RIGHT TO SOIL MY NAME.
I'VE BEEN SHUT AWAY FOR A WHILE.
PAID A FINE FOR MY CONCEALED WEAPONS CHARGE, BUT...
...WITH ALL THE CARDS ON THE TABLE, *KOFF* I CAN'T HELP BUT FEEL THAT I'VE WON AGAIN.

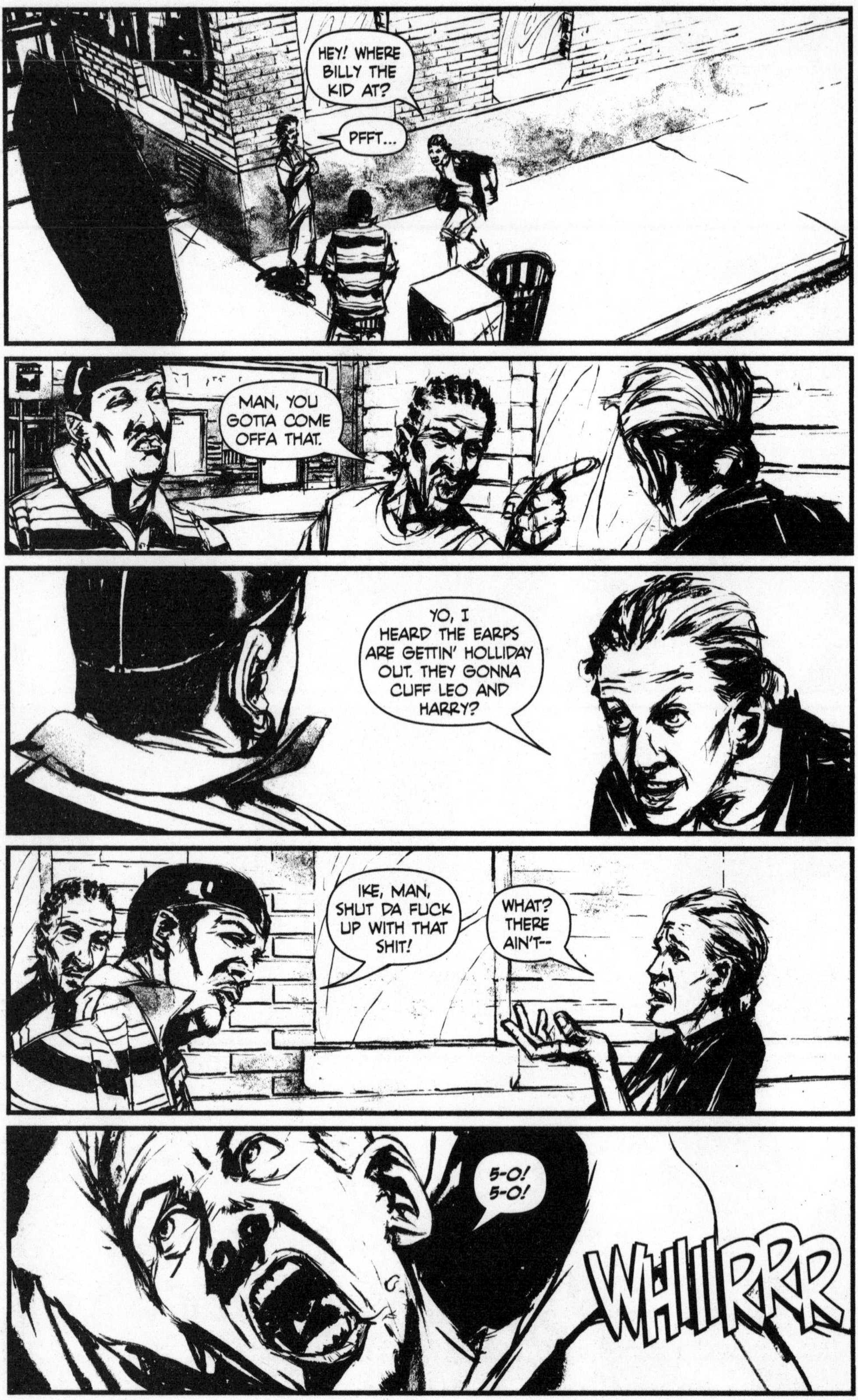
HEY! WHERE BILLY THE KID AT?
PFFT...
MAN, YOU GOTTA COME OFFA THAT.
YO, I HEARD THE EARPS ARE GETTIN' HOLLIDAY OUT. THEY GONNA CUFF LEO AND HARRY?
IKE, MAN, SHUT DA FUCK UP WITH THAT SHIT!
WHAT? THERE AIN'T--
5-O! 5-O!
WHIIRRR

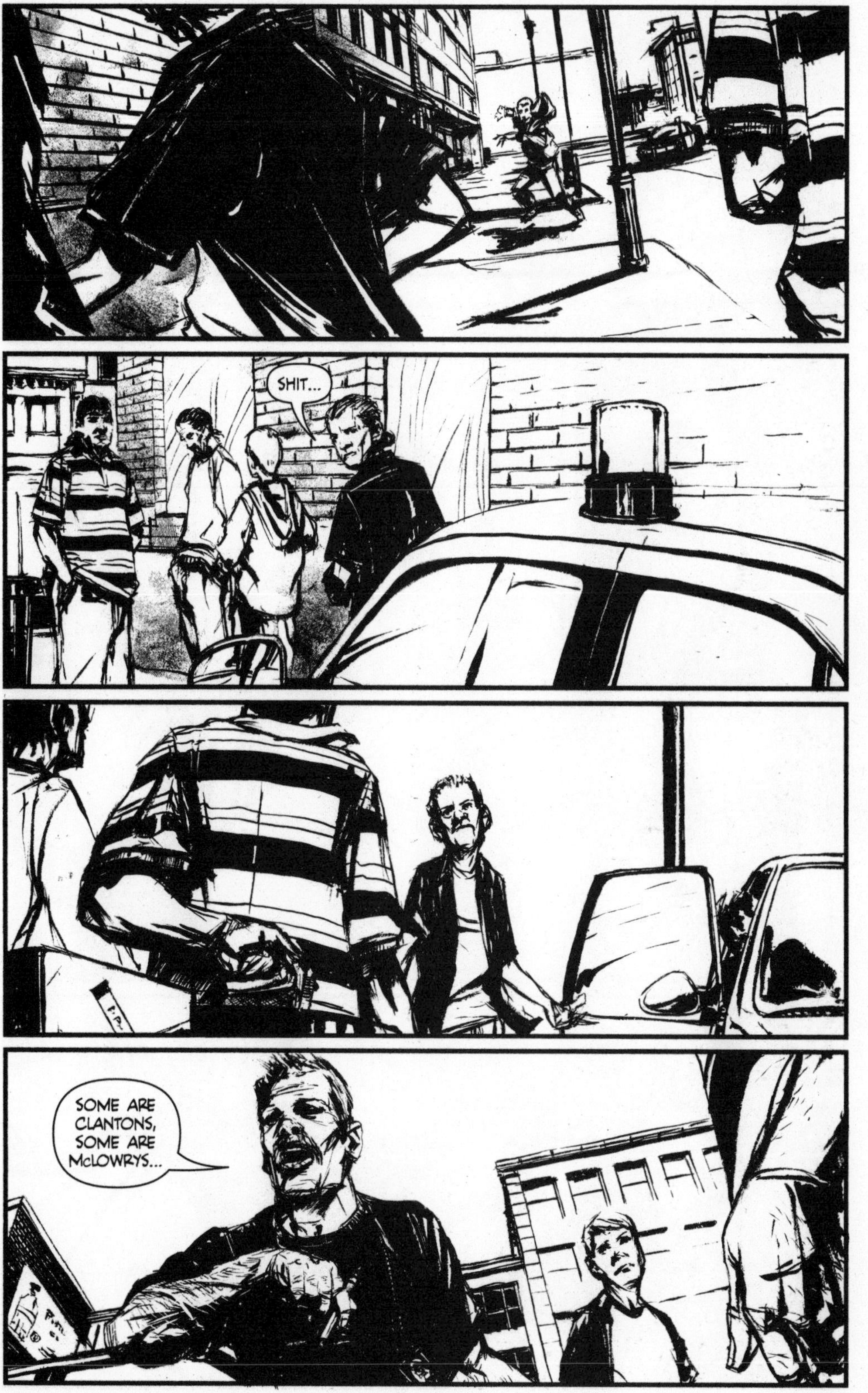
SHIT...
SOME ARE CLANTONS, SOME ARE McLOWRYS...

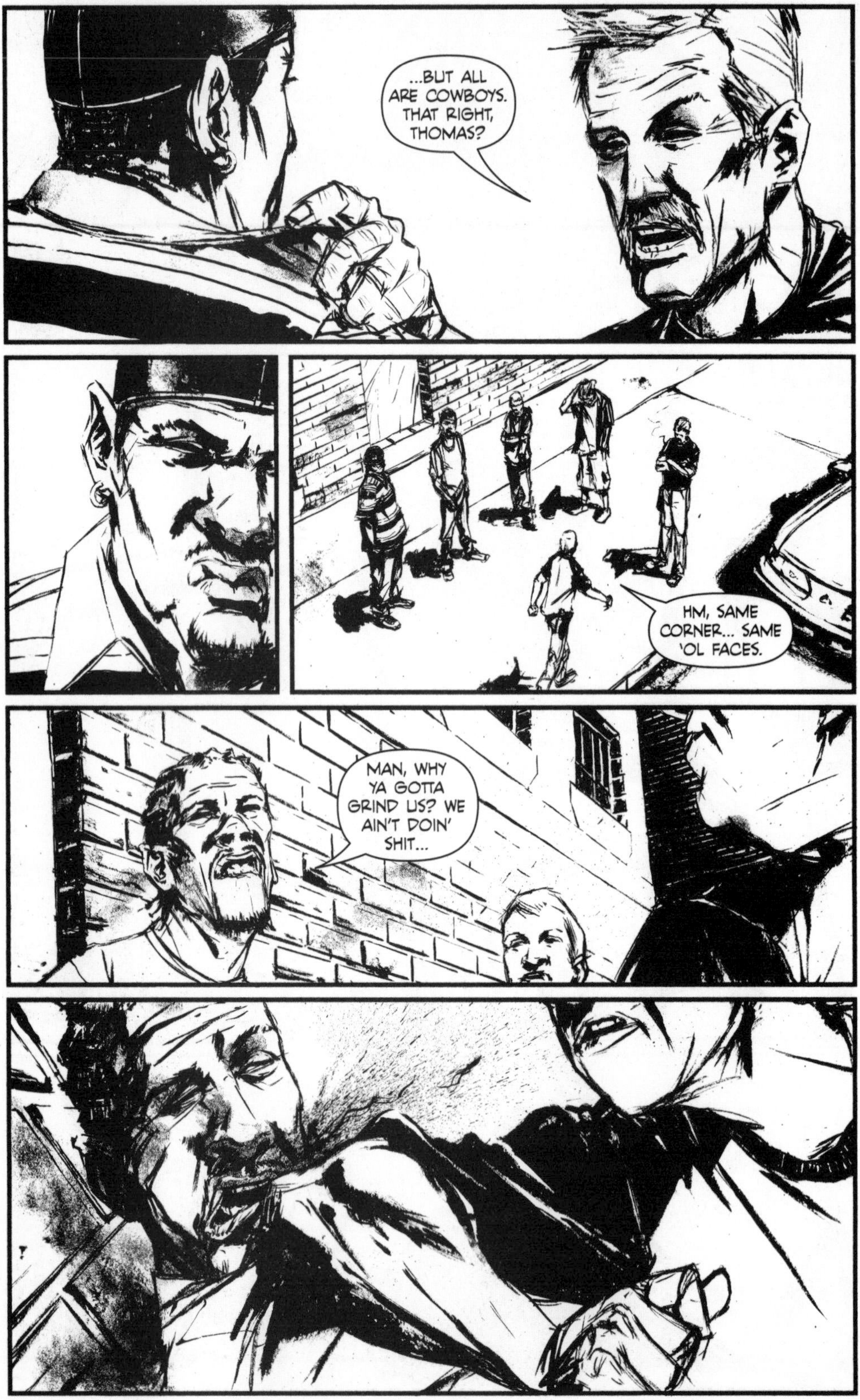
...BUT ALL
ARE COWBOYS.
THAT RIGHT,
THOMAS?
HM, SAME
CORNER... SAME
'OL FACES.
MAN, WHY
YA GOTTA
GRIND US? WE
AIN'T DOIN'
SHIT...

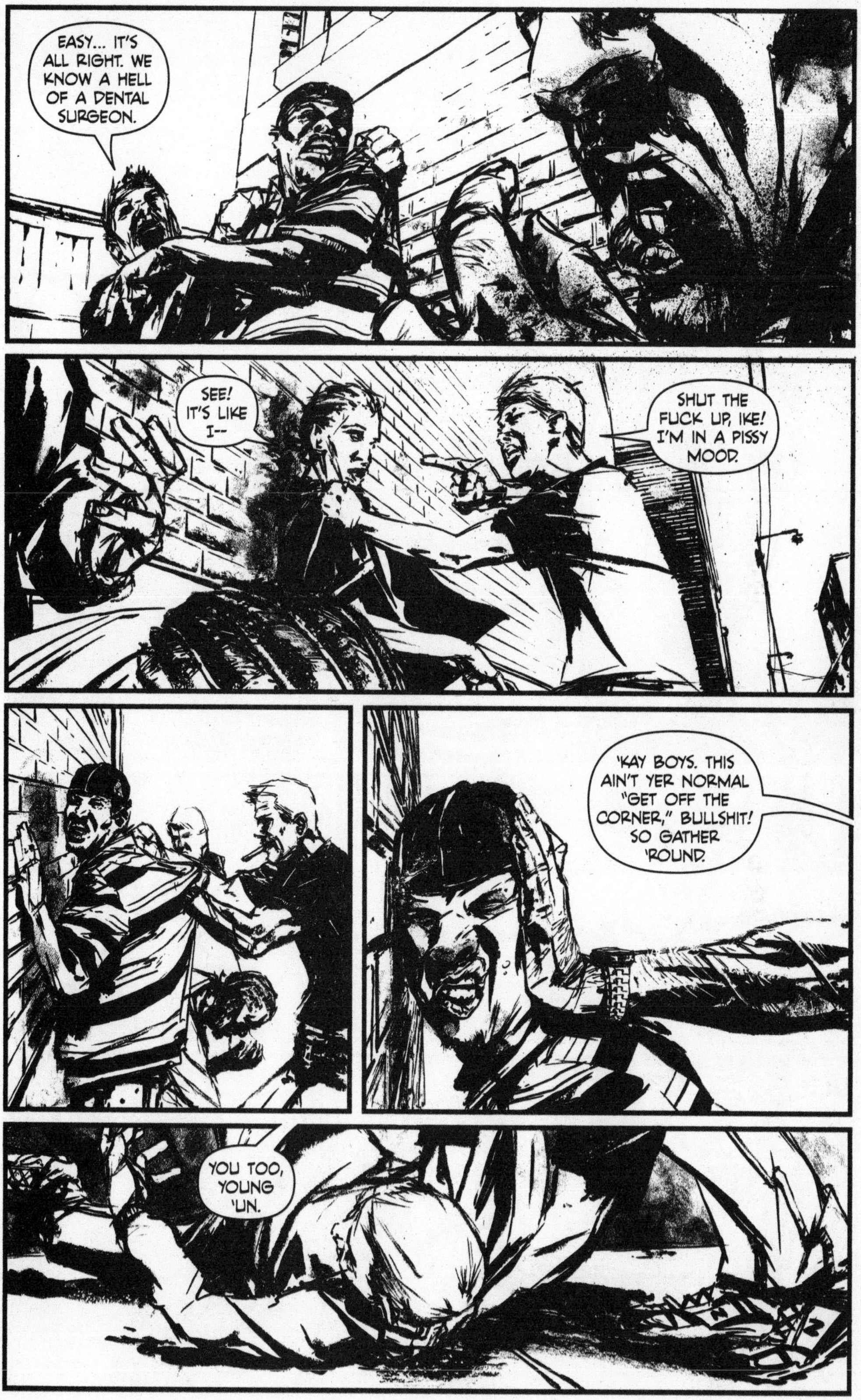
EASY... IT'S ALL RIGHT. WE KNOW A HELL OF A DENTAL SURGEON.
SEE! IT'S LIKE I--
SHUT THE FUCK UP, IKE! I'M IN A PISSY MOOD.
'KAY BOYS. THIS AIN'T YER NORMAL "GET OFF THE CORNER," BULLSHIT! SO GATHER 'ROUND.
YOU TOO, YOUNG 'UN.

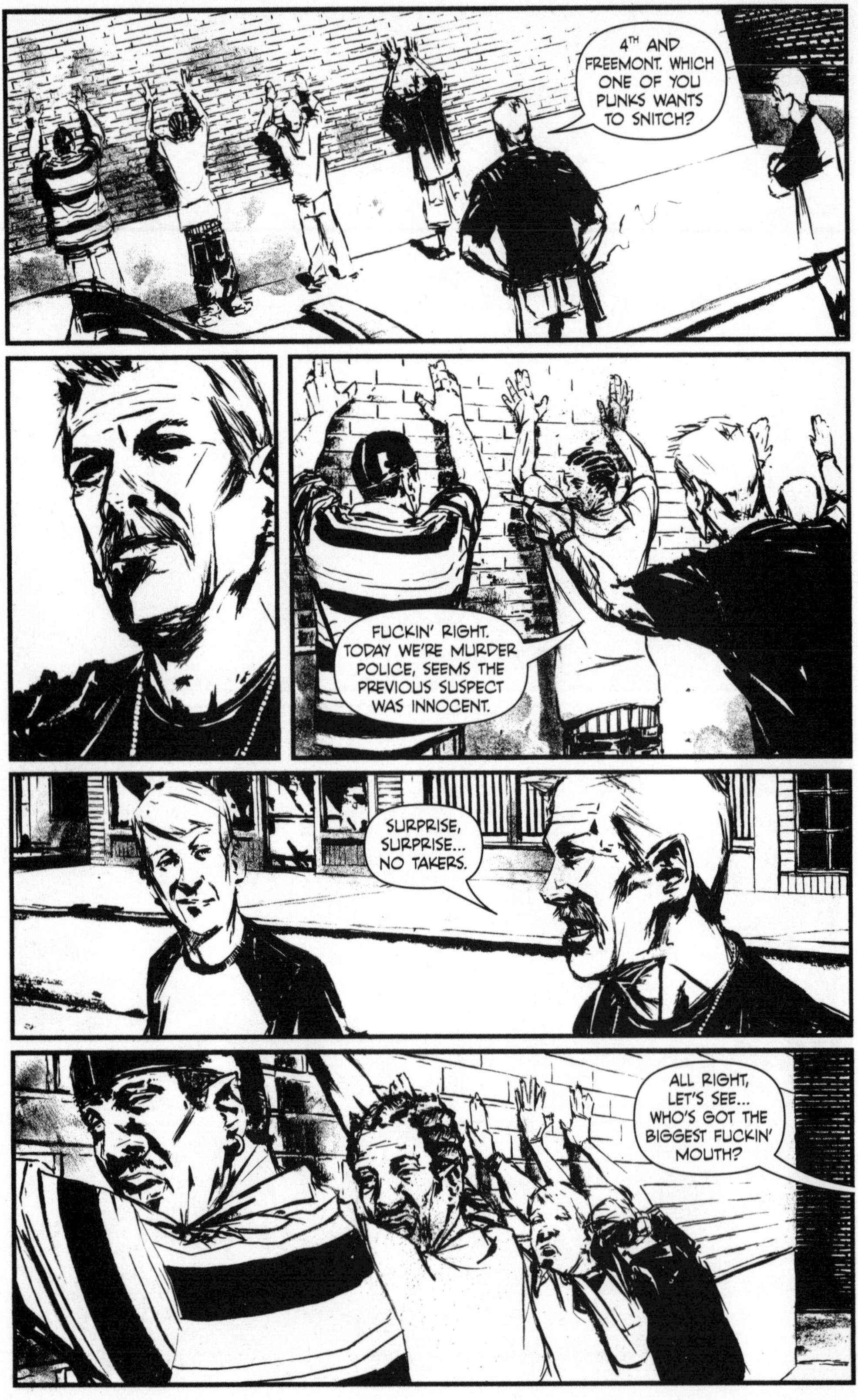
4TH AND FREEMONT. WHICH ONE OF YOU PUNKS WANTS TO SNITCH?
FUCKIN' RIGHT. TODAY WE'RE MURDER POLICE, SEEMS THE PREVIOUS SUSPECT WAS INNOCENT.
SURPRISE, SURPRISE... NO TAKERS.
ALL RIGHT, LET'S SEE... WHO'S GOT THE BIGGEST FUCKIN' MOUTH?

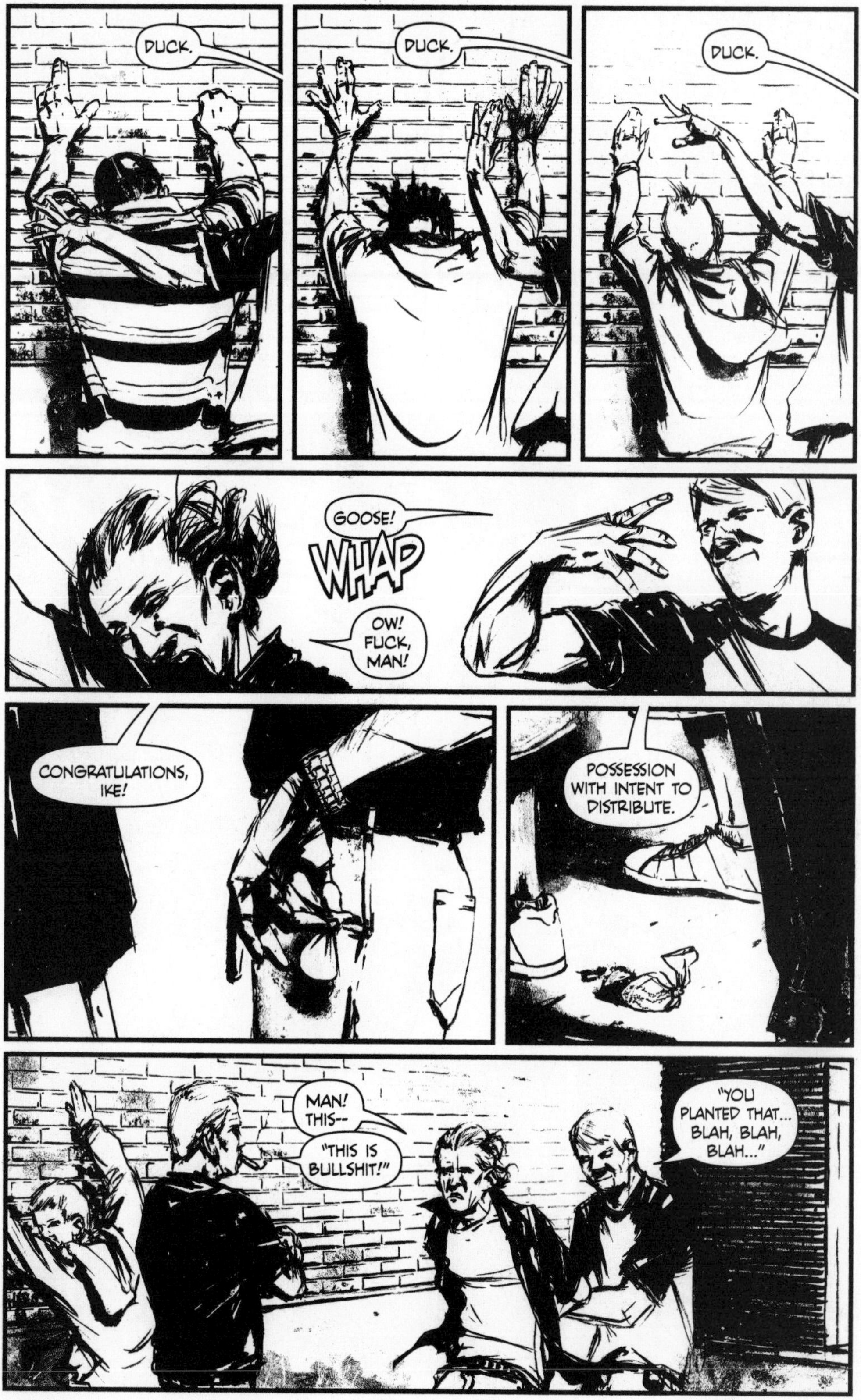
DUCK.
DUCK.
DUCK.
GOOSE!
WHAP
OW! FUCK, MAN!
CONGRATULATIONS, IKE!
POSSESSION WITH INTENT TO DISTRIBUTE.
MAN! THIS--
"THIS IS BULLSHIT!"
"YOU PLANTED THAT... BLAH, BLAH, BLAH..."

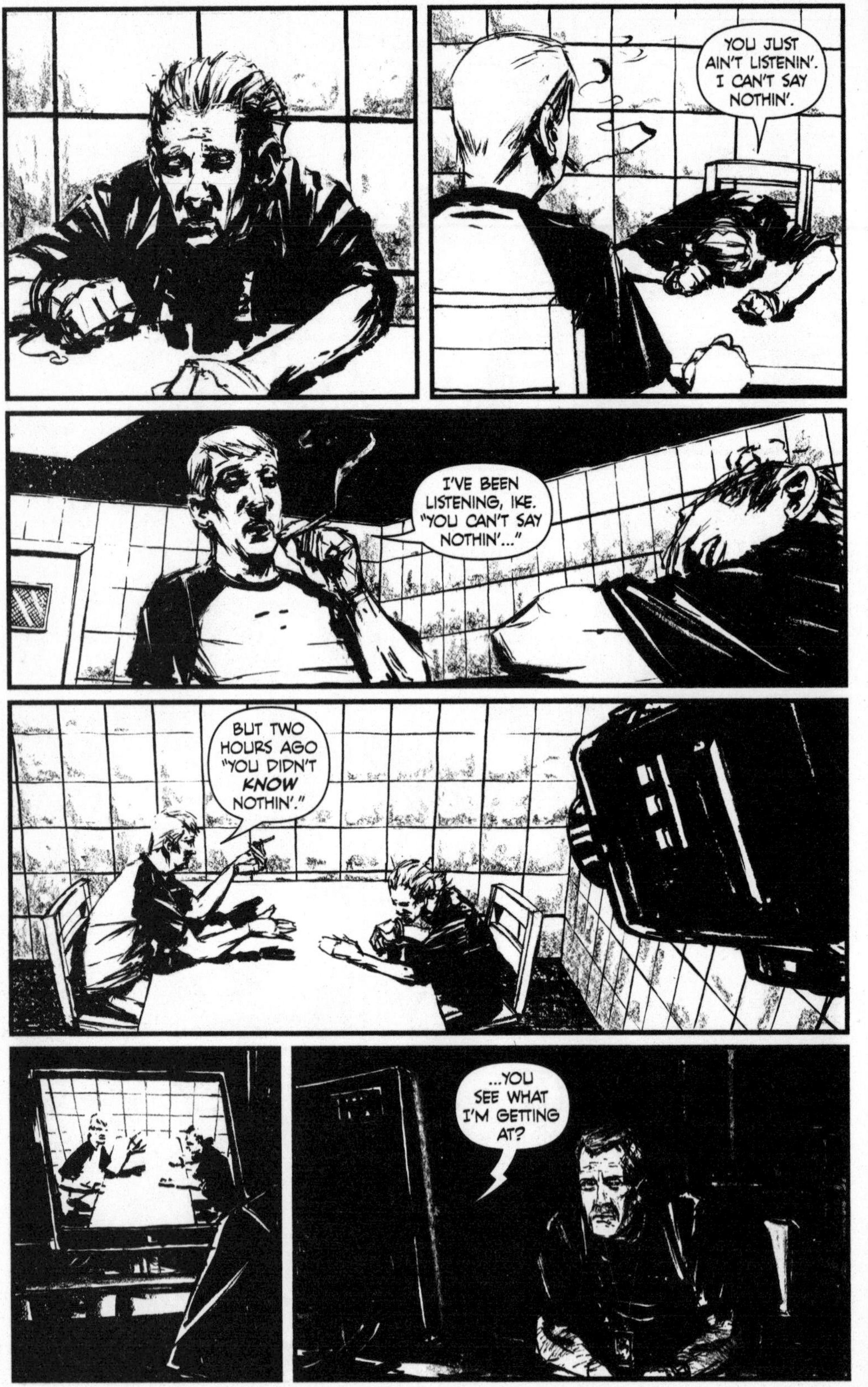
YOU JUST AIN'T LISTENIN'. I CAN'T SAY NOTHIN'.
I'VE BEEN LISTENING, IKE. "YOU CAN'T SAY NOTHIN'..."
BUT TWO HOURS AGO "YOU DIDN'T KNOW NOTHIN'."
...YOU SEE WHAT I'M GETTING AT?

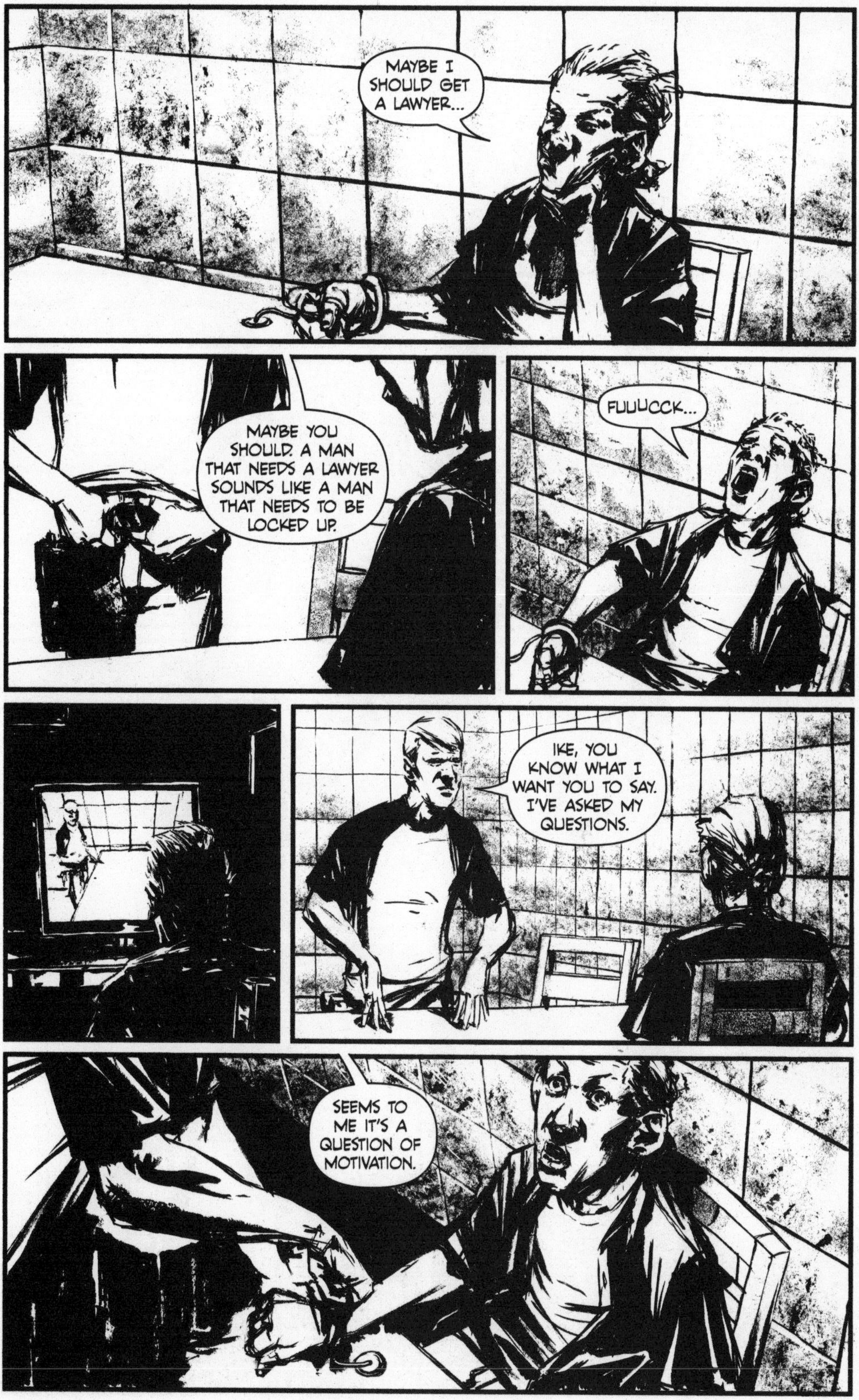
MAYBE I SHOULD GET A LAWYER...
MAYBE YOU SHOULD. A MAN THAT NEEDS A LAWYER SOUNDS LIKE A MAN THAT NEEDS TO BE LOCKED UP.
FUUUCCK...
IKE, YOU KNOW WHAT I WANT YOU TO SAY. I'VE ASKED MY QUESTIONS.
SEEMS TO ME IT'S A QUESTION OF MOTIVATION.

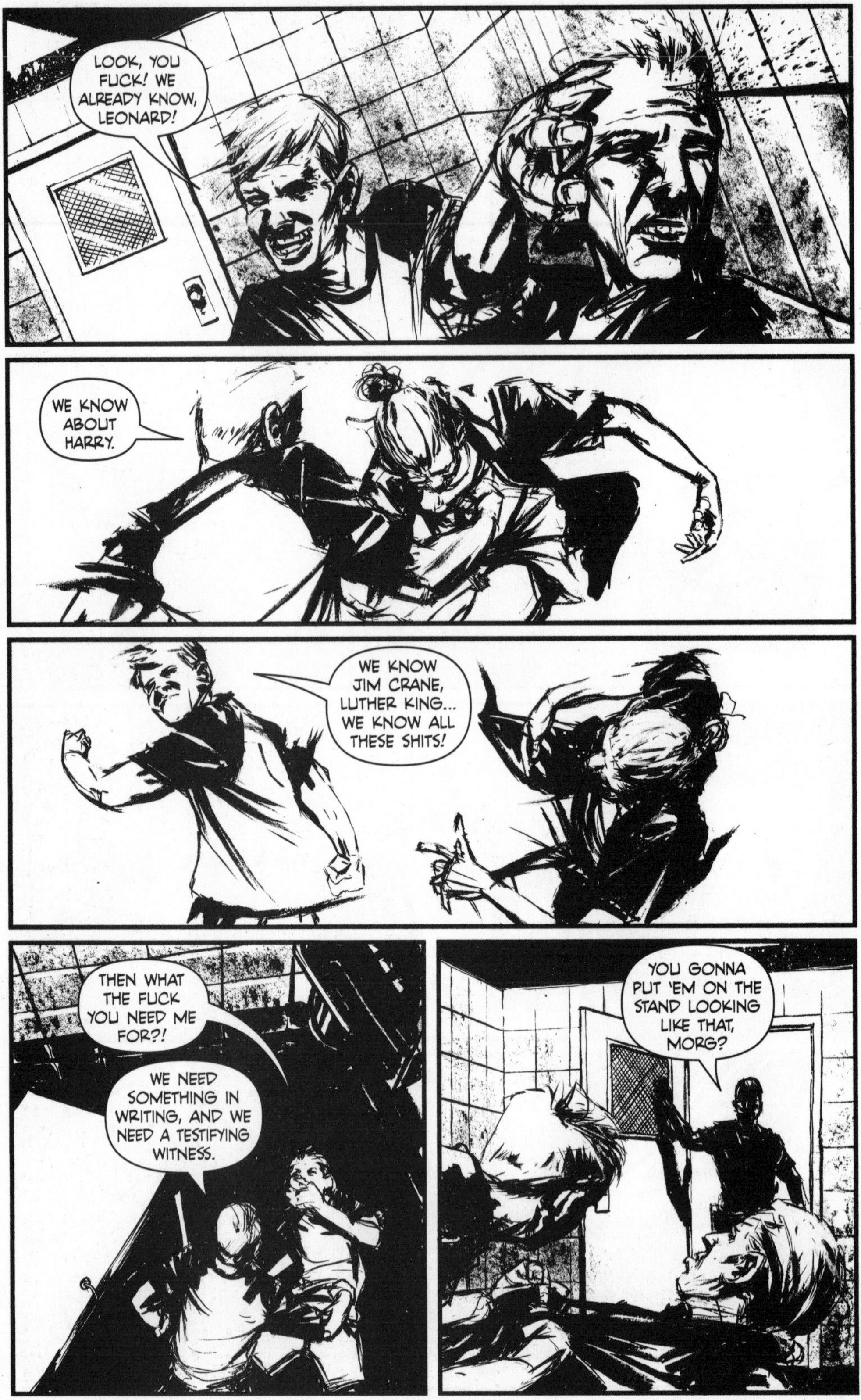
LOOK, YOU FUCK! WE ALREADY KNOW, LEONARD!
WE KNOW ABOUT HARRY.
WE KNOW JIM CRANE, LUTHER KING... WE KNOW ALL THESE SHITS!
THEN WHAT THE FUCK YOU NEED ME FOR?!
WE NEED SOMETHING IN WRITING, AND WE NEED A TESTIFYING WITNESS.
YOU GONNA PUT 'EM ON THE STAND LOOKING LIKE THAT, MORG?

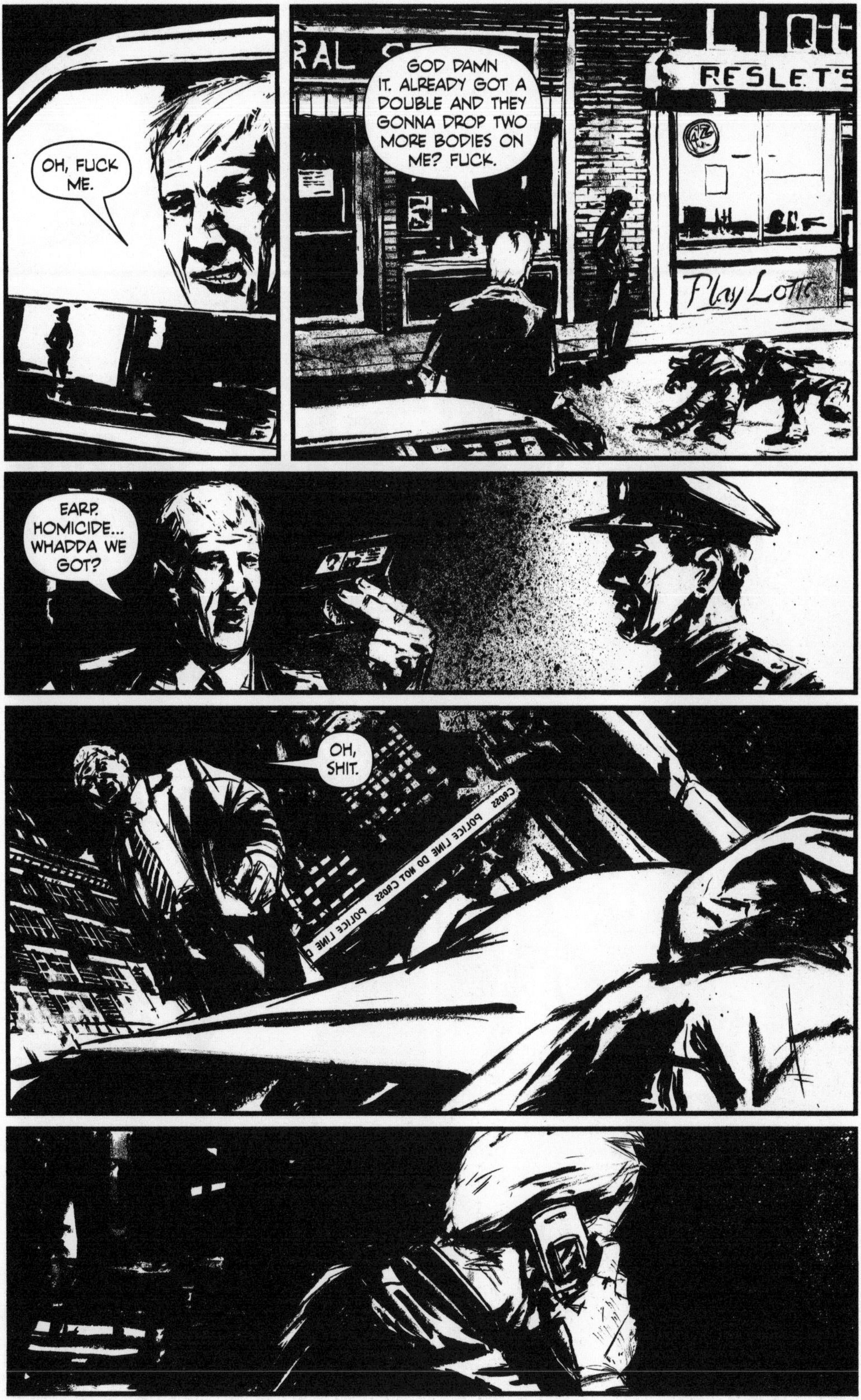
OH, FUCK ME.
RESLET'S
GOD DAMN IT. ALREADY GOT A DOUBLE AND THEY GONNA DROP TWO MORE BODIES ON ME? FUCK.
EARP. HOMICIDE... WHADDA WE GOT?
OH, SHIT.
POLICE LINE DO NOT CROSS

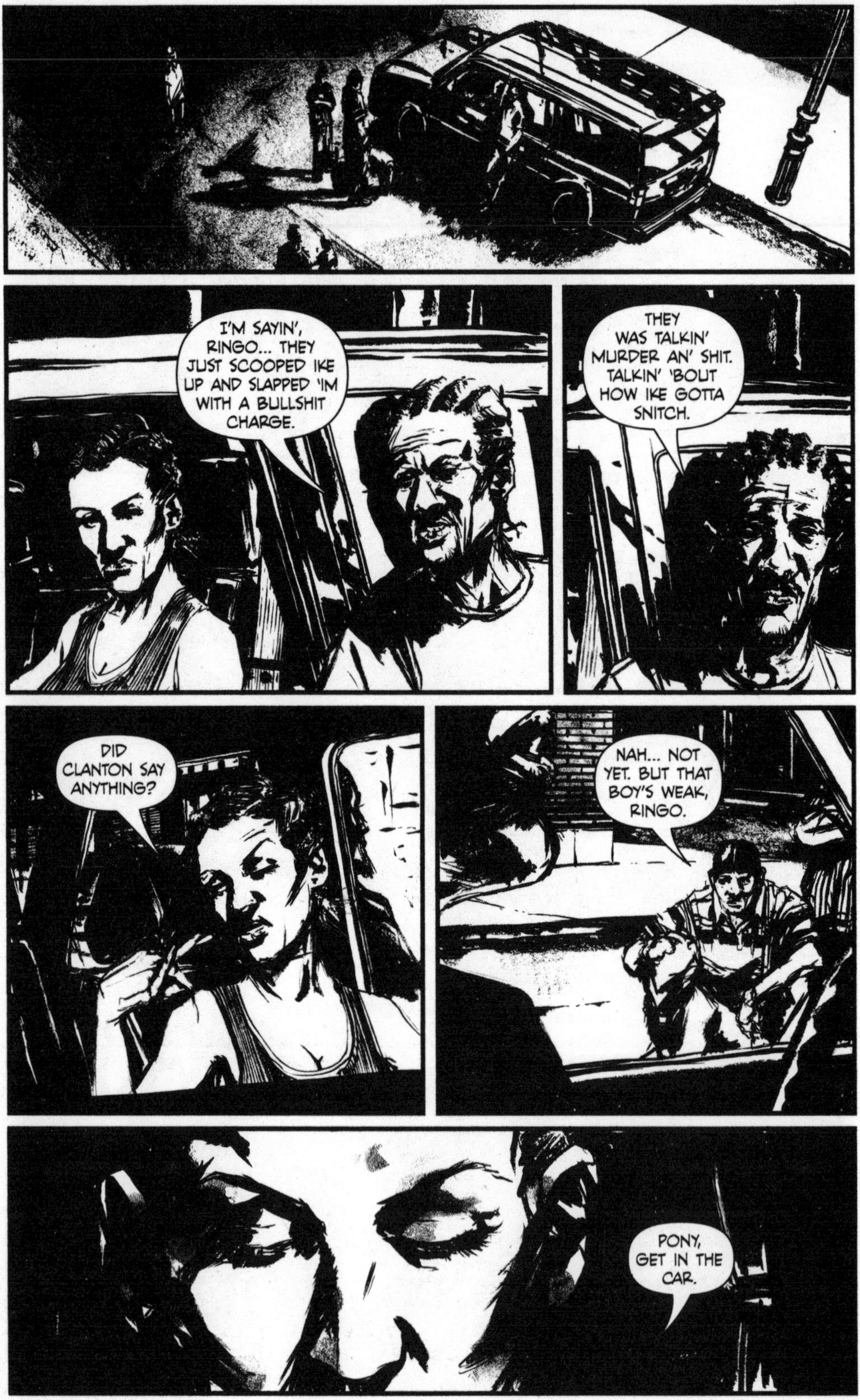
I'M SAYIN', RINGO... THEY JUST SCOOPED IKE UP AND SLAPPED 'IM WITH A BULLSHIT CHARGE.
THEY WAS TALKIN' MURDER AN' SHIT. TALKIN' 'BOUT HOW IKE GOTTA SNITCH.
DID CLANTON SAY ANYTHING?
NAH... NOT YET. BUT THAT BOY'S WEAK, RINGO.
PONY, GET IN THE CAR.

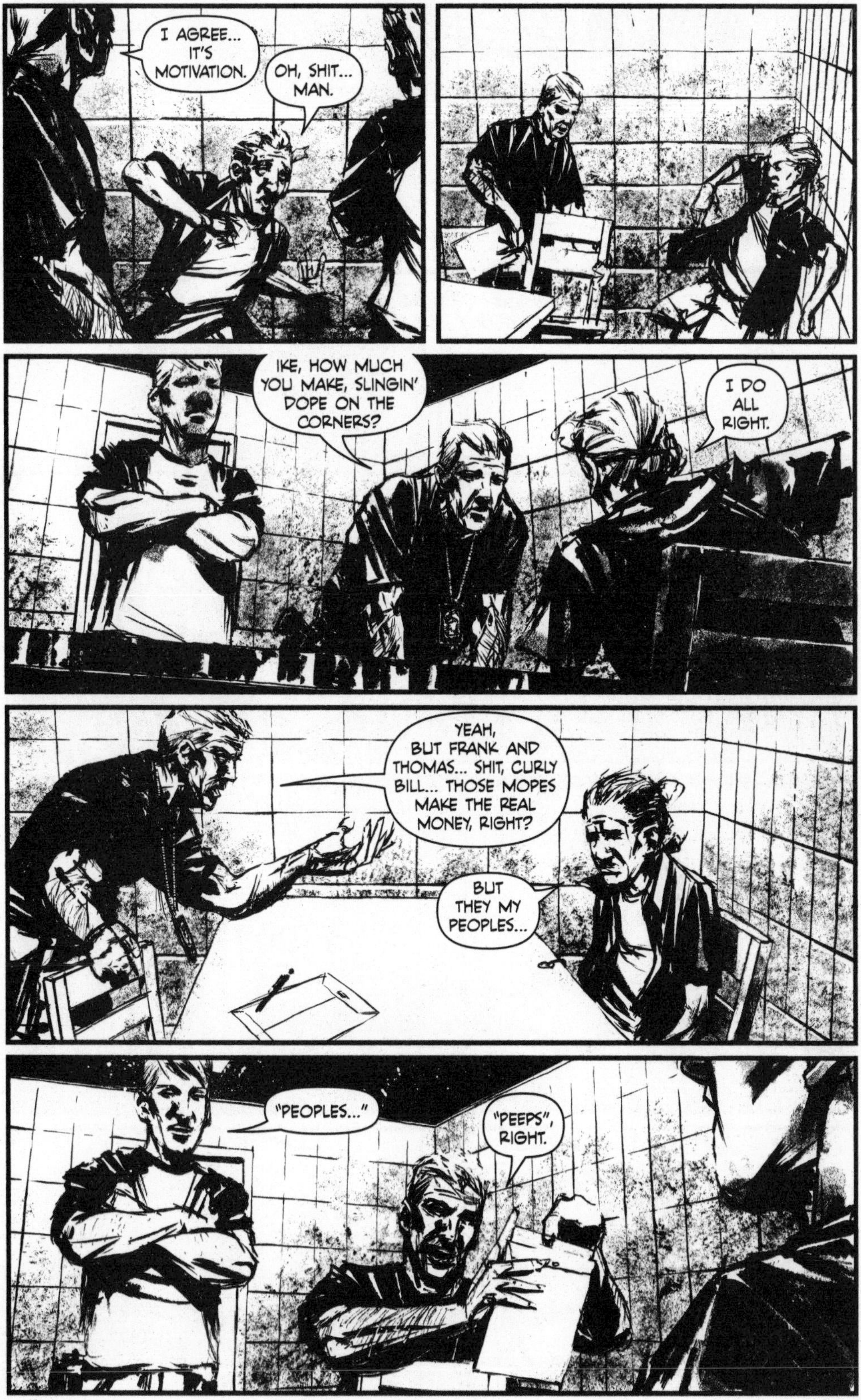
I AGREE... IT'S MOTIVATION.
OH, SHIT... MAN.
IKE, HOW MUCH YOU MAKE, SLINGIN' DOPE ON THE CORNERS?
I DO ALL RIGHT.
YEAH, BUT FRANK AND THOMAS... SHIT, CURLY BILL... THOSE MOPES MAKE THE REAL MONEY, RIGHT?
BUT THEY MY PEOPLES...
"PEOPLES..."
"PEEPS", RIGHT.

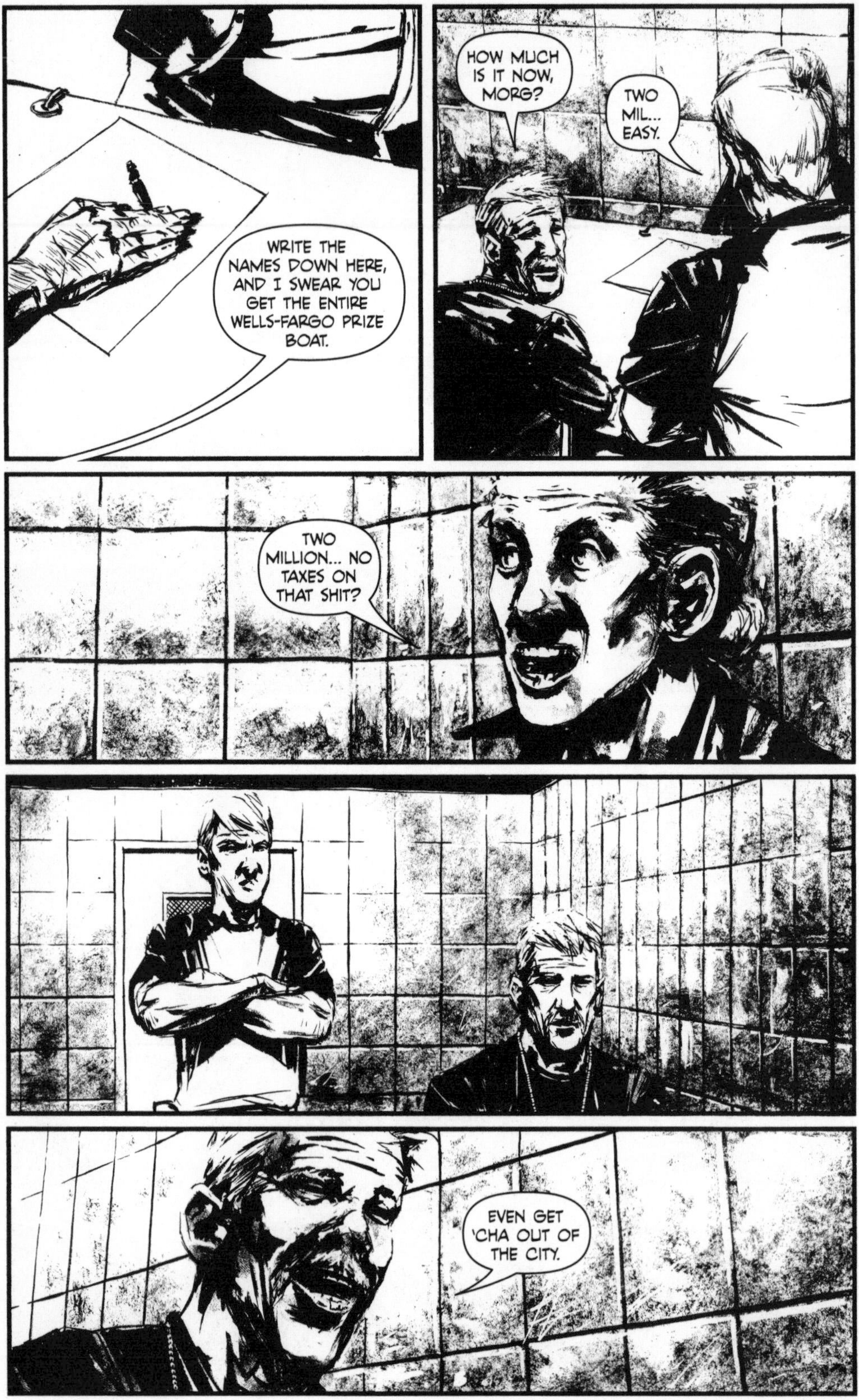
WRITE THE NAMES DOWN HERE, AND I SWEAR YOU GET THE ENTIRE WELLS-FARGO PRIZE BOAT.
HOW MUCH IS IT NOW, MORG?
TWO MIL... EASY.
TWO MILLION... NO TAXES ON THAT SHIT?
EVEN GET 'CHA OUT OF THE CITY.

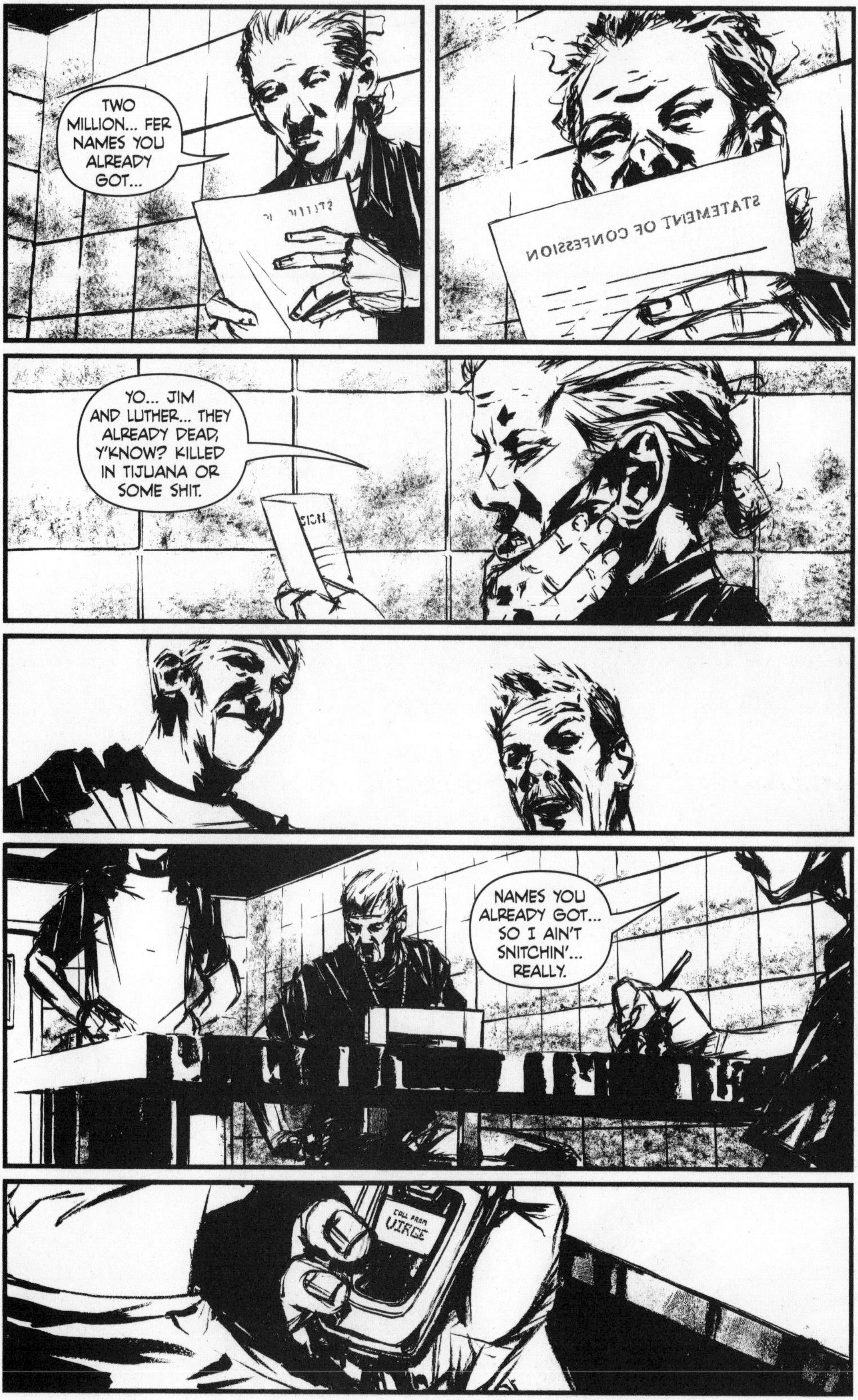
TWO MILLION... FER NAMES YOU ALREADY GOT...
YO... JIM AND LUTHER... THEY ALREADY DEAD, Y'KNOW? KILLED IN TIJUANA OR SOME SHIT.
NAMES YOU ALREADY GOT... SO I AIN'T SNITCHIN'... REALLY.
CALL FROM VIRGE

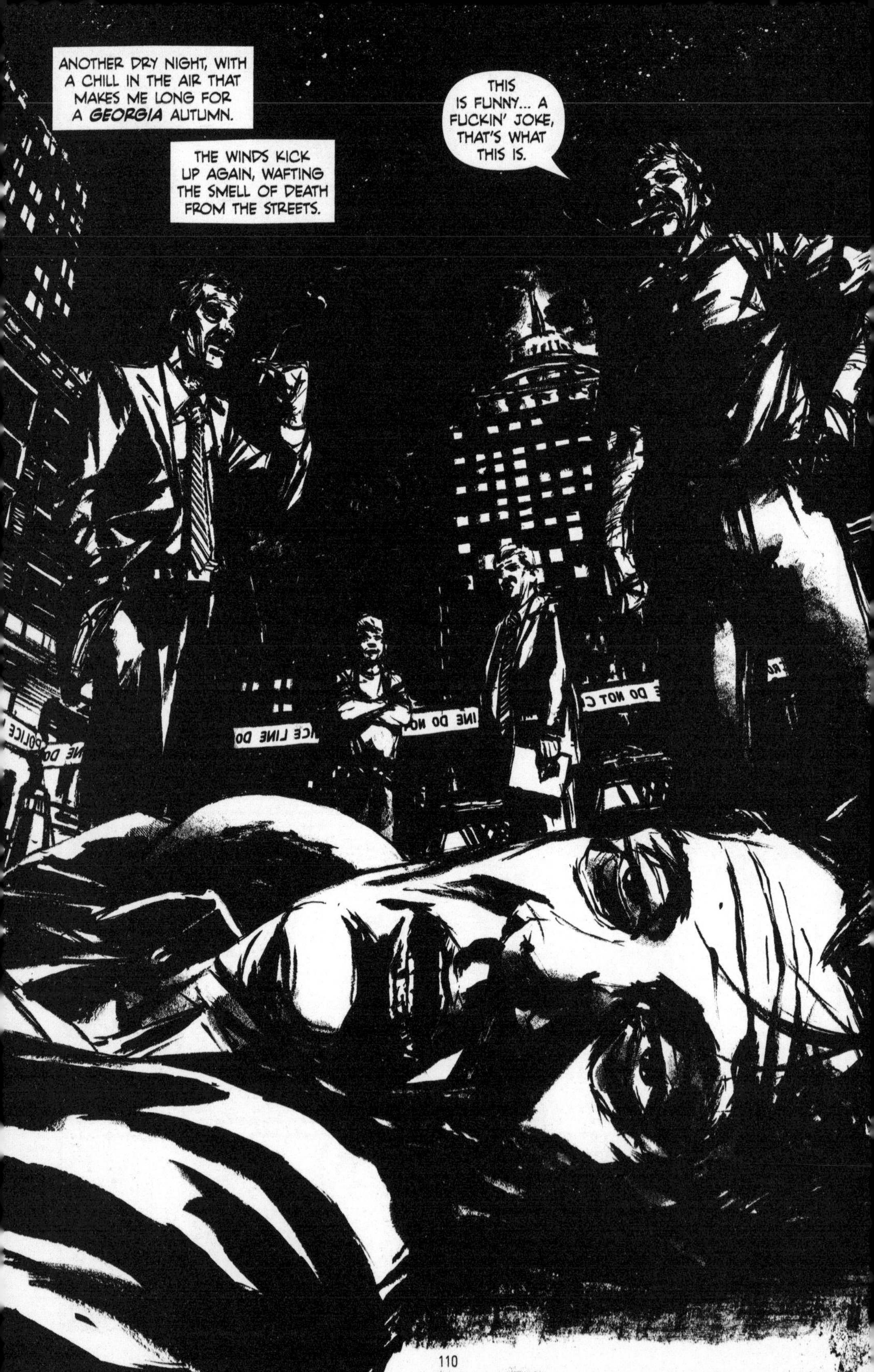
ANOTHER DRY NIGHT, WITH A CHILL IN THE AIR THAT MAKES ME LONG FOR A *GEORGIA* AUTUMN.
THE WINDS KICK UP AGAIN, WAFTING THE SMELL OF DEATH FROM THE STREETS.
THIS IS FUNNY... A FUCKIN' JOKE, THAT'S WHAT THIS IS.

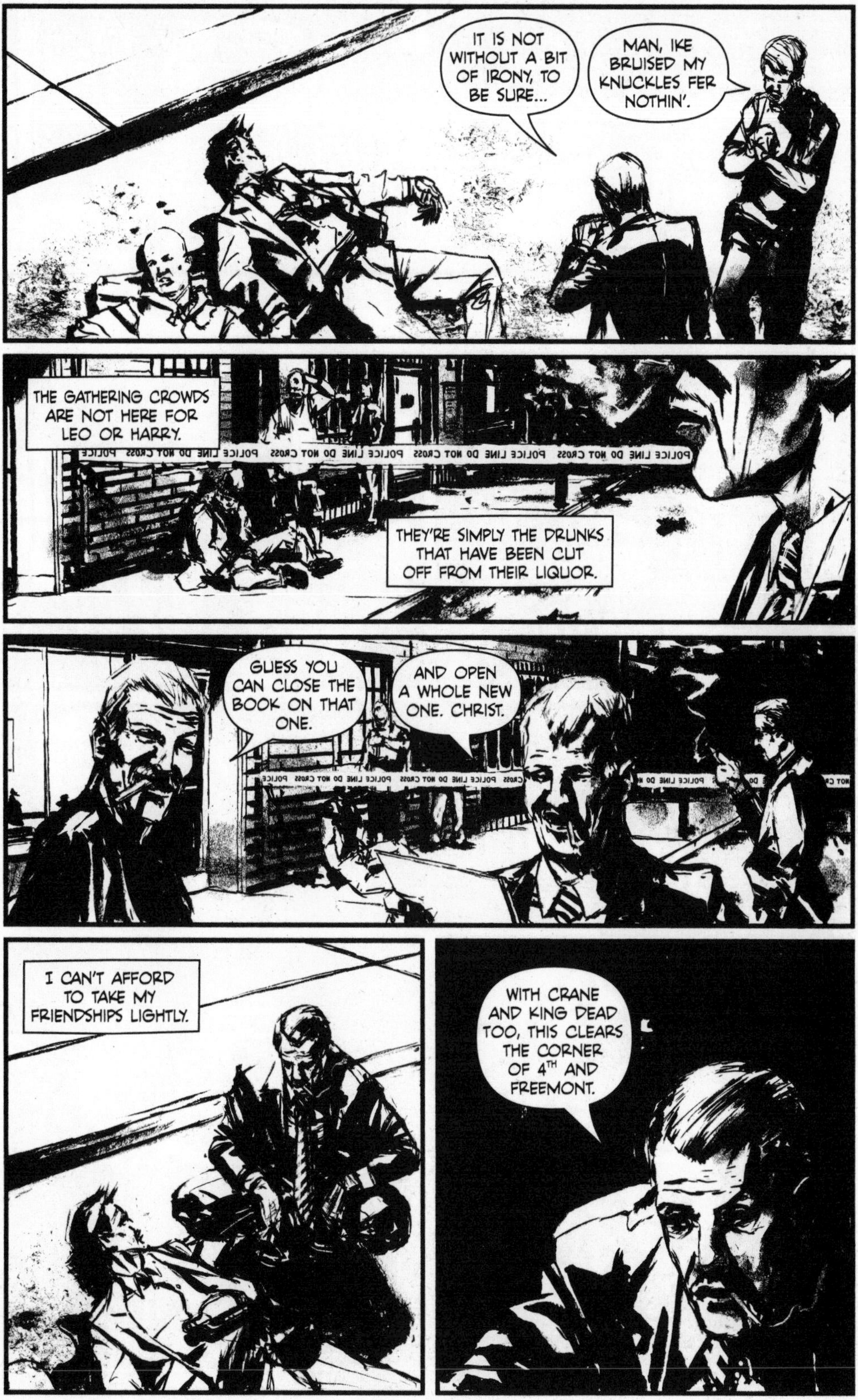
IT IS NOT WITHOUT A BIT OF IRONY, TO BE SURE...
MAN, IKE BRUISED MY KNUCKLES FER NOTHIN'.
THE GATHERING CROWDS ARE NOT HERE FOR LEO OR HARRY.
THEY'RE SIMPLY THE DRUNKS THAT HAVE BEEN CUT OFF FROM THEIR LIQUOR.
GUESS YOU CAN CLOSE THE BOOK ON THAT ONE.
AND OPEN A WHOLE NEW ONE. CHRIST.
I CAN'T AFFORD TO TAKE MY FRIENDSHIPS LIGHTLY.
WITH CRANE AND KING DEAD TOO, THIS CLEARS THE CORNER OF 4TH AND FREEMONT.

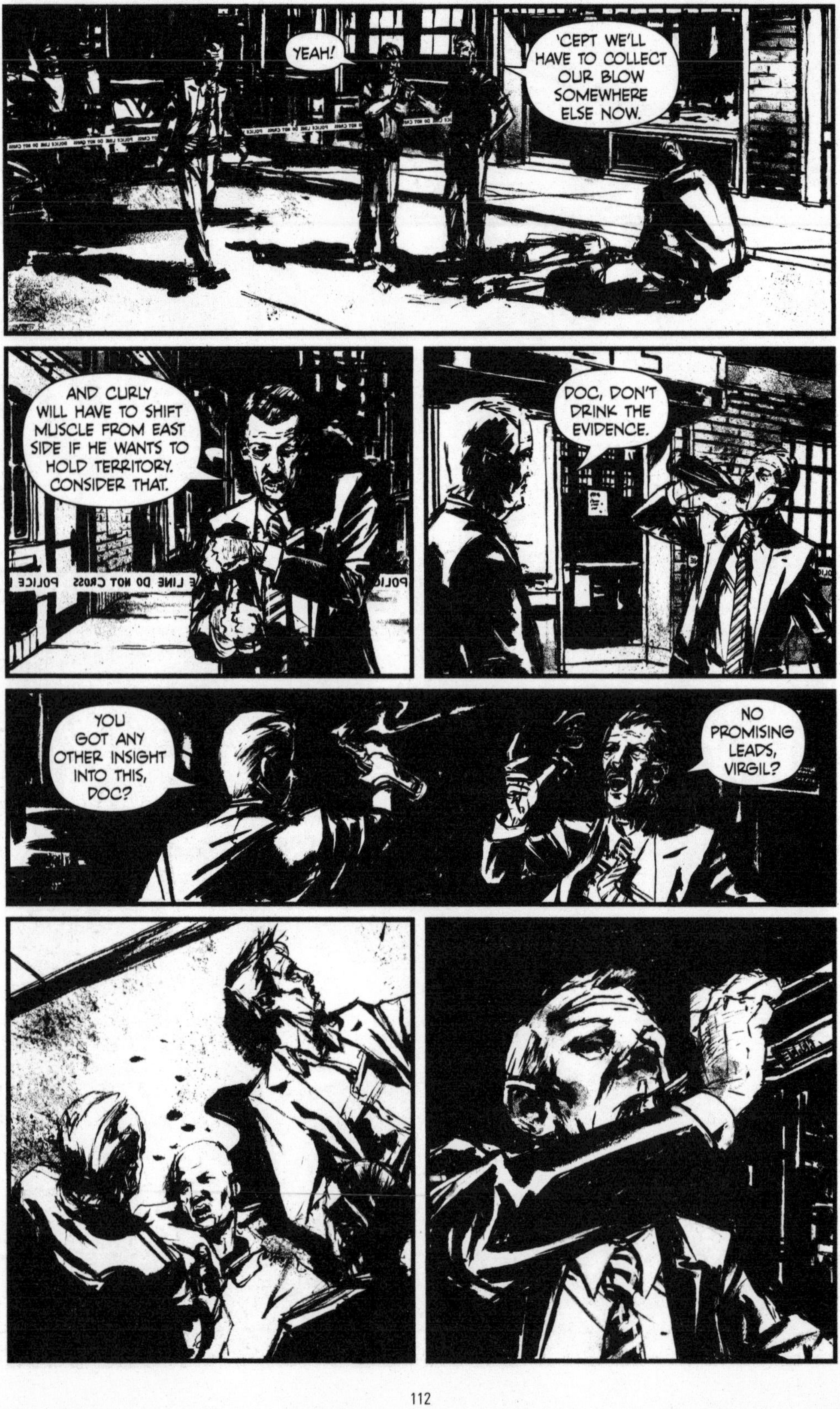
YEAH!
'CEPT WE'LL HAVE TO COLLECT OUR BLOW SOMEWHERE ELSE NOW.
AND CURLY WILL HAVE TO SHIFT MUSCLE FROM EAST SIDE IF HE WANTS TO HOLD TERRITORY. CONSIDER THAT.
DOC, DON'T DRINK THE EVIDENCE.
YOU GOT ANY OTHER INSIGHT INTO THIS, DOC?
NO PROMISING LEADS, VIRGIL?

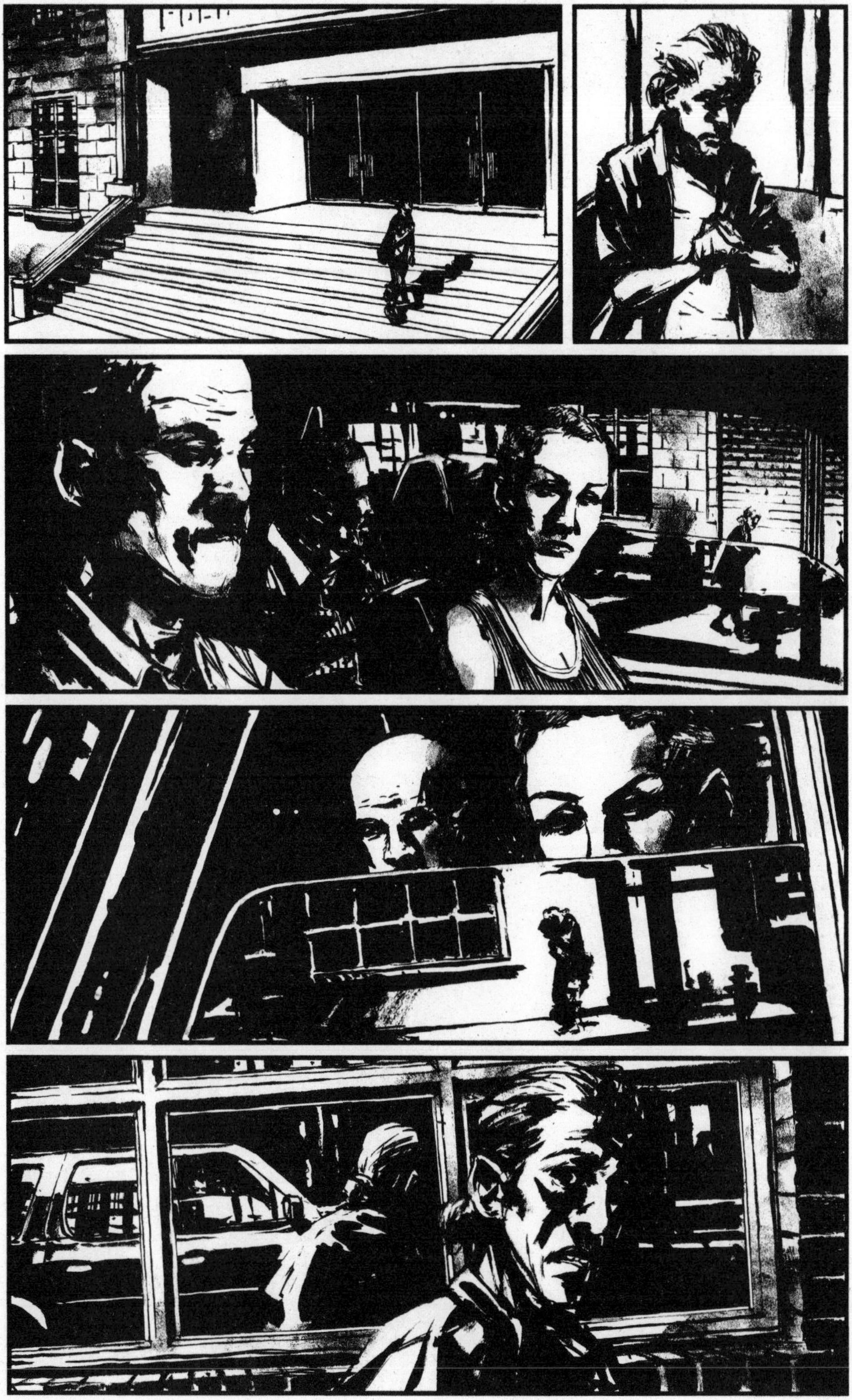

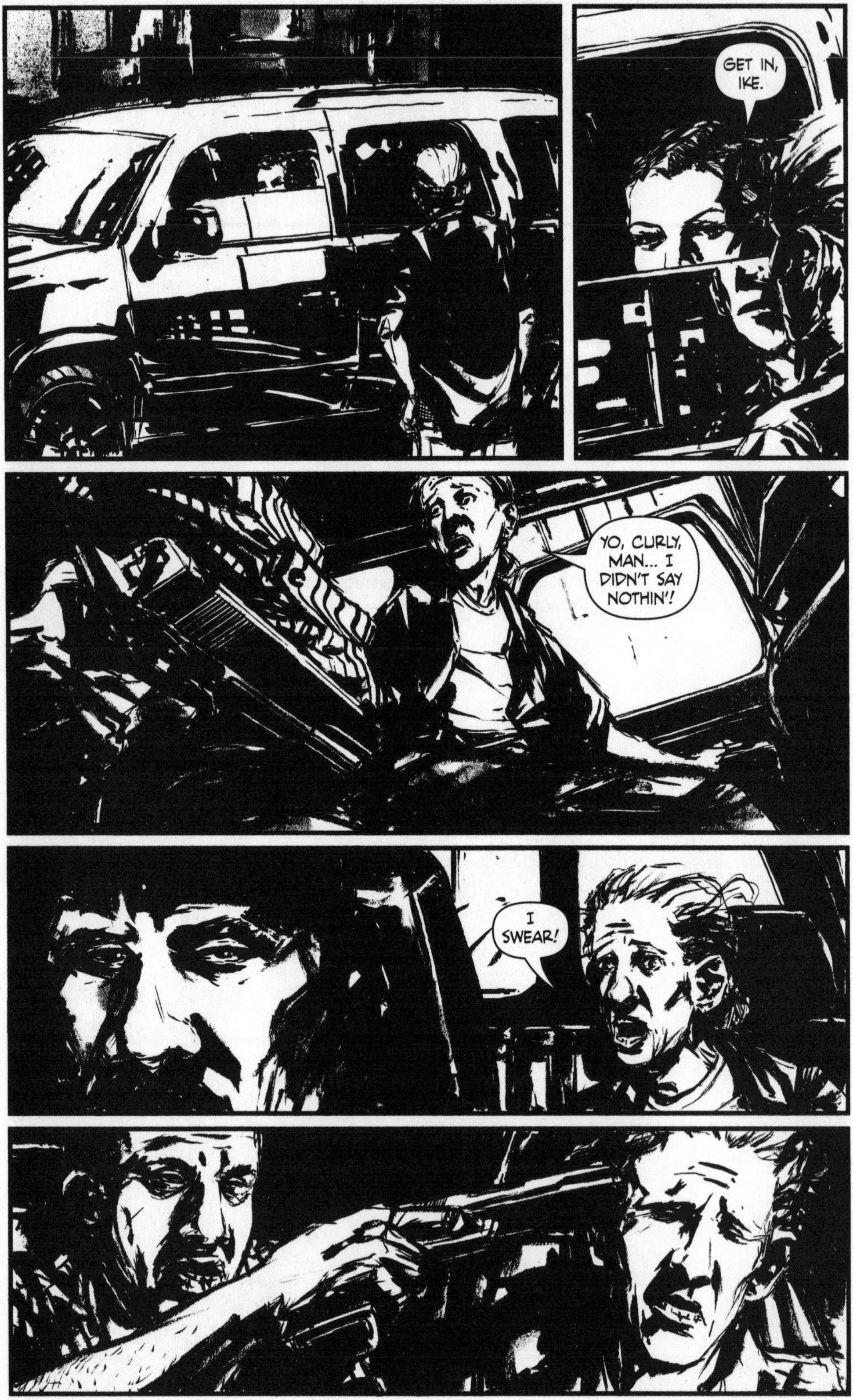
GET IN, IKE.
YO, CURLY, MAN... I DIDN'T SAY NOTHIN'!
I SWEAR!

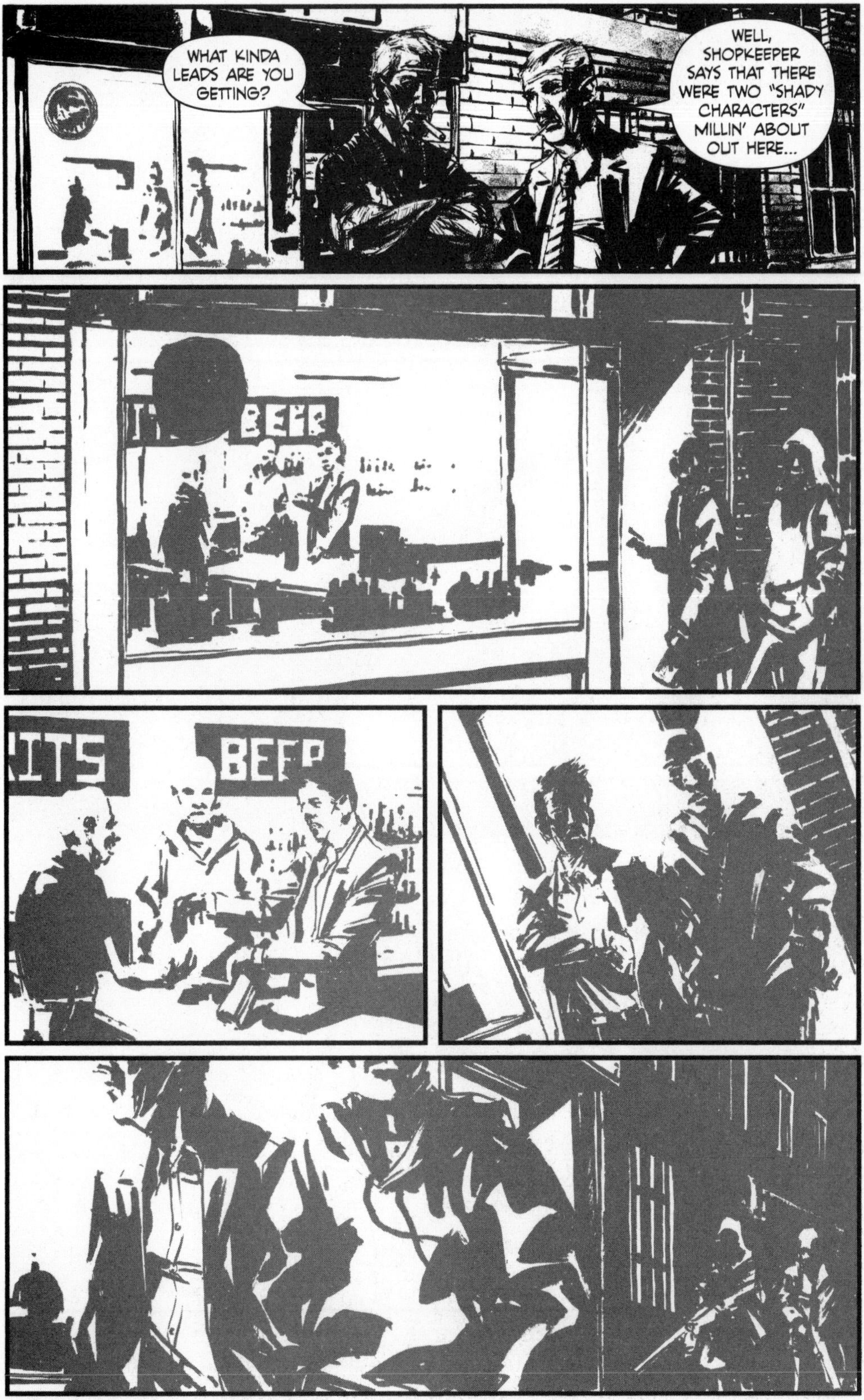
WHAT KINDA LEADS ARE YOU GETTING?
WELL, SHOPKEEPER SAYS THAT THERE WERE TWO "SHADY CHARACTERS" MILLIN' ABOUT OUT HERE...

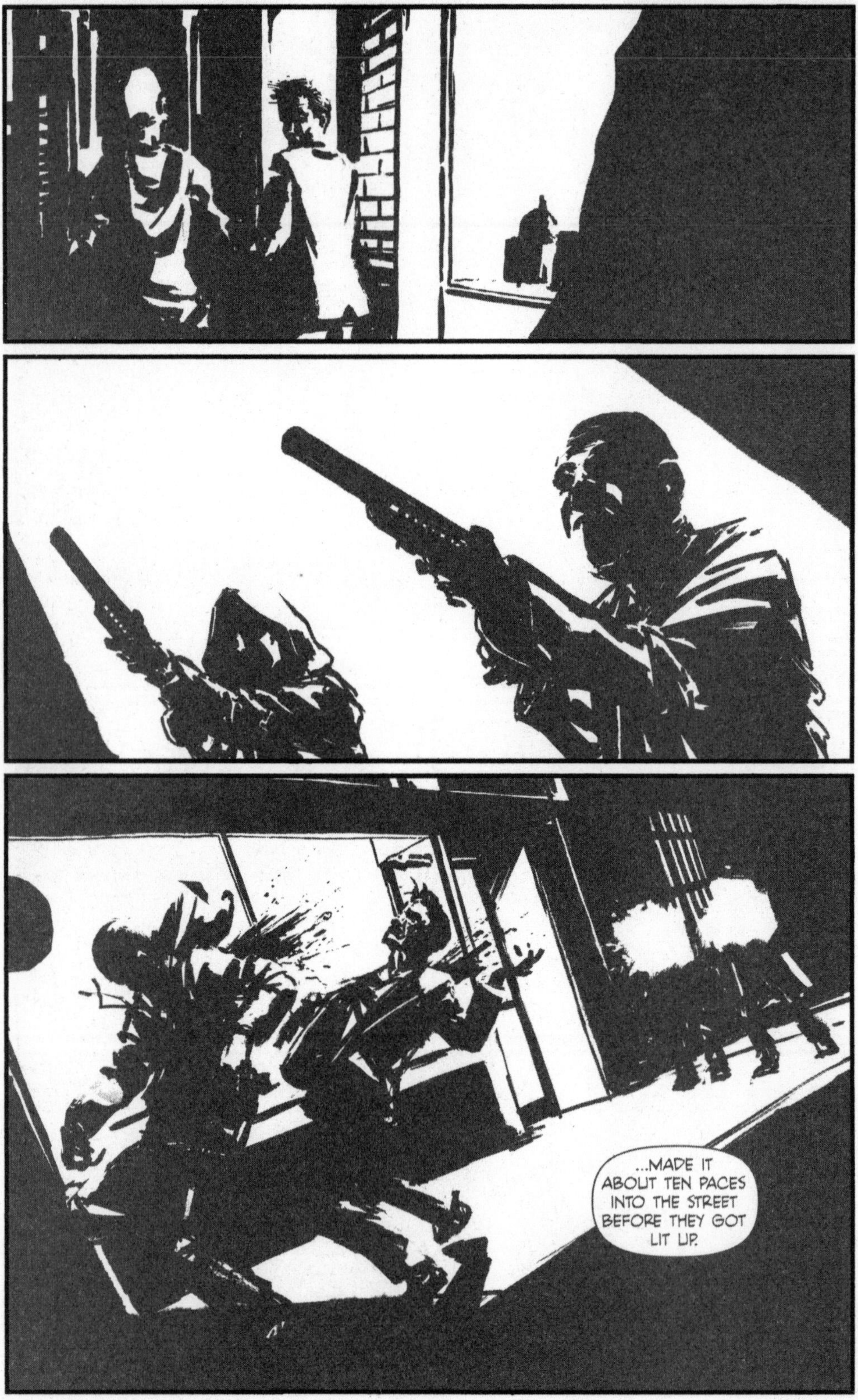
...MADE IT ABOUT TEN PACES INTO THE STREET BEFORE THEY GOT LIT UP.

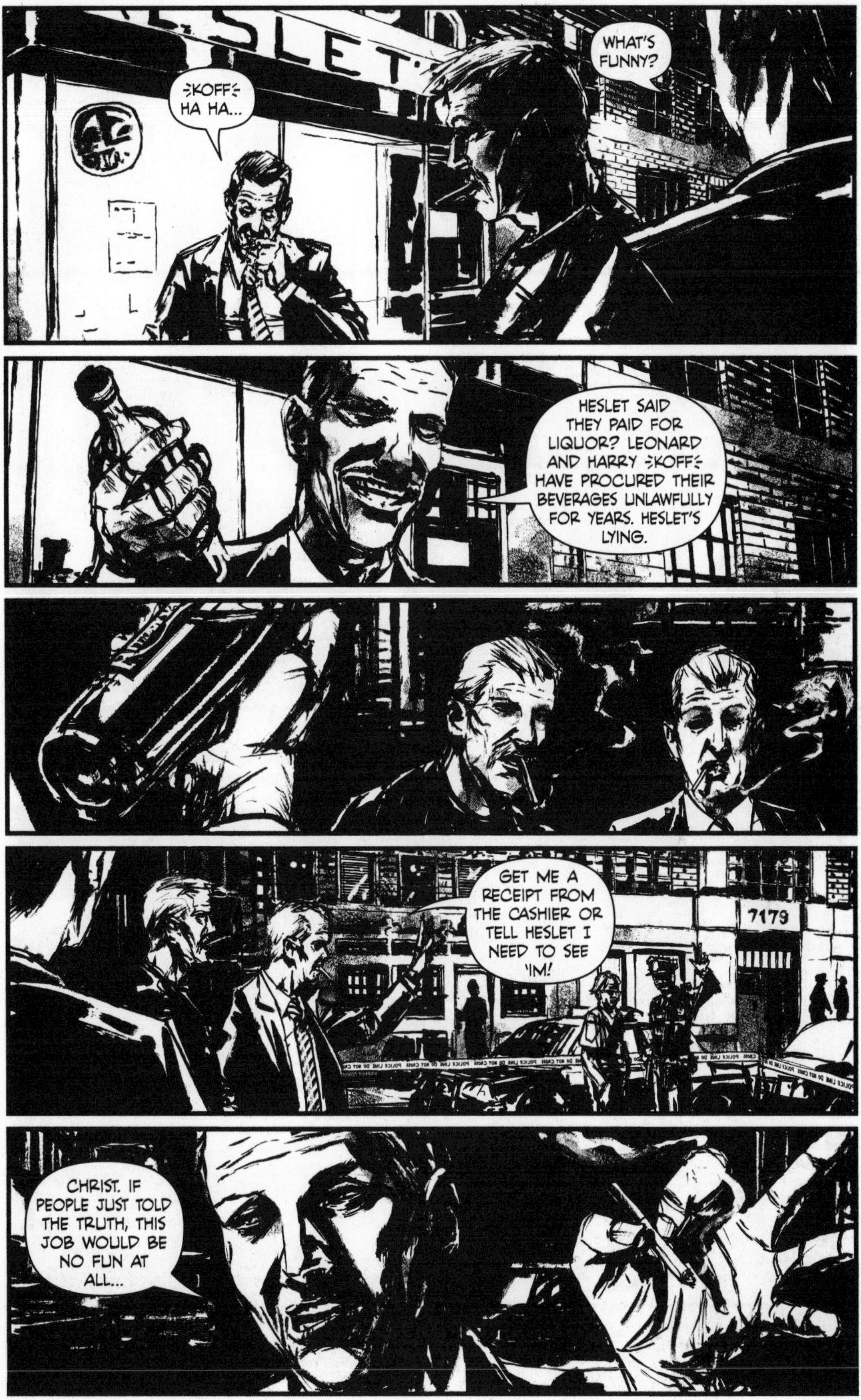
-KOFF- HA HA...
WHAT'S FUNNY?
HESLET SAID THEY PAID FOR LIQUOR? LEONARD AND HARRY -KOFF- HAVE PROCURED THEIR BEVERAGES UNLAWFULLY FOR YEARS. HESLET'S LYING.
GET ME A RECEIPT FROM THE CASHIER OR TELL HESLET I NEED TO SEE 'IM!
7179
CHRIST. IF PEOPLE JUST TOLD THE TRUTH, THIS JOB WOULD BE NO FUN AT ALL...

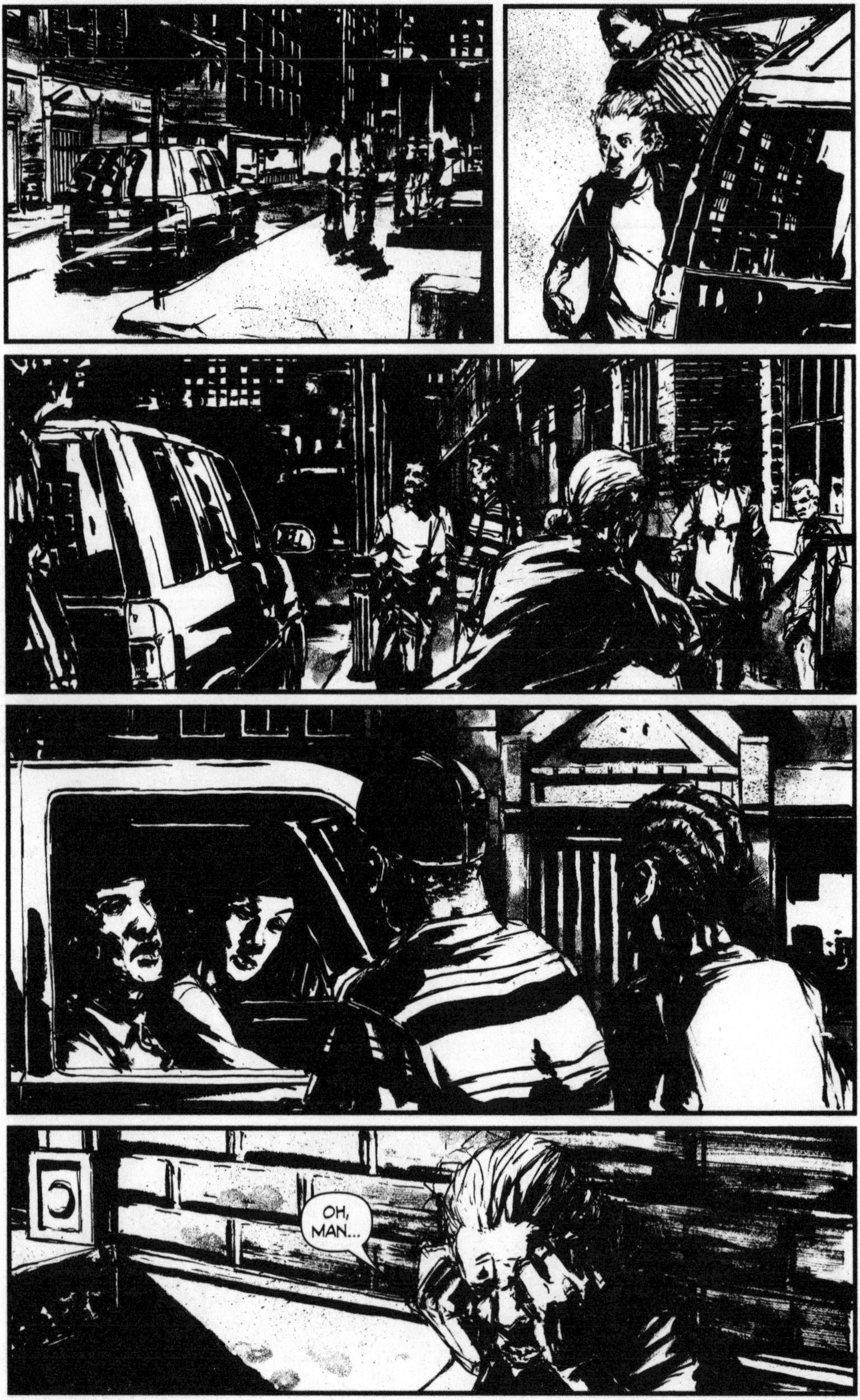
OH, MAN...

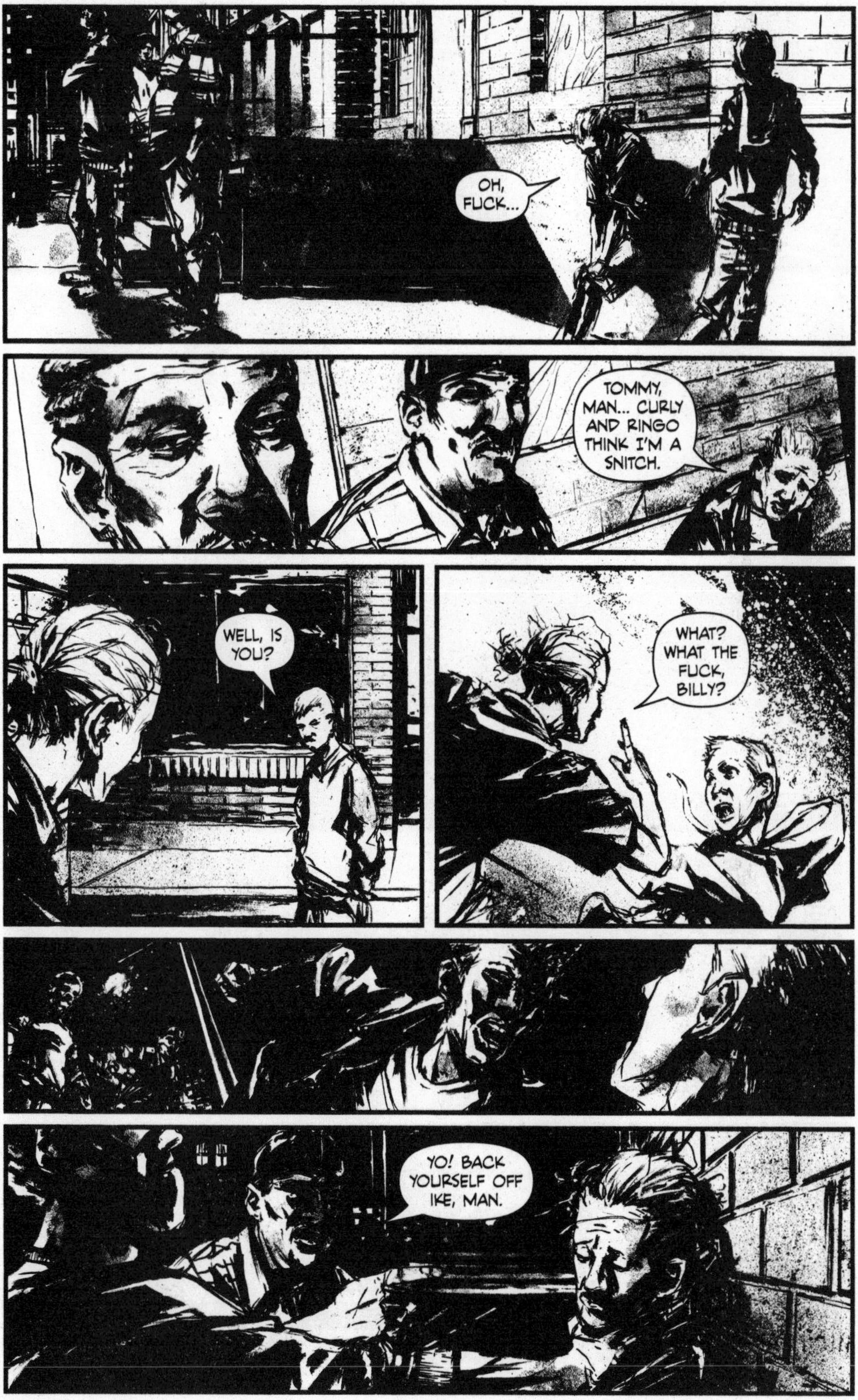
OH, FUCK...
TOMMY, MAN... CURLY AND RINGO THINK I'M A SNITCH.
WELL, IS YOU?
WHAT? WHAT THE FUCK, BILLY?
YO! BACK YOURSELF OFF IKE, MAN.

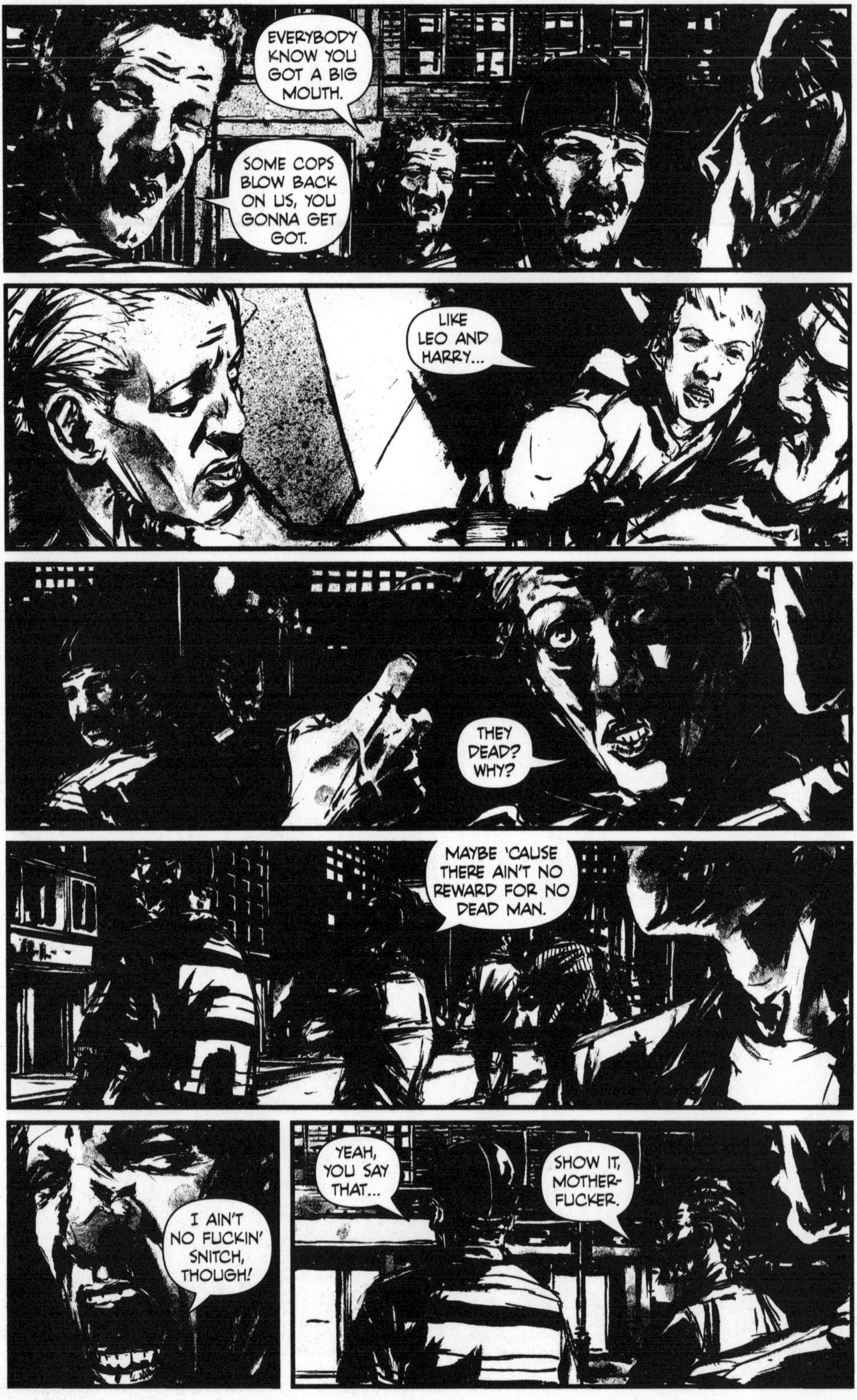
EVERYBODY KNOW YOU GOT A BIG MOUTH.
SOME COPS BLOW BACK ON US, YOU GONNA GET GOT.
LIKE LEO AND HARRY...
THEY DEAD? WHY?
MAYBE 'CAUSE THERE AIN'T NO REWARD FOR NO DEAD MAN.
I AIN'T NO FUCKIN' SNITCH, THOUGH!
YEAH, YOU SAY THAT...
SHOW IT, MOTHER-FUCKER.

CHAPTER FIVE

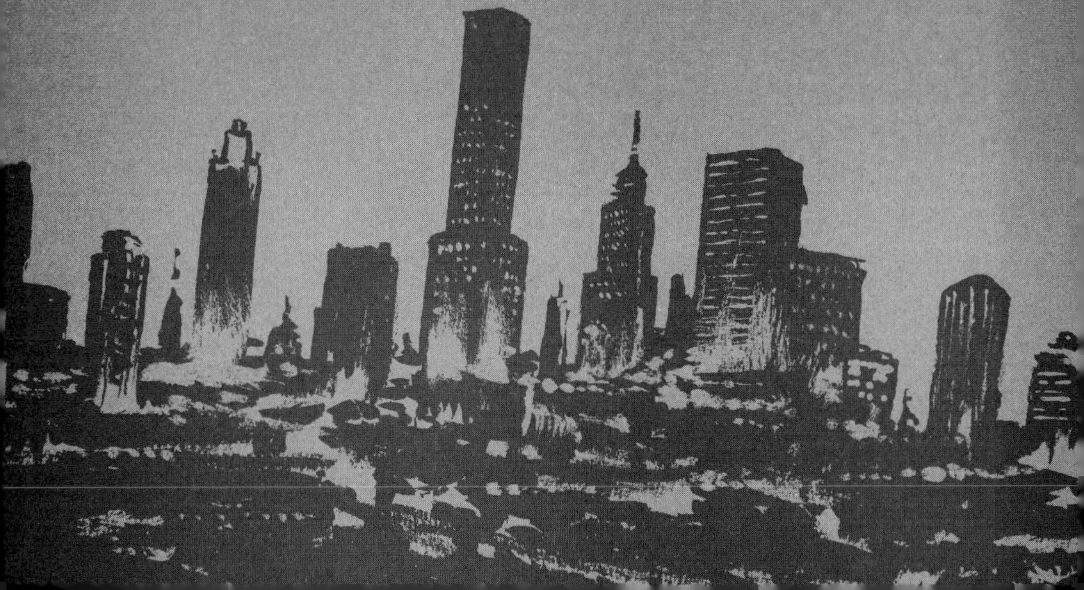

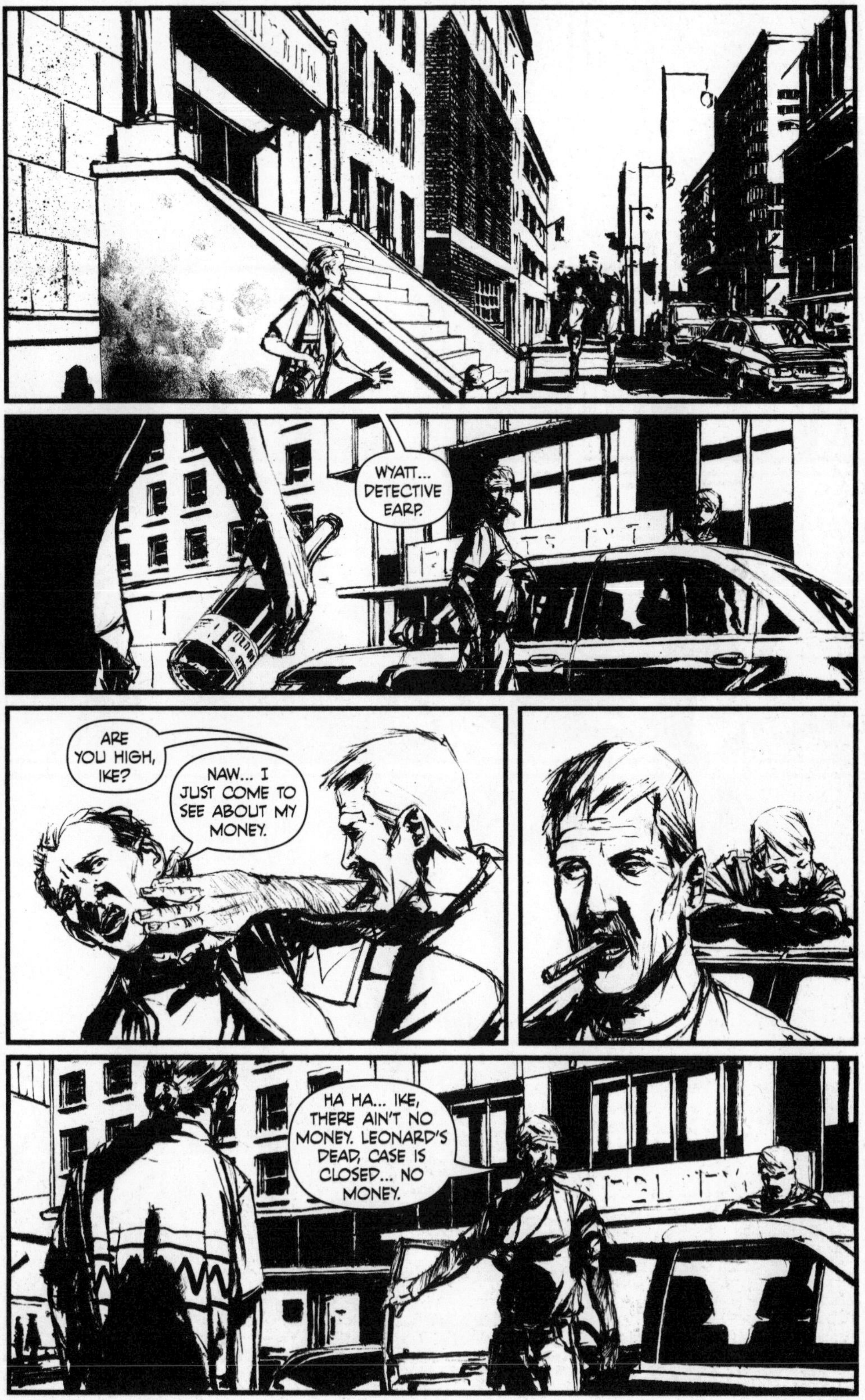
WYATT... DETECTIVE EARP.
ARE YOU HIGH, IKE?
NAW... I JUST COME TO SEE ABOUT MY MONEY.
HA HA... IKE, THERE AIN'T NO MONEY. LEONARD'S DEAD, CASE IS CLOSED... NO MONEY.

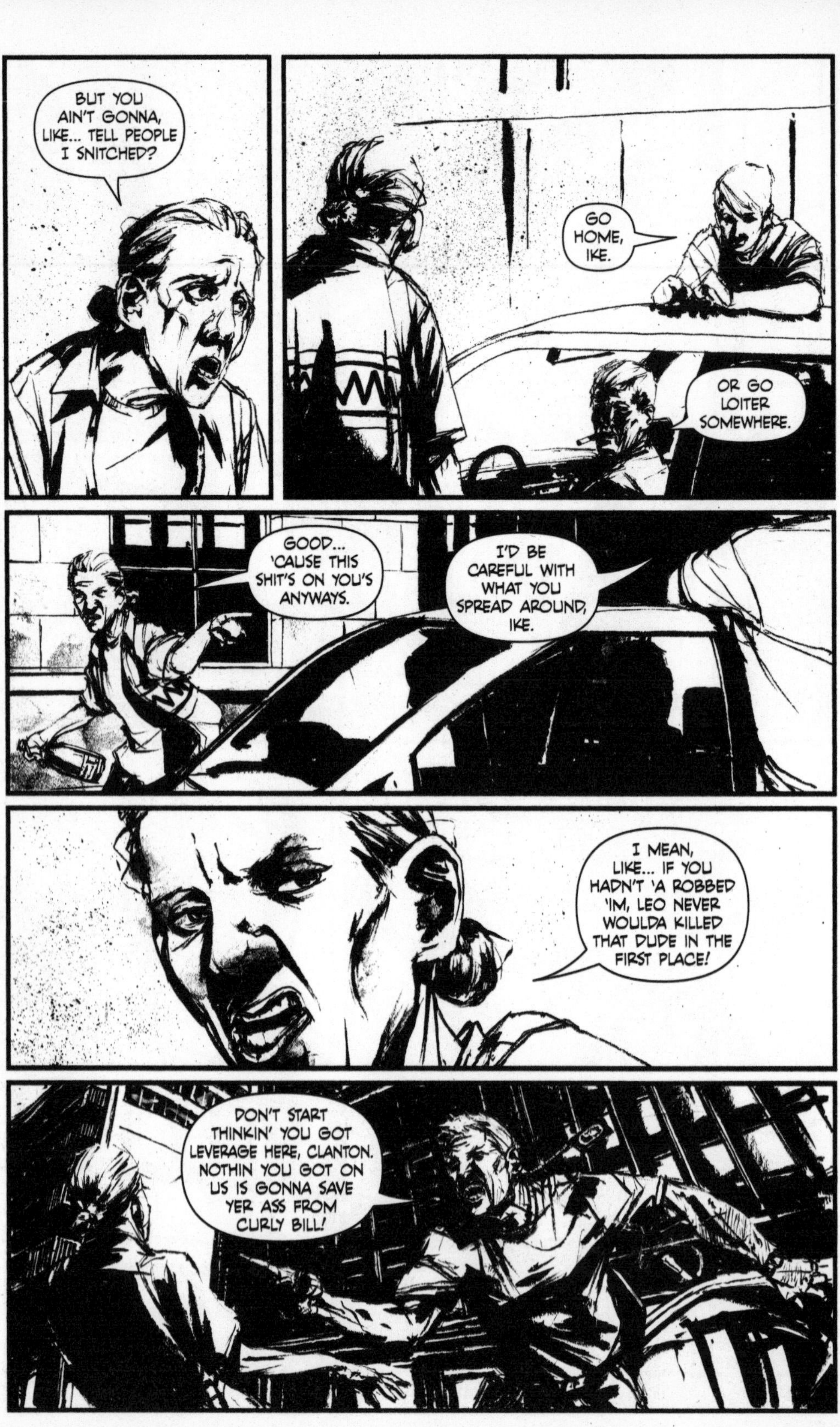
BUT YOU AIN'T GONNA, LIKE... TELL PEOPLE I SNITCHED?
GO HOME, IKE.
OR GO LOITER SOMEWHERE.
GOOD... 'CAUSE THIS SHIT'S ON YOU'S ANYWAYS.
I'D BE CAREFUL WITH WHAT YOU SPREAD AROUND, IKE.
I MEAN, LIKE... IF YOU HADN'T 'A ROBBED 'IM, LEO NEVER WOULDA KILLED THAT DUDE IN THE FIRST PLACE!
DON'T START THINKIN' YOU GOT LEVERAGE HERE, CLANTON. NOTHIN YOU GOT ON US IS GONNA SAVE YER ASS FROM CURLY BILL!

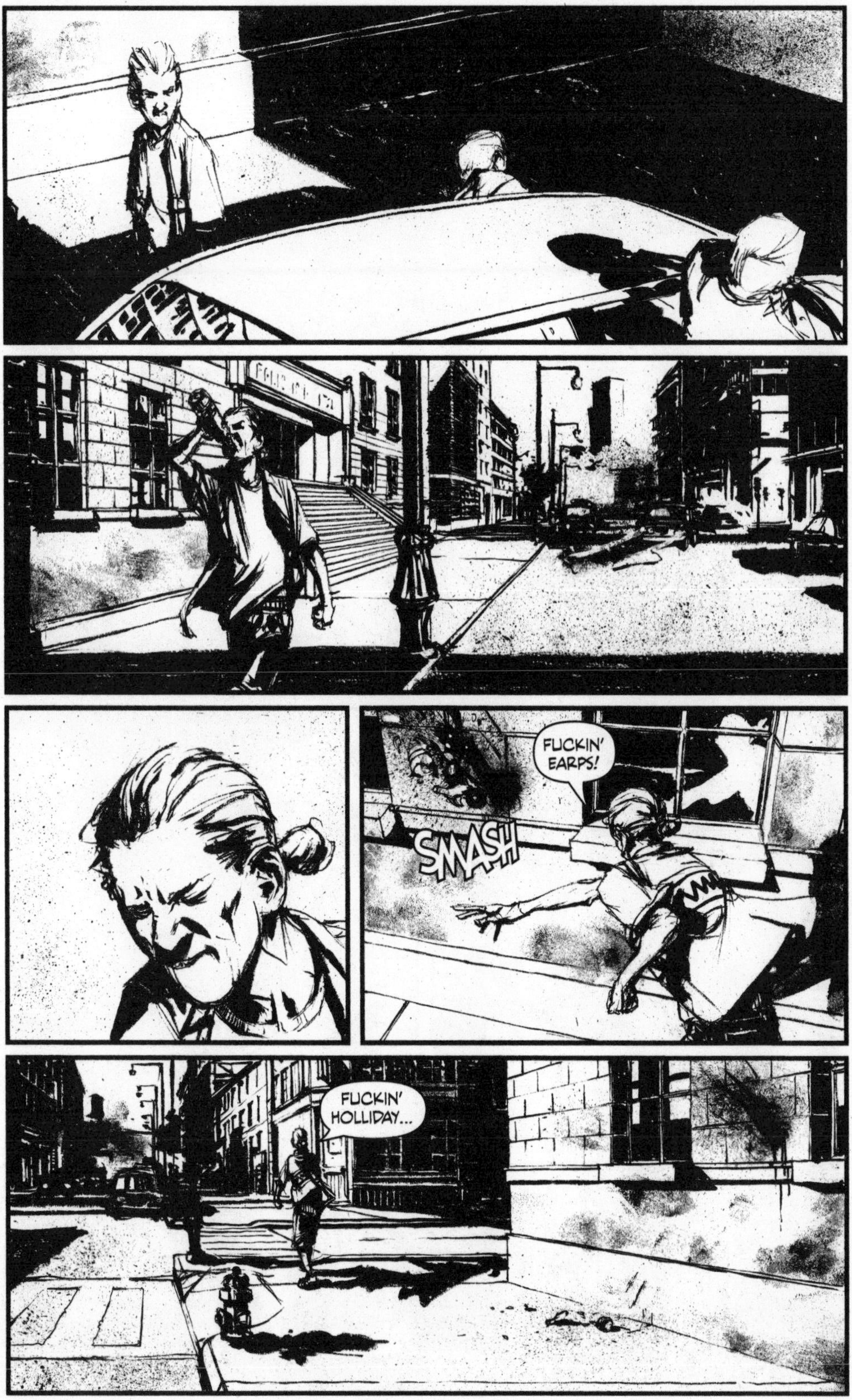
FUCKIN' EARPS!
SMASH
FUCKIN' HOLLIDAY...

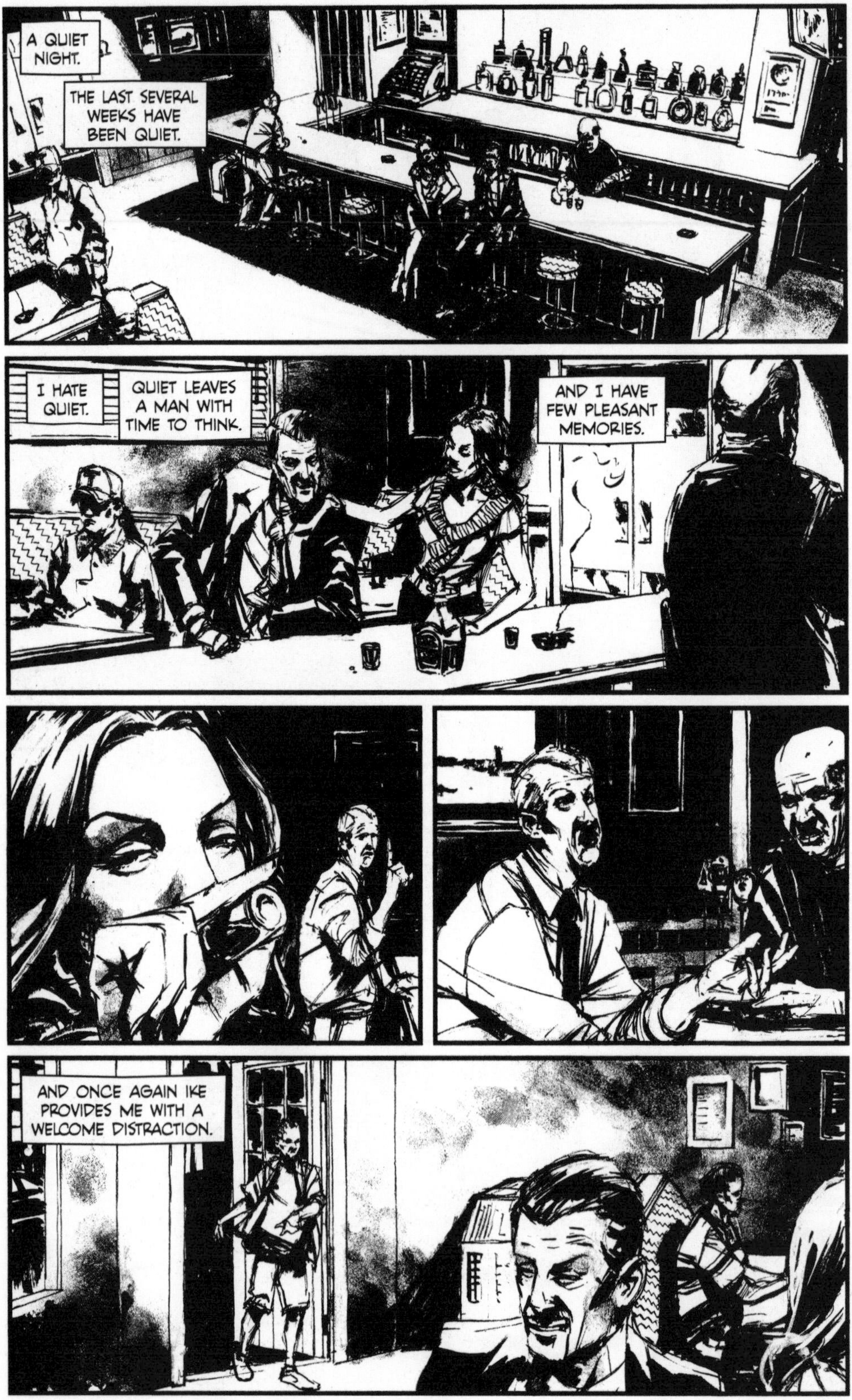
A QUIET NIGHT.
THE LAST SEVERAL WEEKS HAVE BEEN QUIET.
I HATE QUIET.
QUIET LEAVES A MAN WITH TIME TO THINK.
AND I HAVE FEW PLEASANT MEMORIES.
AND ONCE AGAIN IKE PROVIDES ME WITH A WELCOME DISTRACTION.

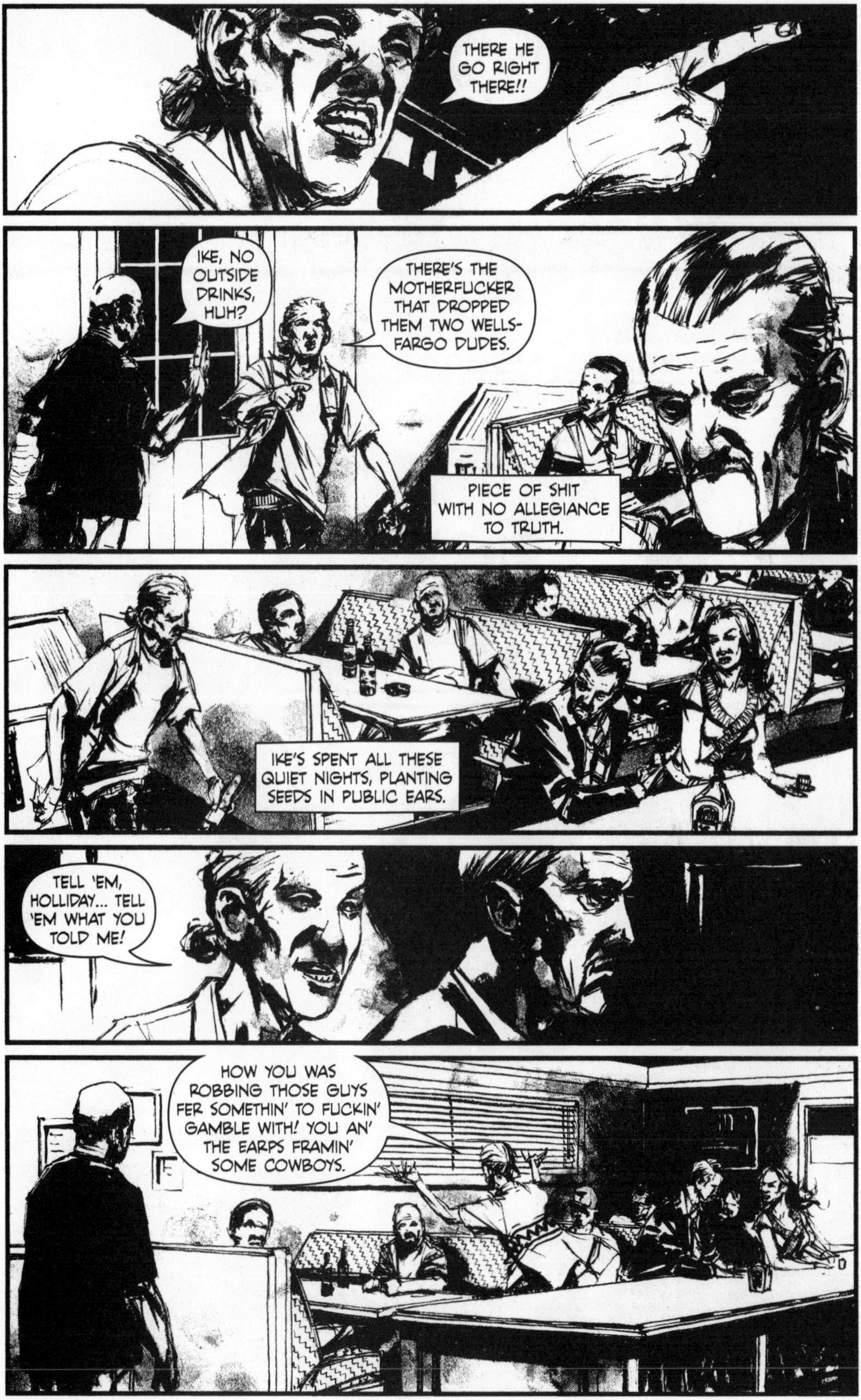
THERE HE GO RIGHT THERE!!
IKE, NO OUTSIDE DRINKS, HUH?
THERE'S THE MOTHERFUCKER THAT DROPPED THEM TWO WELLS-FARGO DUDES.
PIECE OF SHIT WITH NO ALLEGIANCE TO TRUTH.
IKE'S SPENT ALL THESE QUIET NIGHTS, PLANTING SEEDS IN PUBLIC EARS.
TELL 'EM, HOLLIDAY... TELL 'EM WHAT YOU TOLD ME!
HOW YOU WAS ROBBING THOSE GUYS FER SOMETHIN' TO FUCKIN' GAMBLE WITH! YOU AN' THE EARPS FRAMIN' SOME COWBOYS.

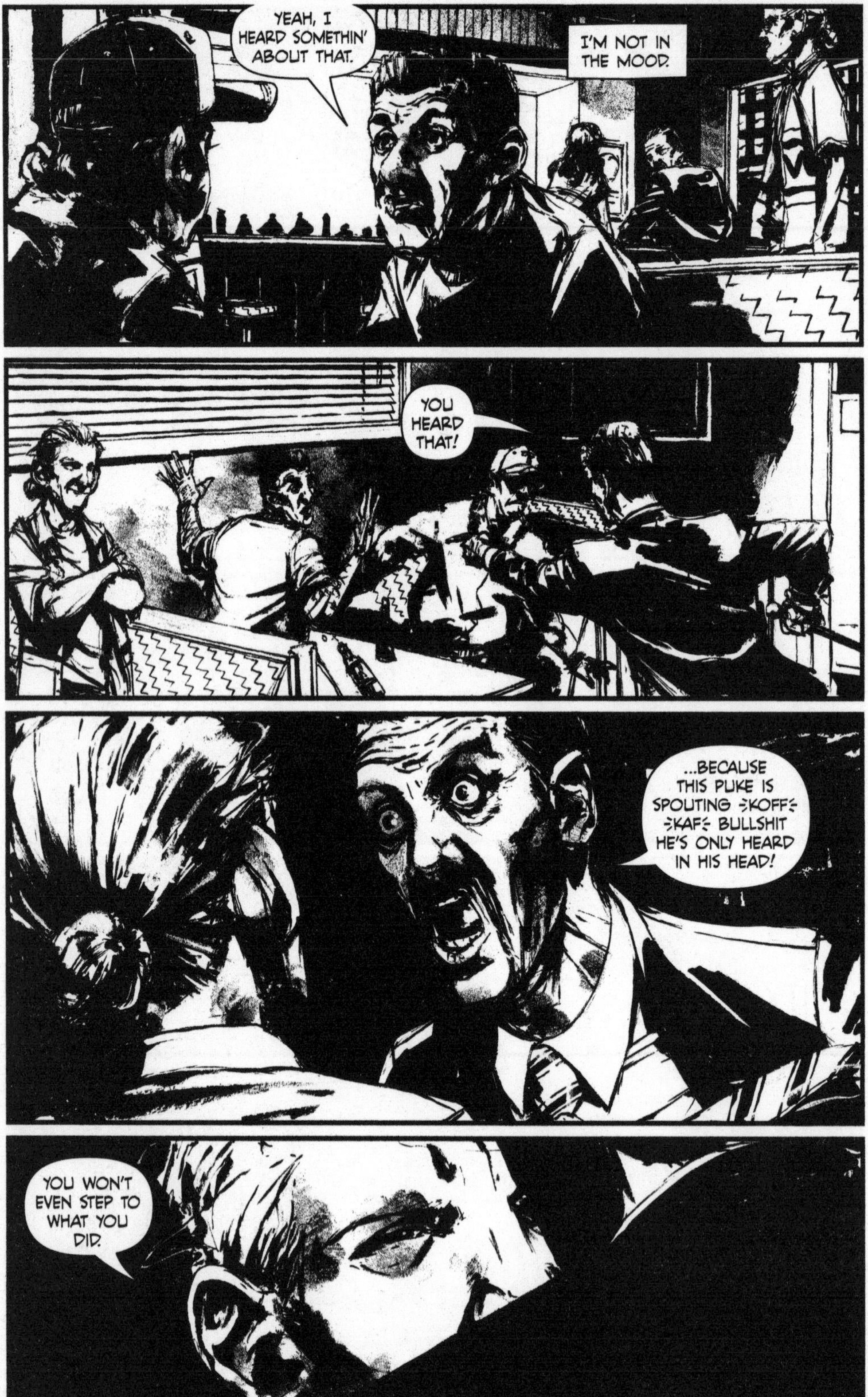
YEAH, I HEARD SOMETHIN' ABOUT THAT.
I'M NOT IN THE MOOD.
YOU HEARD THAT!
...BECAUSE THIS PUKE IS SPOUTING -KOFF- -KAF- BULLSHIT HE'S ONLY HEARD IN HIS HEAD!
YOU WON'T EVEN STEP TO WHAT YOU DID.

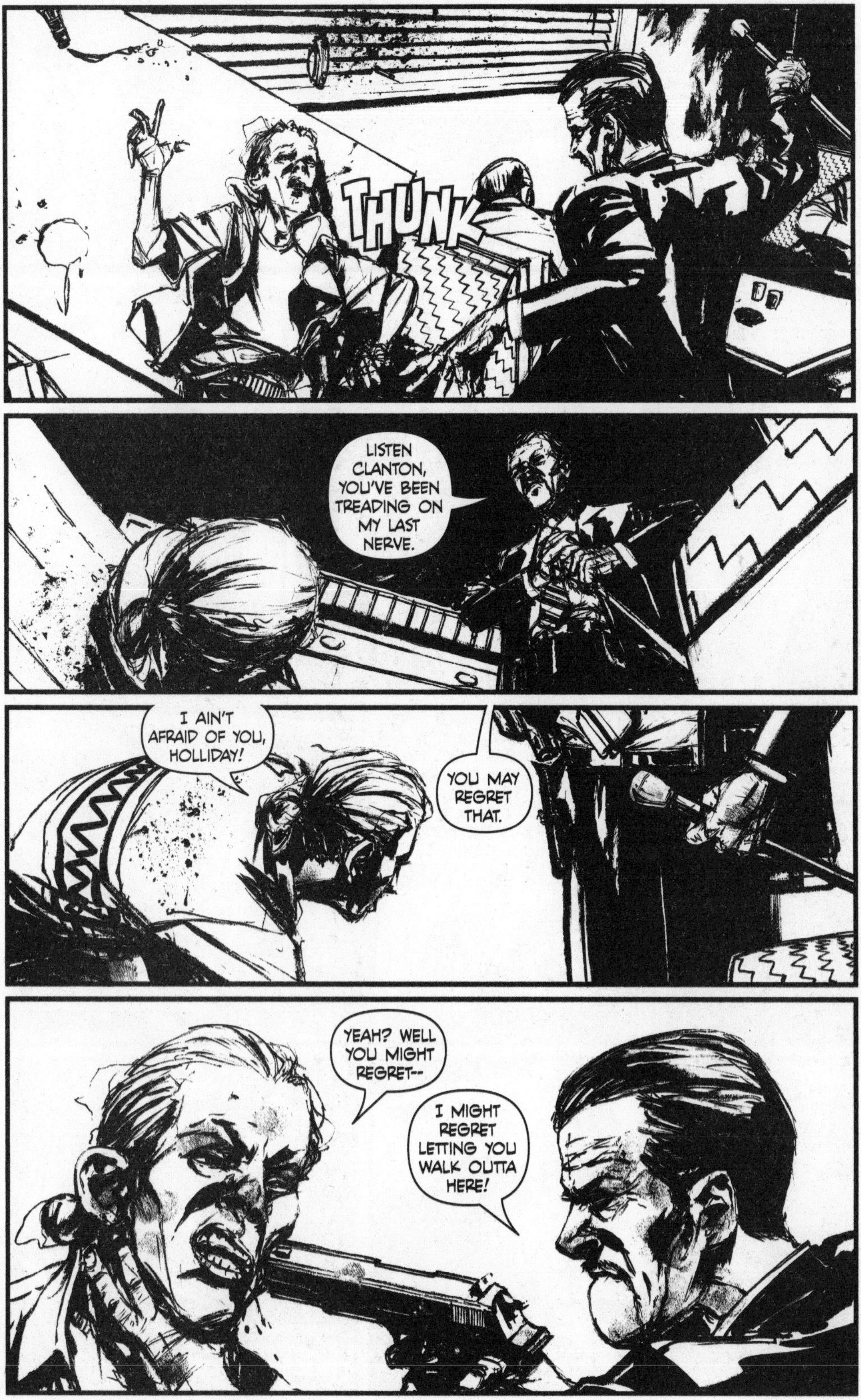
THUNK
LISTEN CLANTON, YOU'VE BEEN TREADING ON MY LAST NERVE.
I AIN'T AFRAID OF YOU, HOLLIDAY!
YOU MAY REGRET THAT.
YEAH? WELL YOU MIGHT REGRET--
I MIGHT REGRET LETTING YOU WALK OUTTA HERE!

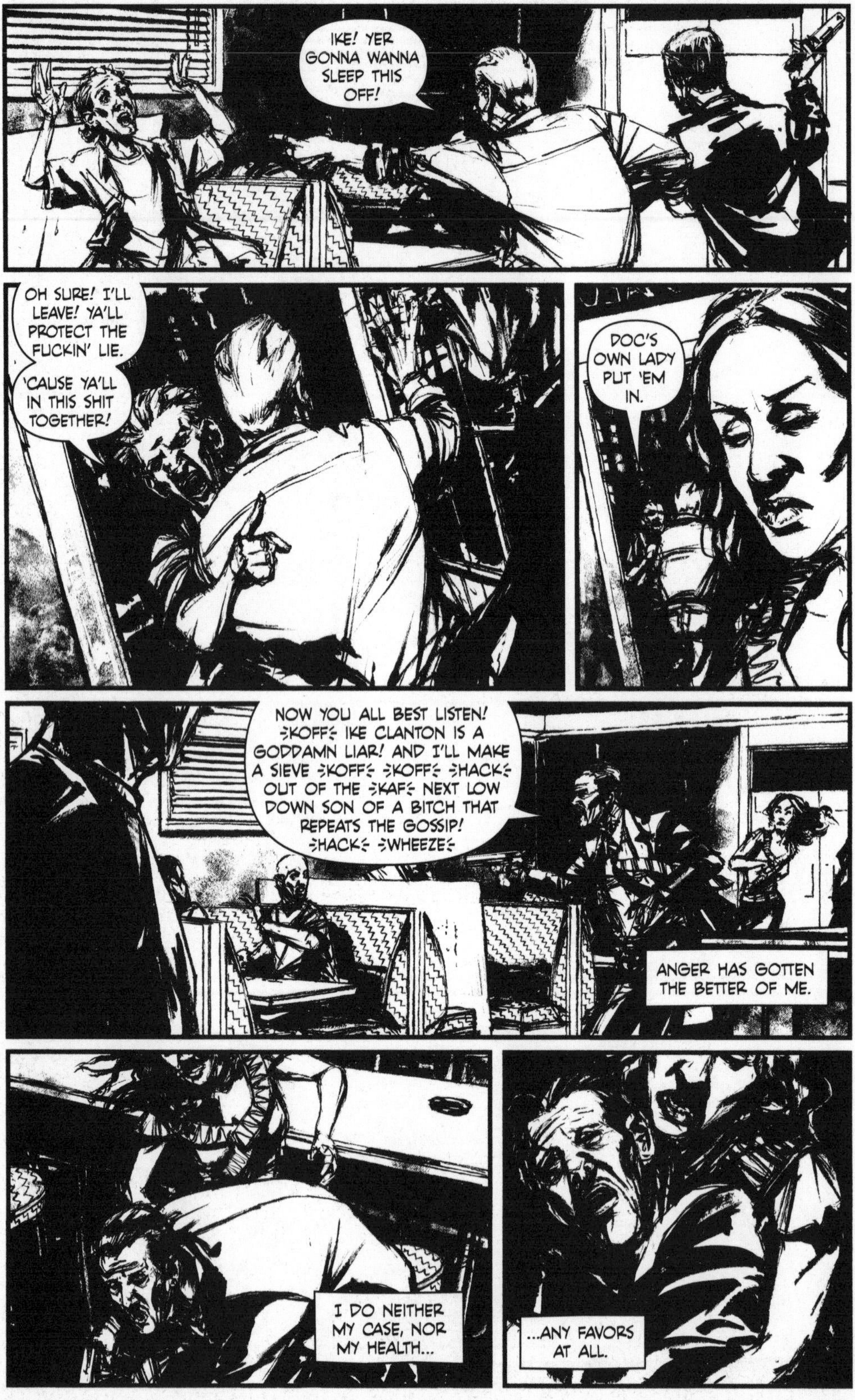
IKE! YER GONNA WANNA SLEEP THIS OFF!
OH SURE! I'LL LEAVE! YA'LL PROTECT THE FUCKIN' LIE.
'CAUSE YA'LL IN THIS SHIT TOGETHER!
DOC'S OWN LADY PUT 'EM IN.
NOW YOU ALL BEST LISTEN! -KOFF- IKE CLANTON IS A GODDAMN LIAR! AND I'LL MAKE A SIEVE -KOFF- -KOFF- -HACK- OUT OF THE -KAF- NEXT LOW DOWN SON OF A BITCH THAT REPEATS THE GOSSIP! -HACK- -WHEEZE-
ANGER HAS GOTTEN THE BETTER OF ME.
I DO NEITHER MY CASE, NOR MY HEALTH...
...ANY FAVORS AT ALL.

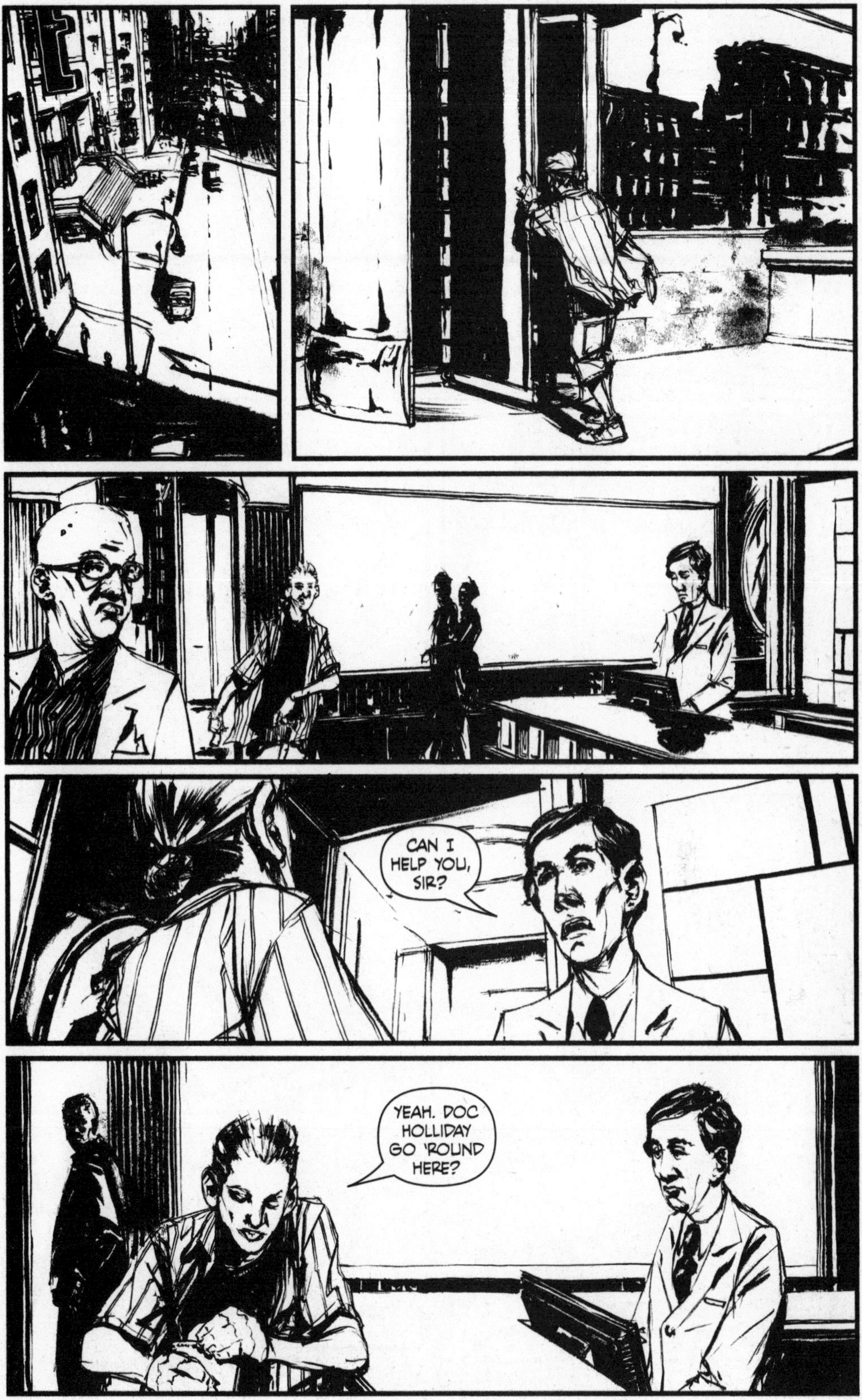
CAN I HELP YOU, SIR?
YEAH. DOC HOLLIDAY GO 'ROUND HERE?

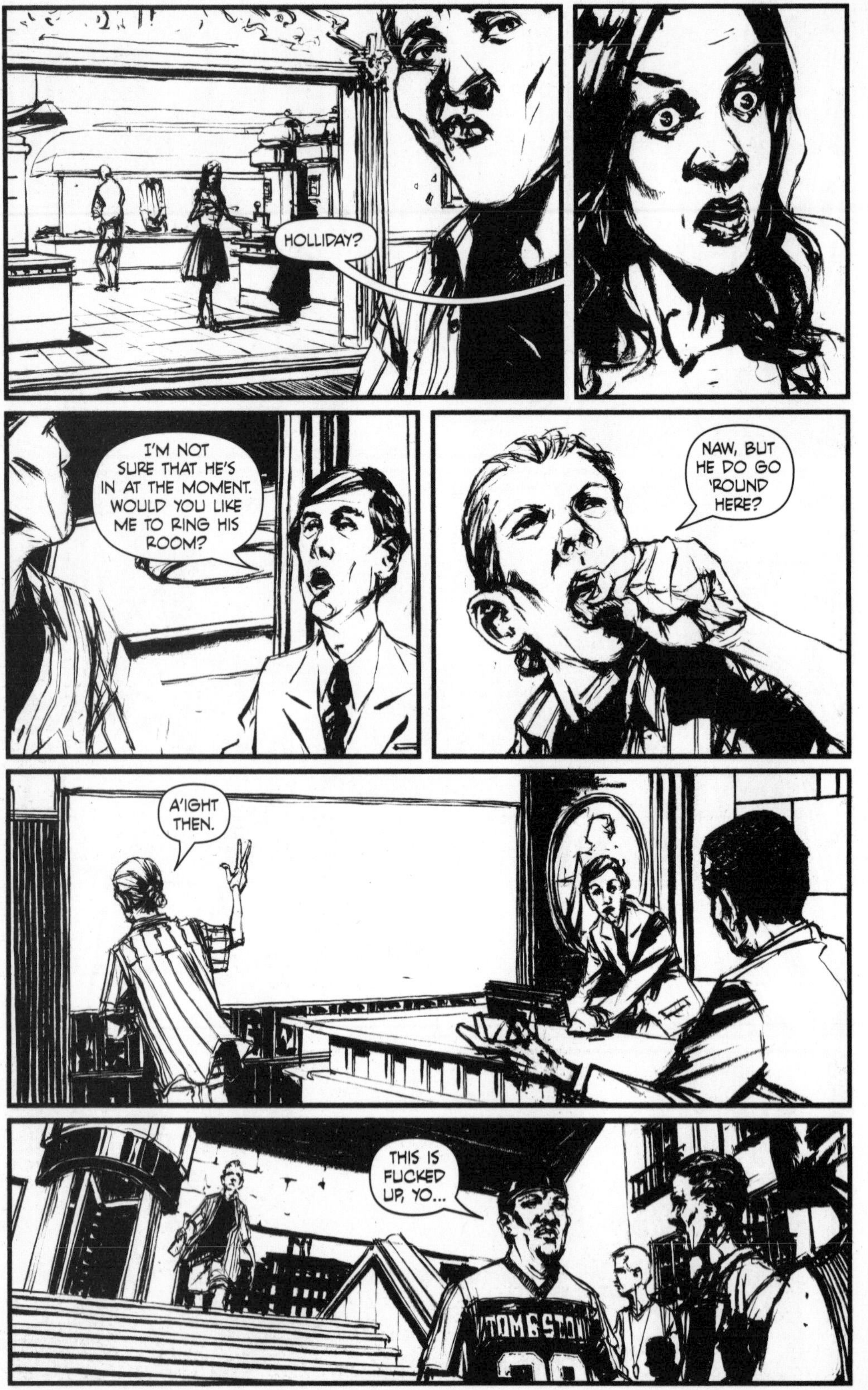
HOLLIDAY?
I'M NOT SURE THAT HE'S IN AT THE MOMENT. WOULD YOU LIKE ME TO RING HIS ROOM?
NAW, BUT HE DO GO 'ROUND HERE?
A'IGHT THEN.
THIS IS FUCKED UP, YO...
TOMBSTO

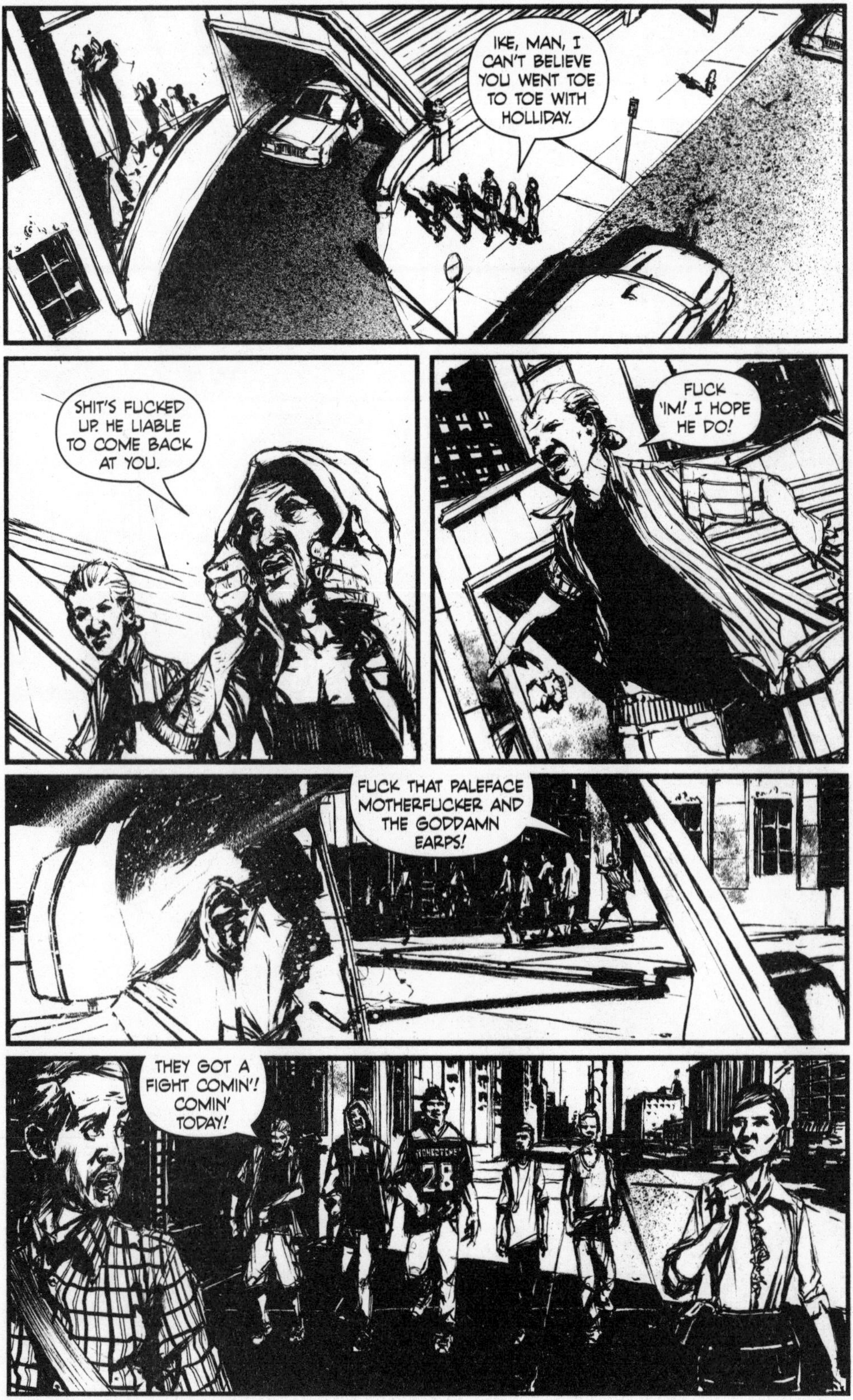
IKE, MAN, I CAN'T BELIEVE YOU WENT TOE TO TOE WITH HOLLIDAY.
SHIT'S FUCKED UP. HE LIABLE TO COME BACK AT YOU.
FUCK 'IM! I HOPE HE DO!
FUCK THAT PALEFACE MOTHERFUCKER AND THE GODDAMN EARPS!
THEY GOT A FIGHT COMIN'! COMIN' TODAY!

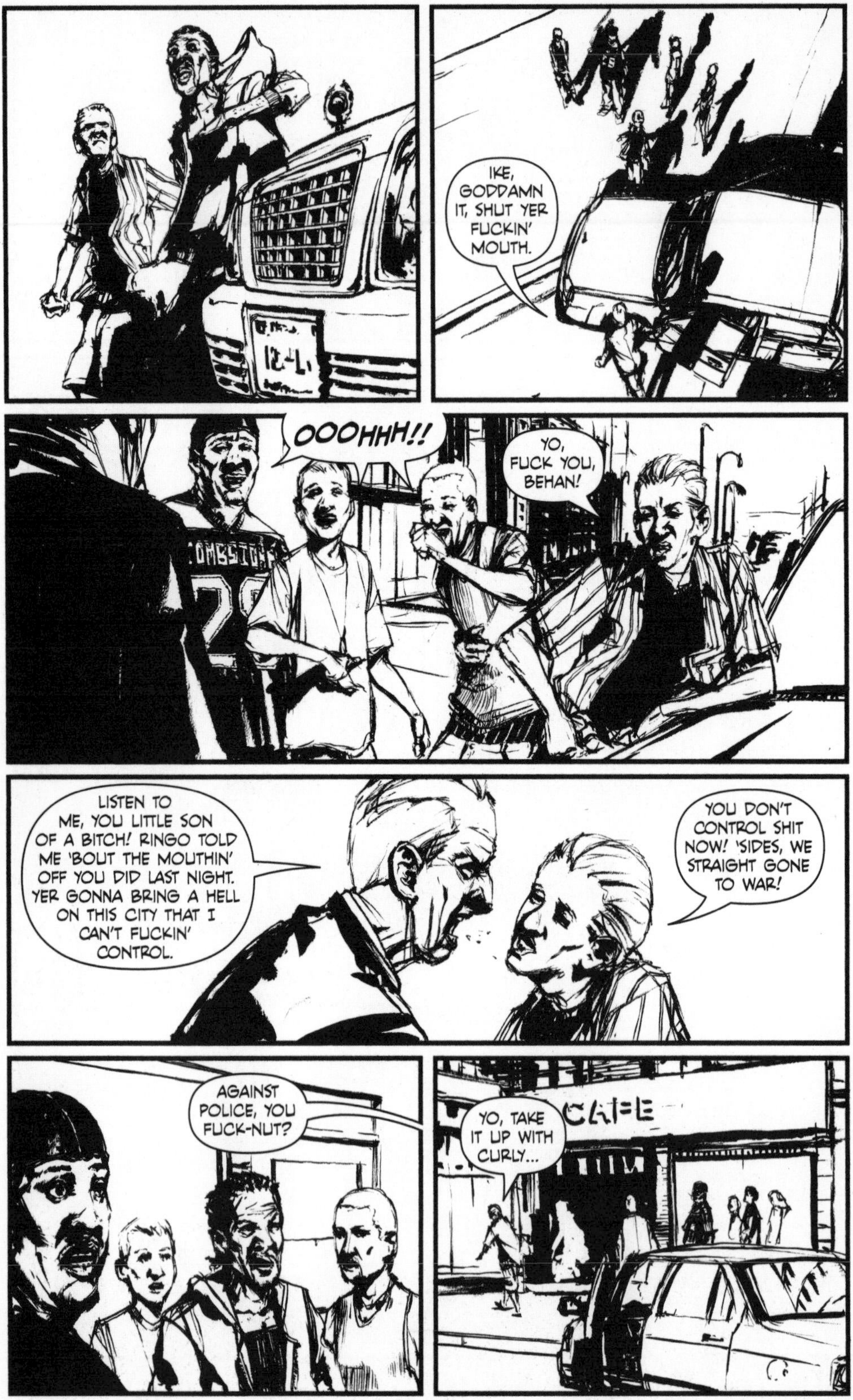
IKE, GODDAMN IT, SHUT YER FUCKIN' MOUTH.
OOOHHH!!
YO, FUCK YOU, BEHAN!
LISTEN TO ME, YOU LITTLE SON OF A BITCH! RINGO TOLD ME 'BOUT THE MOUTHIN' OFF YOU DID LAST NIGHT. YER GONNA BRING A HELL ON THIS CITY THAT I CAN'T FUCKIN' CONTROL.
YOU DON'T CONTROL SHIT NOW! 'SIDES, WE STRAIGHT GONE TO WAR!
AGAINST POLICE, YOU FUCK-NUT?
CAFE
YO, TAKE IT UP WITH CURLY...

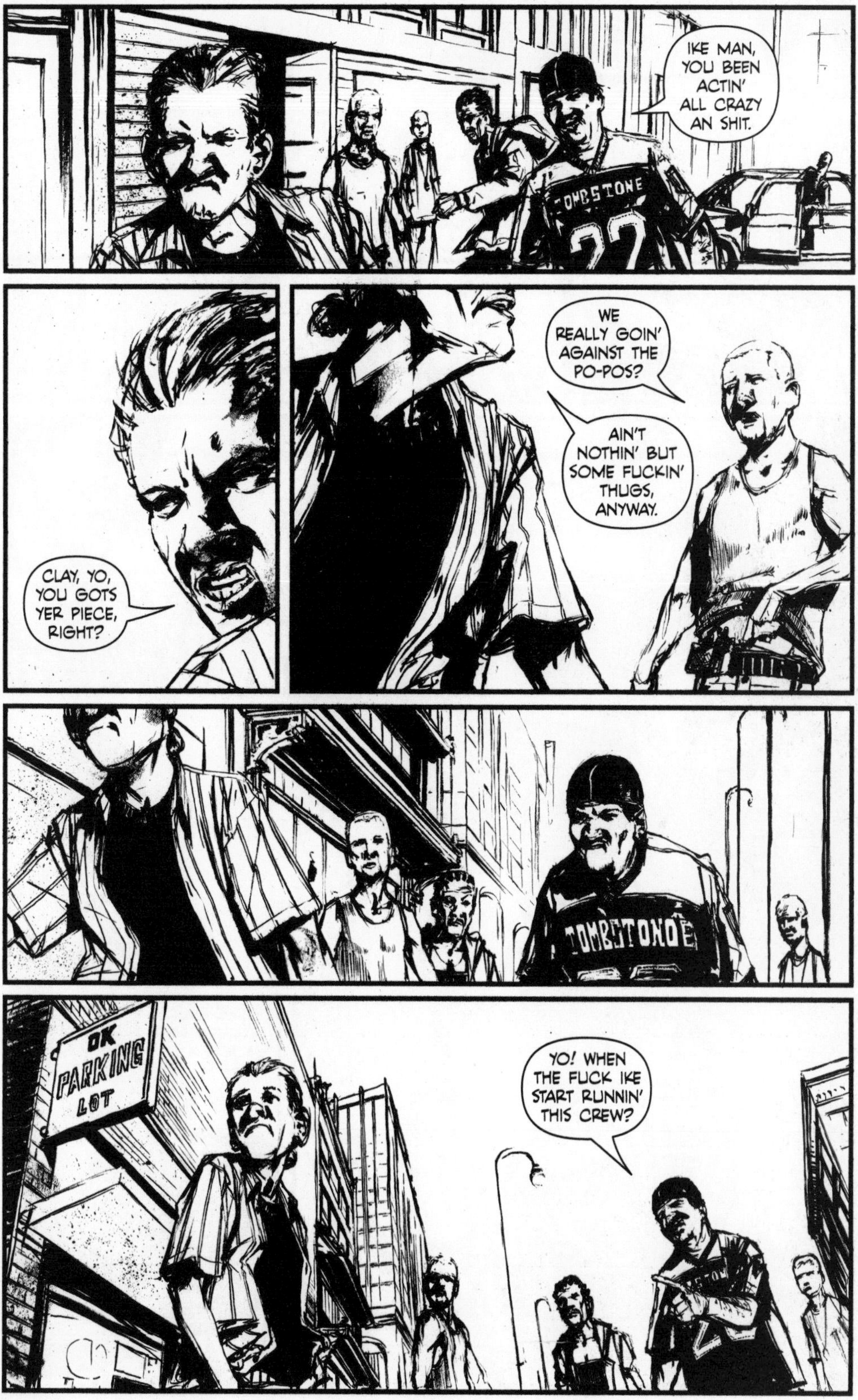
IKE MAN, YOU BEEN ACTIN' ALL CRAZY AN SHIT.
TOMBSTONE
CLAY, YO, YOU GOTS YER PIECE, RIGHT?
WE REALLY GOIN' AGAINST THE PO-POS?
AIN'T NOTHIN' BUT SOME FUCKIN' THUGS, ANYWAY.
OK PARKING LOT
YO! WHEN THE FUCK IKE START RUNNIN' THIS CREW?

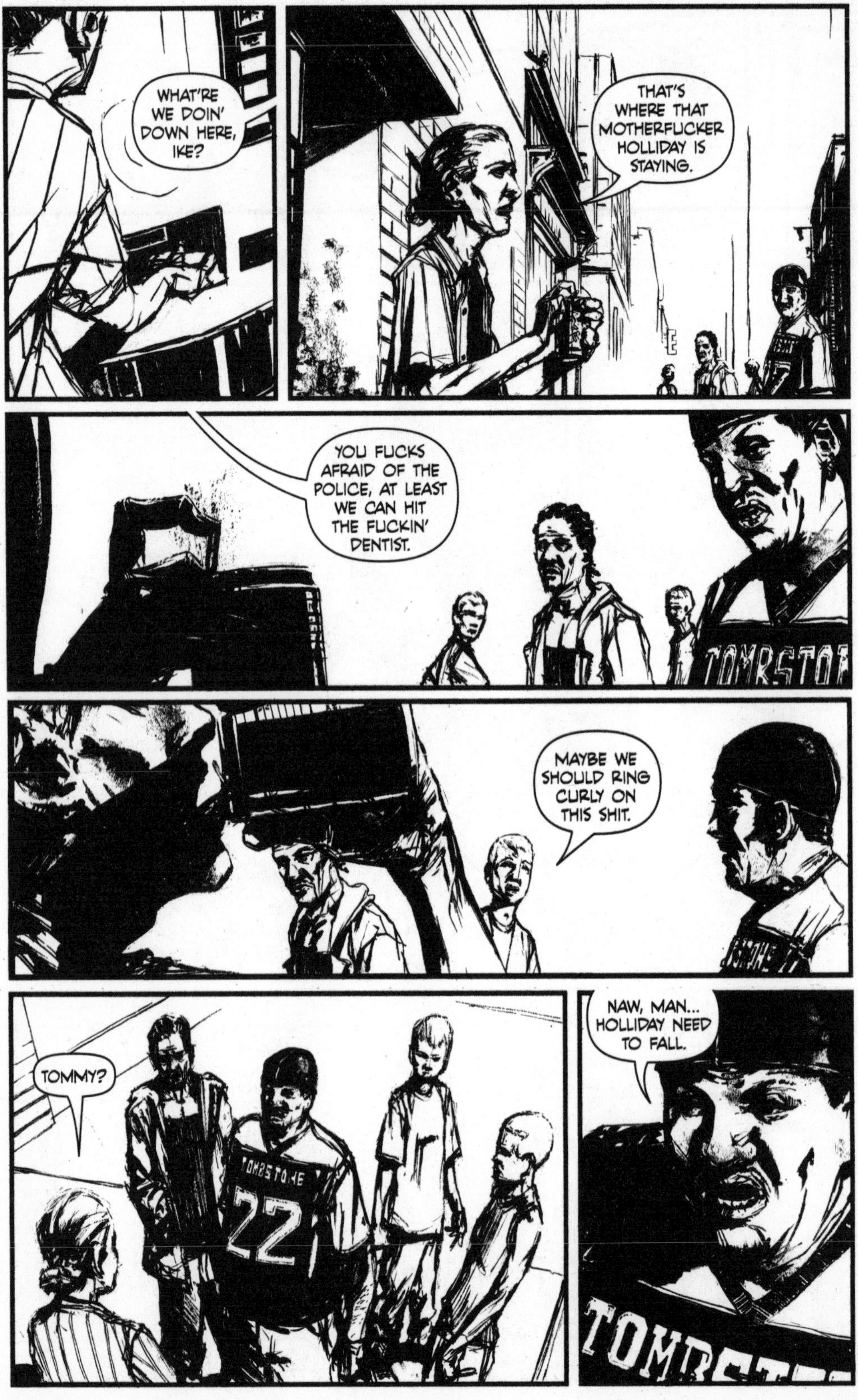
WHAT'RE WE DOIN' DOWN HERE, IKE?
THAT'S WHERE THAT MOTHERFUCKER HOLLIDAY IS STAYING.
YOU FUCKS AFRAID OF THE POLICE, AT LEAST WE CAN HIT THE FUCKIN' DENTIST.
TOMBSTO
MAYBE WE SHOULD RING CURLY ON THIS SHIT.
TOMMY?
TOMBSTONE
22
NAW, MAN... HOLLIDAY NEED TO FALL.
TOMBST

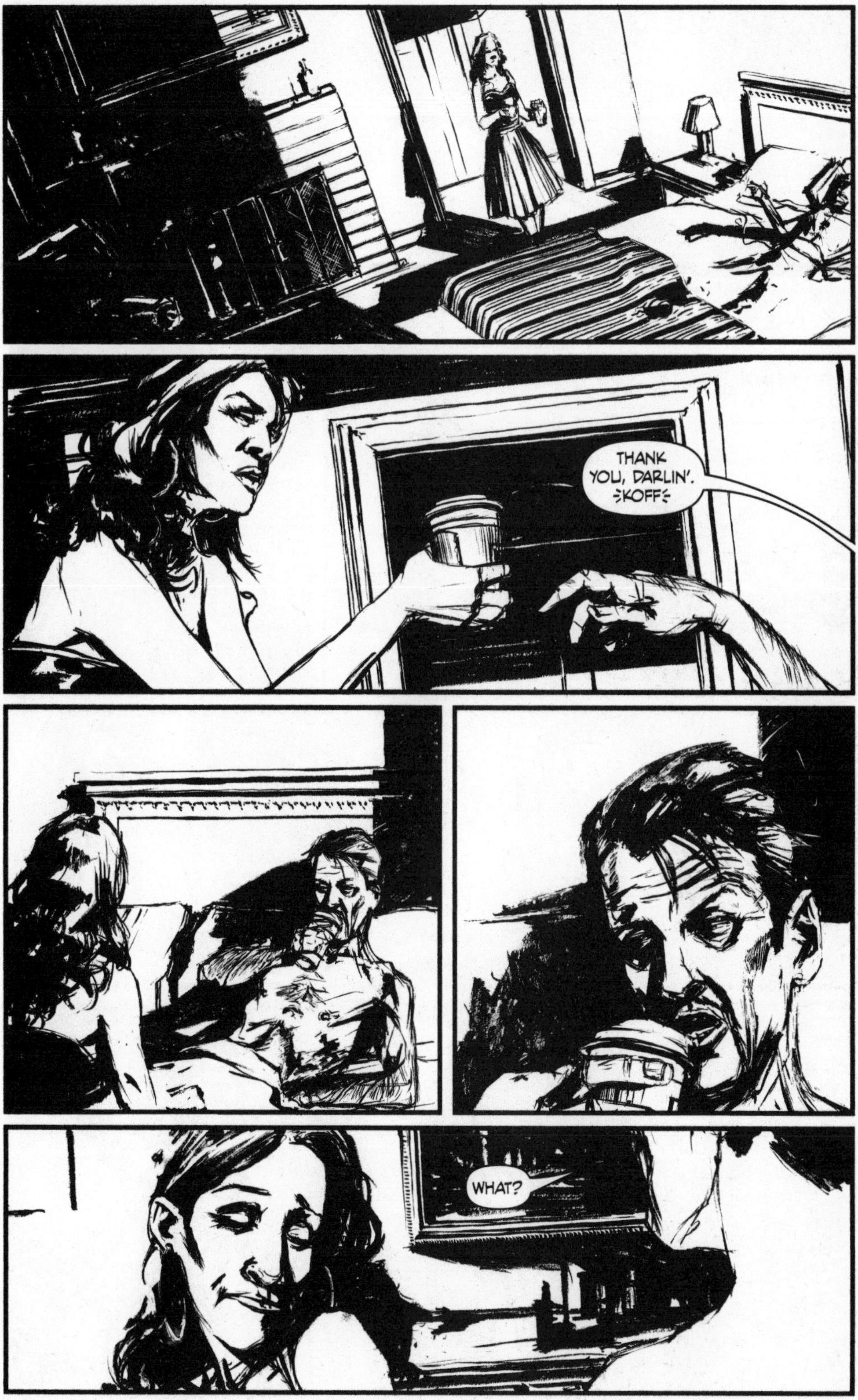
THANK YOU, DARLIN'. ✳KOFF✳
WHAT?

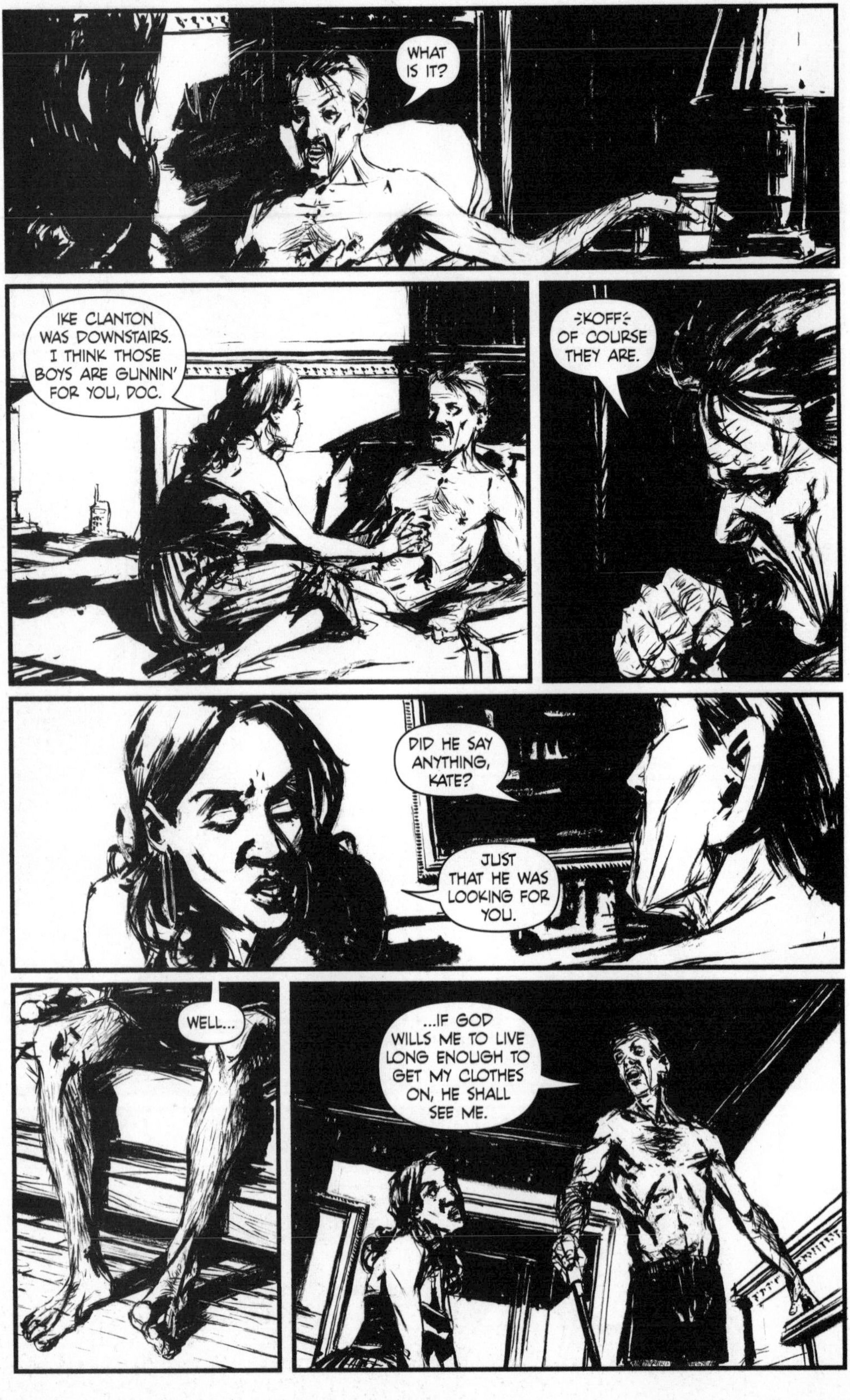
WHAT IS IT?
IKE CLANTON WAS DOWNSTAIRS. I THINK THOSE BOYS ARE GUNNIN' FOR YOU, DOC.
≈KOFF≈ OF COURSE THEY ARE.
DID HE SAY ANYTHING, KATE?
JUST THAT HE WAS LOOKING FOR YOU.
WELL...
...IF GOD WILLS ME TO LIVE LONG ENOUGH TO GET MY CLOTHES ON, HE SHALL SEE ME.

CHAPTER SIX

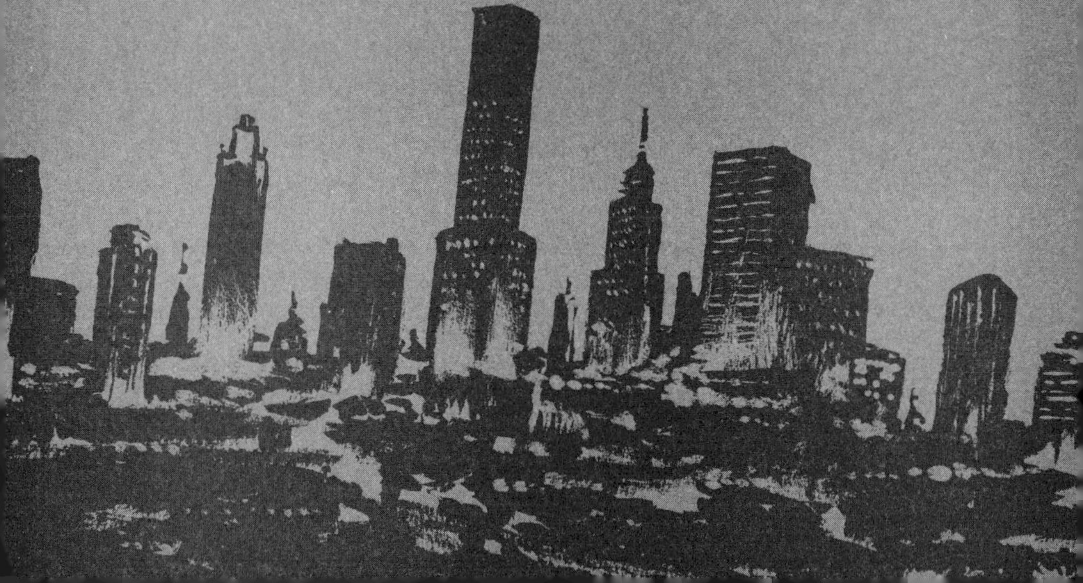

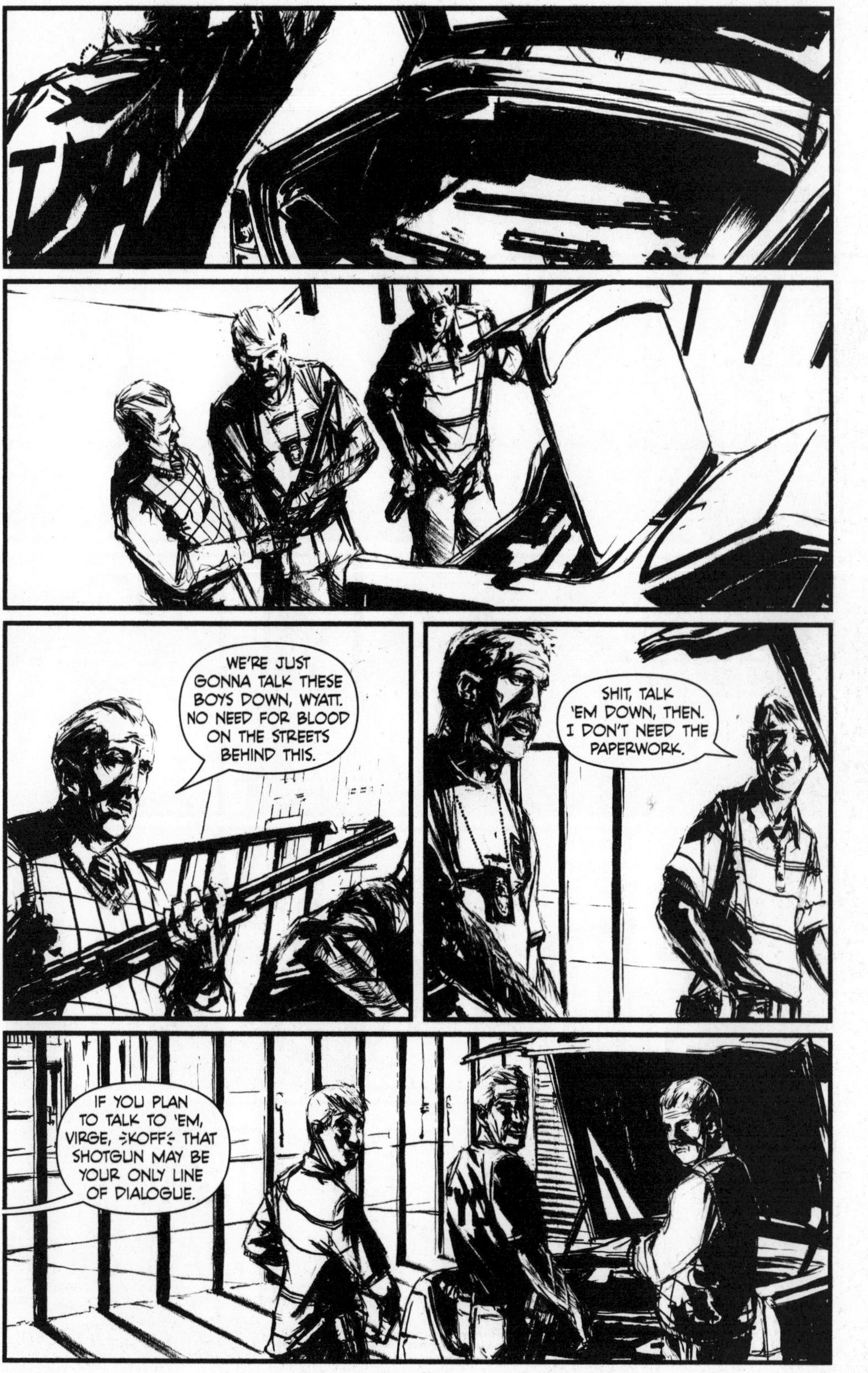
WE'RE JUST GONNA TALK THESE BOYS DOWN, WYATT. NO NEED FOR BLOOD ON THE STREETS BEHIND THIS.
SHIT, TALK 'EM DOWN, THEN. I DON'T NEED THE PAPERWORK.
IF YOU PLAN TO TALK TO 'EM, VIRGE, ≈KOFF≈ THAT SHOTGUN MAY BE YOUR ONLY LINE OF DIALOGUE.

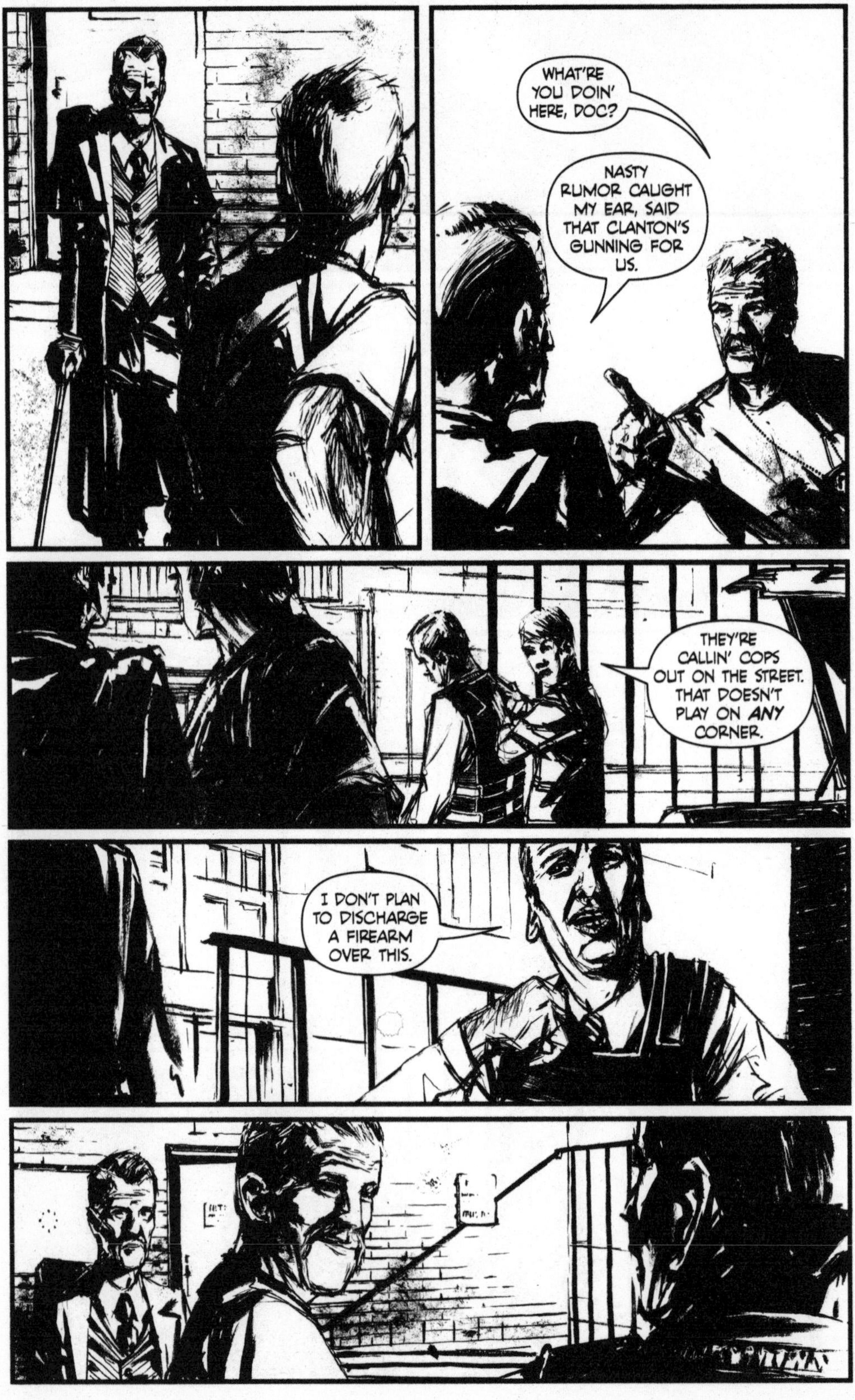
WHAT'RE YOU DOIN' HERE, DOC?
NASTY RUMOR CAUGHT MY EAR, SAID THAT CLANTON'S GUNNING FOR US.
THEY'RE CALLIN' COPS OUT ON THE STREET. THAT DOESN'T PLAY ON *ANY* CORNER.
I DON'T PLAN TO DISCHARGE A FIREARM OVER THIS.

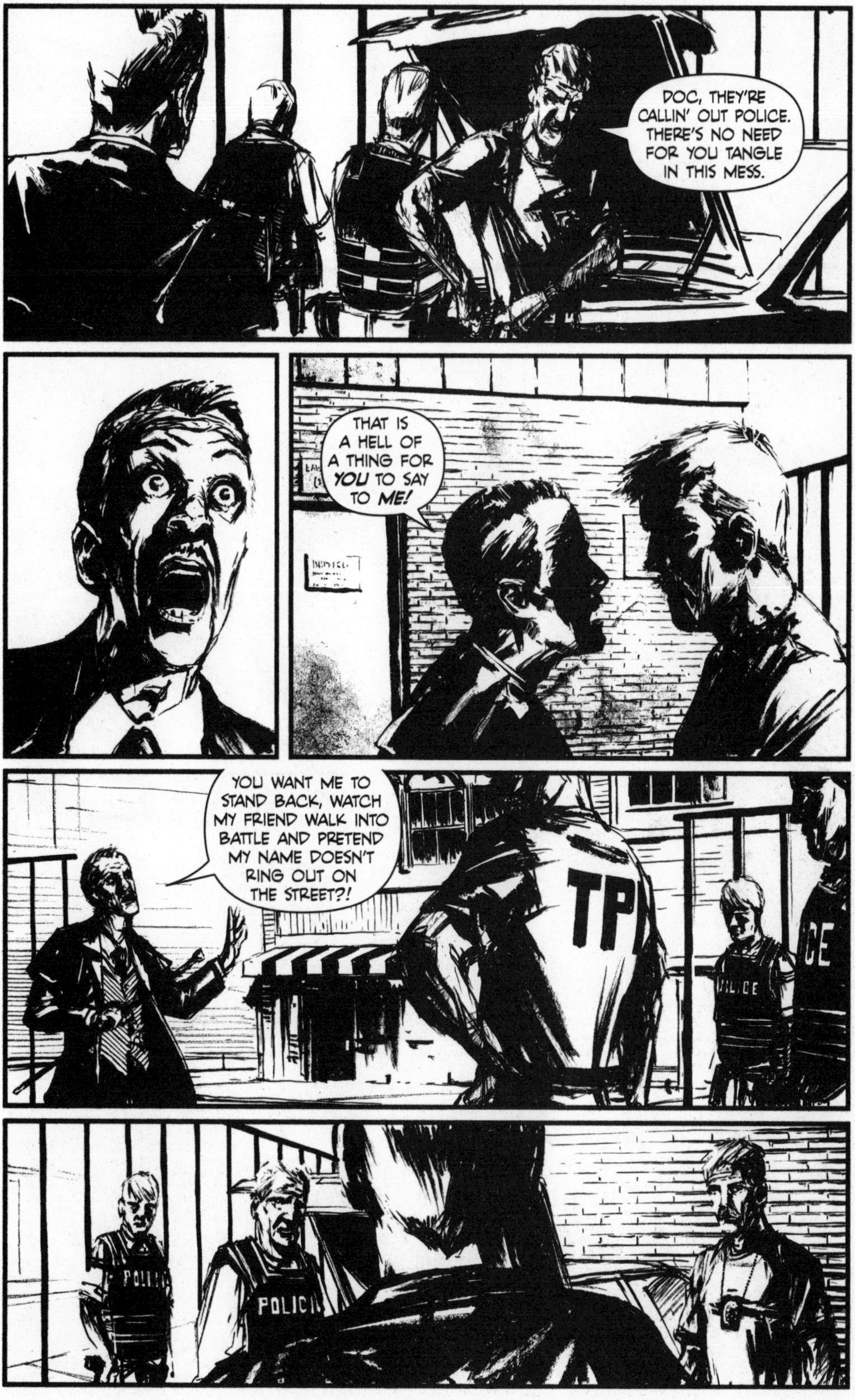
DOC, THEY'RE CALLIN' OUT POLICE. THERE'S NO NEED FOR YOU TANGLE IN THIS MESS.
THAT IS A HELL OF A THING FOR *YOU* TO SAY TO *ME!*
YOU WANT ME TO STAND BACK, WATCH MY FRIEND WALK INTO BATTLE AND PRETEND MY NAME DOESN'T RING OUT ON THE STREET?!

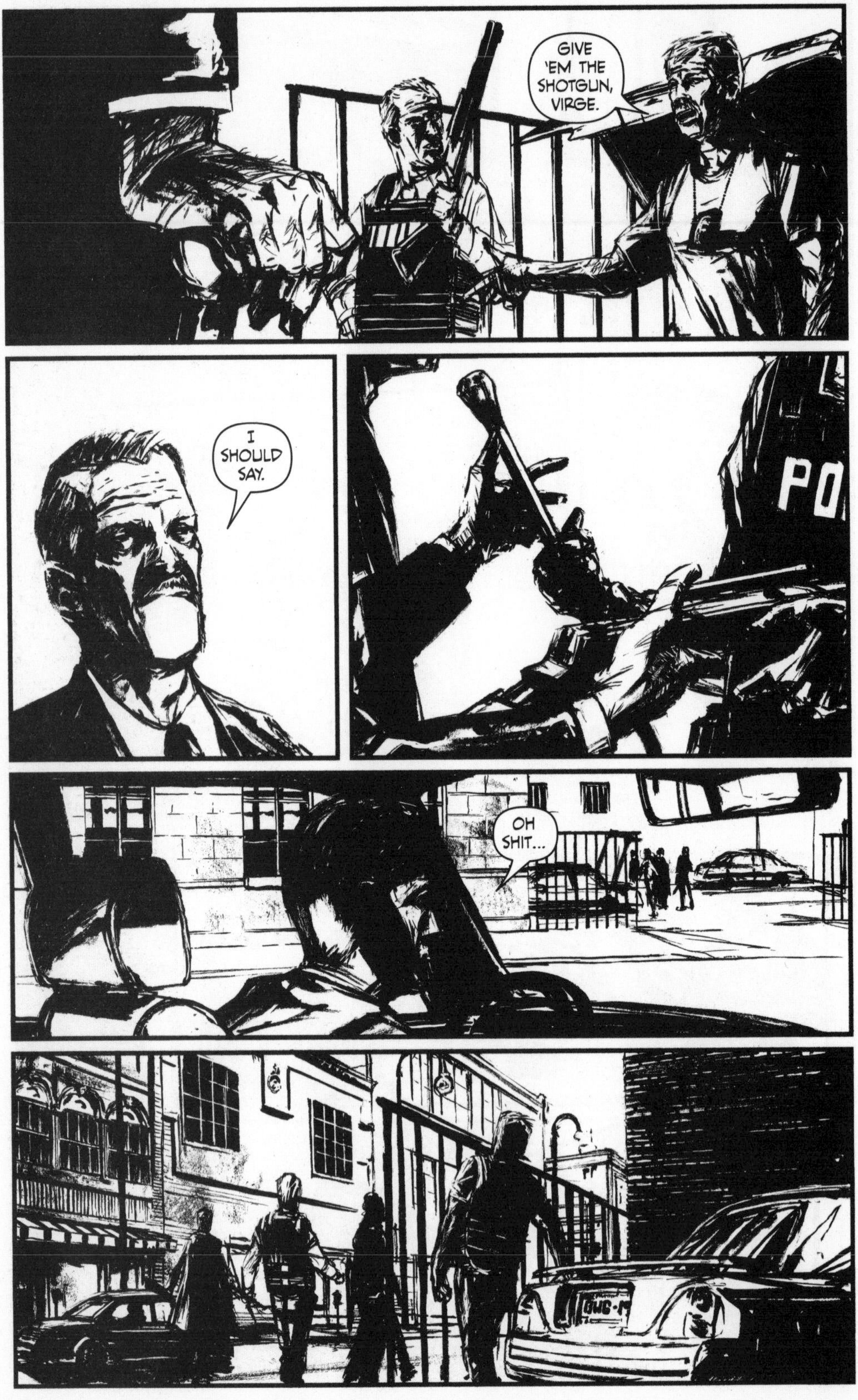
GIVE 'EM THE SHOTGUN, VIRGE.
I SHOULD SAY.
PO
OH SHIT...

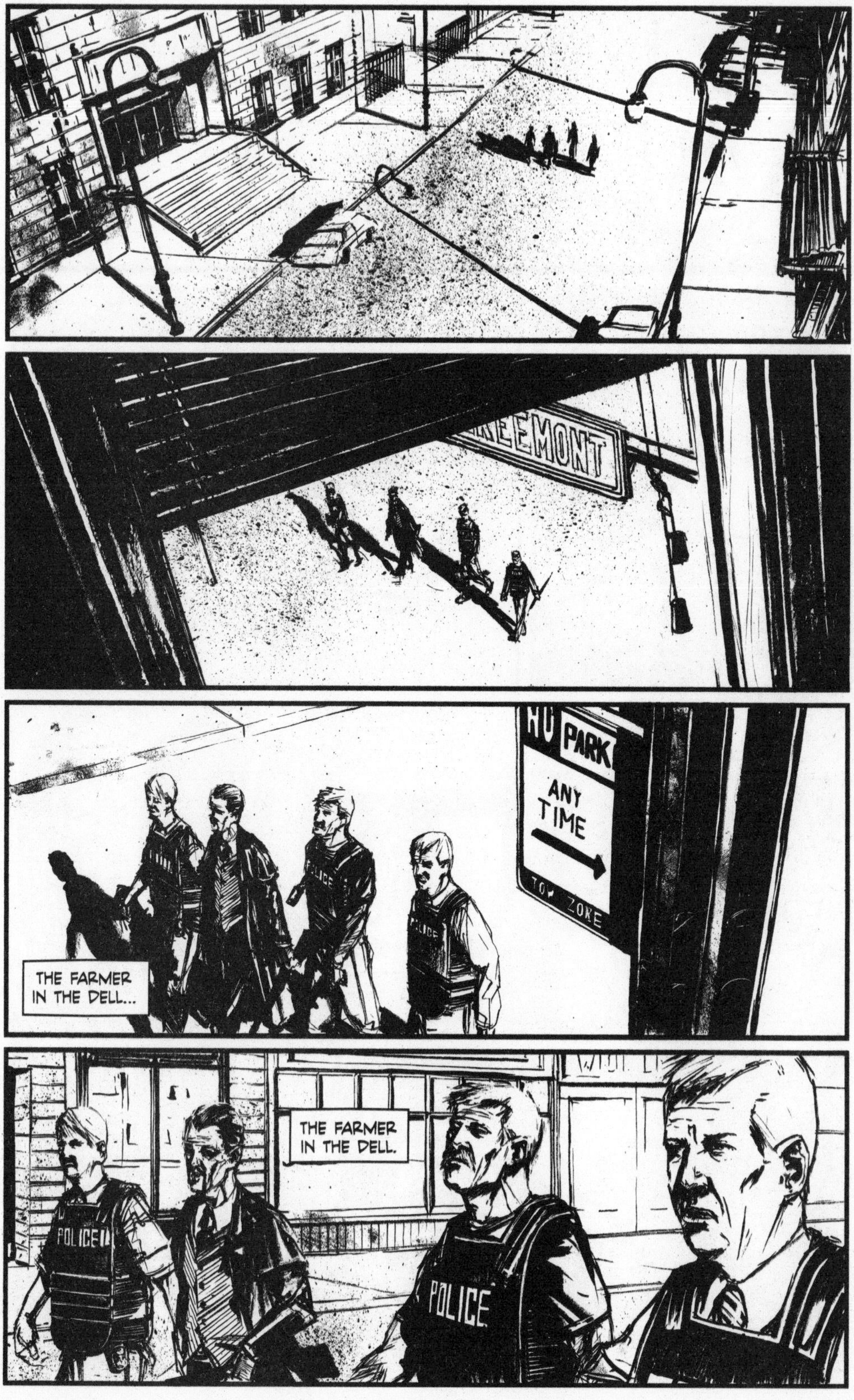

KLEEMONT
NO PARK
ANY TIME
TOW ZONE
THE FARMER IN THE DELL...
POLICE
THE FARMER IN THE DELL.
POLICE
POLICE

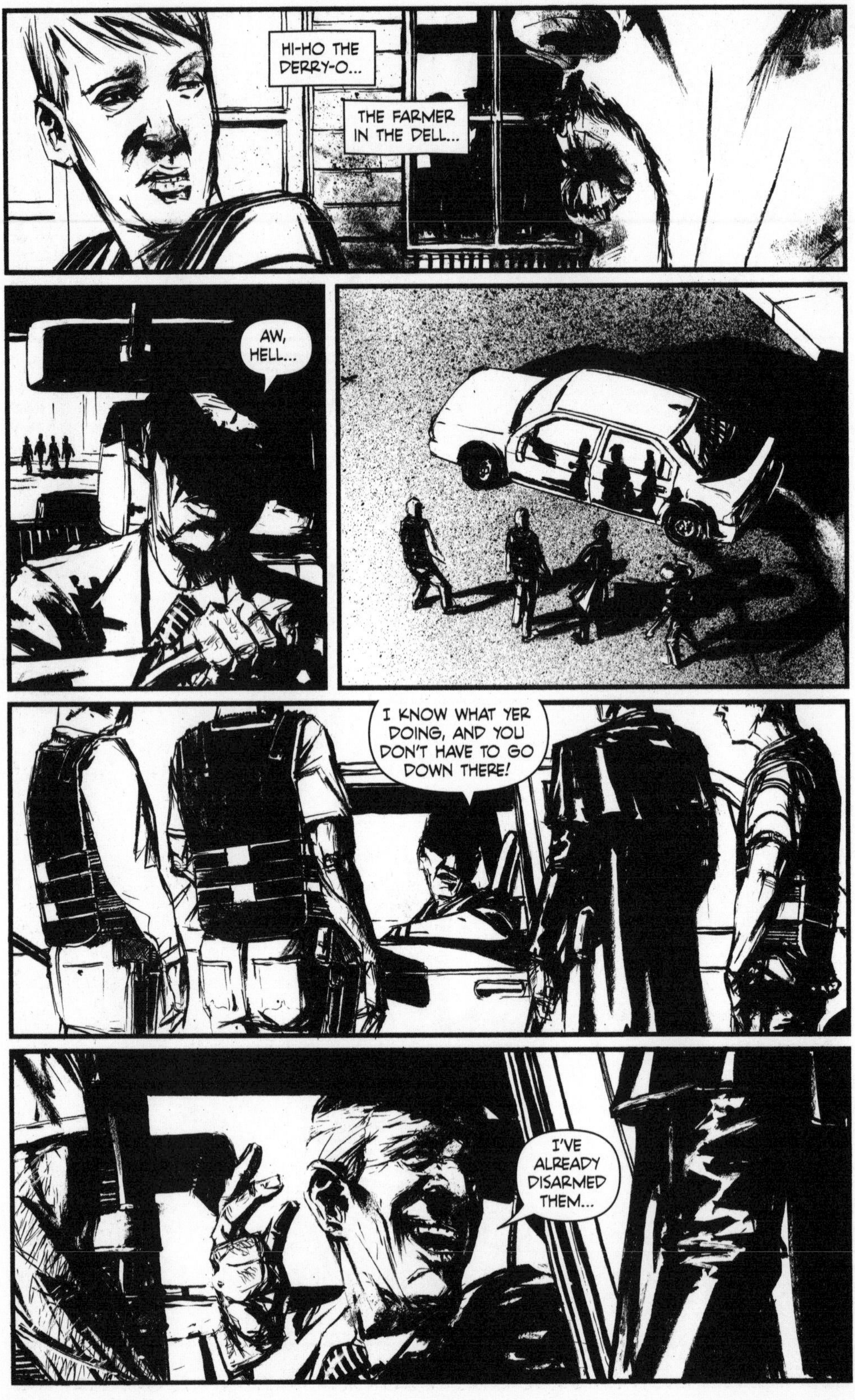
HI-HO THE DERRY-O...
THE FARMER IN THE DELL...
AW, HELL...
I KNOW WHAT YER DOING, AND YOU DON'T HAVE TO GO DOWN THERE!
I'VE ALREADY DISARMED THEM...

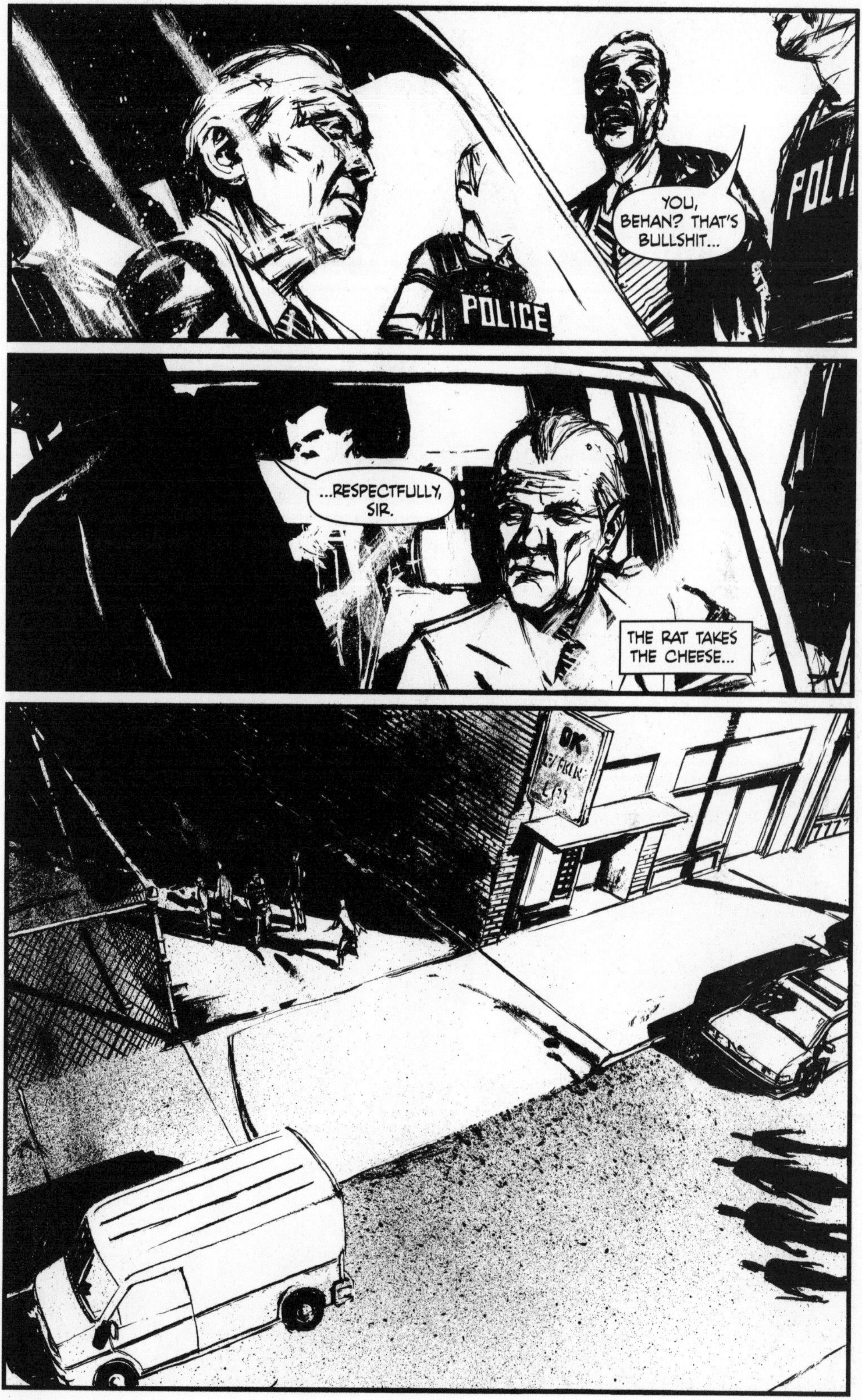
YOU, BEHAN? THAT'S BULLSHIT...
...RESPECTFULLY, SIR.
THE RAT TAKES THE CHEESE...

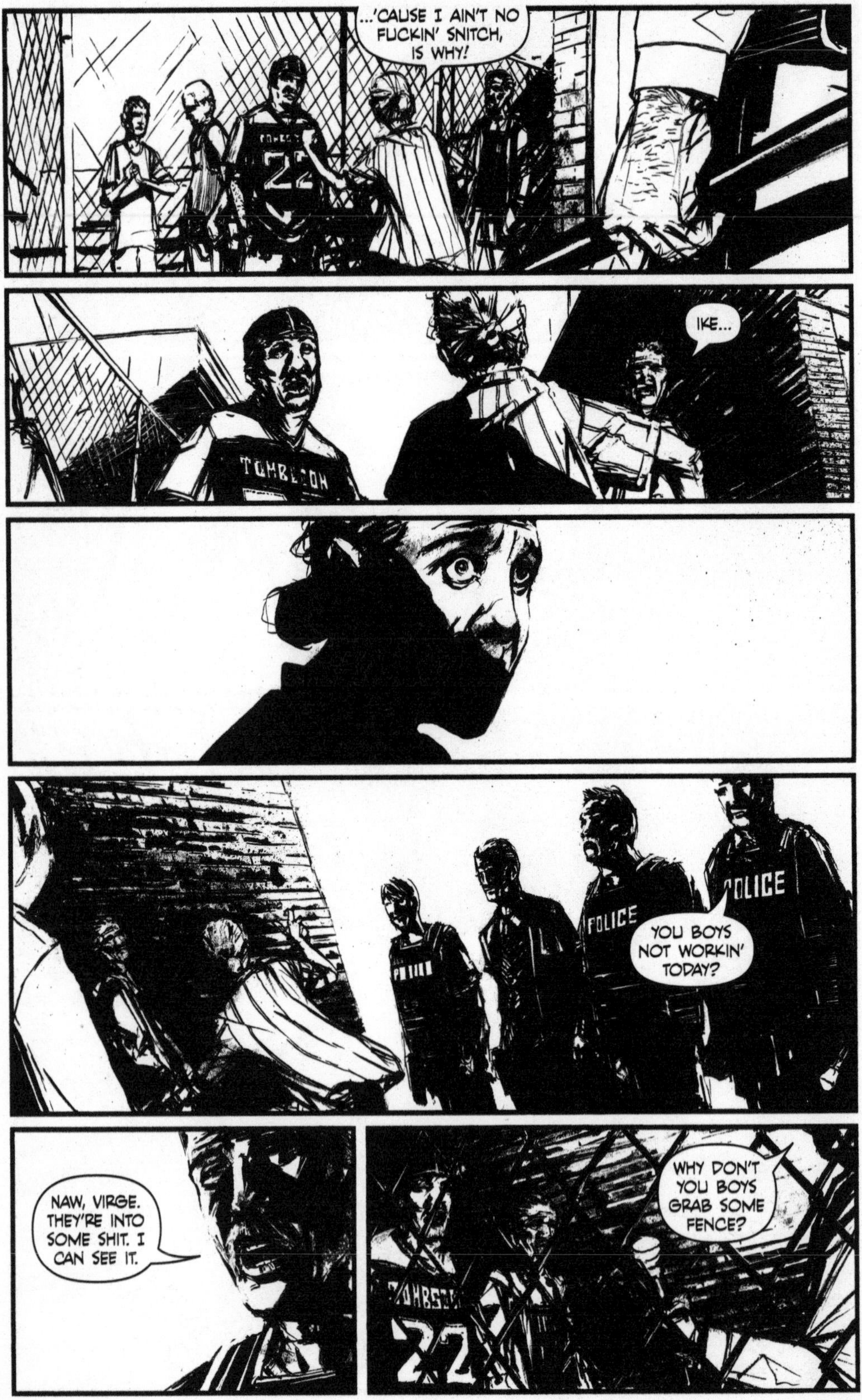
...'CAUSE I AIN'T NO FUCKIN' SNITCH, IS WHY!
IKE...
POLICE
POLICE
YOU BOYS NOT WORKIN' TODAY?
NAW, VIRGE. THEY'RE INTO SOME SHIT. I CAN SEE IT.
WHY DON'T YOU BOYS GRAB SOME FENCE?

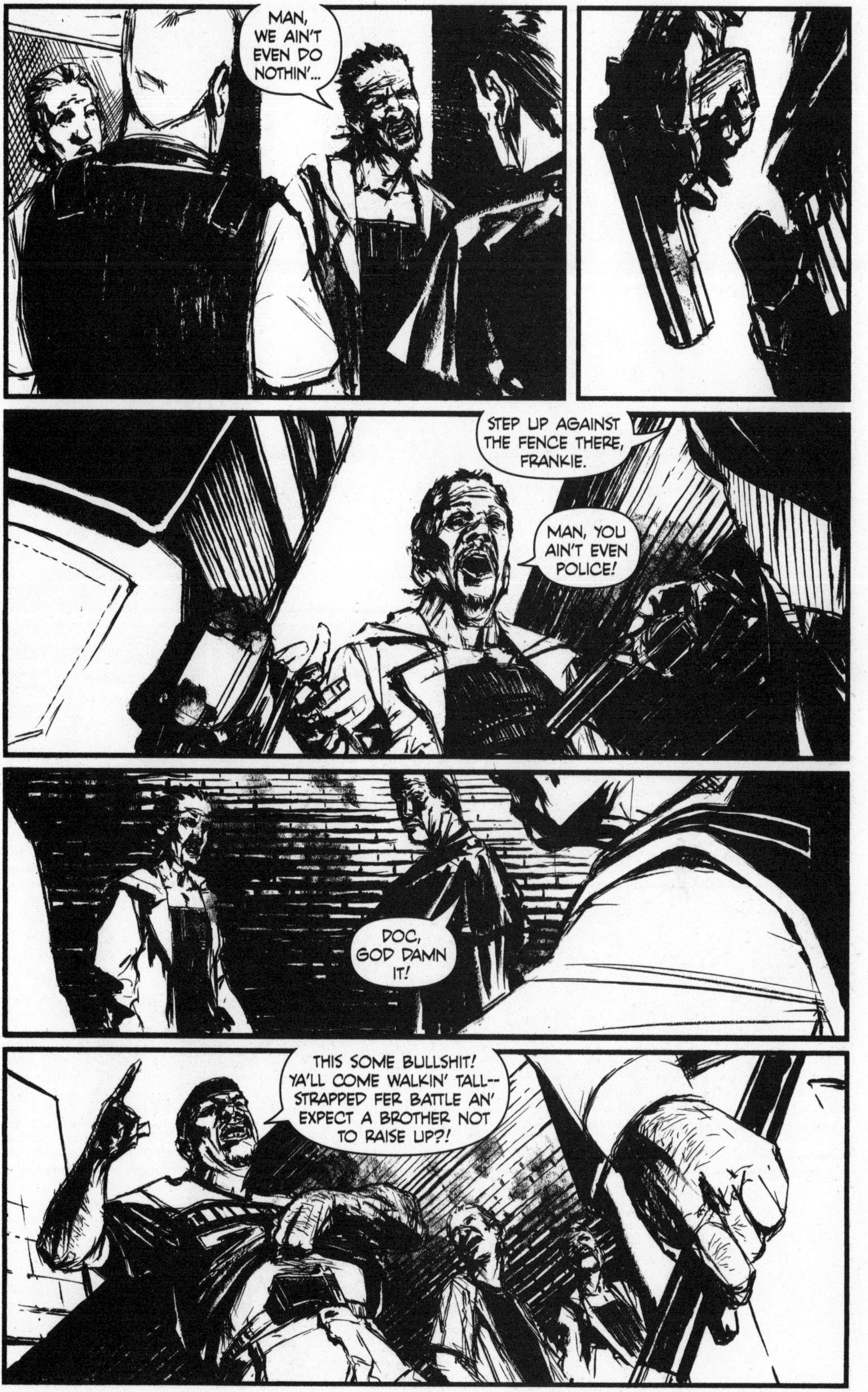
MAN, WE AIN'T EVEN DO NOTHIN'...
STEP UP AGAINST THE FENCE THERE, FRANKIE.
MAN, YOU AIN'T EVEN POLICE!
DOC, GOD DAMN IT!
THIS SOME BULLSHIT! YA'LL COME WALKIN' TALL-- STRAPPED FER BATTLE AN' EXPECT A BROTHER NOT TO RAISE UP?!

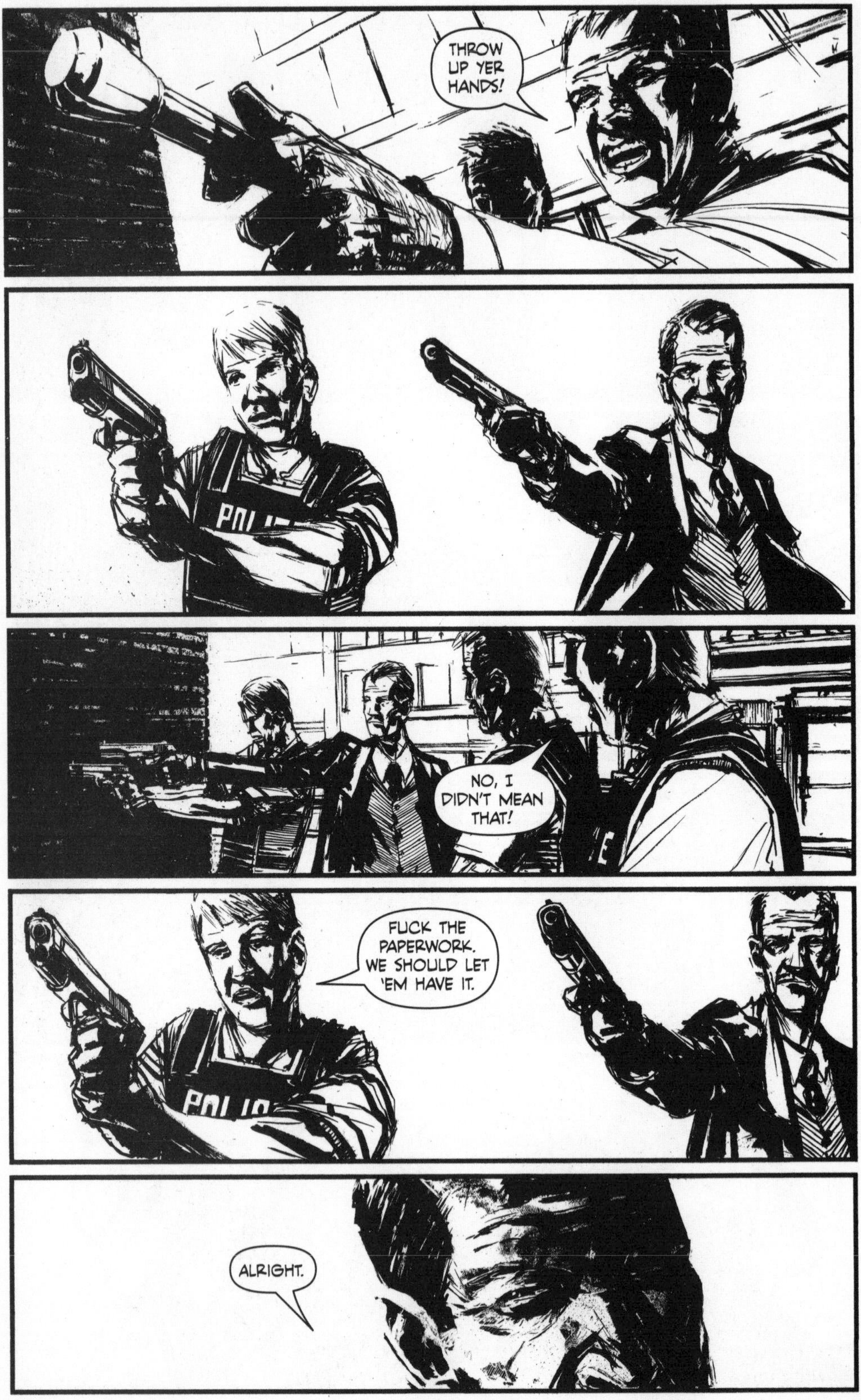
THROW UP YER HANDS!
NO, I DIDN'T MEAN THAT!
FUCK THE PAPERWORK. WE SHOULD LET 'EM HAVE IT.
ALRIGHT.

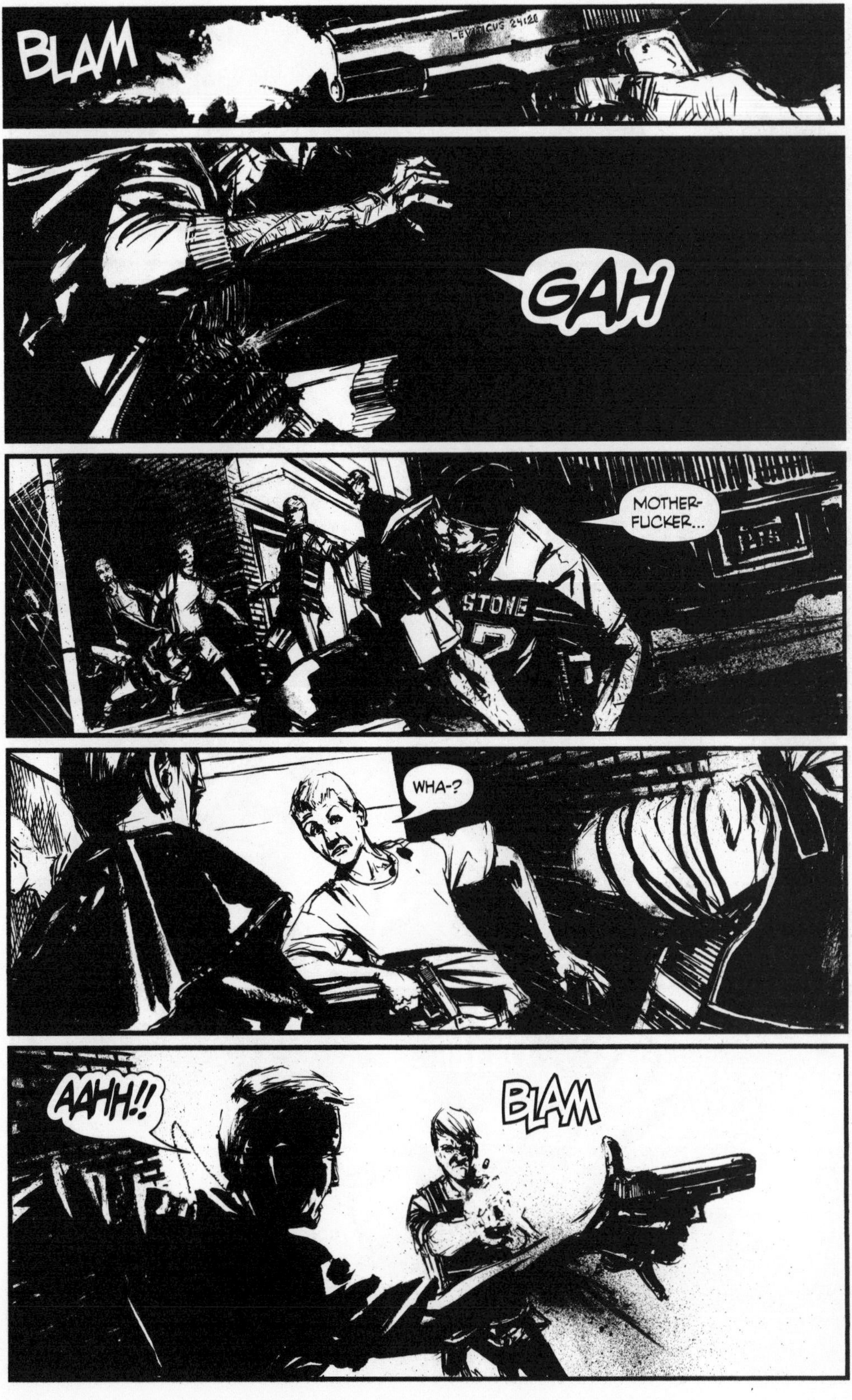
BLAM
LEVITICUS 24:20
GAH
MOTHER-FUCKER...
STONE
WHA-?
AAHH!!
BLAM

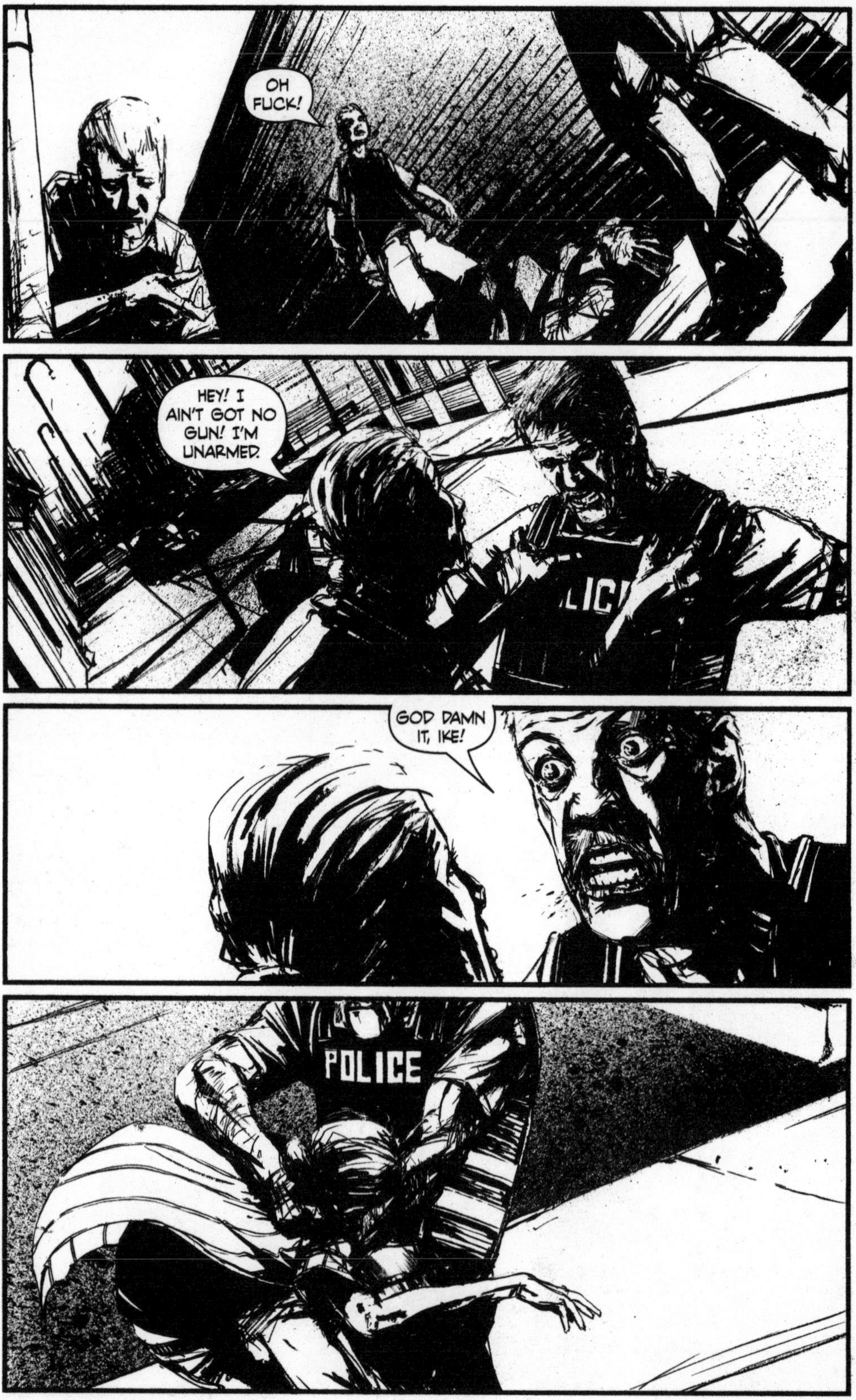
OH FUCK!
HEY! I AIN'T GOT NO GUN! I'M UNARMED.
LICI
GOD DAMN IT, IKE!
POLICE

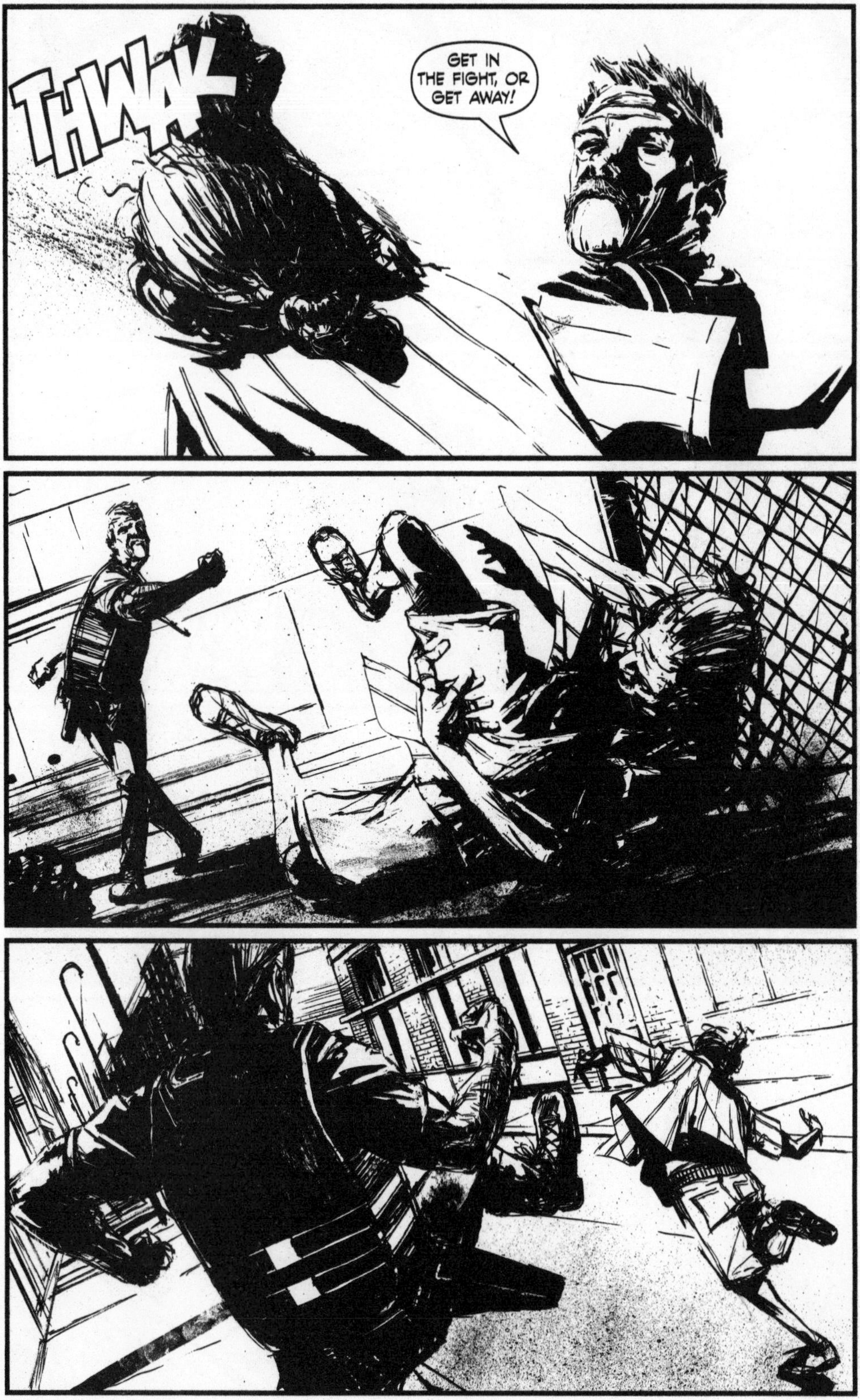
THWAK
GET IN THE FIGHT, OR GET AWAY!

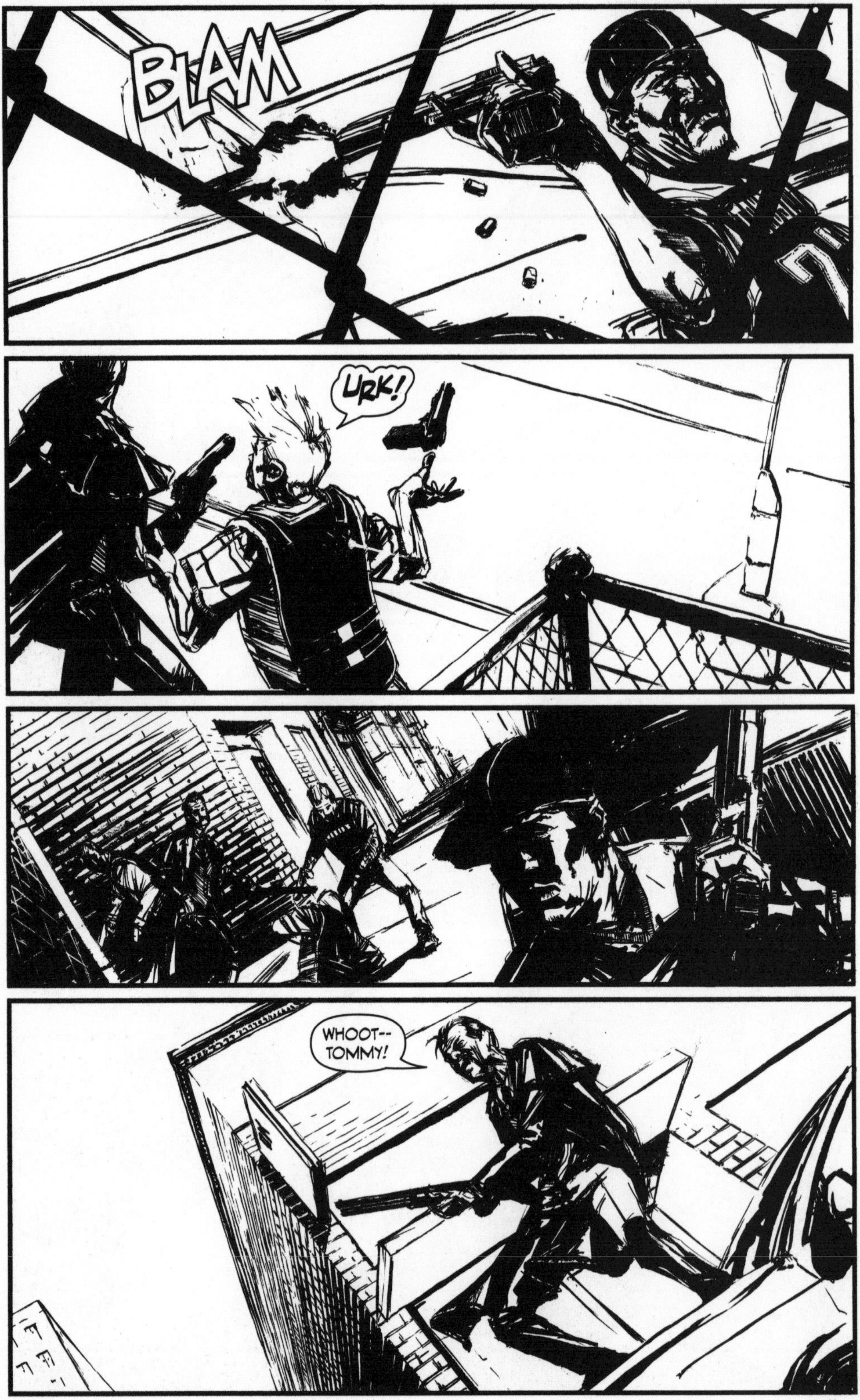
BLAM
URK!
WHOOT--
TOMMY!

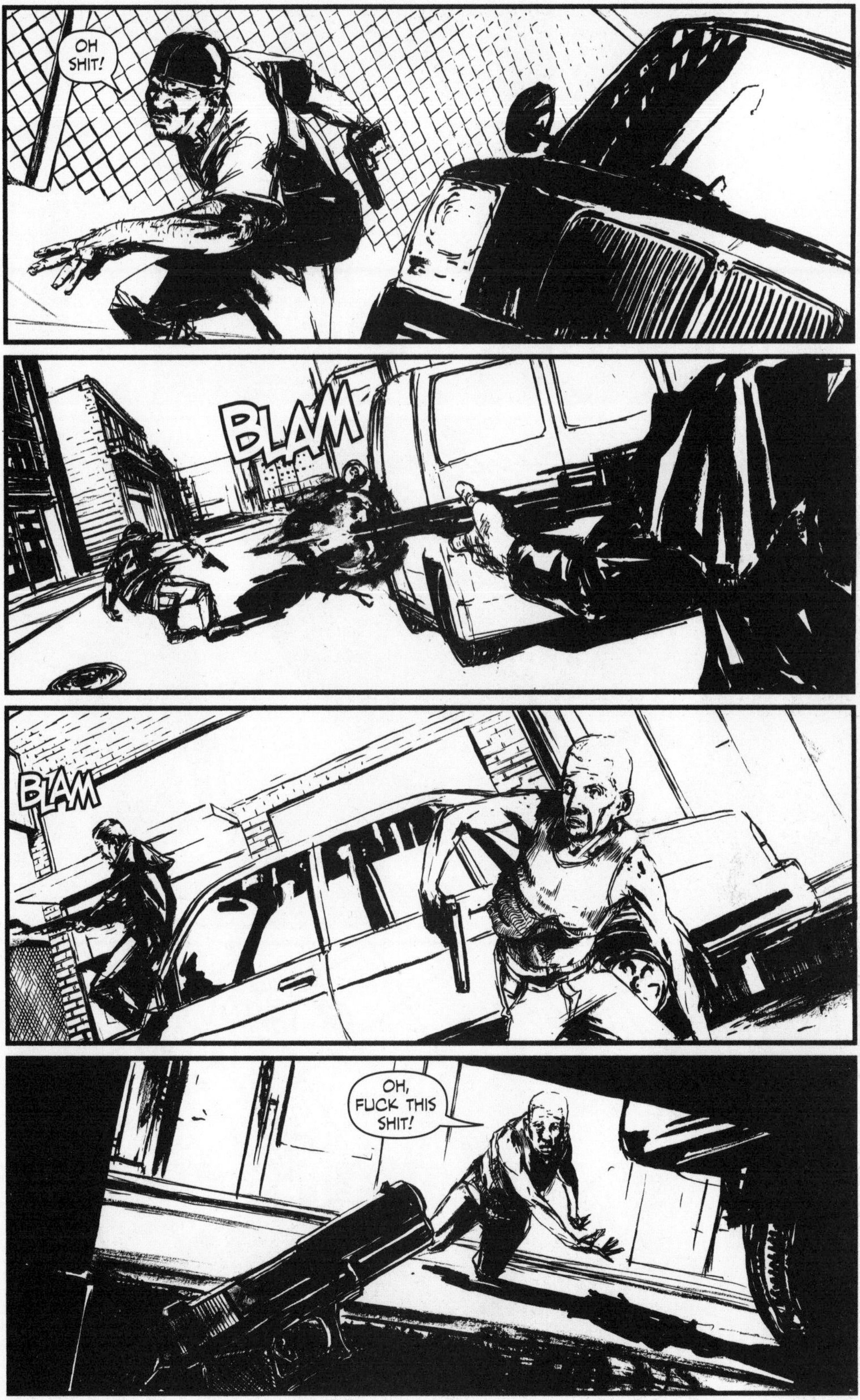
OH SHIT!
BLAM
BLAM
OH, FUCK THIS SHIT!

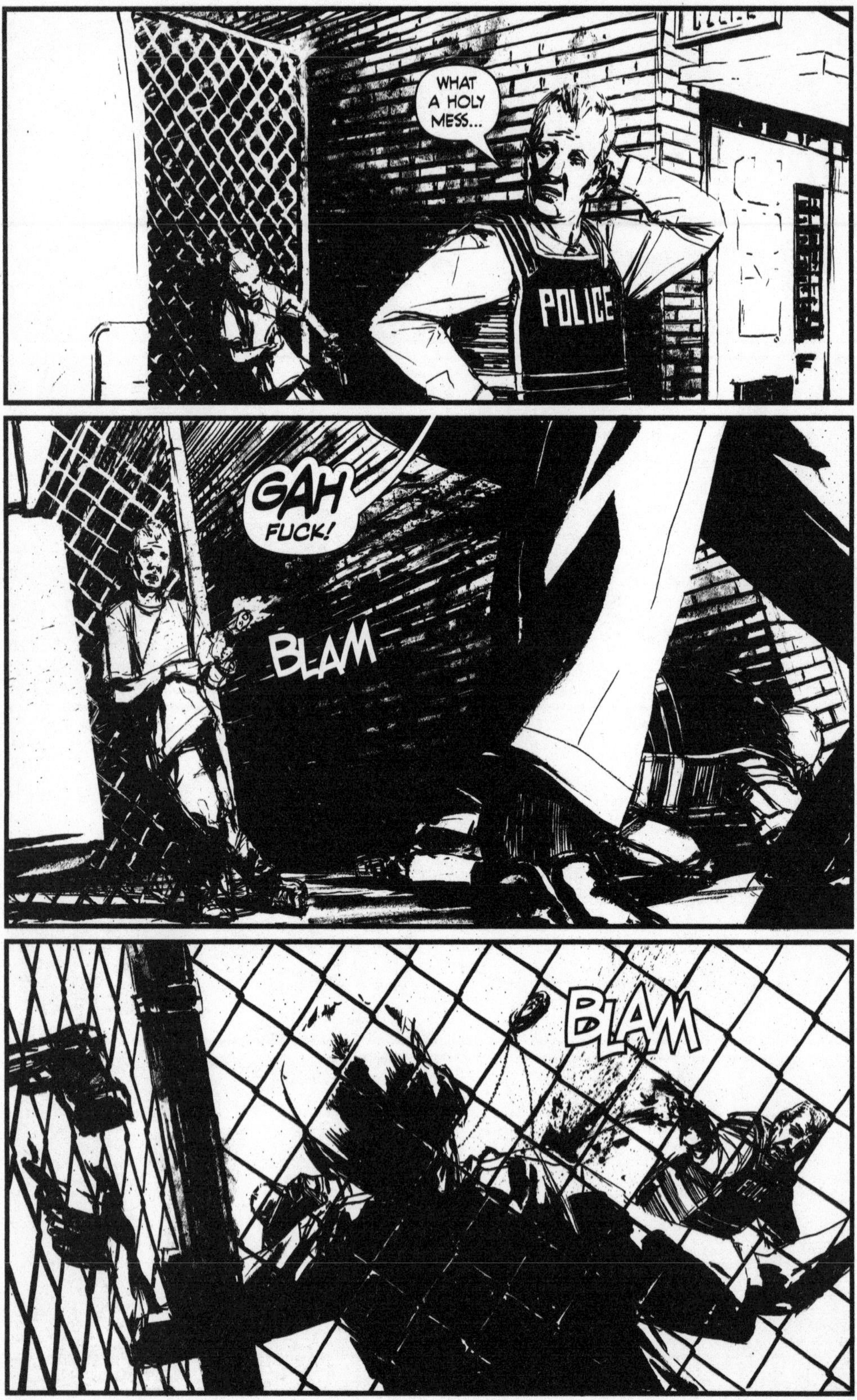
WHAT A HOLY MESS...
POLICE
GAH FUCK!
BLAM
BLAM

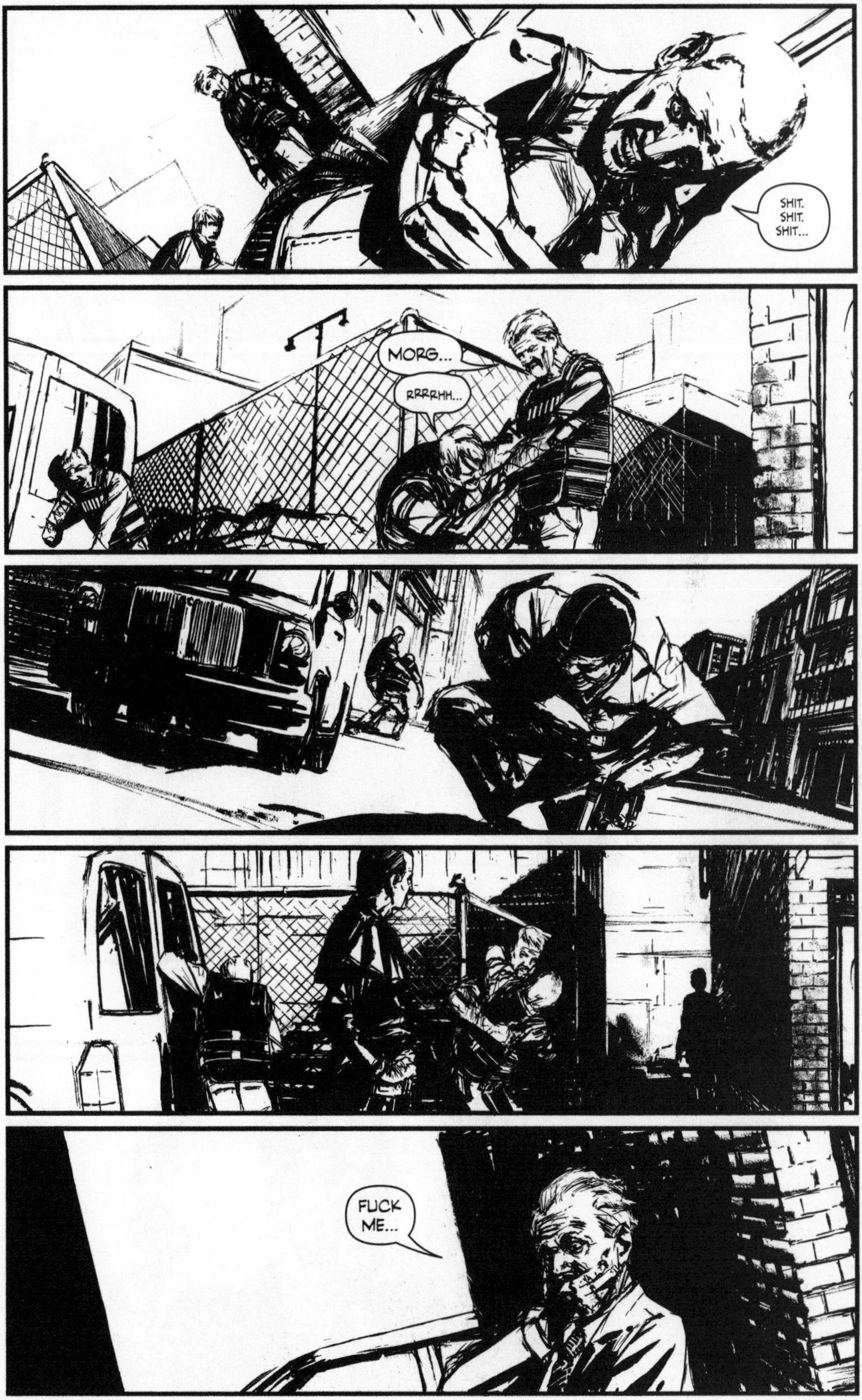
SHIT. SHIT. SHIT...
MORG...
RRRRHH...
FUCK ME...

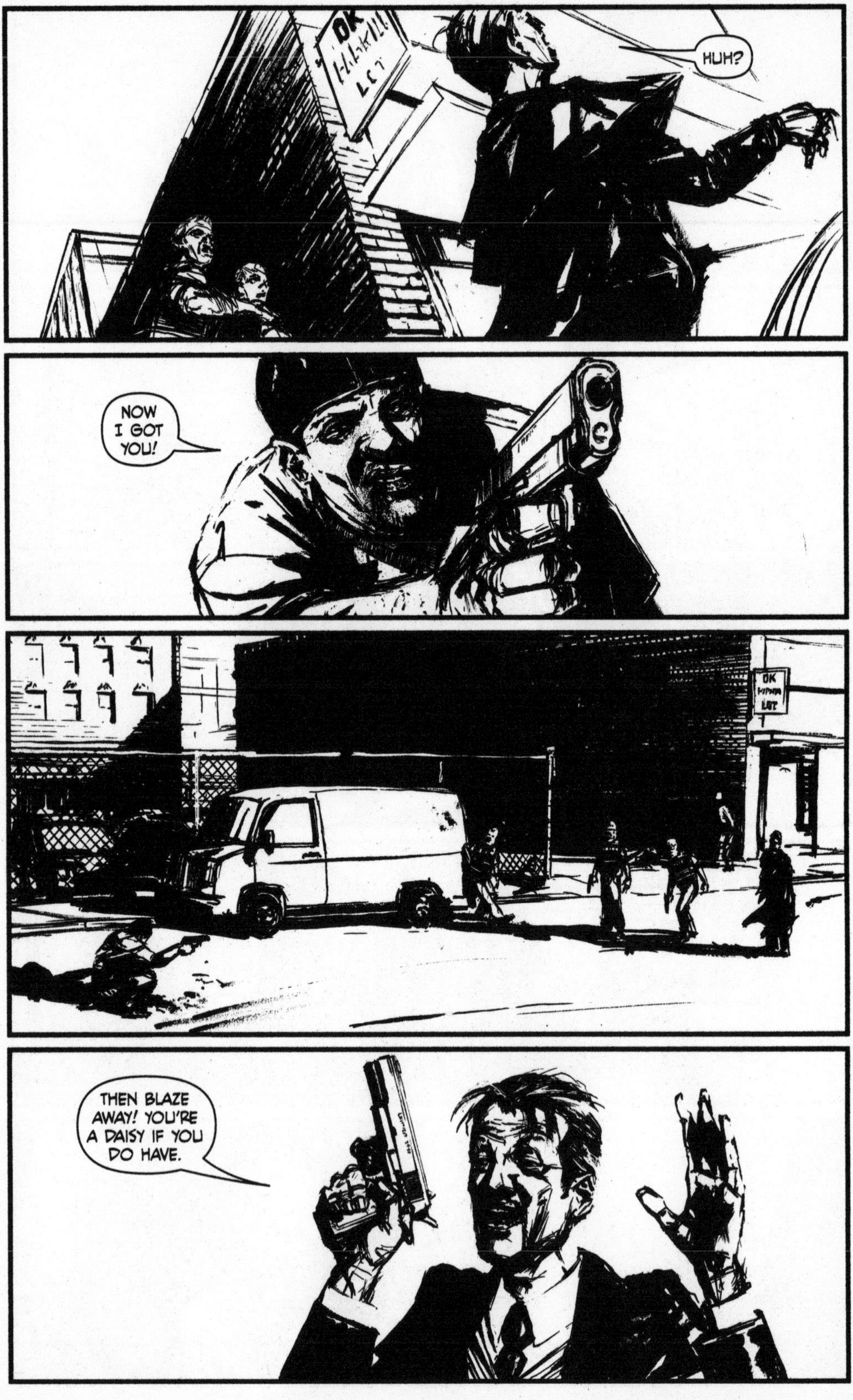
HUH?
NOW I GOT YOU!
THEN BLAZE AWAY! YOU'RE A DAISY IF YOU DO HAVE.

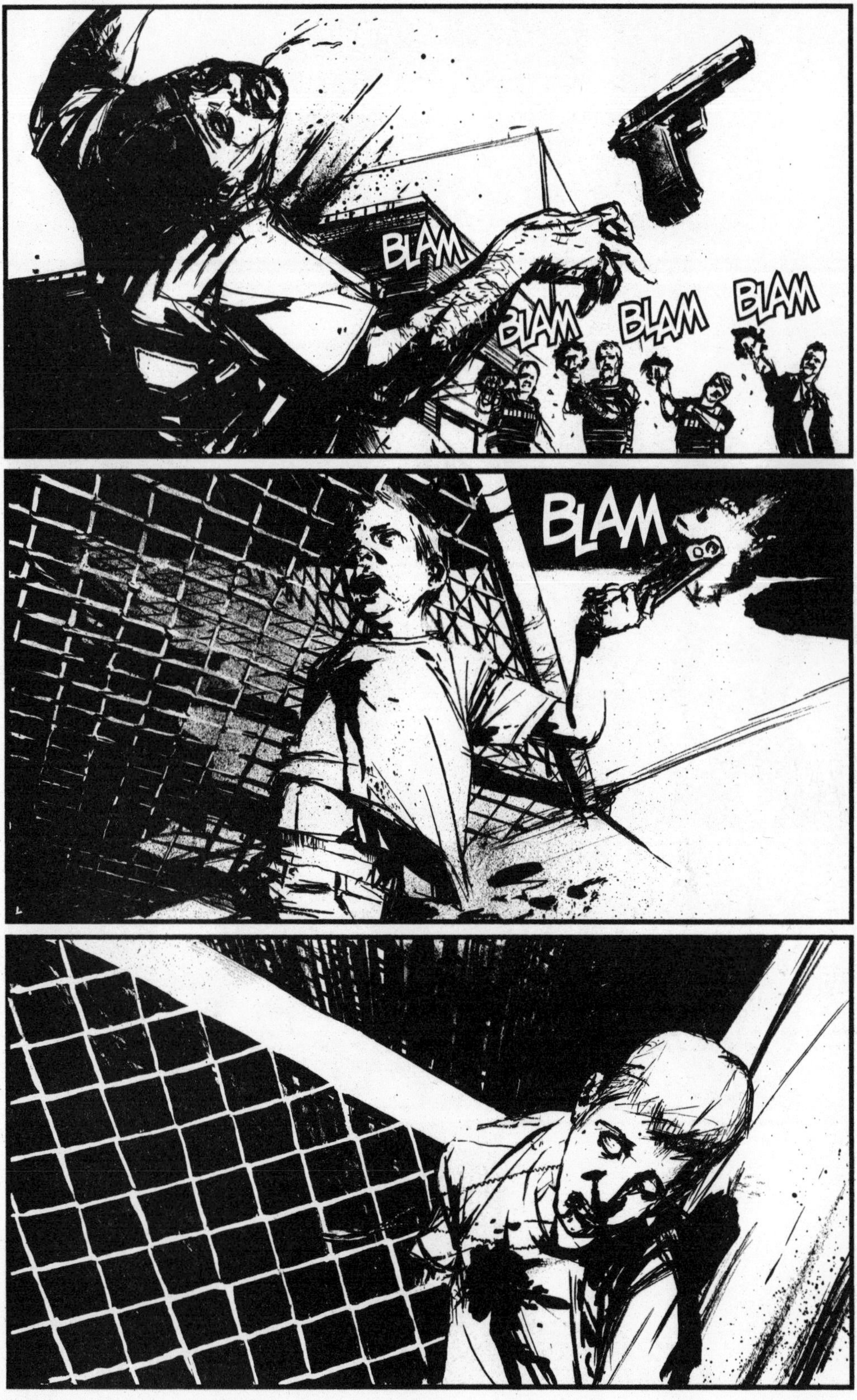
BLAM
BLAM
BLAM
BLAM
BLAM

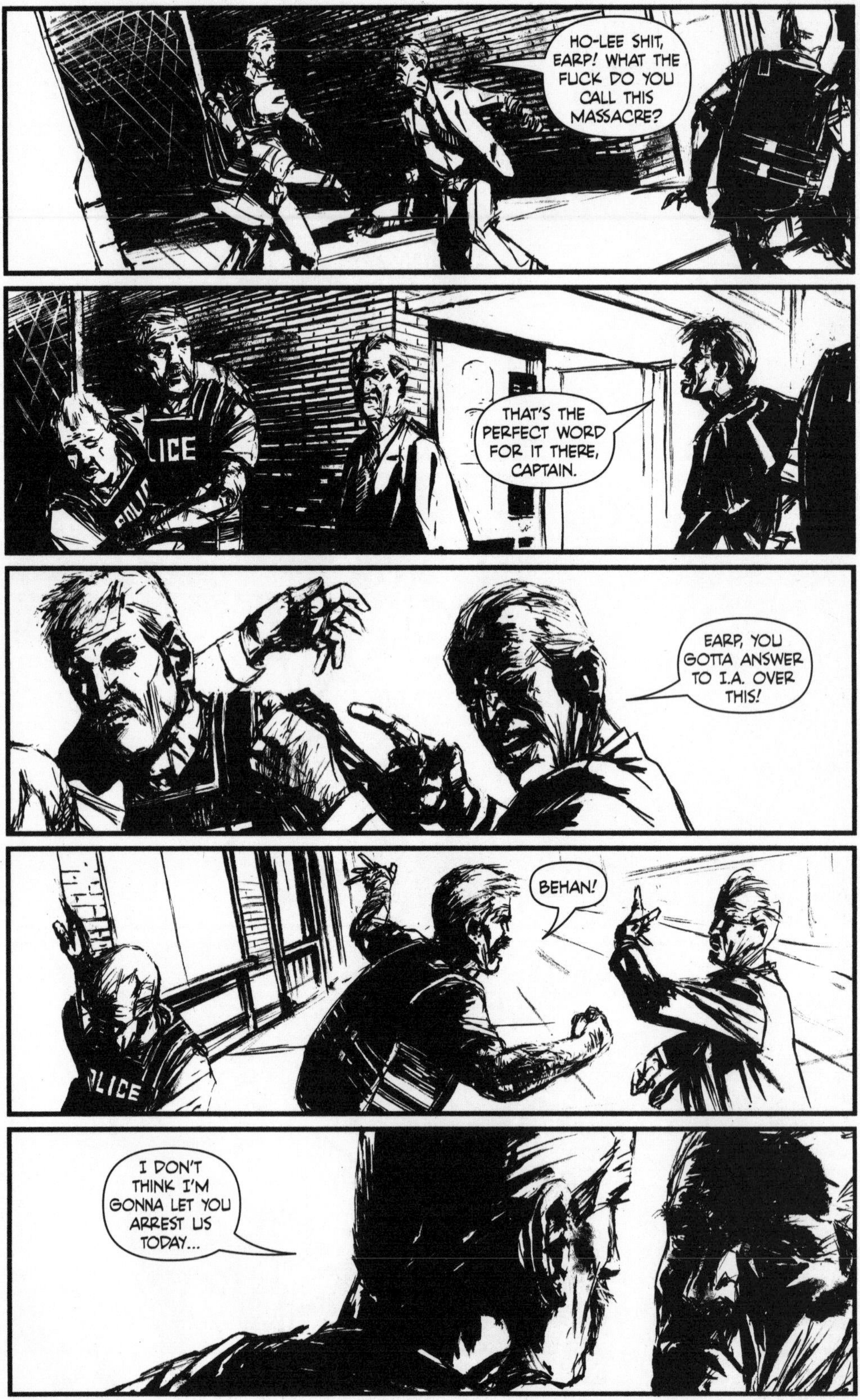
HO-LEE SHIT, EARP! WHAT THE FUCK DO YOU CALL THIS MASSACRE?
THAT'S THE PERFECT WORD FOR IT THERE, CAPTAIN.
LICE
EARP, YOU GOTTA ANSWER TO I.A. OVER THIS!
BEHAN!
LICE
I DON'T THINK I'M GONNA LET YOU ARREST US TODAY...

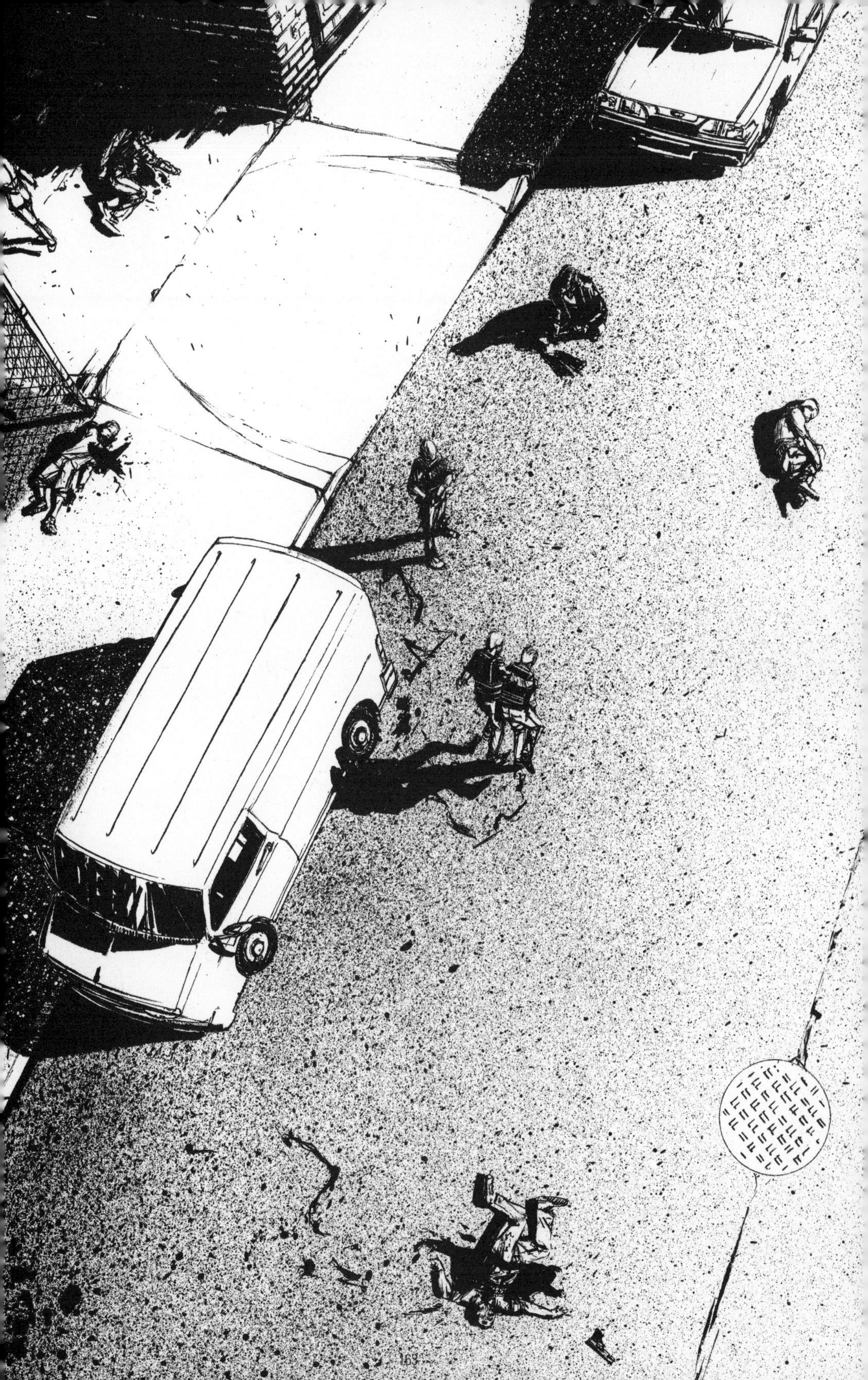

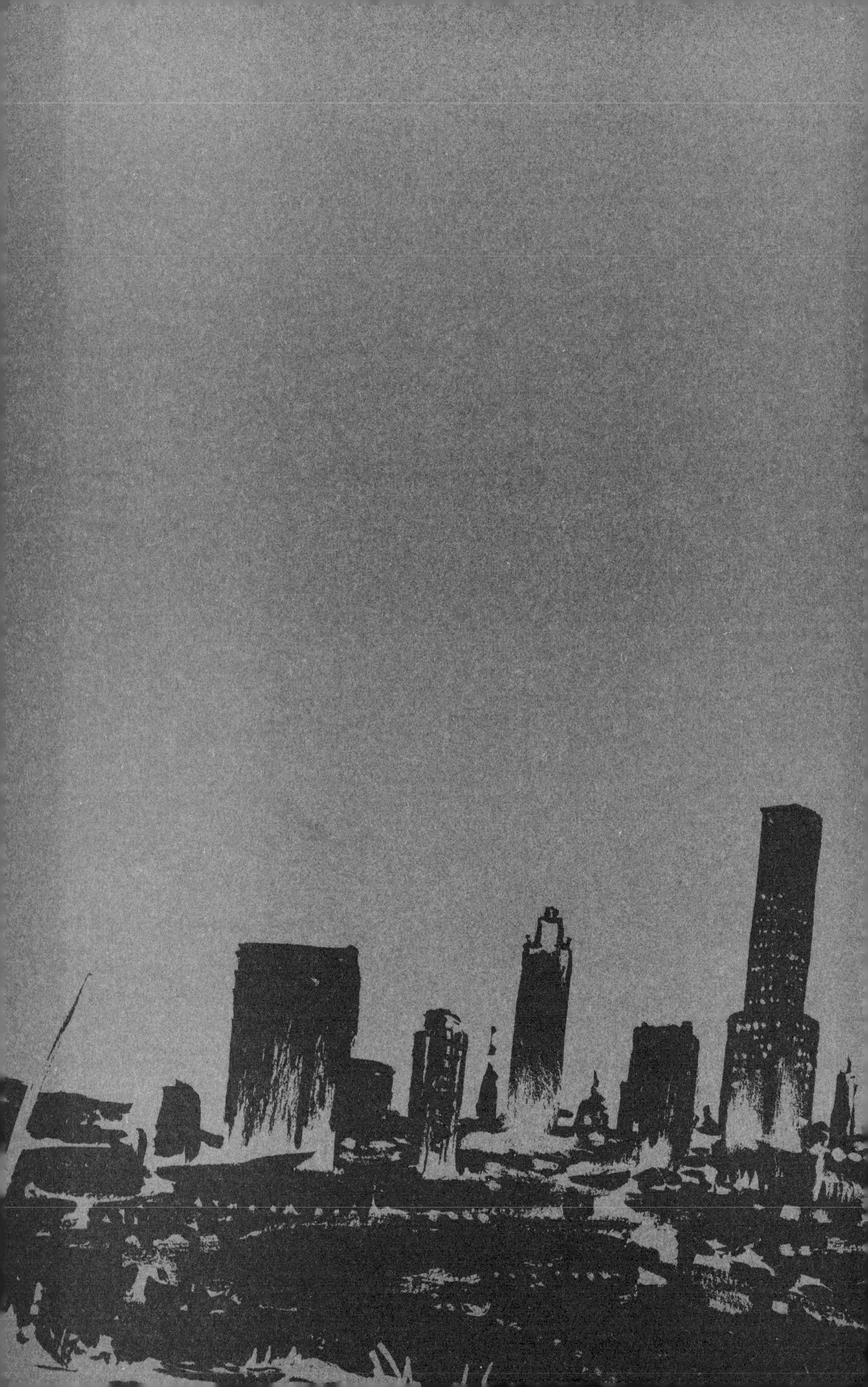

CHAPTER SEVEN

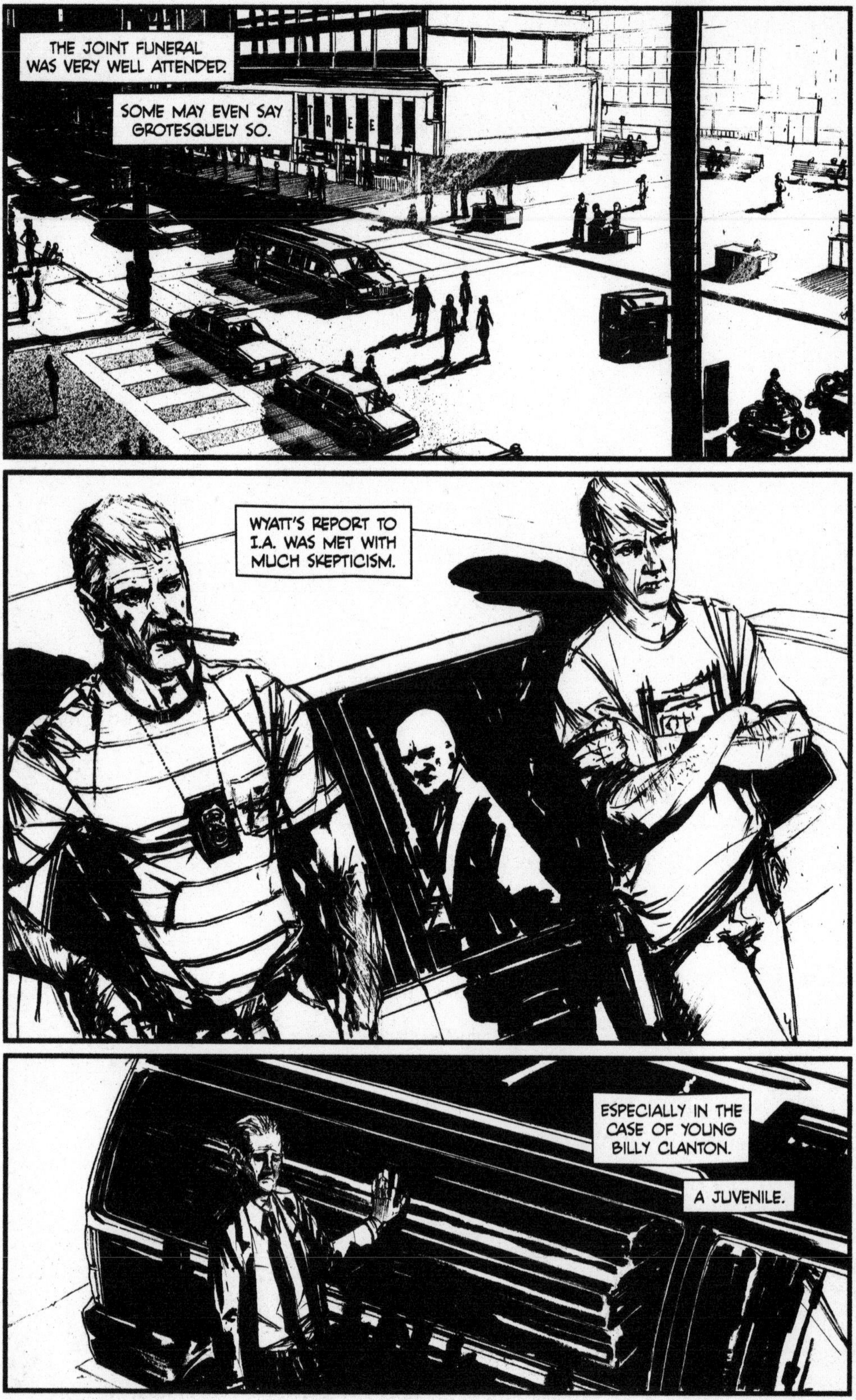
THE JOINT FUNERAL WAS VERY WELL ATTENDED.
SOME MAY EVEN SAY GROTESQUELY SO.
WYATT'S REPORT TO I.A. WAS MET WITH MUCH SKEPTICISM.
ESPECIALLY IN THE CASE OF YOUNG BILLY CLANTON.
A JUVENILE.

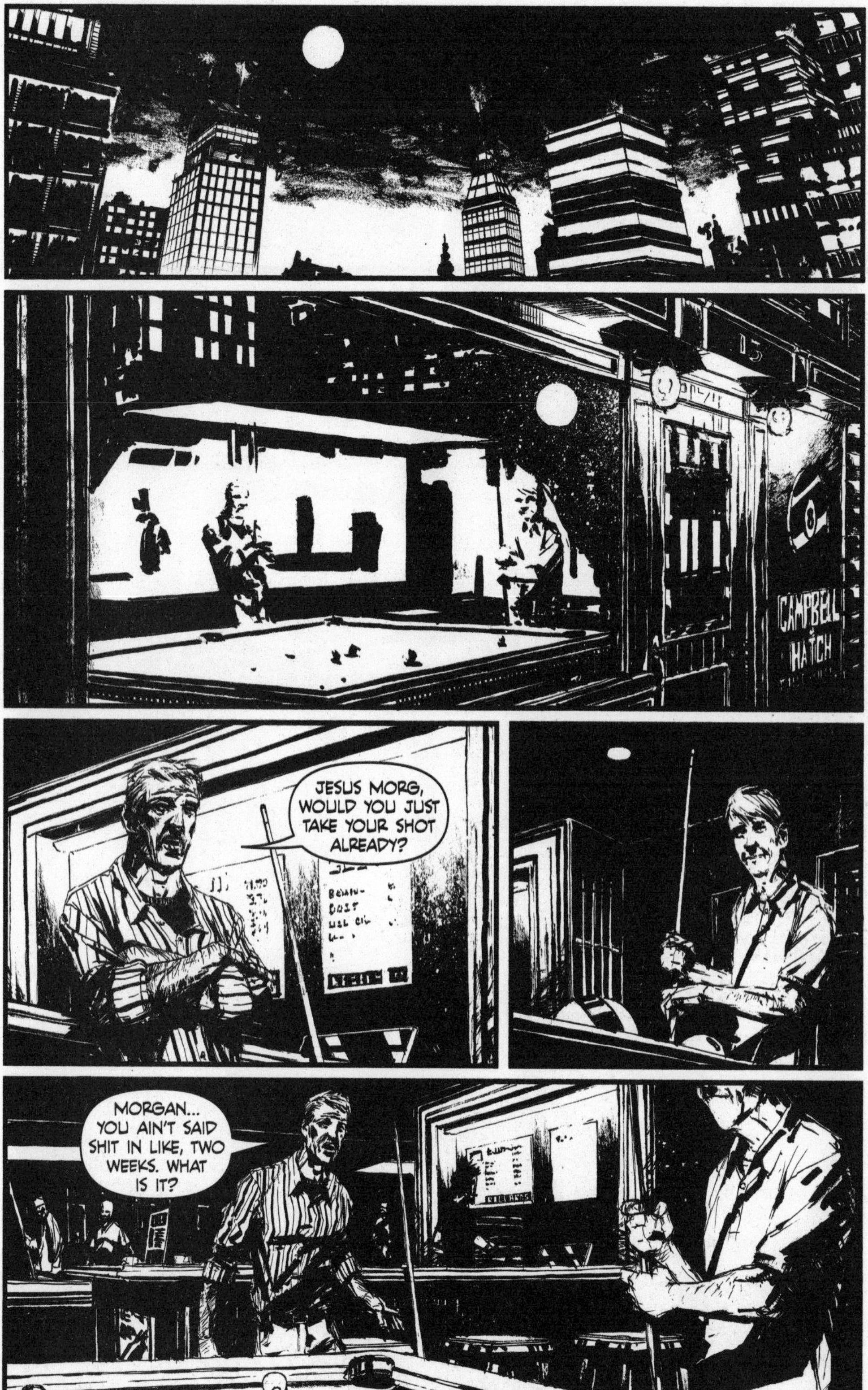
CAMPBELL
HATCH
JESUS MORG, WOULD YOU JUST TAKE YOUR SHOT ALREADY?
MORGAN... YOU AIN'T SAID SHIT IN LIKE, TWO WEEKS. WHAT IS IT?

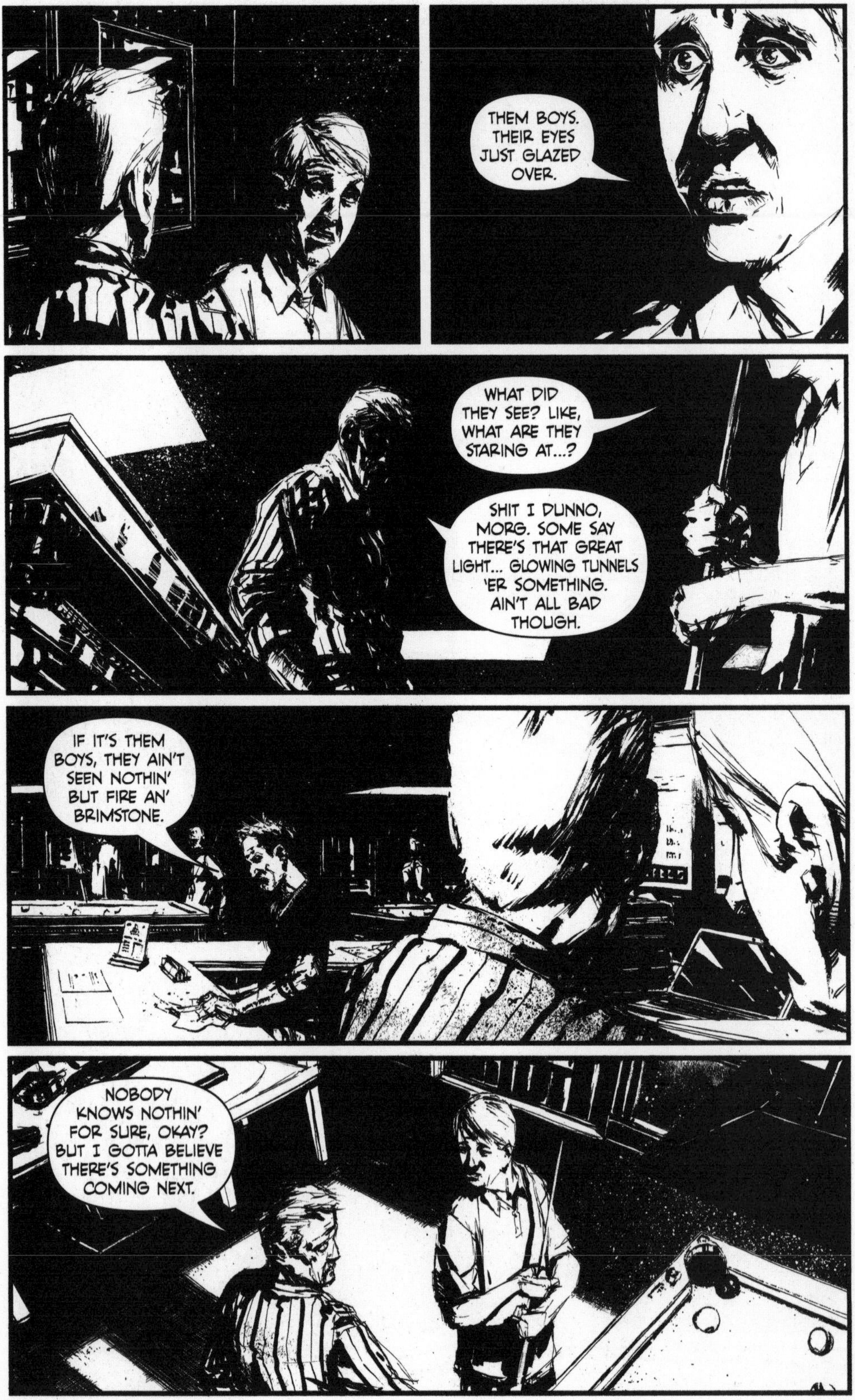
THEM BOYS. THEIR EYES JUST GLAZED OVER.
WHAT DID THEY SEE? LIKE, WHAT ARE THEY STARING AT...?
SHIT I DUNNO, MORG. SOME SAY THERE'S THAT GREAT LIGHT... GLOWING TUNNELS 'ER SOMETHING. AIN'T ALL BAD THOUGH.
IF IT'S THEM BOYS, THEY AIN'T SEEN NOTHIN' BUT FIRE AN' BRIMSTONE.
NOBODY KNOWS NOTHIN' FOR SURE, OKAY? BUT I GOTTA BELIEVE THERE'S SOMETHING COMING NEXT.

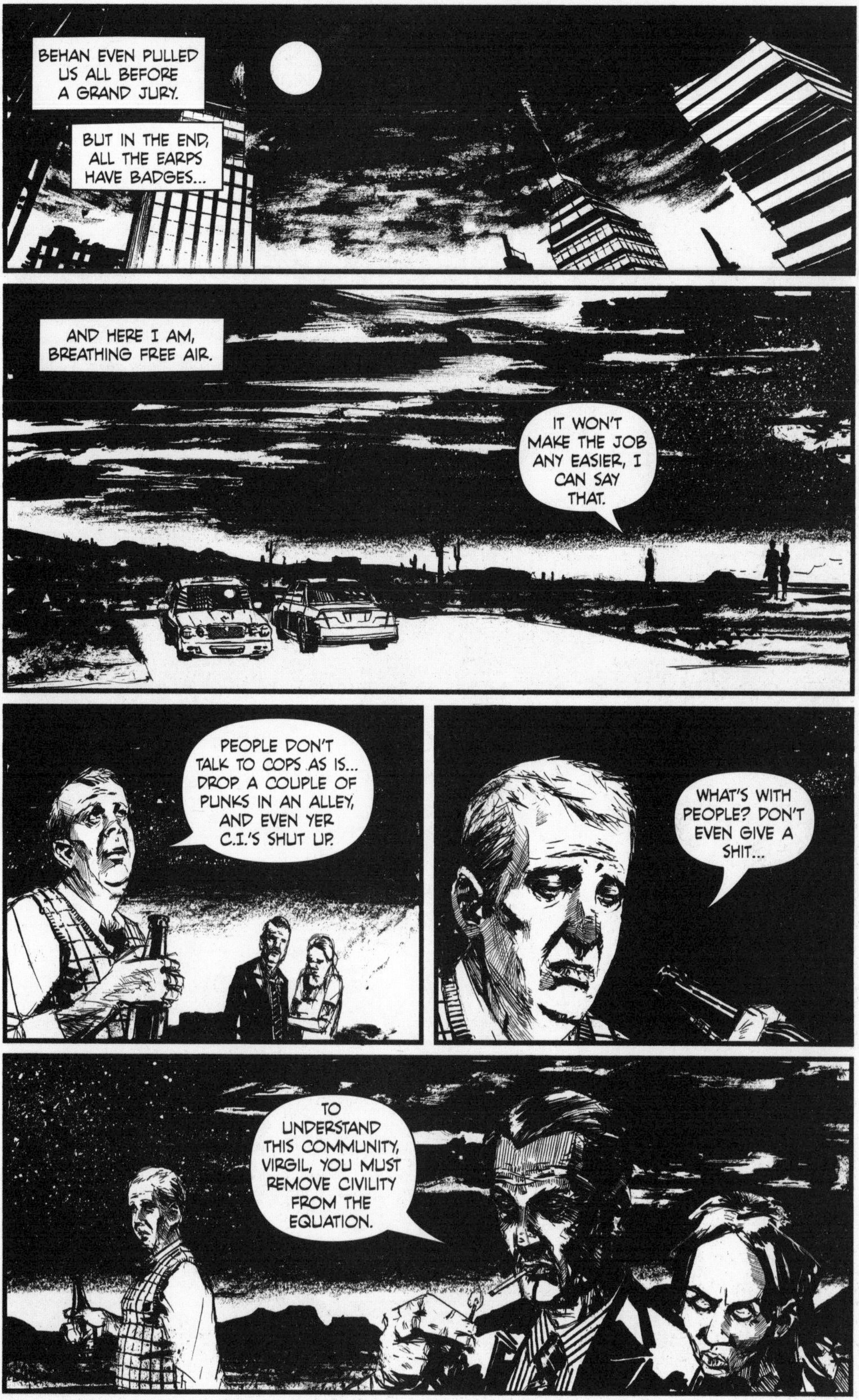
BEHAN EVEN PULLED US ALL BEFORE A GRAND JURY.
BUT IN THE END, ALL THE EARPS HAVE BADGES...
AND HERE I AM, BREATHING FREE AIR.
IT WON'T MAKE THE JOB ANY EASIER, I CAN SAY THAT.
PEOPLE DON'T TALK TO COPS AS IS... DROP A COUPLE OF PUNKS IN AN ALLEY, AND EVEN YER C.I.'S SHUT UP.
WHAT'S WITH PEOPLE? DON'T EVEN GIVE A SHIT...
TO UNDERSTAND THIS COMMUNITY, VIRGIL, YOU MUST REMOVE CIVILITY FROM THE EQUATION.

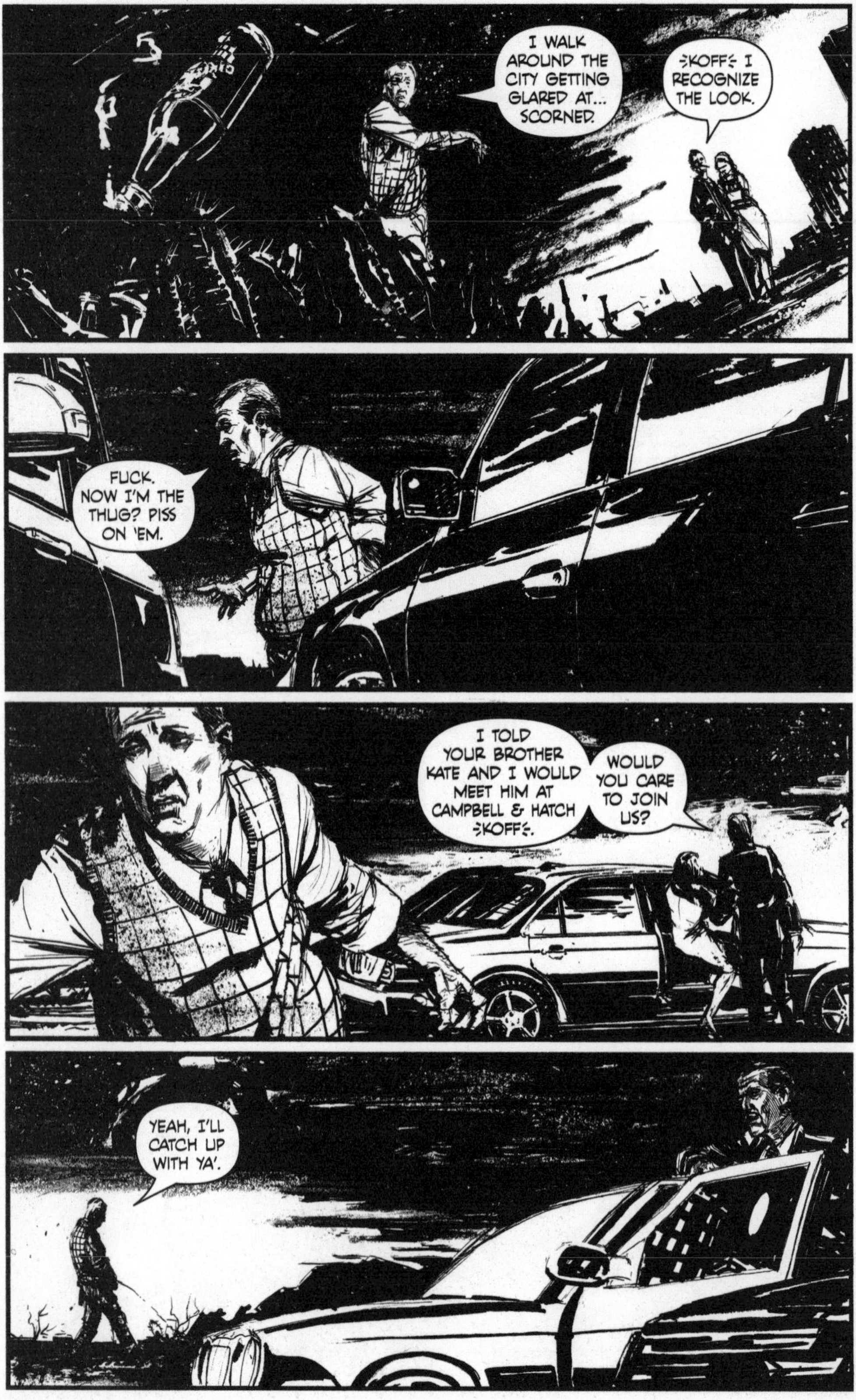
I WALK AROUND THE CITY GETTING GLARED AT... SCORNED.
≈KOFF≈ I RECOGNIZE THE LOOK.
FUCK. NOW I'M THE THUG? PISS ON 'EM.
I TOLD YOUR BROTHER KATE AND I WOULD MEET HIM AT CAMPBELL & HATCH ≈KOFF≈.
WOULD YOU CARE TO JOIN US?
YEAH, I'LL CATCH UP WITH YA'.

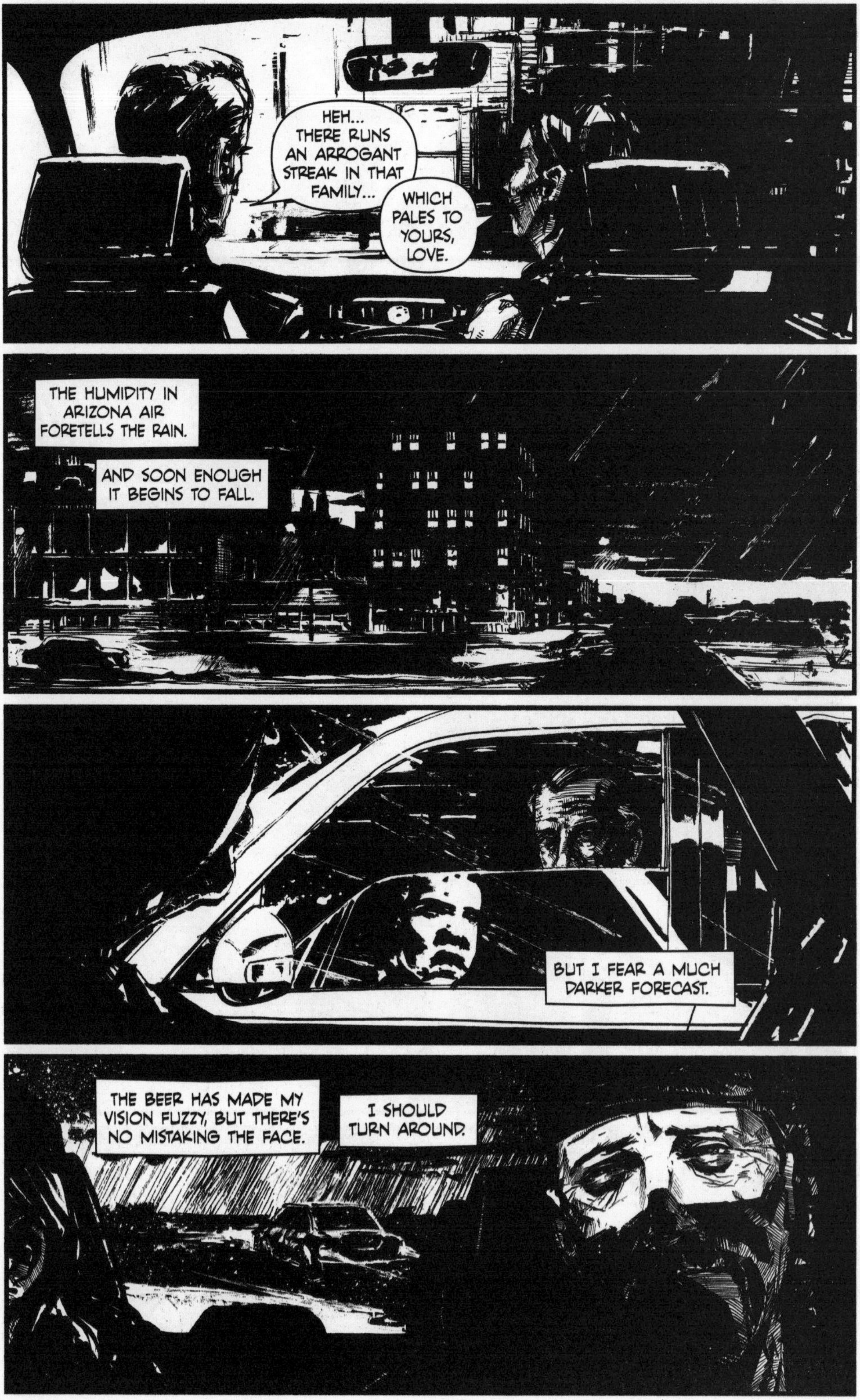
HEH... THERE RUNS AN ARROGANT STREAK IN THAT FAMILY...
WHICH PALES TO YOURS, LOVE.
THE HUMIDITY IN ARIZONA AIR FORETELLS THE RAIN.
AND SOON ENOUGH IT BEGINS TO FALL.
BUT I FEAR A MUCH DARKER FORECAST.
THE BEER HAS MADE MY VISION FUZZY, BUT THERE'S NO MISTAKING THE FACE.
I SHOULD TURN AROUND.

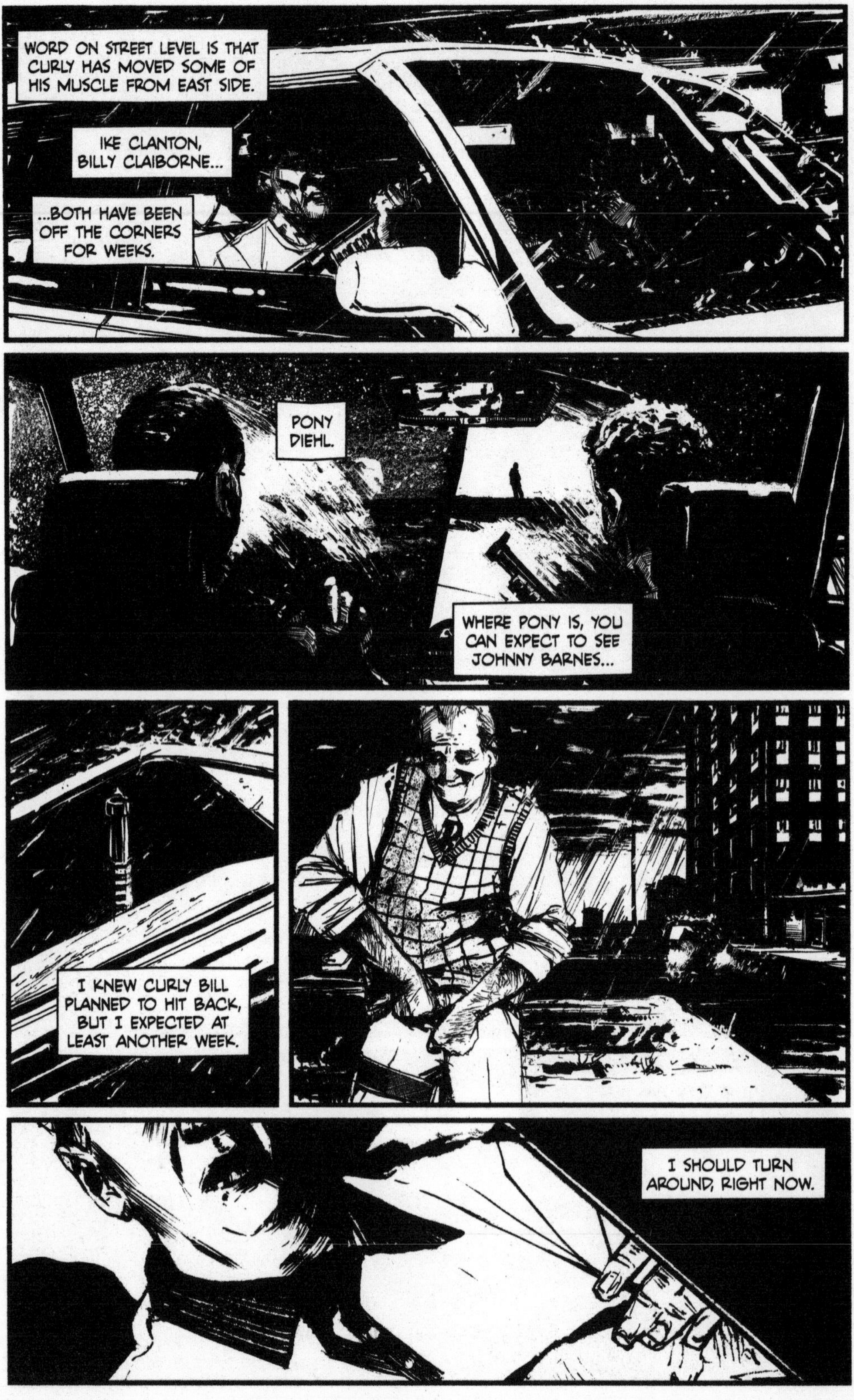
WORD ON STREET LEVEL IS THAT CURLY HAS MOVED SOME OF HIS MUSCLE FROM EAST SIDE.
IKE CLANTON, BILLY CLAIBORNE...
...BOTH HAVE BEEN OFF THE CORNERS FOR WEEKS.
PONY DIEHL.
WHERE PONY IS, YOU CAN EXPECT TO SEE JOHNNY BARNES...
I KNEW CURLY BILL PLANNED TO HIT BACK, BUT I EXPECTED AT LEAST ANOTHER WEEK.
I SHOULD TURN AROUND, RIGHT NOW.

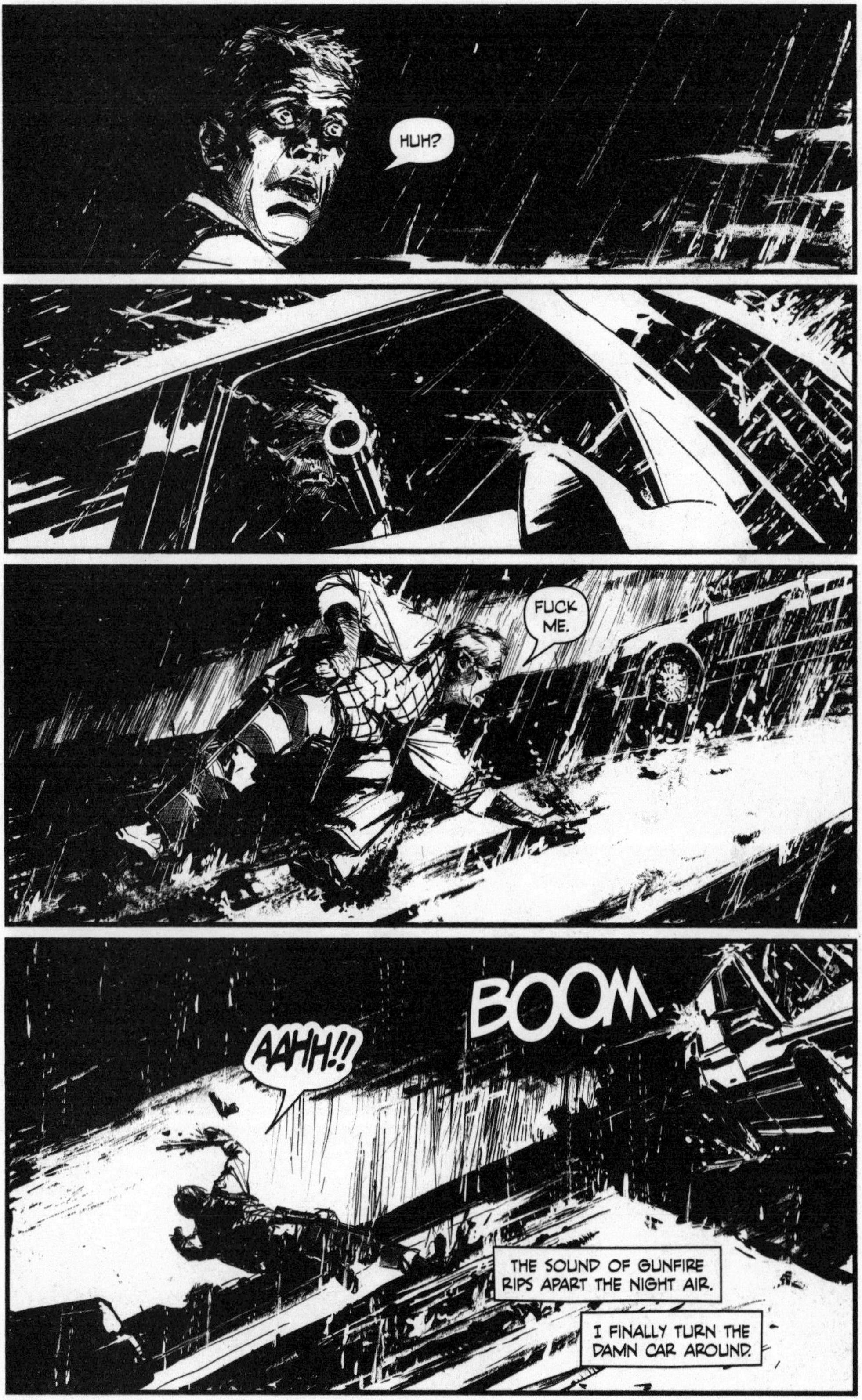
HUH?
FUCK ME.
BOOM.
AAHH!!
THE SOUND OF GUNFIRE RIPS APART THE NIGHT AIR.
I FINALLY TURN THE DAMN CAR AROUND.

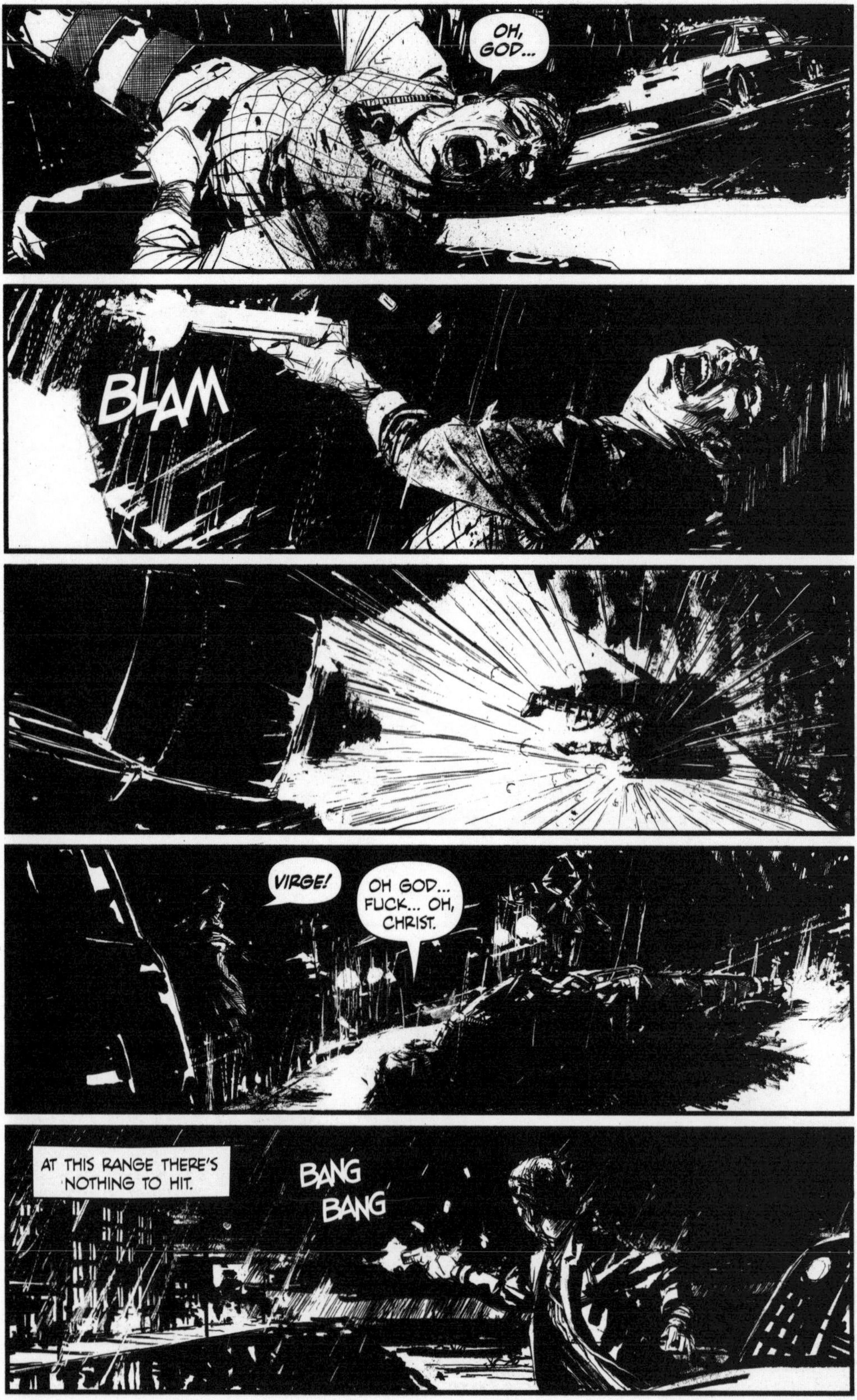
OH, GOD...
BLAM
VIRGE!
OH GOD... FUCK... OH, CHRIST.
AT THIS RANGE THERE'S NOTHING TO HIT.
BANG
BANG

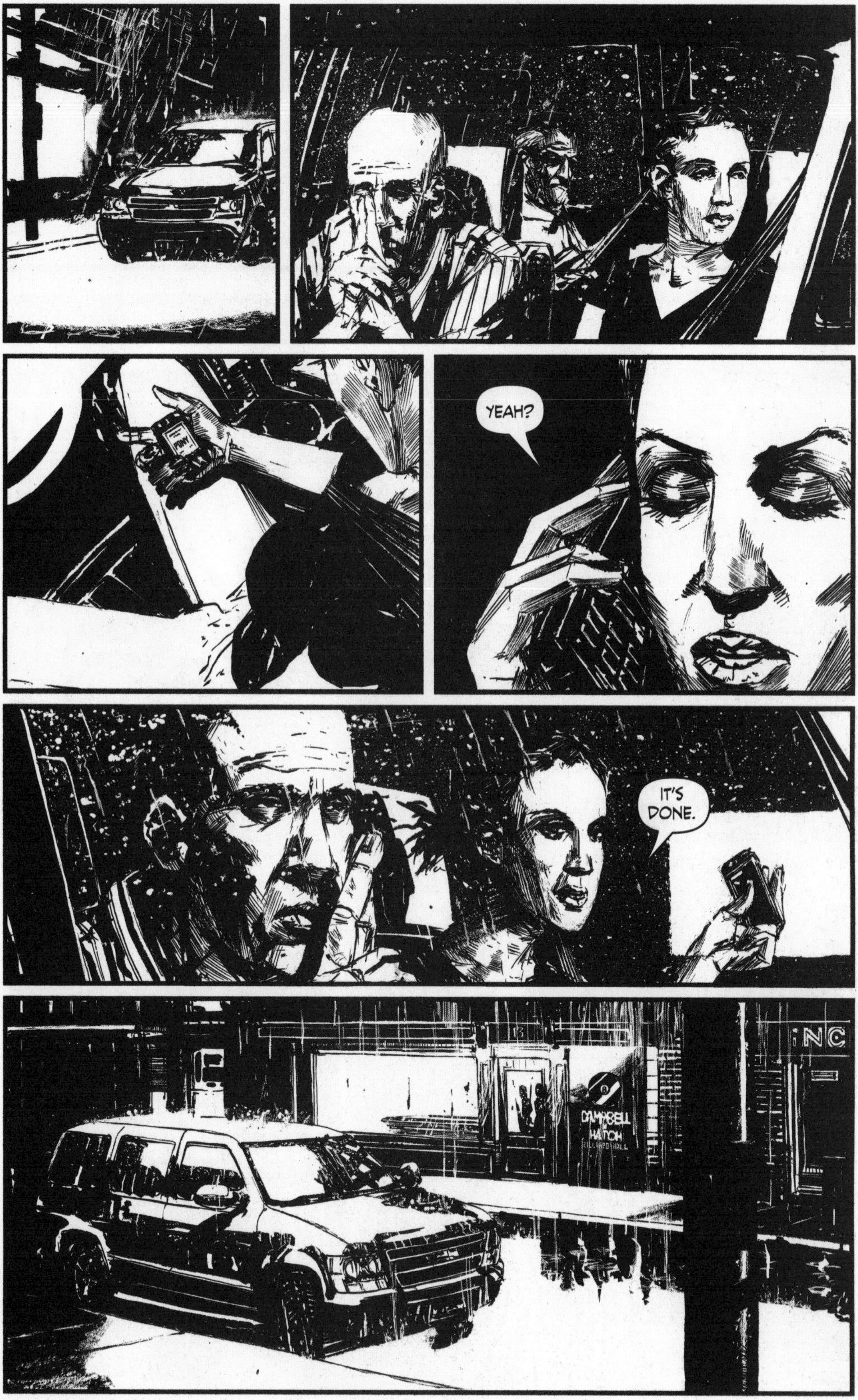
YEAH?
IT'S DONE.

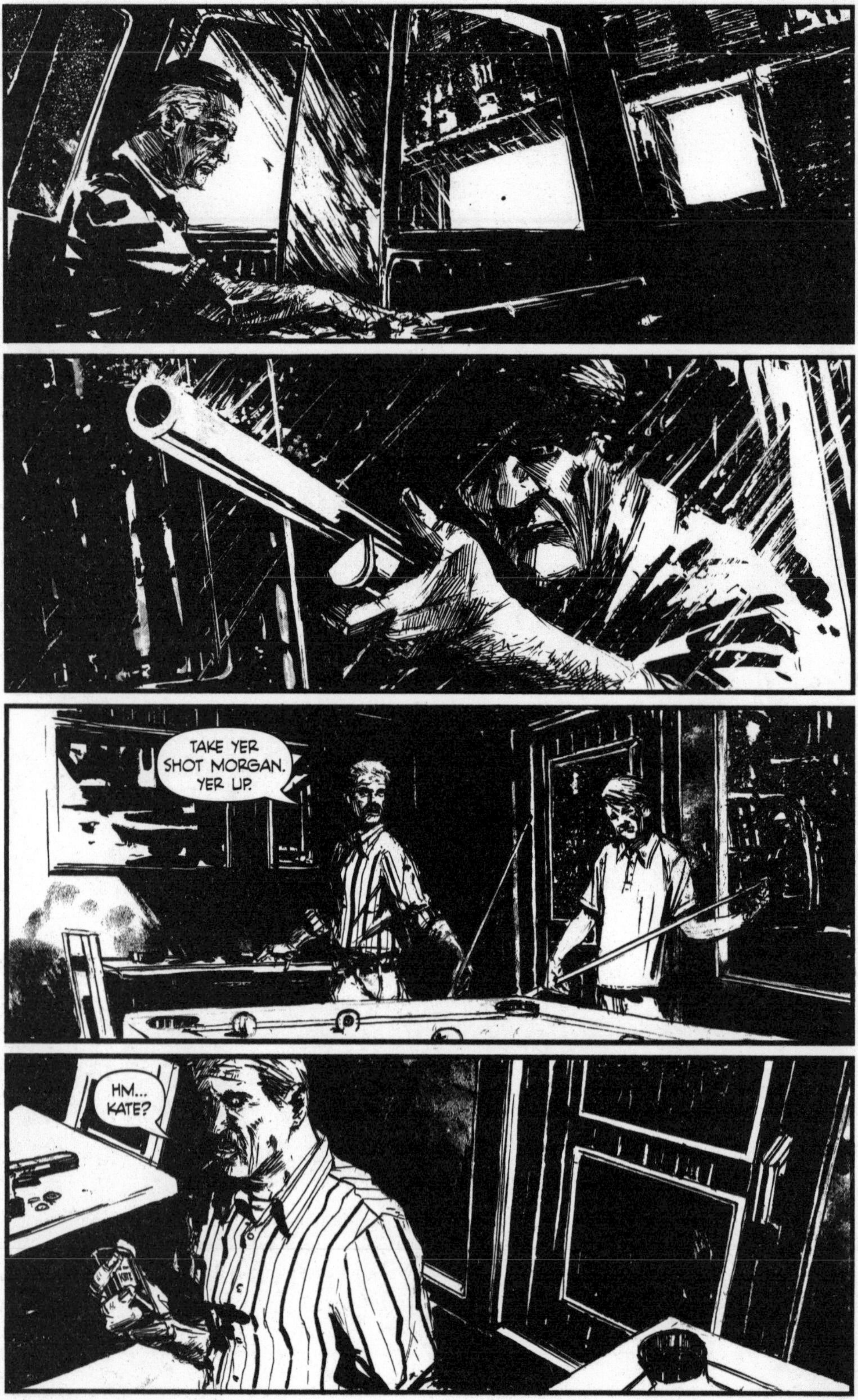
TAKE YER SHOT MORGAN. YER UP.
HM... KATE?

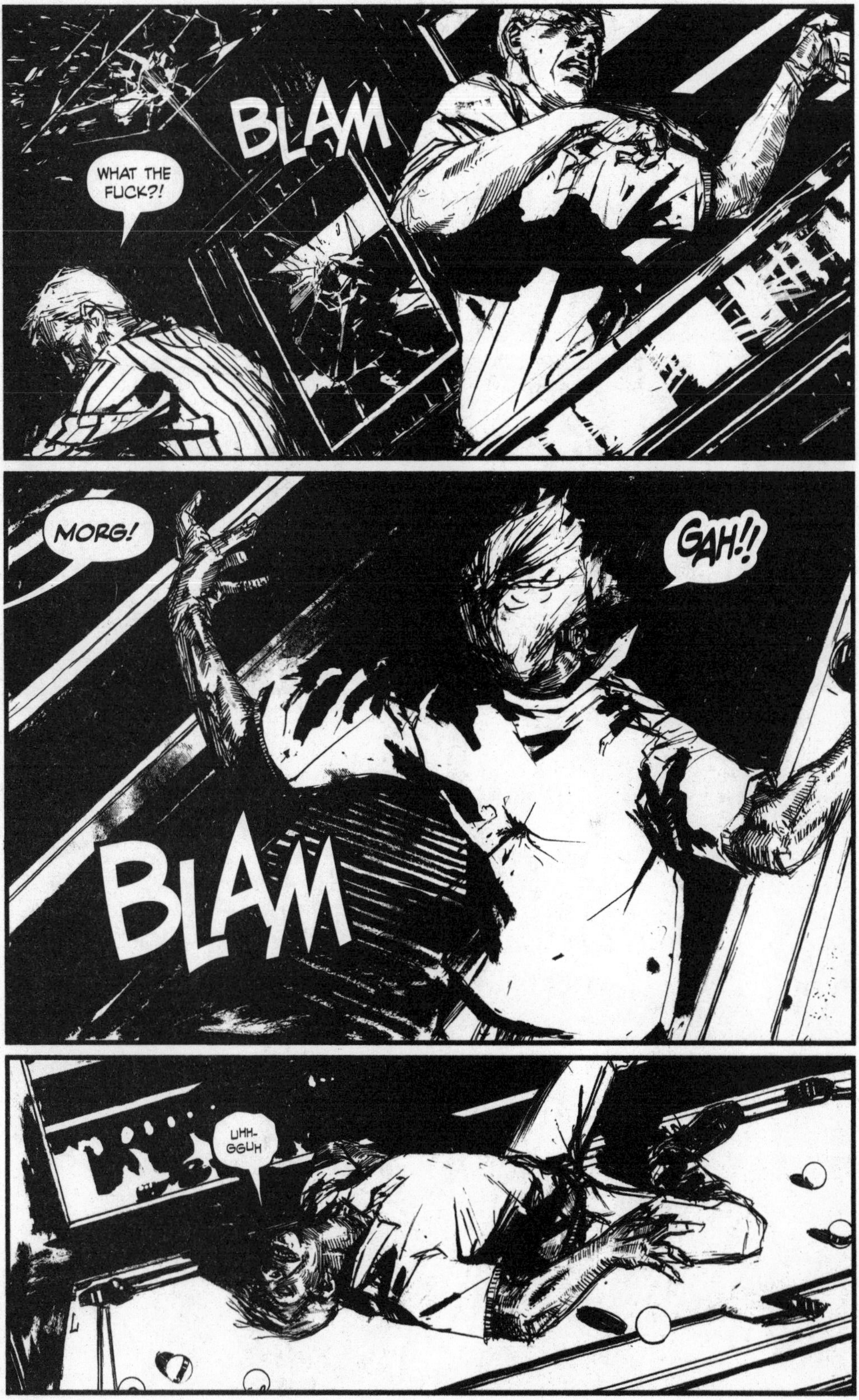
BLAM
WHAT THE FUCK?!
MORG!
GAH!!
BLAM
UHH-GGUH

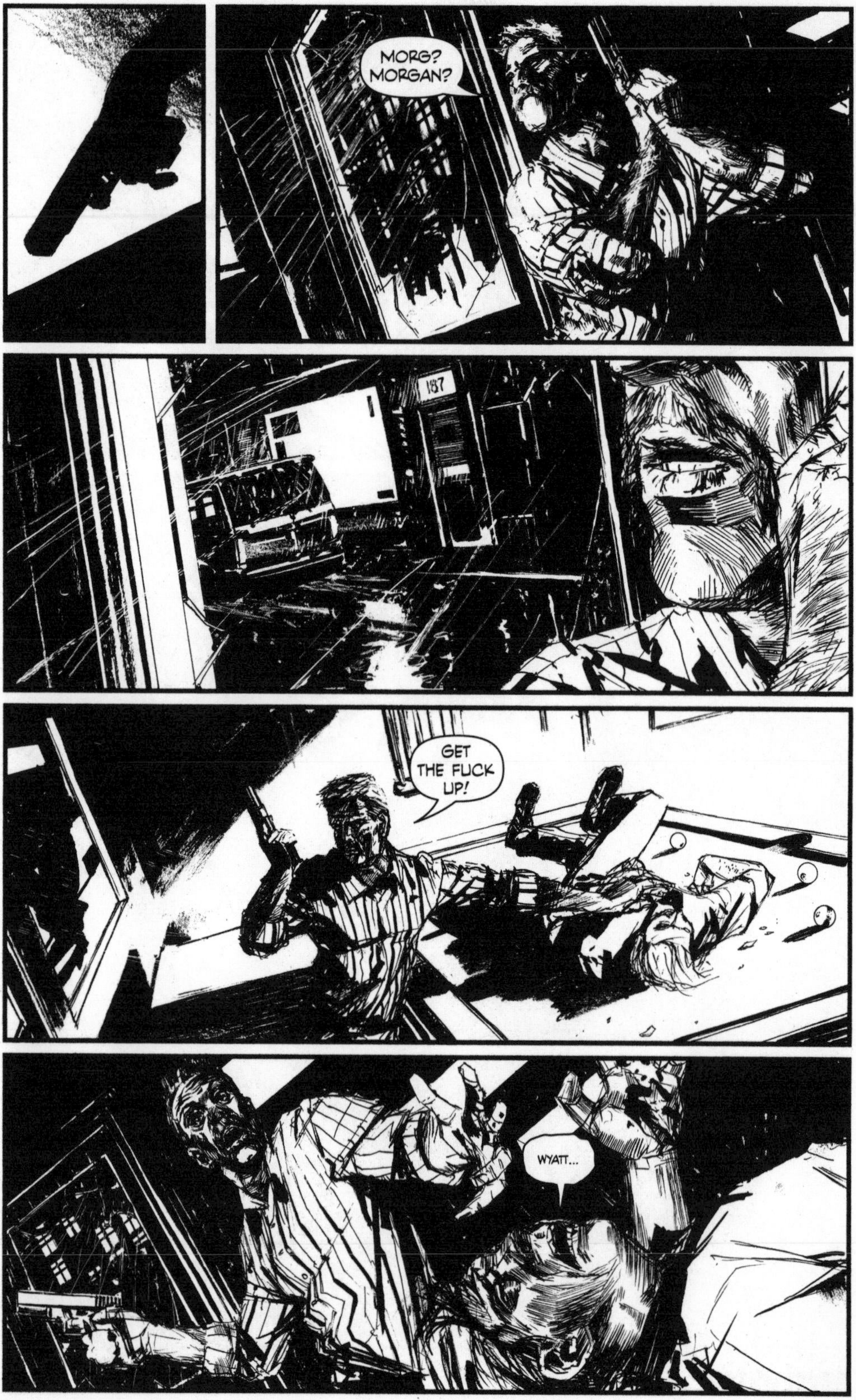
MORG? MORGAN?
GET THE FUCK UP!
WYATT...

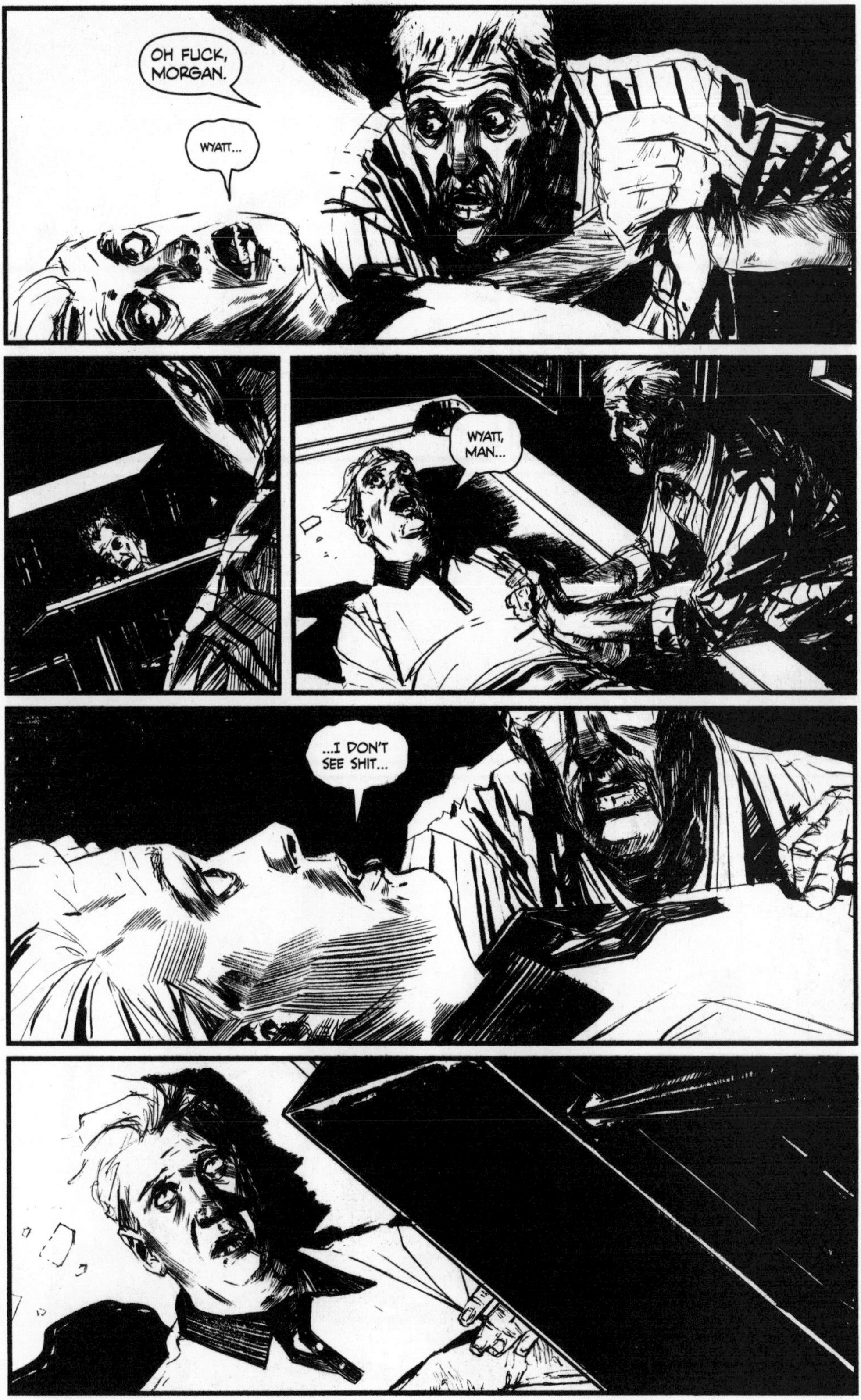
OH FUCK, MORGAN.
WYATT...
WYATT, MAN...
...I DON'T SEE SHIT...

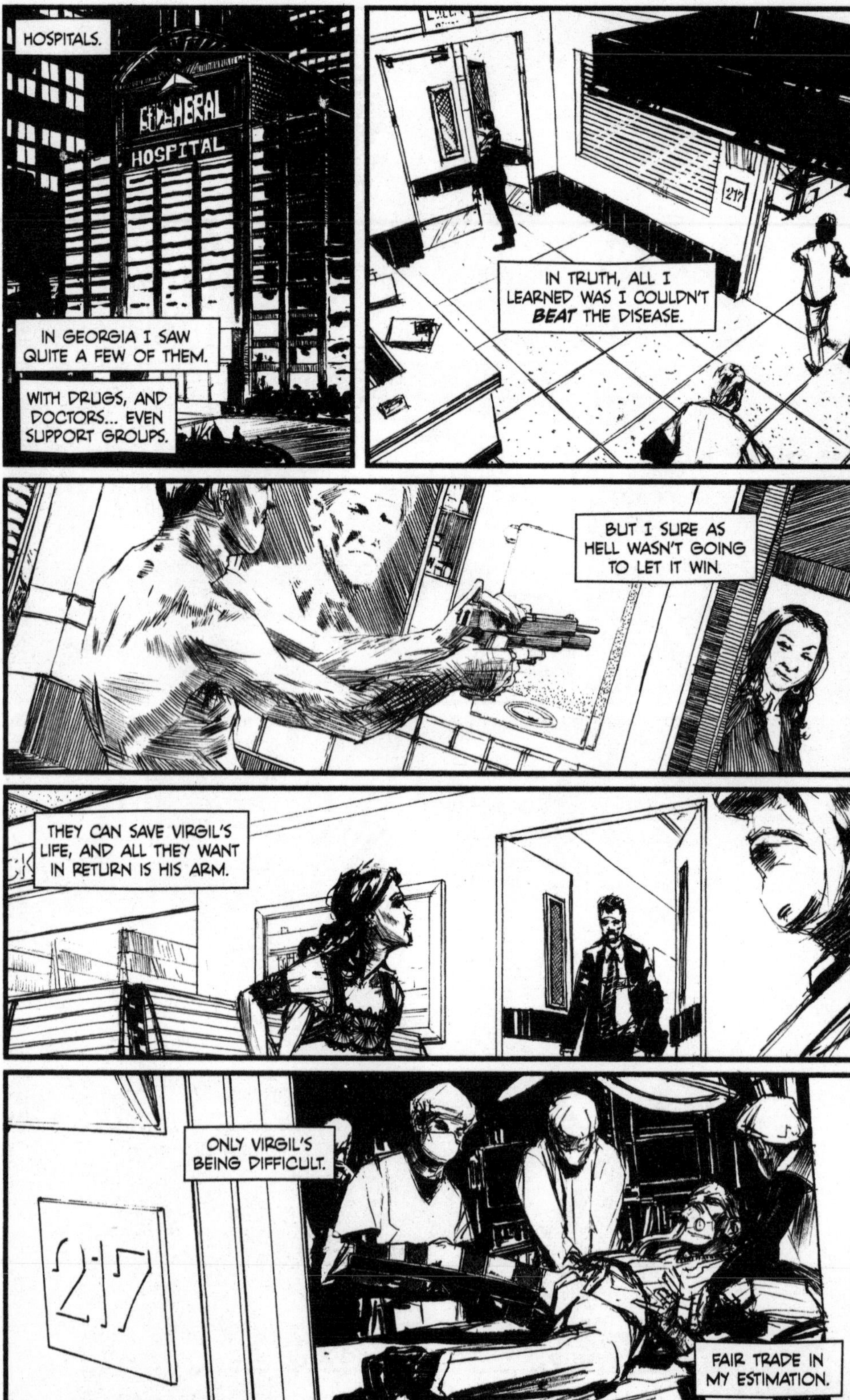
HOSPITALS.
IN GEORGIA I SAW QUITE A FEW OF THEM.
WITH DRUGS, AND DOCTORS... EVEN SUPPORT GROUPS.
IN TRUTH, ALL I LEARNED WAS I COULDN'T BEAT THE DISEASE.
BUT I SURE AS HELL WASN'T GOING TO LET IT WIN.
THEY CAN SAVE VIRGIL'S LIFE, AND ALL THEY WANT IN RETURN IS HIS ARM.
ONLY VIRGIL'S BEING DIFFICULT.
FAIR TRADE IN MY ESTIMATION.

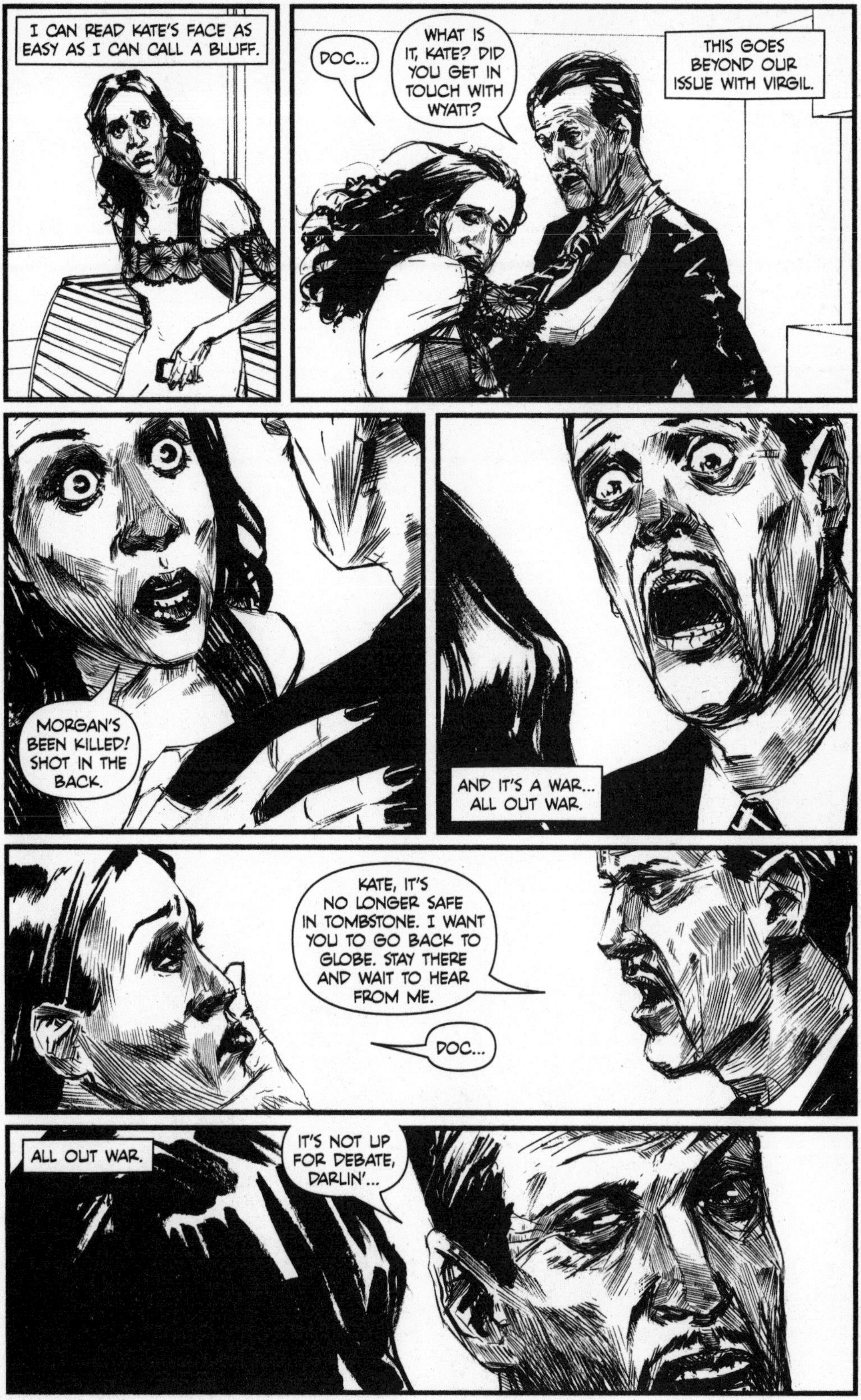
I CAN READ KATE'S FACE AS EASY AS I CAN CALL A BLUFF.
DOC...
WHAT IS IT, KATE? DID YOU GET IN TOUCH WITH WYATT?
THIS GOES BEYOND OUR ISSUE WITH VIRGIL.
MORGAN'S BEEN KILLED! SHOT IN THE BACK.
AND IT'S A WAR... ALL OUT WAR.
KATE, IT'S NO LONGER SAFE IN TOMBSTONE. I WANT YOU TO GO BACK TO GLOBE. STAY THERE AND WAIT TO HEAR FROM ME.
DOC...
ALL OUT WAR.
IT'S NOT UP FOR DEBATE, DARLIN'...

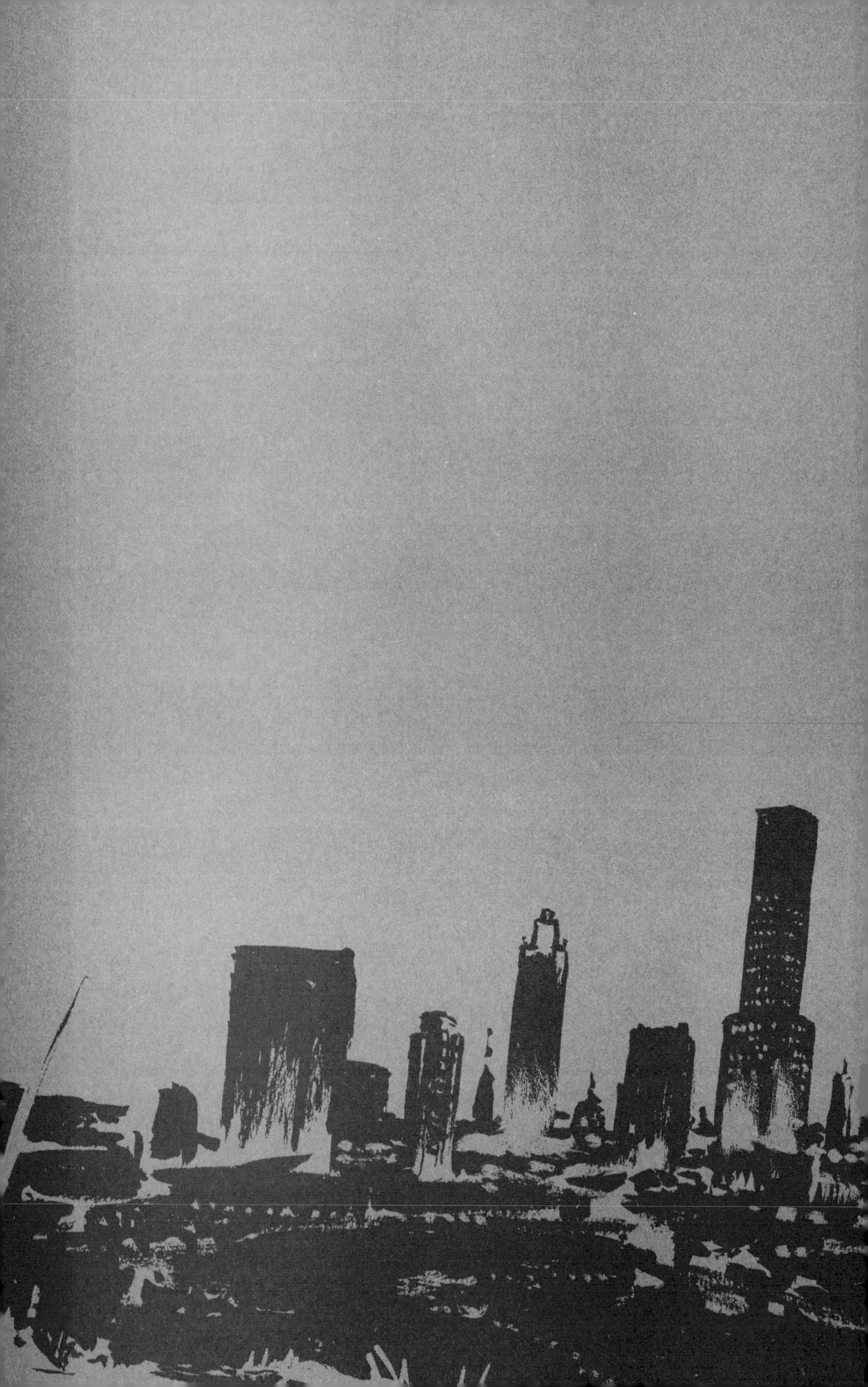

CHAPTER EIGHT

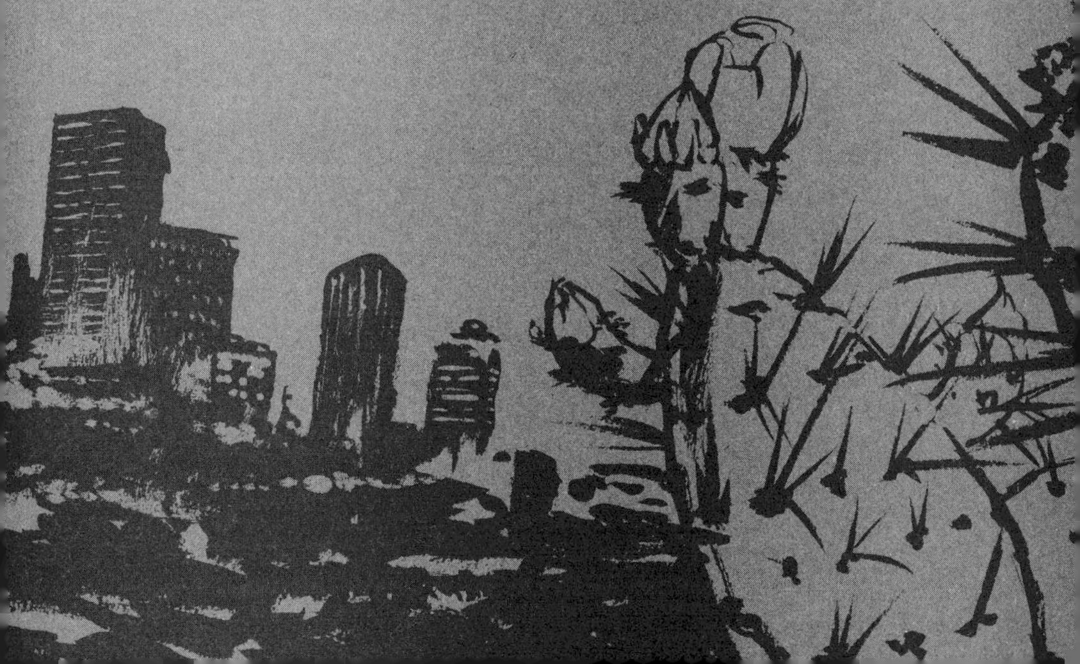

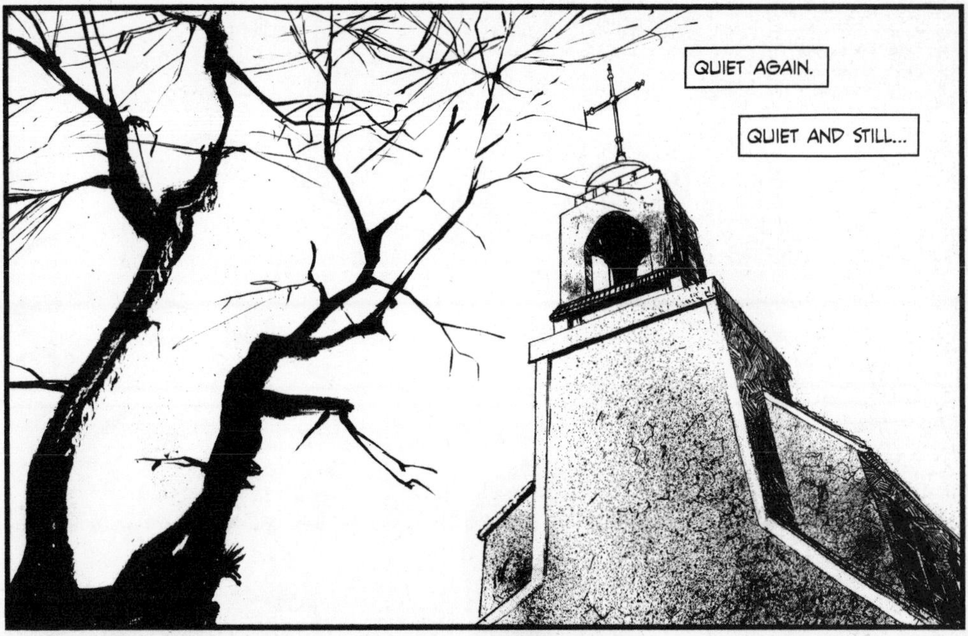
QUIET AGAIN.
QUIET AND STILL...

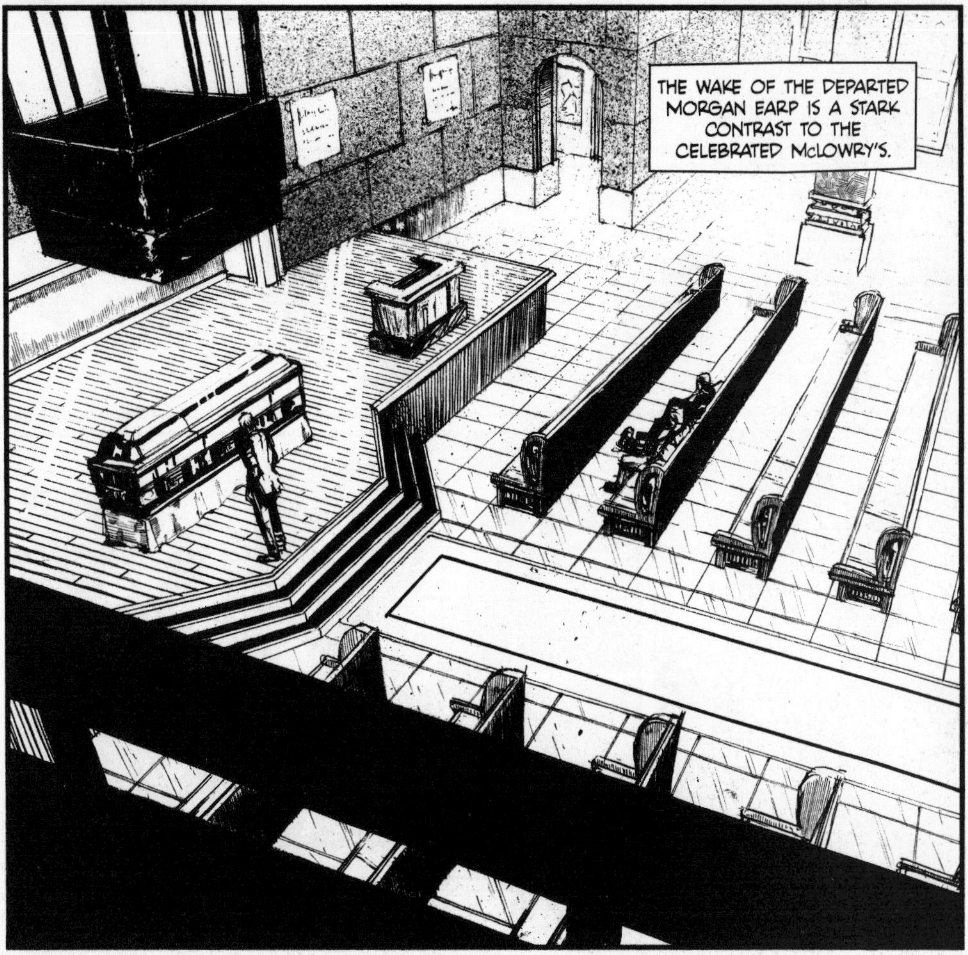
THE WAKE OF THE DEPARTED MORGAN EARP IS A STARK CONTRAST TO THE CELEBRATED McLOWRY'S.

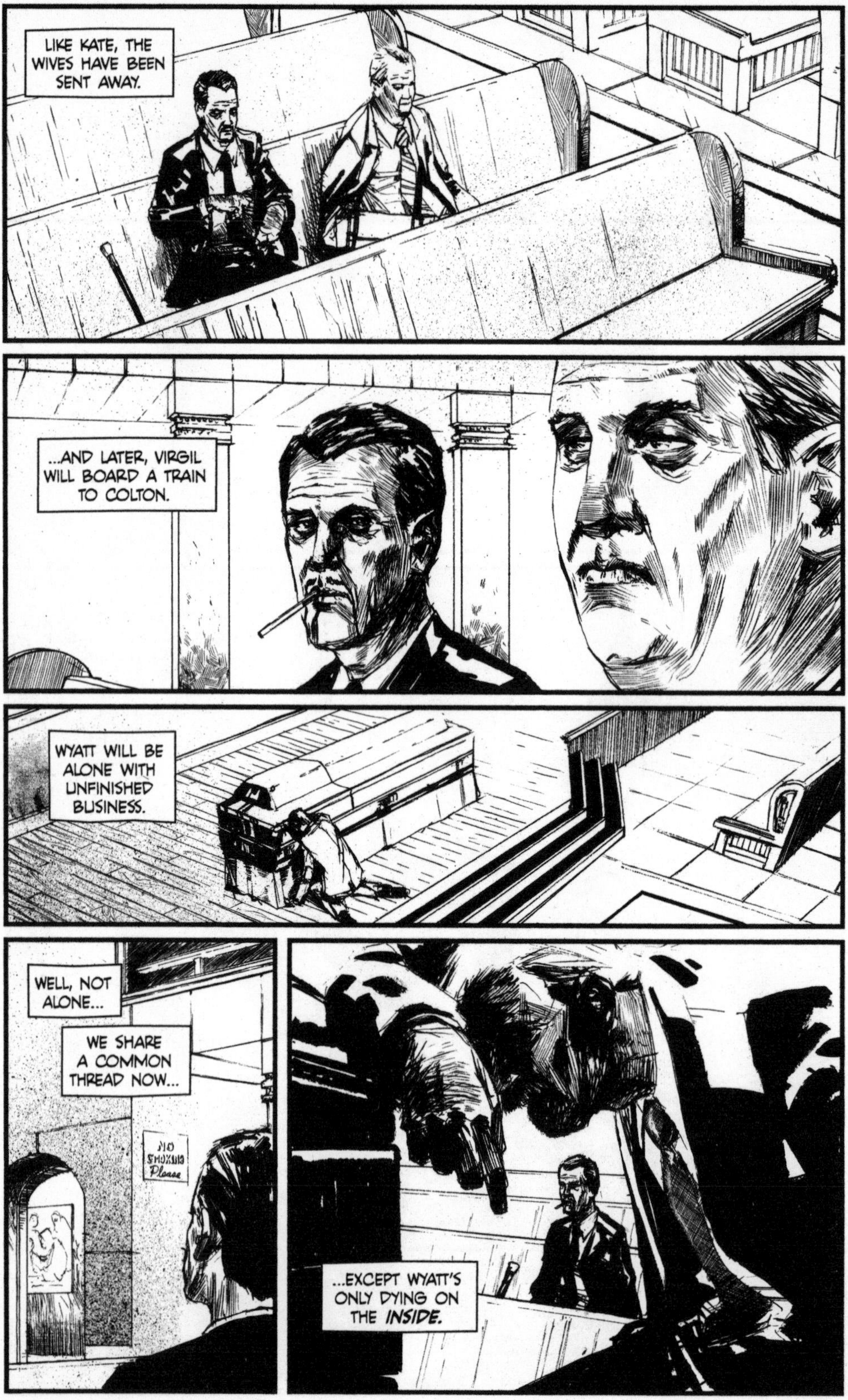
LIKE KATE, THE WIVES HAVE BEEN SENT AWAY.
...AND LATER, VIRGIL WILL BOARD A TRAIN TO COLTON.
WYATT WILL BE ALONE WITH UNFINISHED BUSINESS.
WELL, NOT ALONE...
WE SHARE A COMMON THREAD NOW...
...EXCEPT WYATT'S ONLY DYING ON THE *INSIDE.*

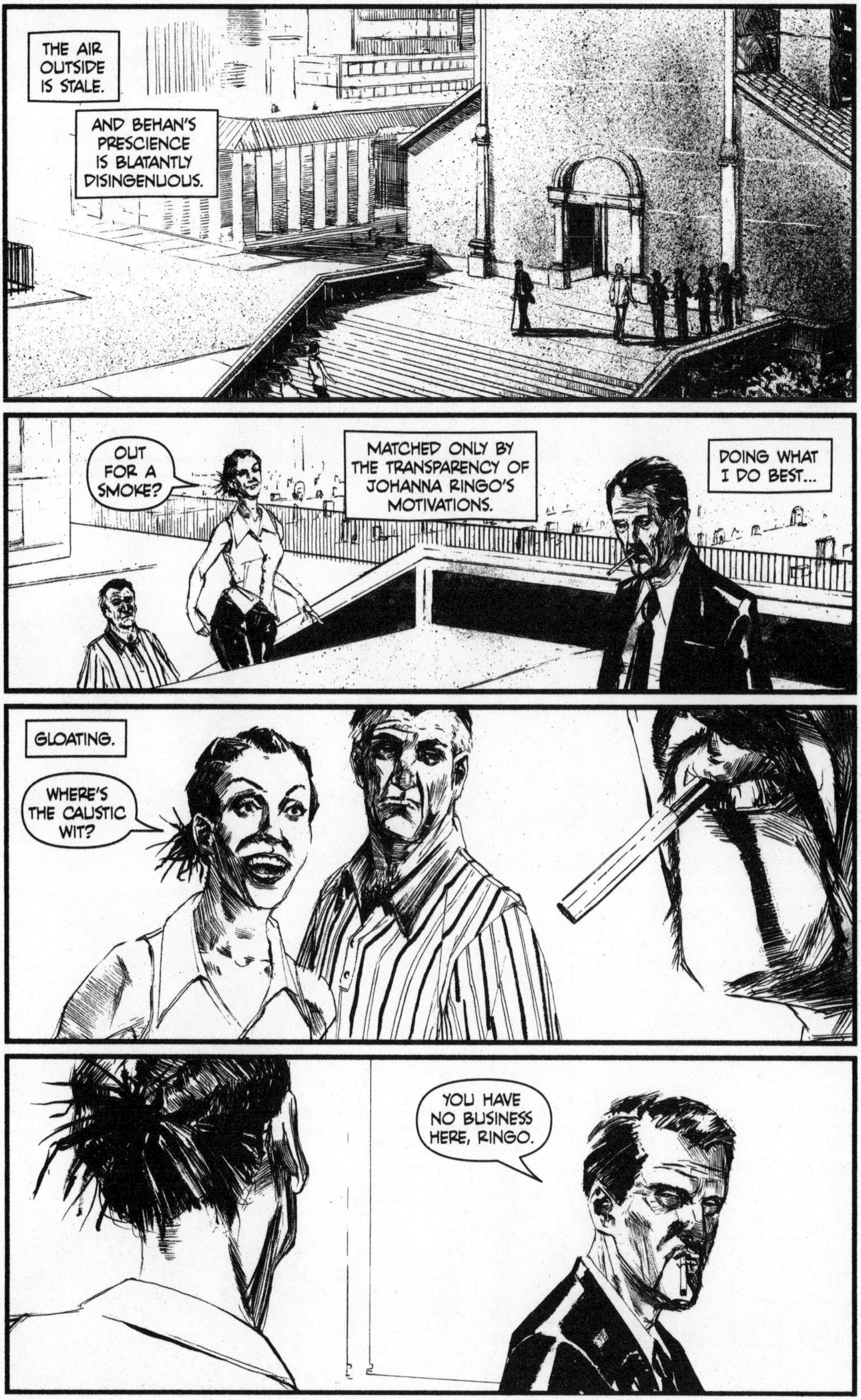
THE AIR OUTSIDE IS STALE.
AND BEHAN'S PRESCIENCE IS BLATANTLY DISINGENUOUS.
OUT FOR A SMOKE?
MATCHED ONLY BY THE TRANSPARENCY OF JOHANNA RINGO'S MOTIVATIONS.
DOING WHAT I DO BEST...
GLOATING.
WHERE'S THE CAUSTIC WIT?
YOU HAVE NO BUSINESS HERE, RINGO.

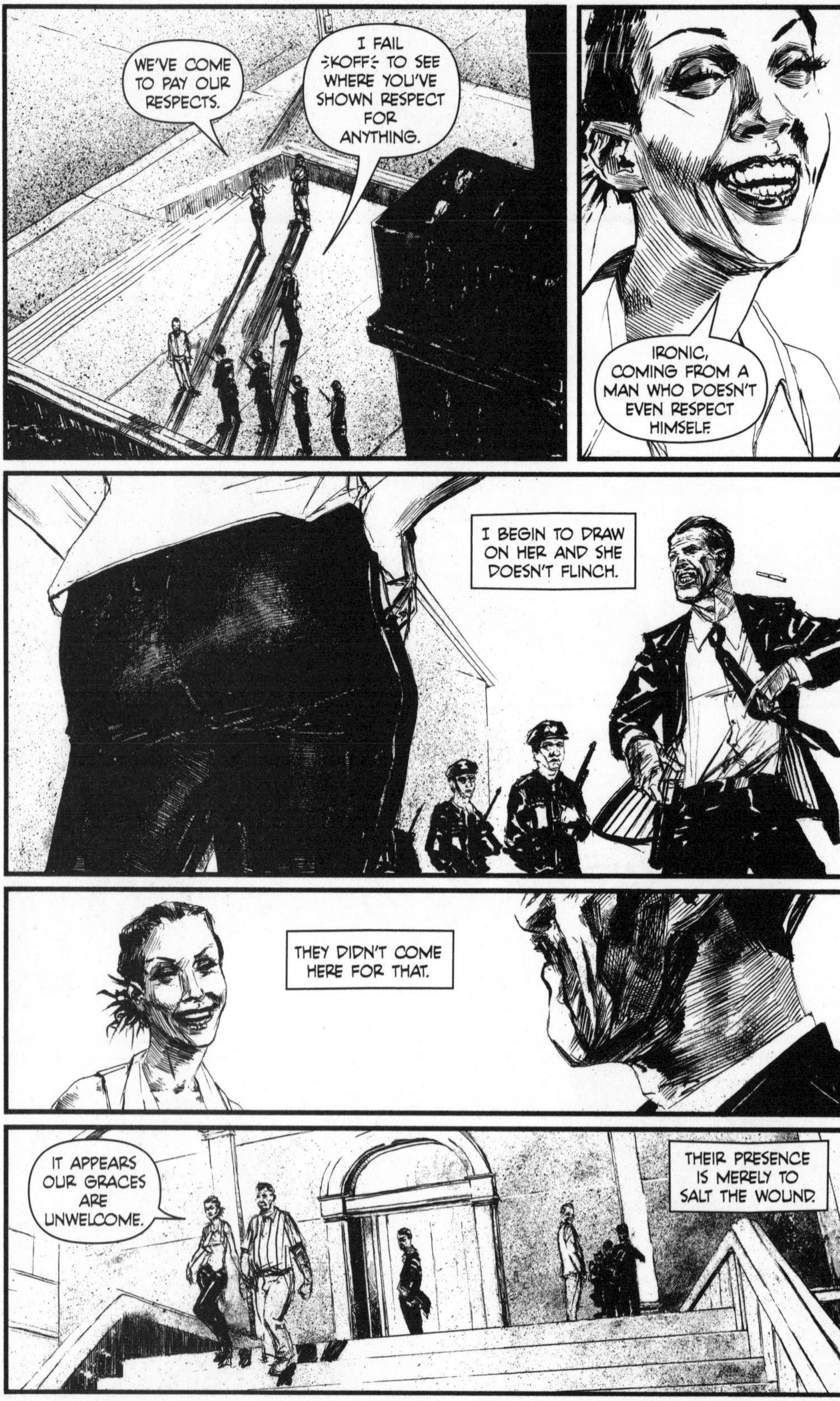
WE'VE COME TO PAY OUR RESPECTS.
I FAIL ≑KOFF≑ TO SEE WHERE YOU'VE SHOWN RESPECT FOR ANYTHING.
IRONIC, COMING FROM A MAN WHO DOESN'T EVEN RESPECT HIMSELF.
I BEGIN TO DRAW ON HER AND SHE DOESN'T FLINCH.
THEY DIDN'T COME HERE FOR THAT.
IT APPEARS OUR GRACES ARE UNWELCOME.
THEIR PRESENCE IS MERELY TO SALT THE WOUND.

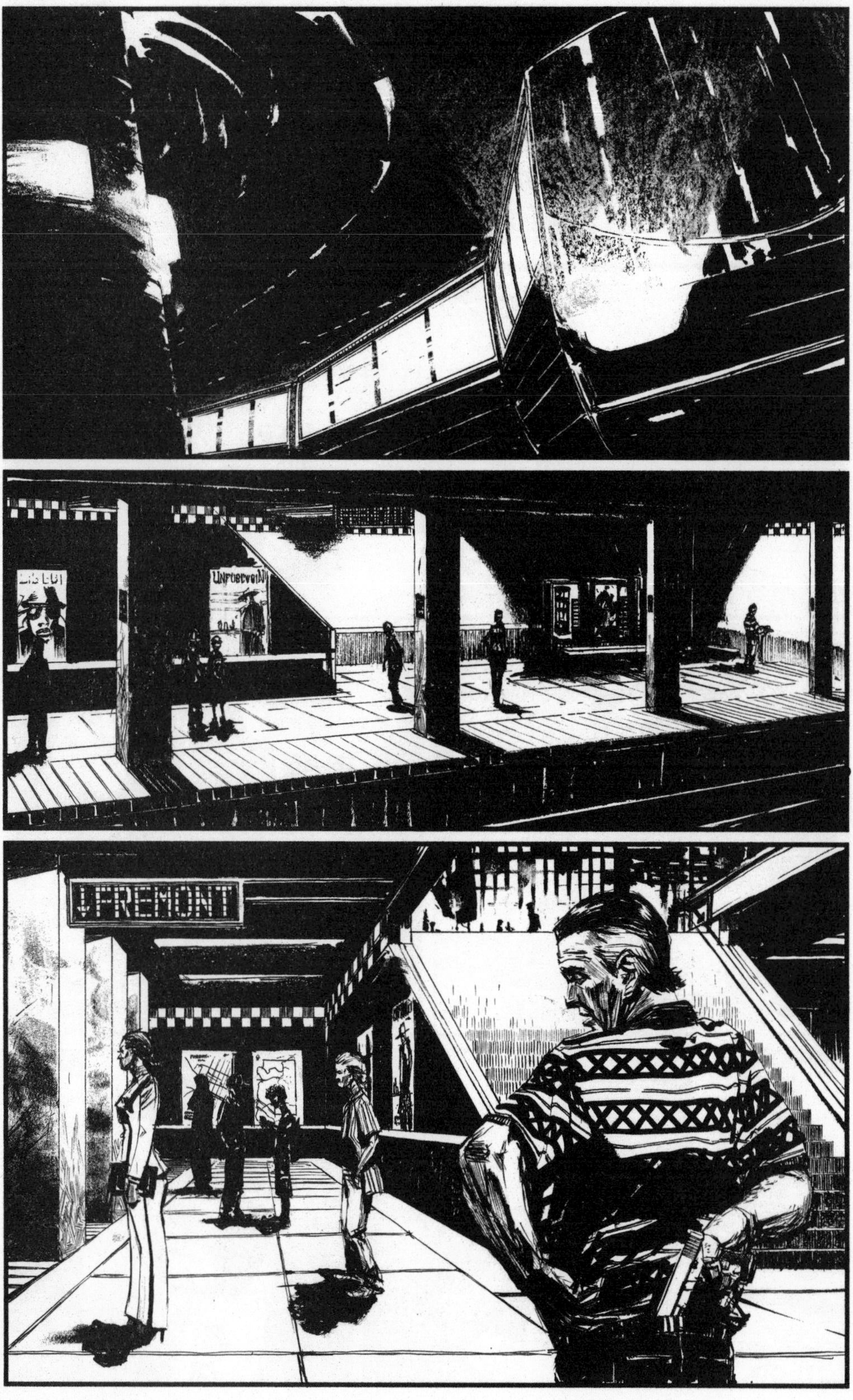
FREMONT

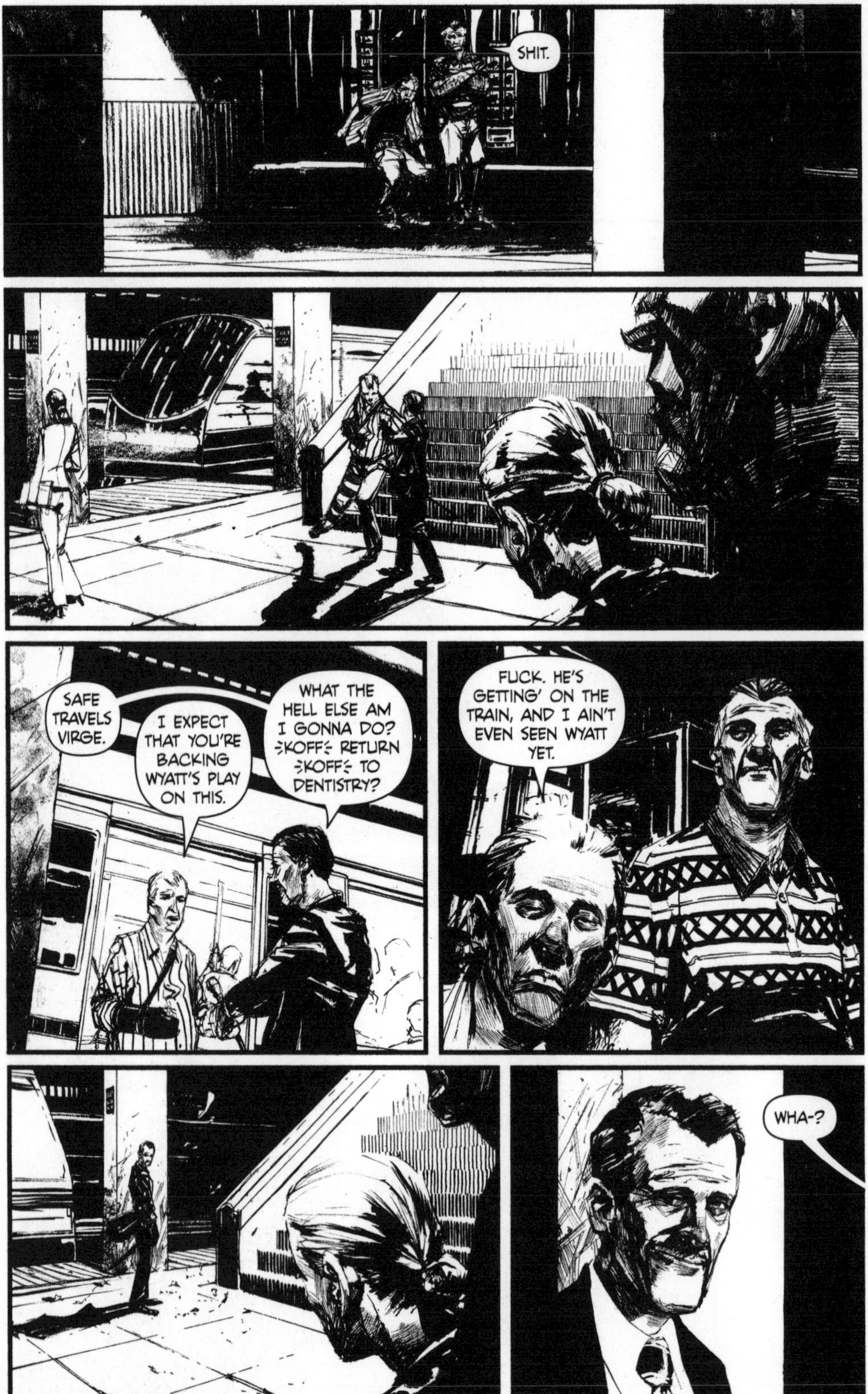

SHIT.
SAFE TRAVELS VIRGE.
I EXPECT THAT YOU'RE BACKING WYATT'S PLAY ON THIS.
WHAT THE HELL ELSE AM I GONNA DO? *KOFF* RETURN *KOFF* TO DENTISTRY?
FUCK. HE'S GETTING' ON THE TRAIN, AND I AIN'T EVEN SEEN WYATT YET.
WHA-?

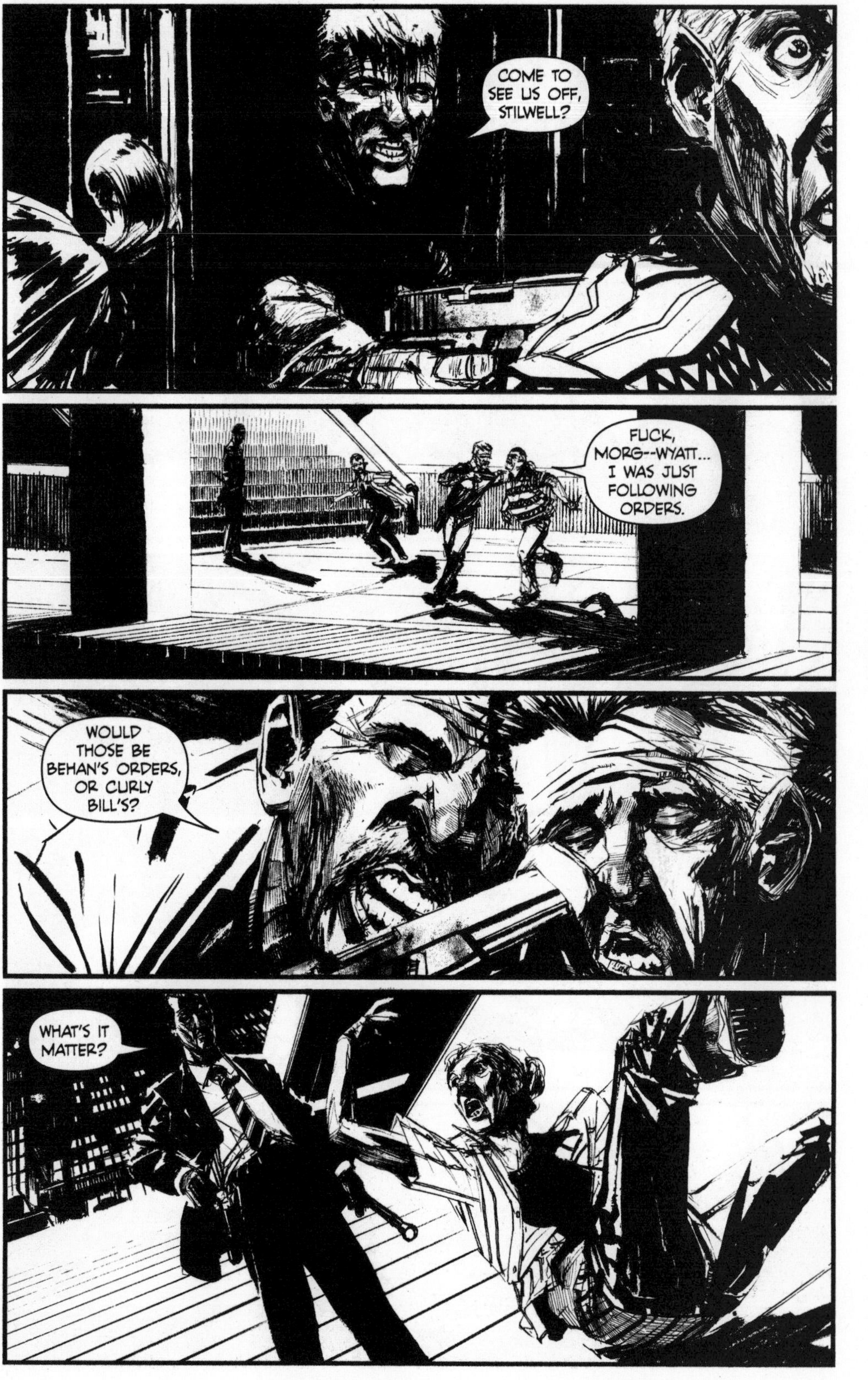
COME TO SEE US OFF, STILWELL?
FUCK, MORG--WYATT... I WAS JUST FOLLOWING ORDERS.
WOULD THOSE BE BEHAN'S ORDERS, OR CURLY BILL'S?
WHAT'S IT MATTER?

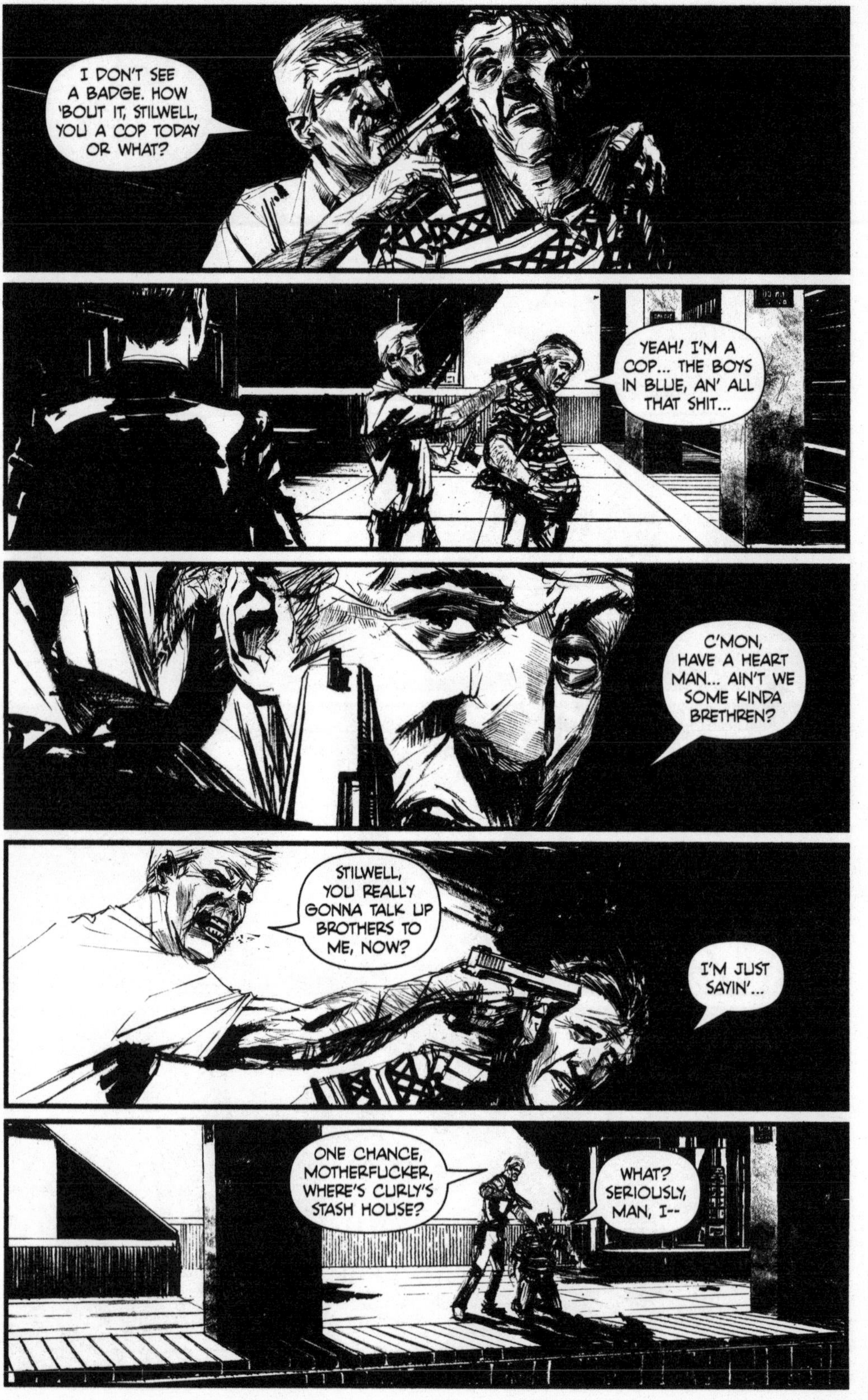
I DON'T SEE A BADGE. HOW 'BOUT IT, STILWELL, YOU A COP TODAY OR WHAT?
YEAH! I'M A COP... THE BOYS IN BLUE, AN' ALL THAT SHIT...
C'MON, HAVE A HEART MAN... AIN'T WE SOME KINDA BRETHREN?
STILWELL, YOU REALLY GONNA TALK UP BROTHERS TO ME, NOW?
I'M JUST SAYIN'...
ONE CHANCE, MOTHERFUCKER, WHERE'S CURLY'S STASH HOUSE?
WHAT? SERIOUSLY, MAN, I--

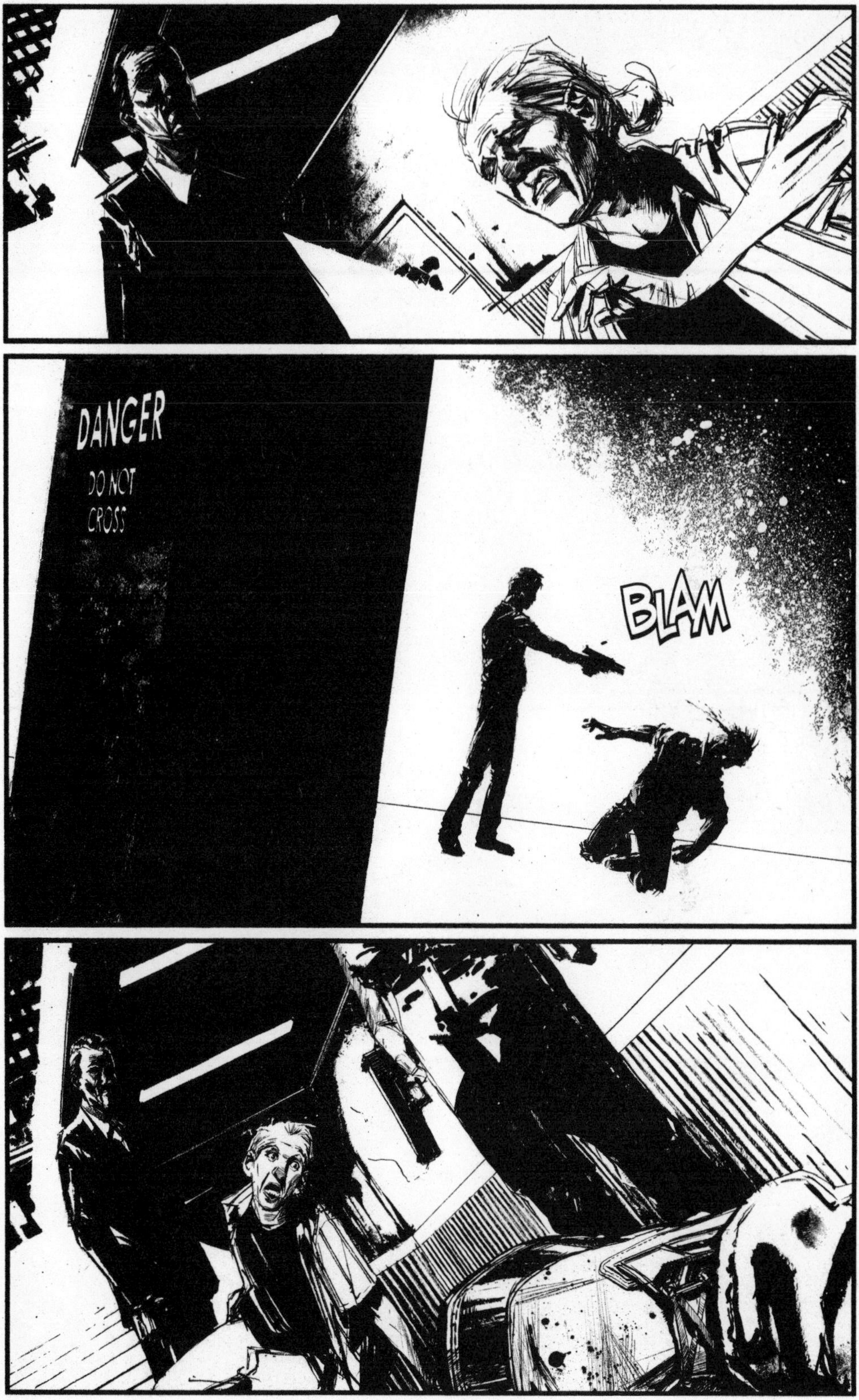
DANGER
DO NOT
CROSS
BLAM

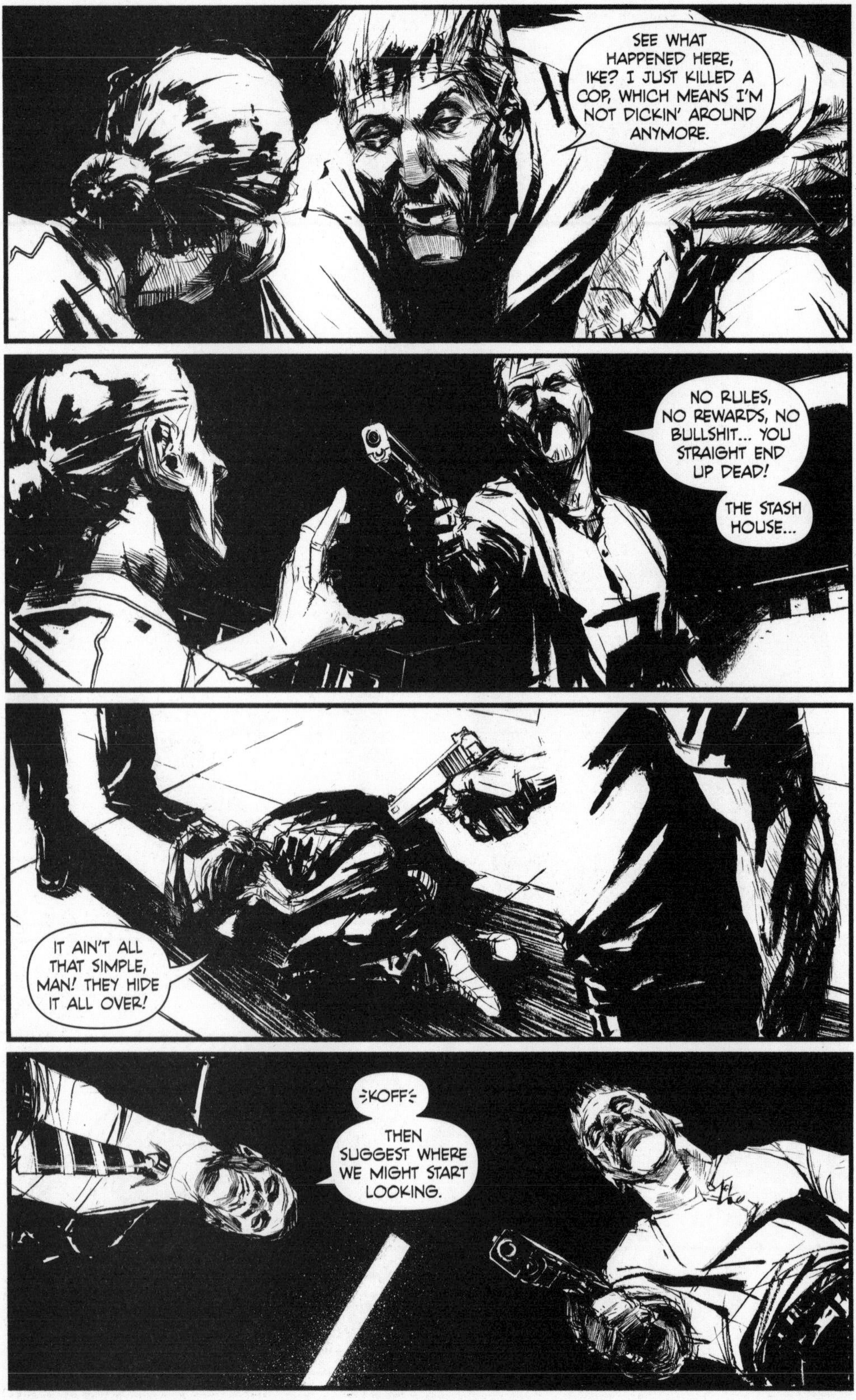
SEE WHAT HAPPENED HERE, IKE? I JUST KILLED A COP, WHICH MEANS I'M NOT DICKIN' AROUND ANYMORE.
NO RULES, NO REWARDS, NO BULLSHIT... YOU STRAIGHT END UP DEAD!
THE STASH HOUSE...
IT AIN'T ALL THAT SIMPLE, MAN! THEY HIDE IT ALL OVER!
KOFF
THEN SUGGEST WHERE WE MIGHT START LOOKING.

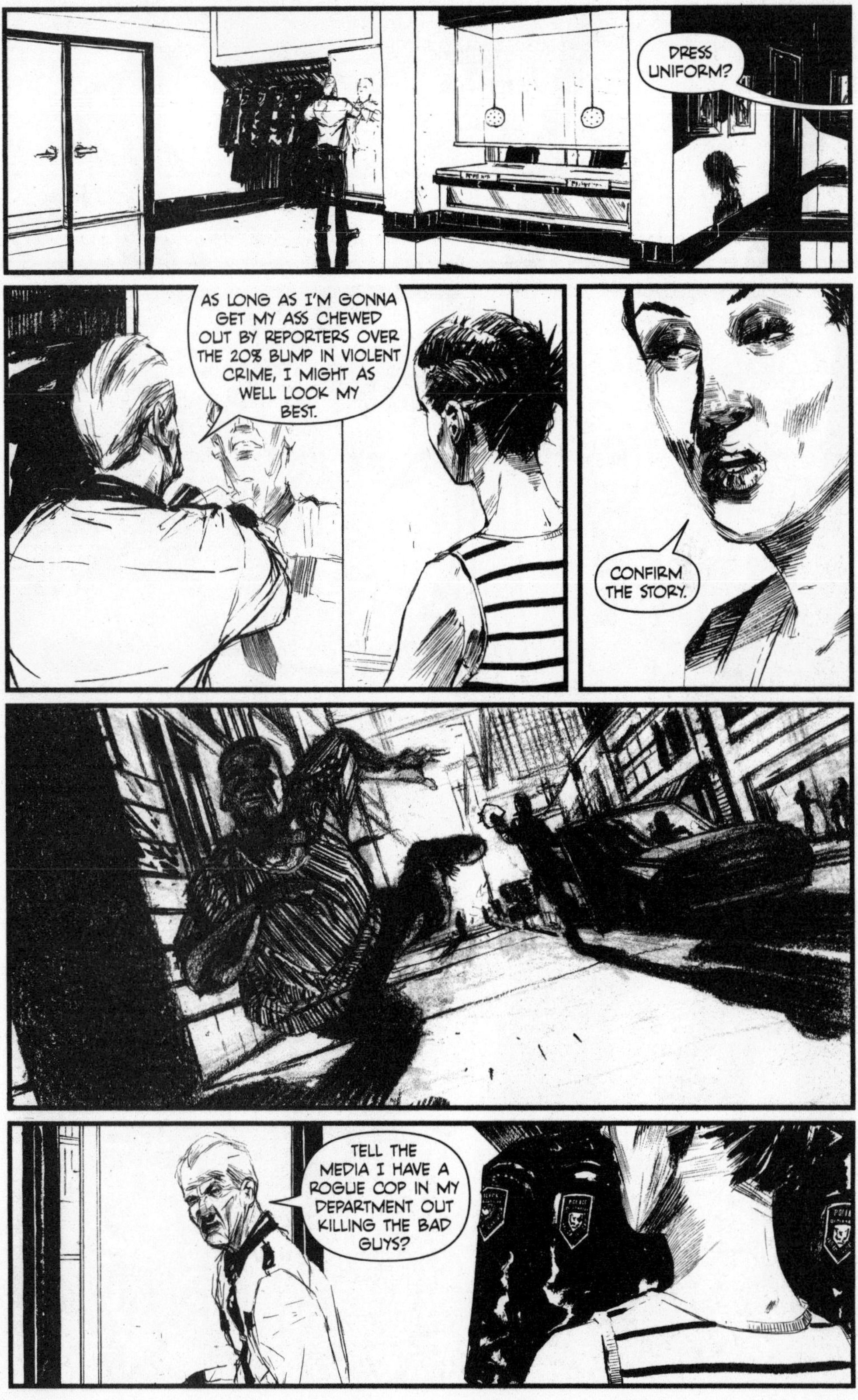
DRESS UNIFORM?
AS LONG AS I'M GONNA GET MY ASS CHEWED OUT BY REPORTERS OVER THE 20% BUMP IN VIOLENT CRIME, I MIGHT AS WELL LOOK MY BEST.
CONFIRM THE STORY.
TELL THE MEDIA I HAVE A ROGUE COP IN MY DEPARTMENT OUT KILLING THE BAD GUYS?

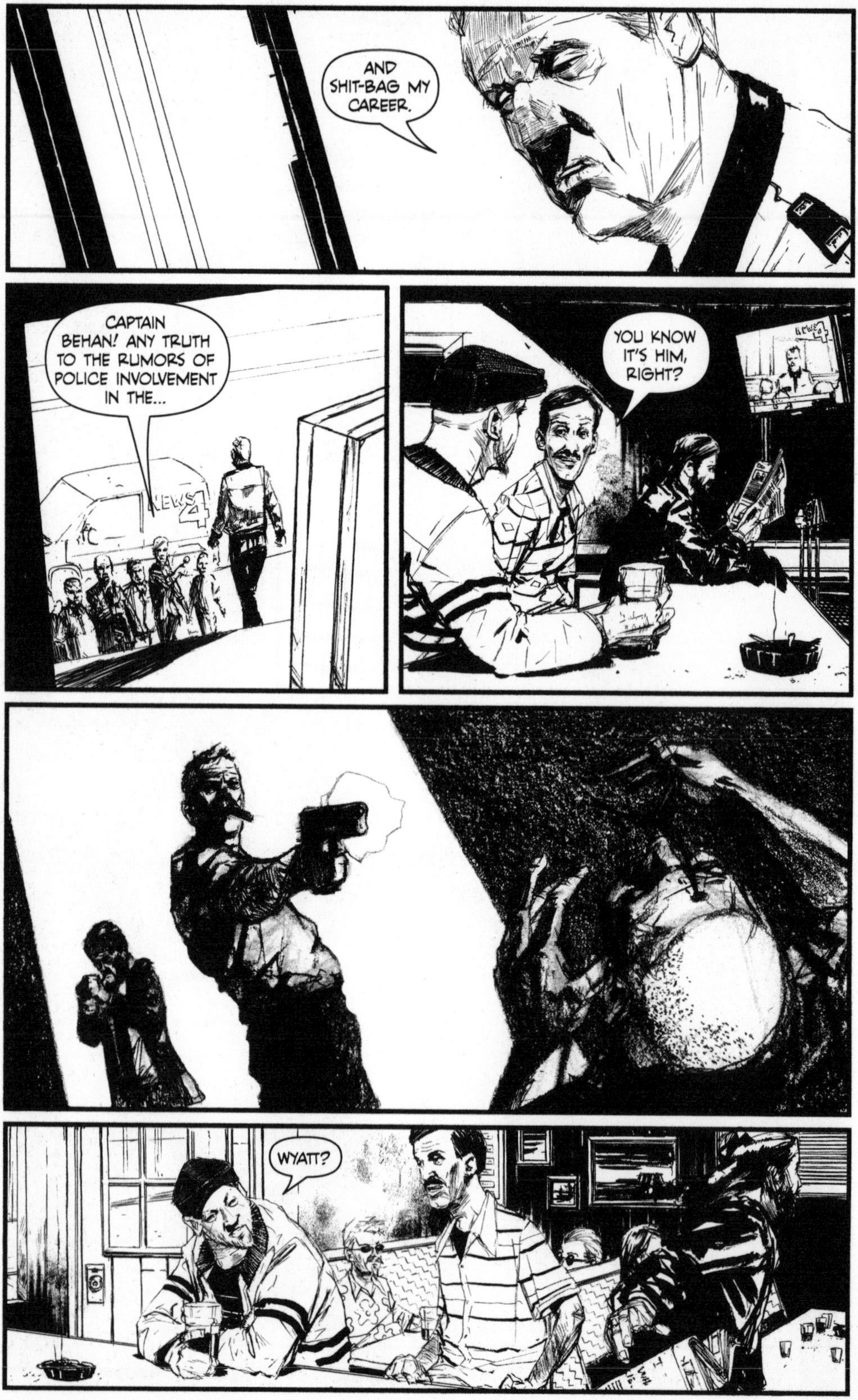
AND SHIT-BAG MY CAREER.
CAPTAIN BEHAN! ANY TRUTH TO THE RUMORS OF POLICE INVOLVEMENT IN THE...
NEWS 4
YOU KNOW IT'S HIM, RIGHT?
WYATT?

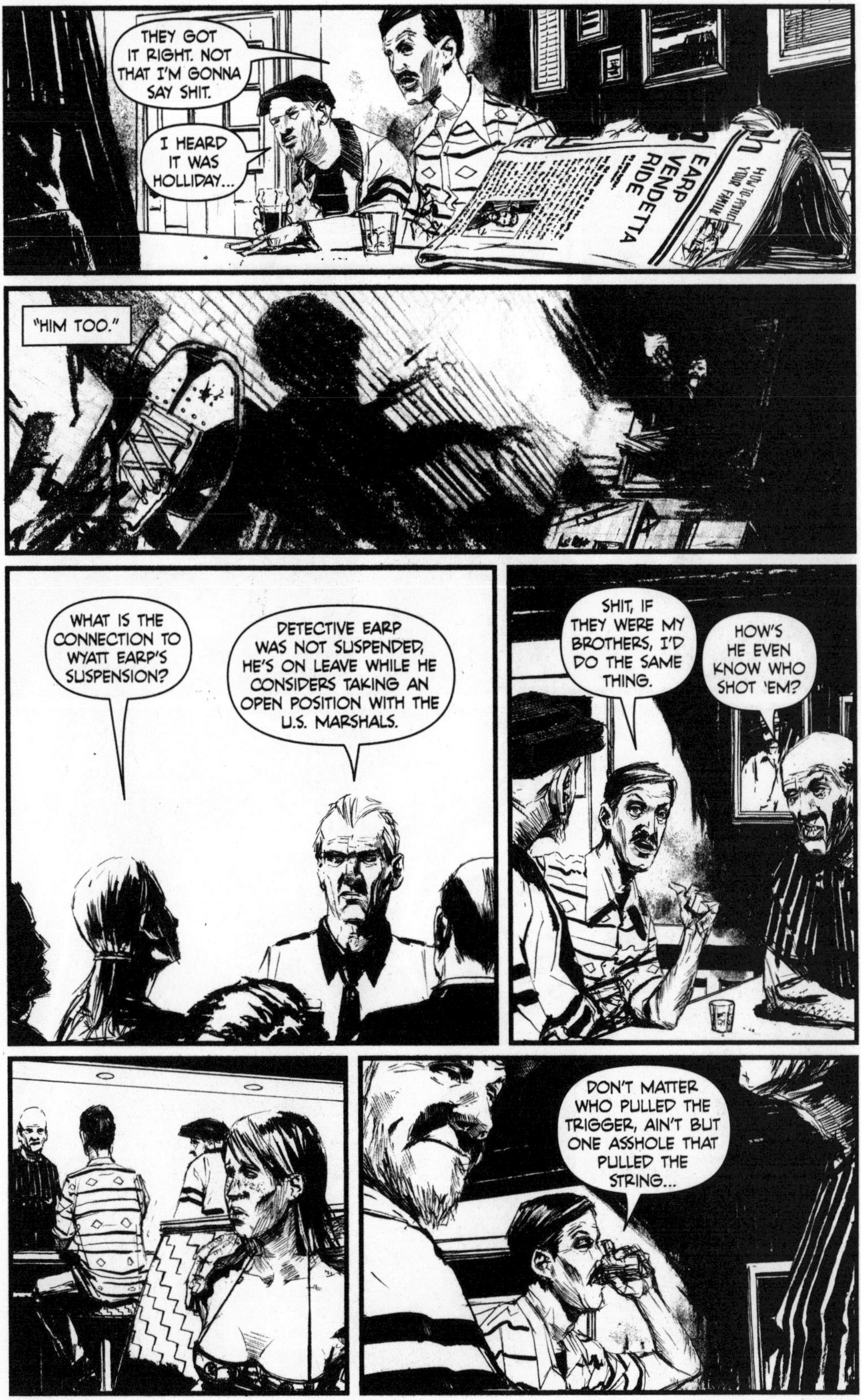
THEY GOT IT RIGHT. NOT THAT I'M GONNA SAY SHIT.
I HEARD IT WAS HOLLIDAY...
EARP VENDETTA RIDE
"HIM TOO."
WHAT IS THE CONNECTION TO WYATT EARP'S SUSPENSION?
DETECTIVE EARP WAS NOT SUSPENDED, HE'S ON LEAVE WHILE HE CONSIDERS TAKING AN OPEN POSITION WITH THE U.S. MARSHALS.
SHIT, IF THEY WERE MY BROTHERS, I'D DO THE SAME THING.
HOW'S HE EVEN KNOW WHO SHOT 'EM?
DON'T MATTER WHO PULLED THE TRIGGER, AIN'T BUT ONE ASSHOLE THAT PULLED THE STRING...

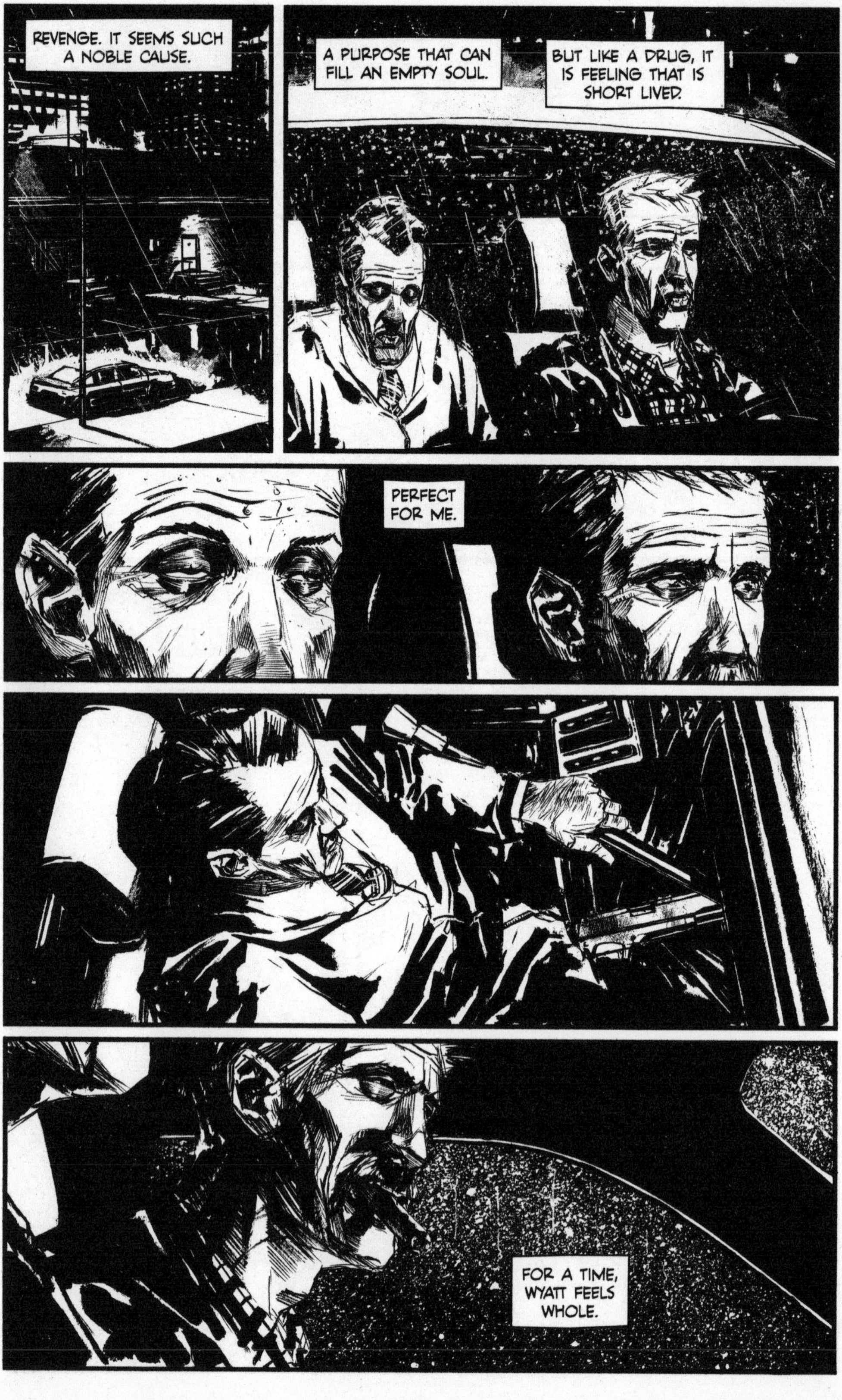
REVENGE. IT SEEMS SUCH A NOBLE CAUSE.
A PURPOSE THAT CAN FILL AN EMPTY SOUL.
BUT LIKE A DRUG, IT IS FEELING THAT IS SHORT LIVED.
PERFECT FOR ME.
FOR A TIME, WYATT FEELS WHOLE.

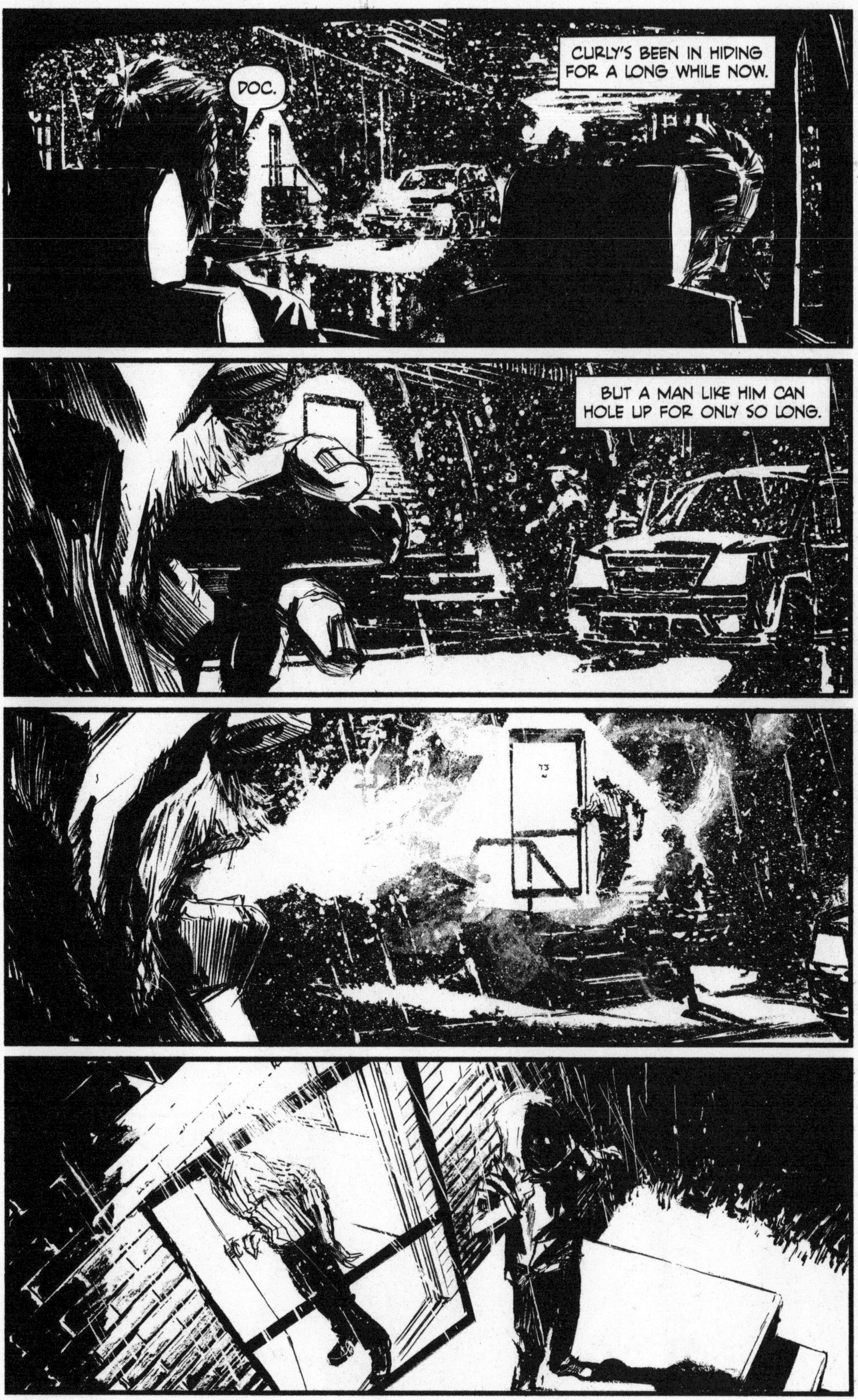
CURLY'S BEEN IN HIDING FOR A LONG WHILE NOW.
DOC.
BUT A MAN LIKE HIM CAN HOLE UP FOR ONLY SO LONG.

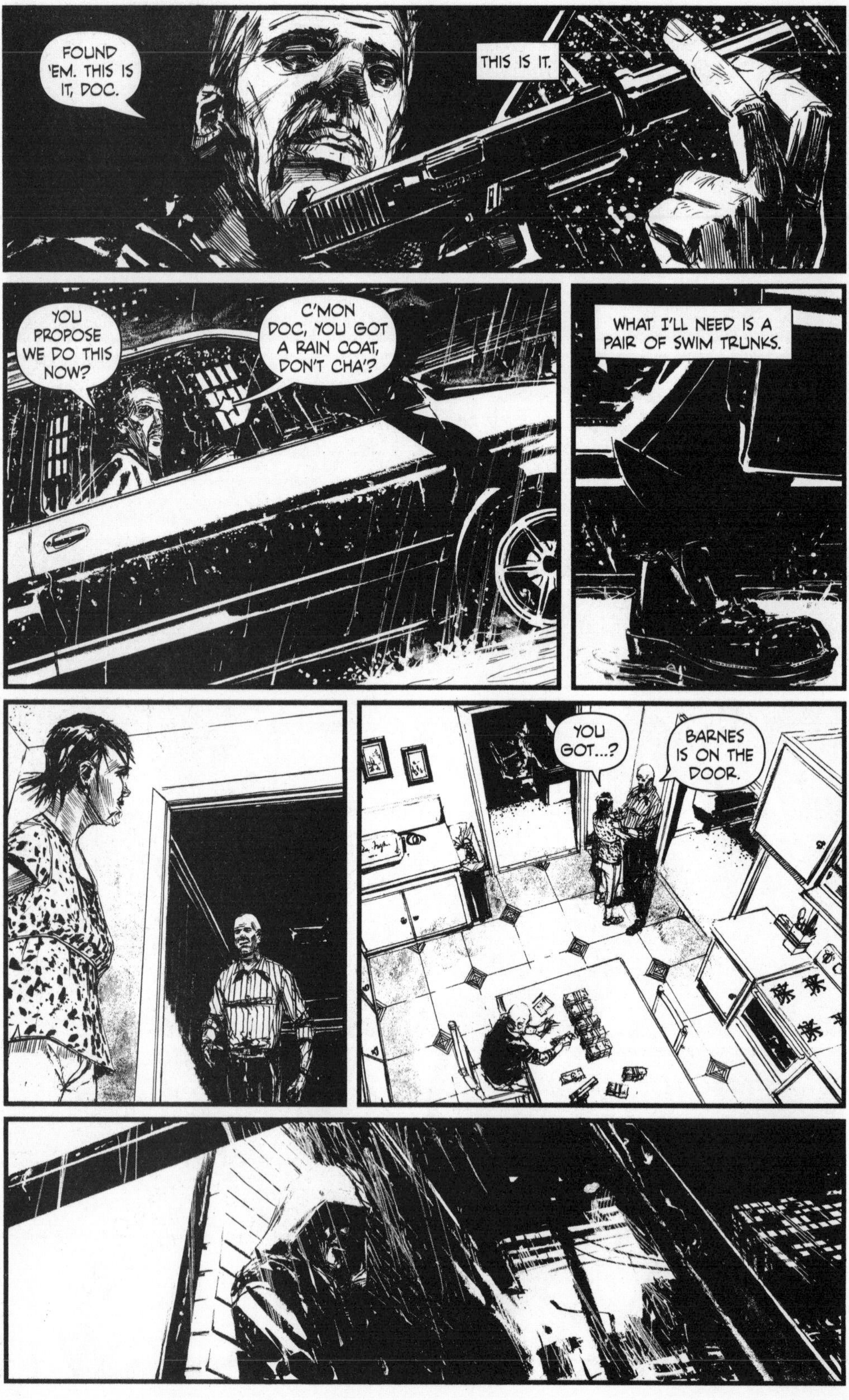
FOUND 'EM. THIS IS IT, DOC.
THIS IS IT.
YOU PROPOSE WE DO THIS NOW?
C'MON DOC, YOU GOT A RAIN COAT, DON'T CHA'?
WHAT I'LL NEED IS A PAIR OF SWIM TRUNKS.
YOU GOT...?
BARNES IS ON THE DOOR.

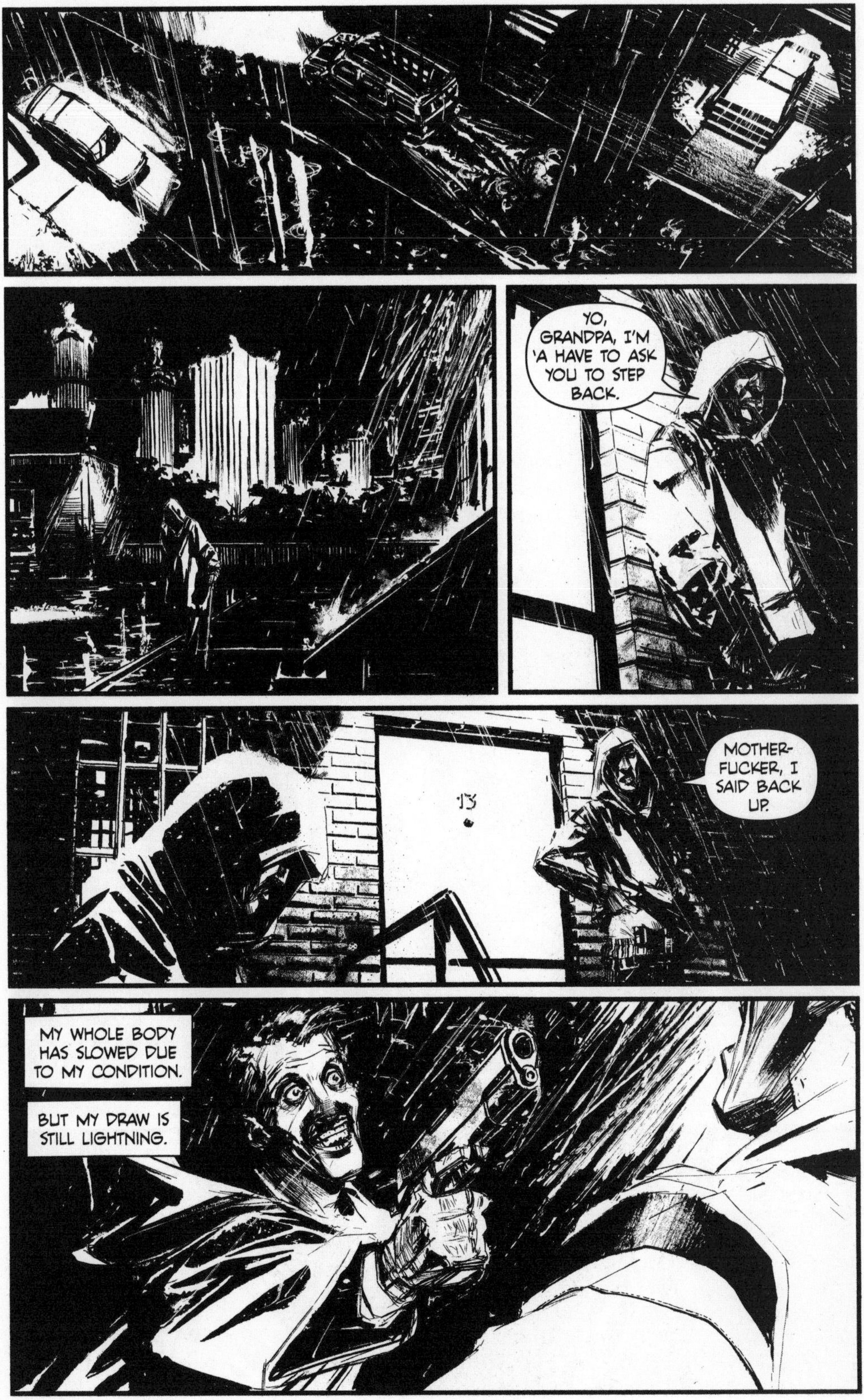
YO, GRANDPA, I'M 'A HAVE TO ASK YOU TO STEP BACK.
13
MOTHER-FUCKER, I SAID BACK UP.
MY WHOLE BODY HAS SLOWED DUE TO MY CONDITION.
BUT MY DRAW IS STILL LIGHTNING.

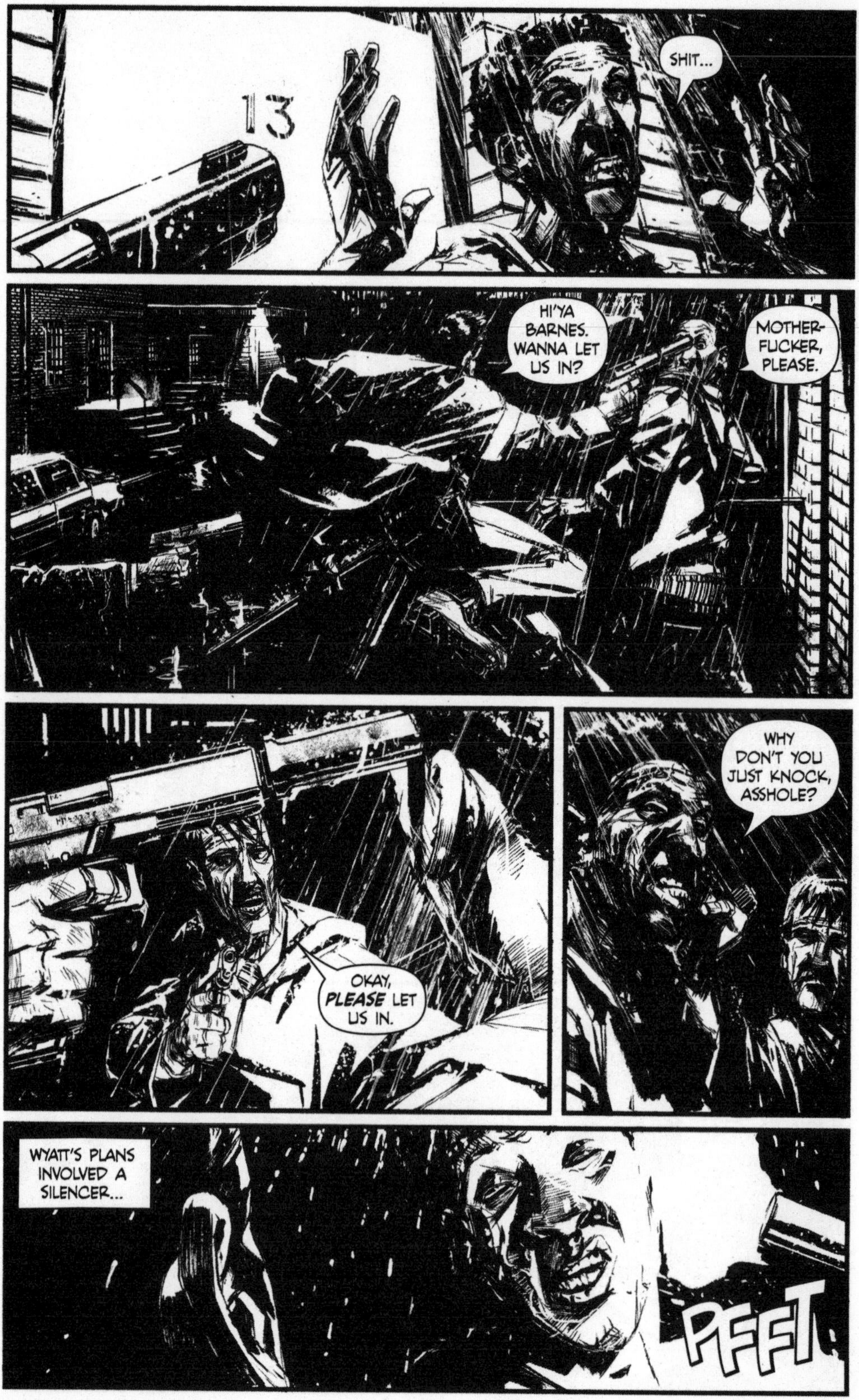

13
SHIT...
HI'YA BARNES. WANNA LET US IN?
MOTHER-FUCKER, PLEASE.
OKAY, PLEASE LET US IN.
WHY DON'T YOU JUST KNOCK, ASSHOLE?
WYATT'S PLANS INVOLVED A SILENCER...
PFFT

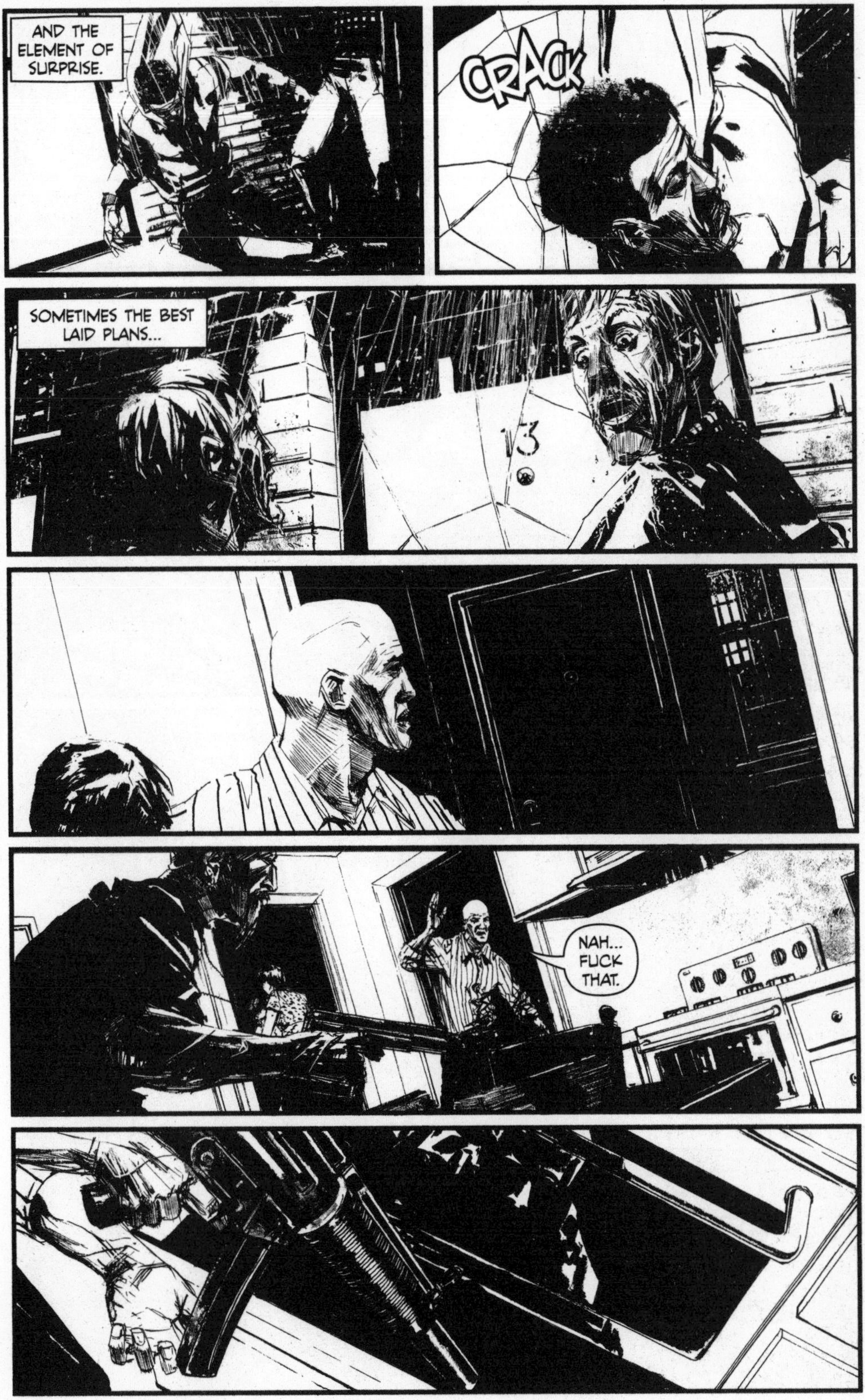
AND THE ELEMENT OF SURPRISE.
CRACK
SOMETIMES THE BEST LAID PLANS...
13
NAH... FUCK THAT.

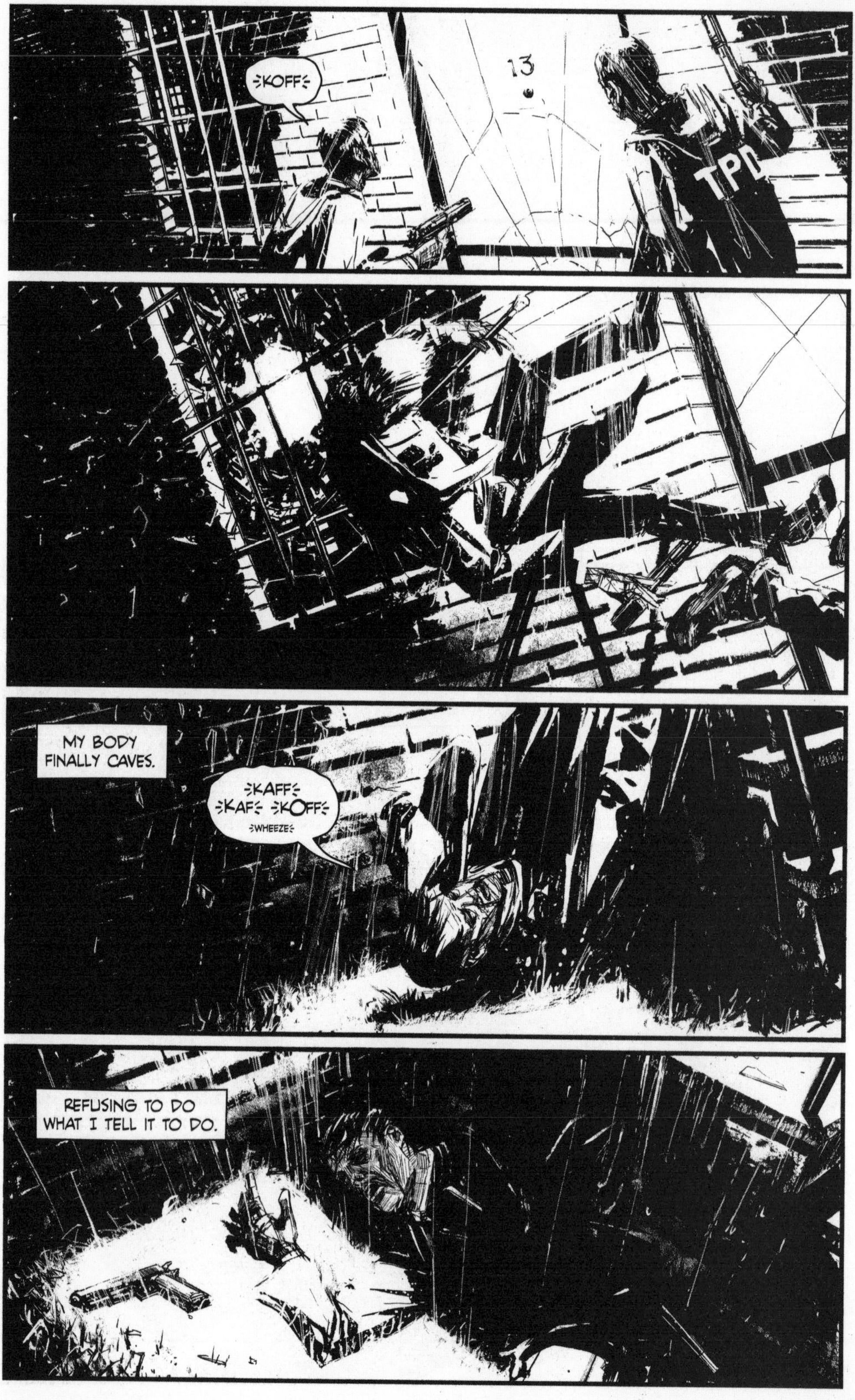
KOFF
13
TPD
MY BODY FINALLY CAVES.
KAFF
KAF KOFF
WHEEZE
REFUSING TO DO WHAT I TELL IT TO DO.

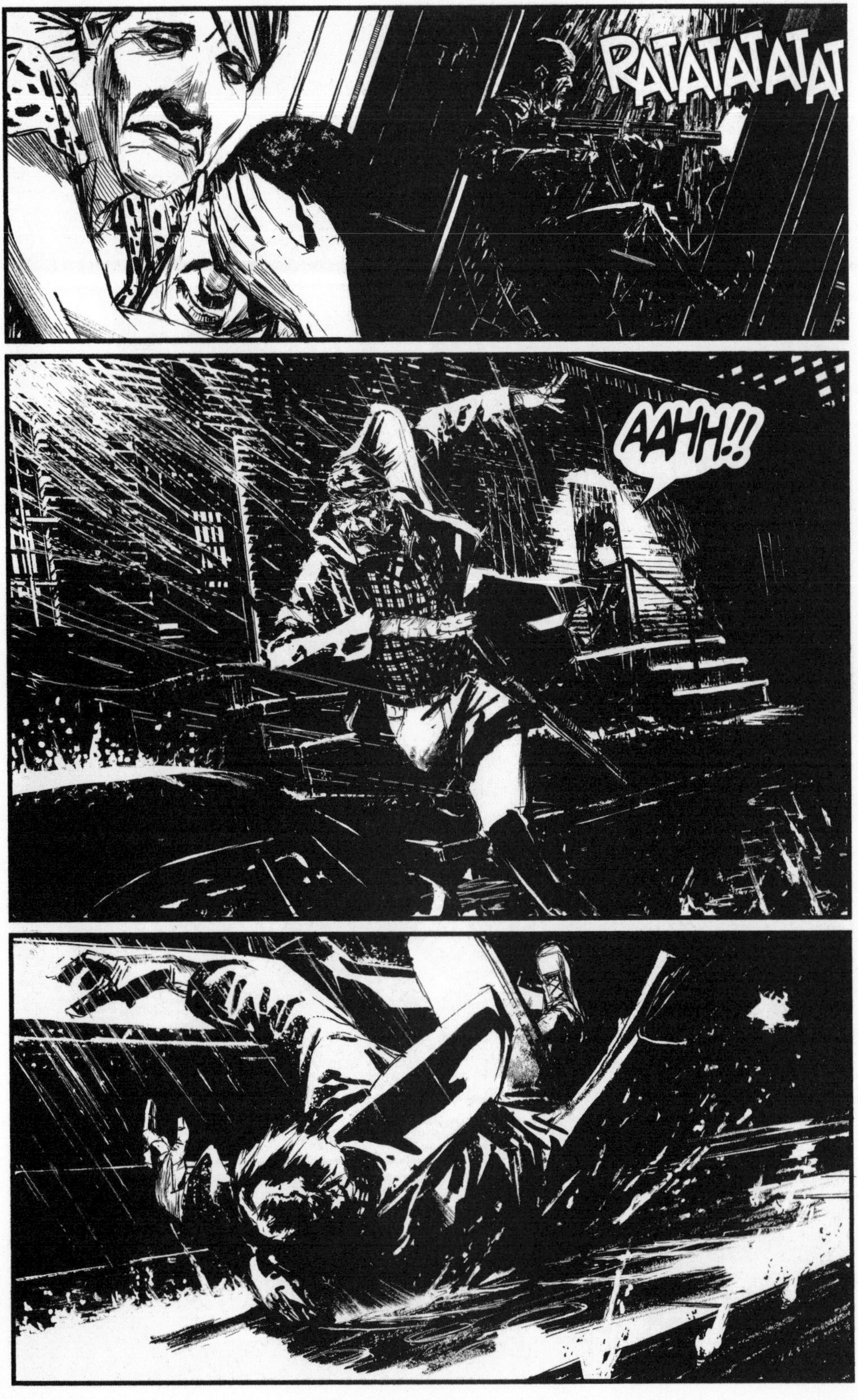
RATATATATAT
AAHH!!

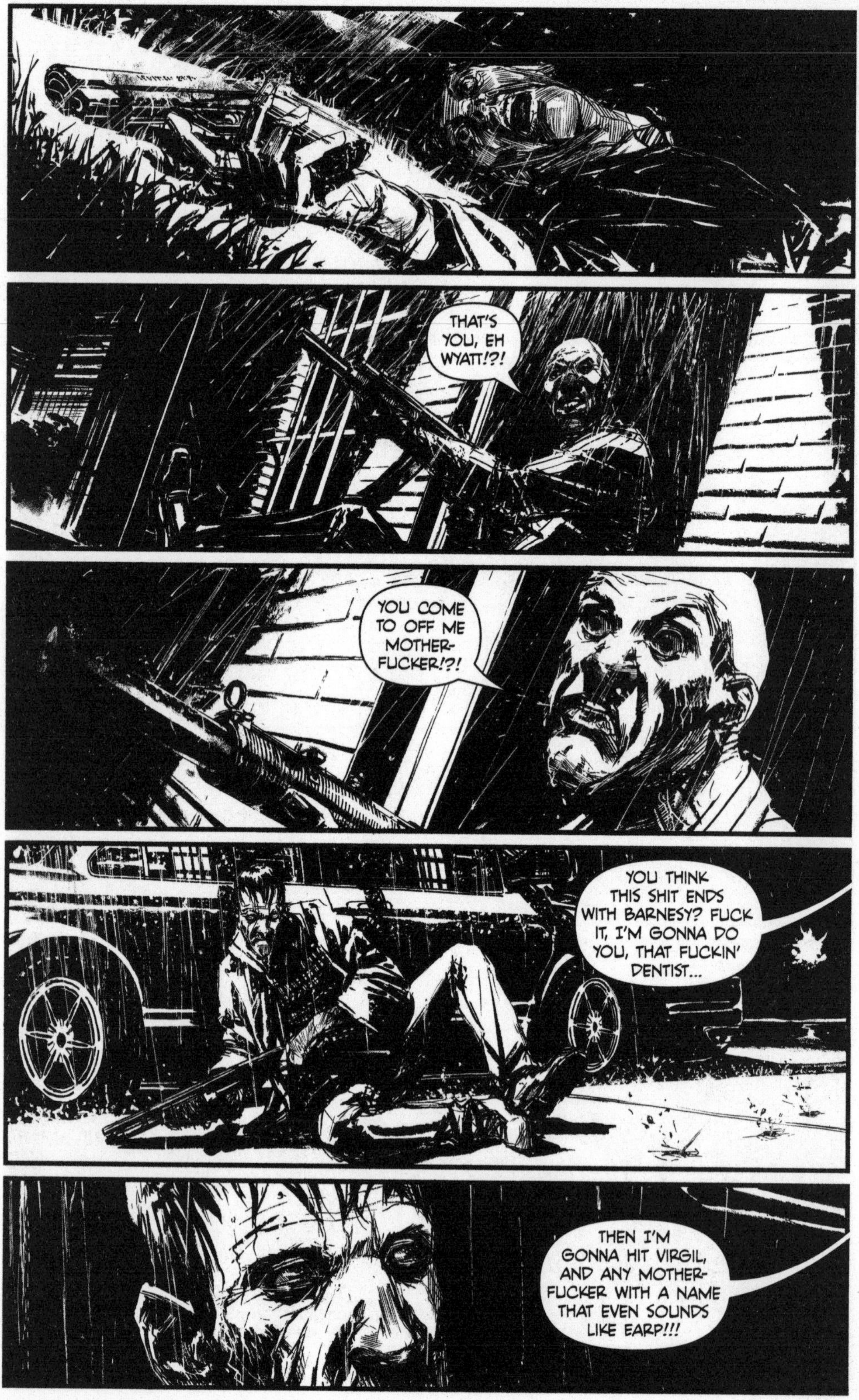
THAT'S YOU, EH WYATT!?!
YOU COME TO OFF ME MOTHER-FUCKER!?!
YOU THINK THIS SHIT ENDS WITH BARNESY? FUCK IT, I'M GONNA DO YOU, THAT FUCKIN' DENTIST...
THEN I'M GONNA HIT VIRGIL, AND ANY MOTHER-FUCKER WITH A NAME THAT EVEN SOUNDS LIKE EARP!!!

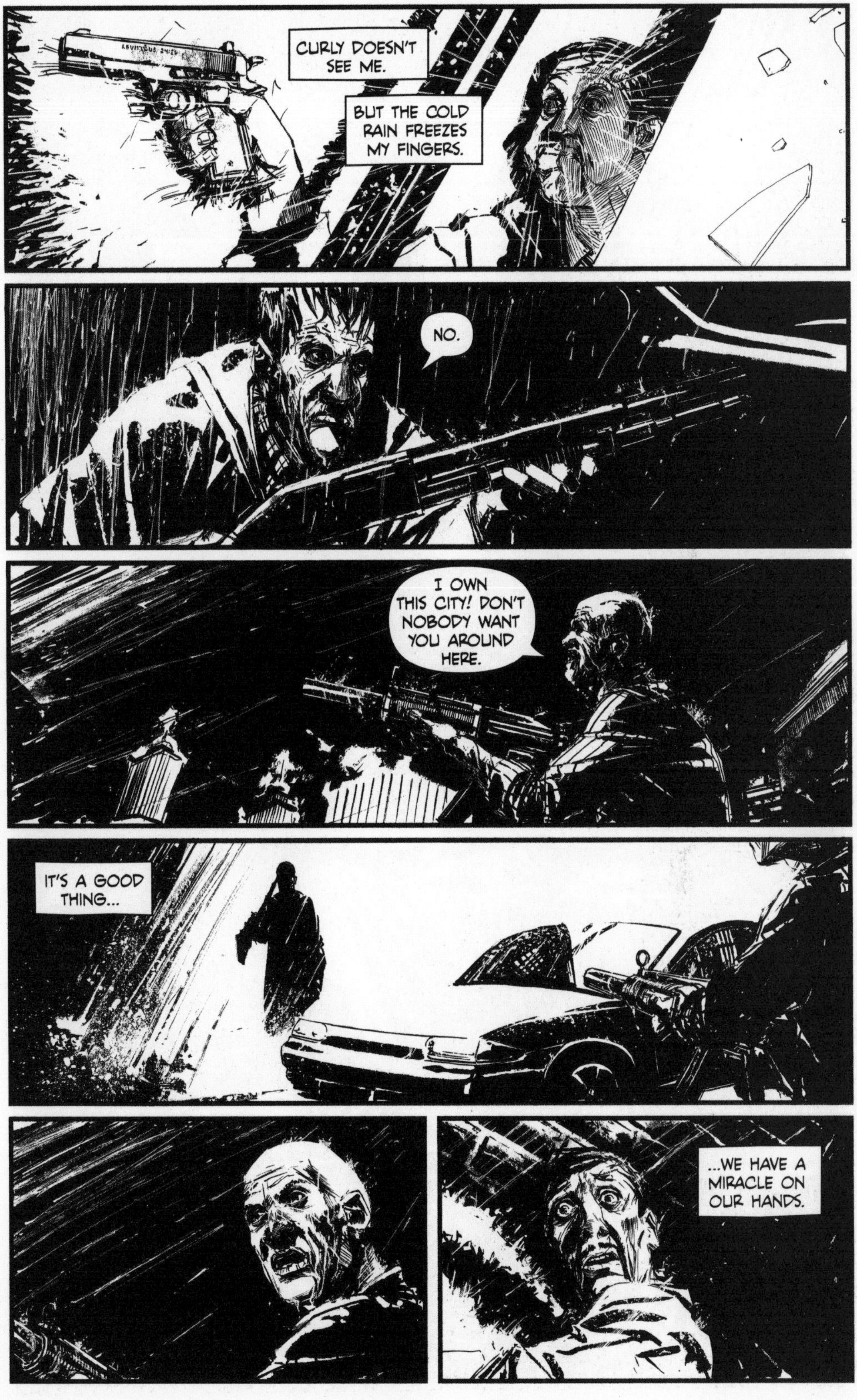
CURLY DOESN'T SEE ME.
BUT THE COLD RAIN FREEZES MY FINGERS.
NO.
I OWN THIS CITY! DON'T NOBODY WANT YOU AROUND HERE.
IT'S A GOOD THING...
...WE HAVE A MIRACLE ON OUR HANDS.

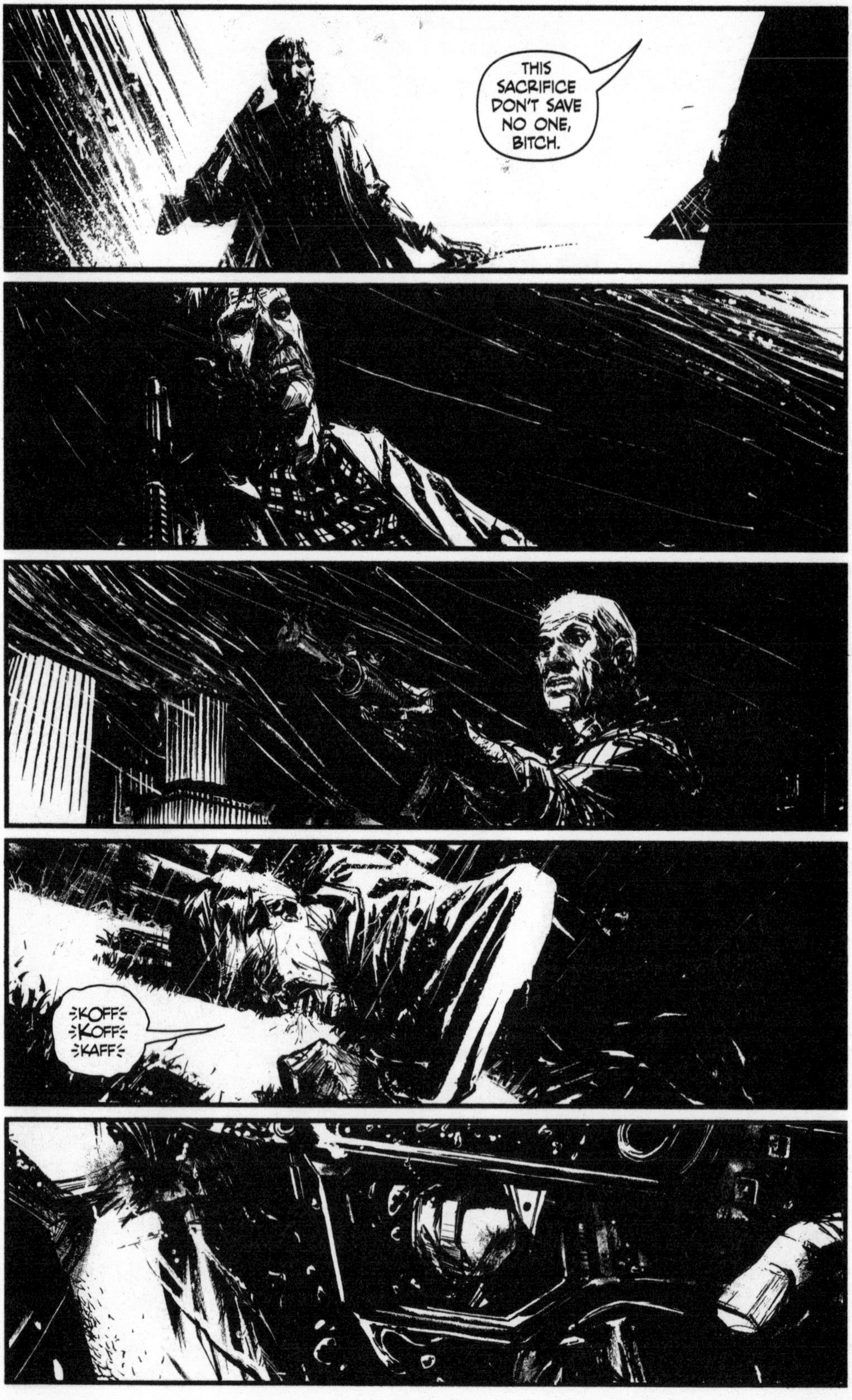
THIS SACRIFICE DON'T SAVE NO ONE, BITCH.
KOFF KOFF KAFF

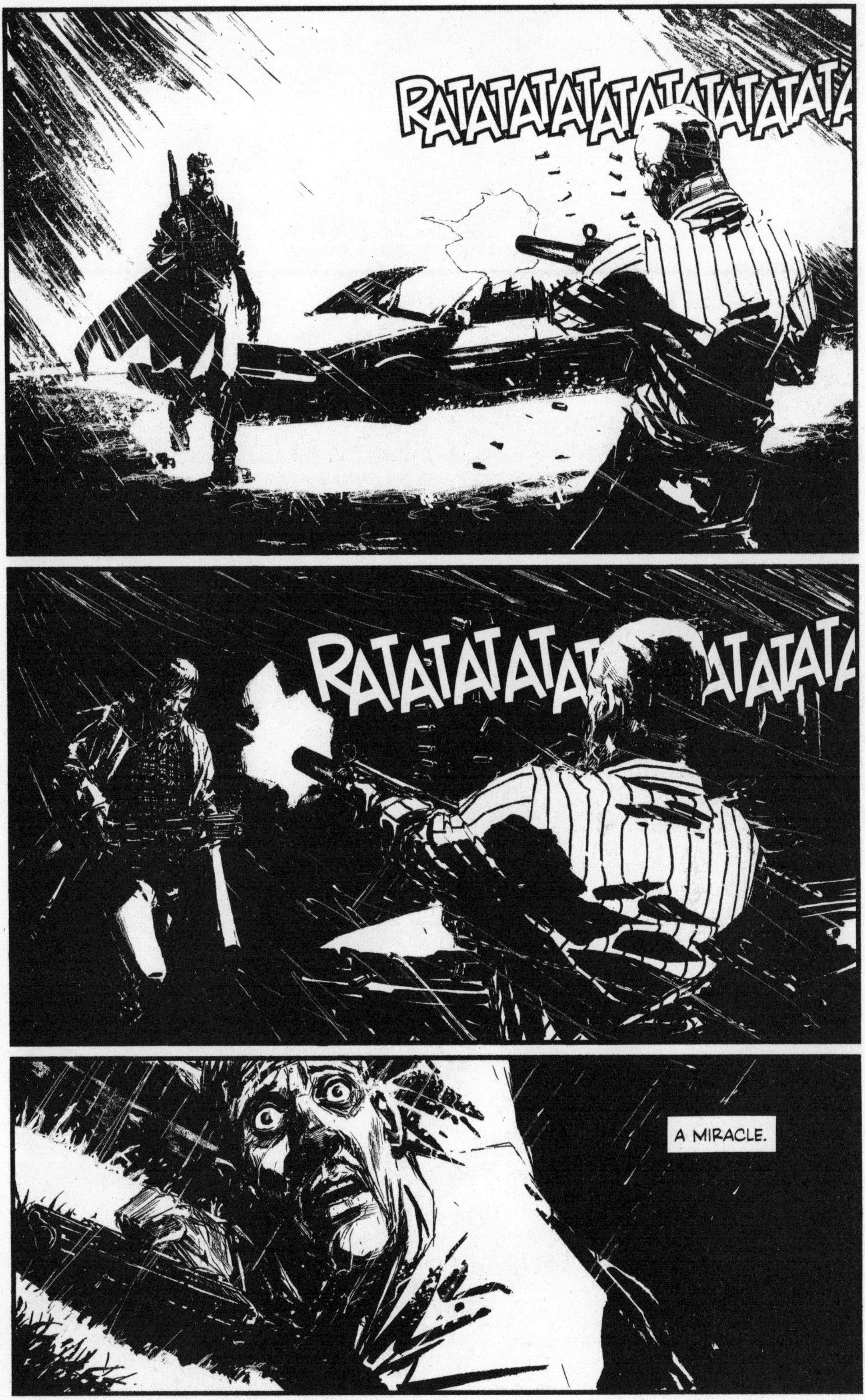
RATATATATATATATATATATA
RATATATATAT ATATATA
A MIRACLE.

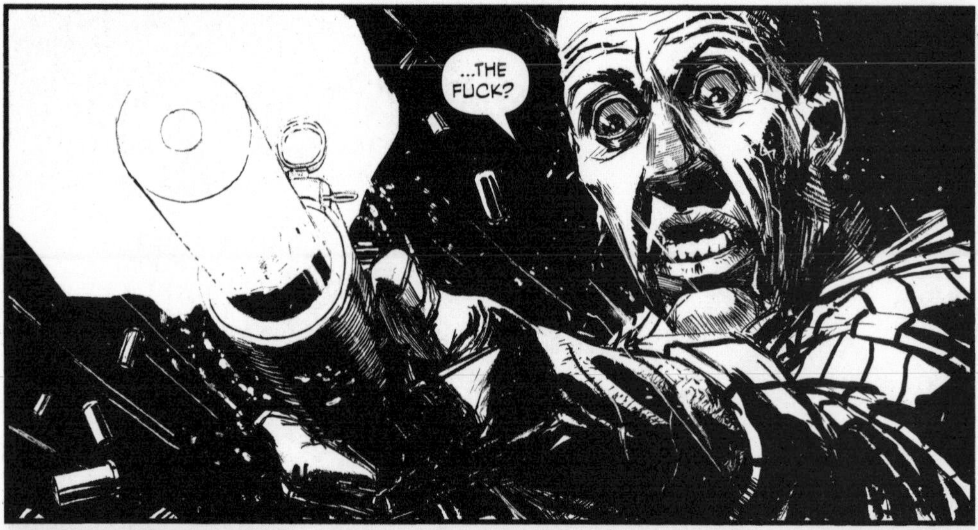
...THE FUCK?

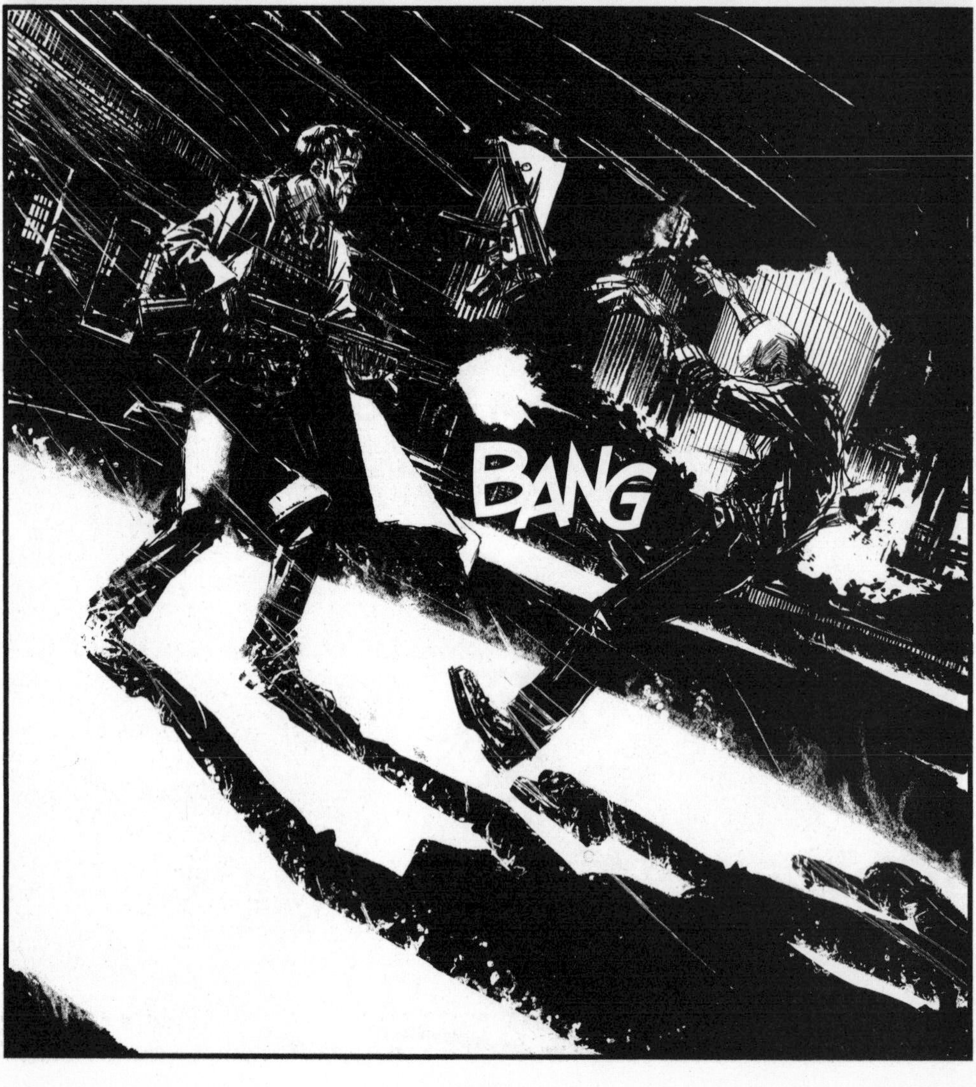
BANG

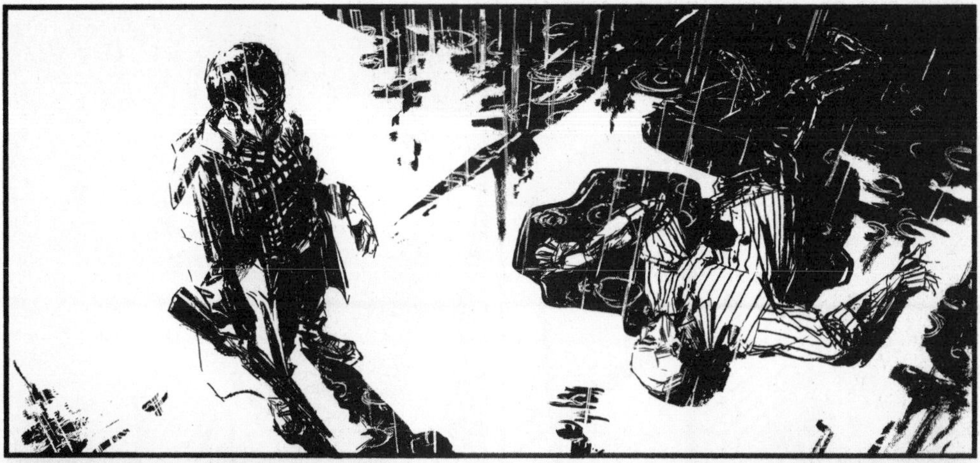

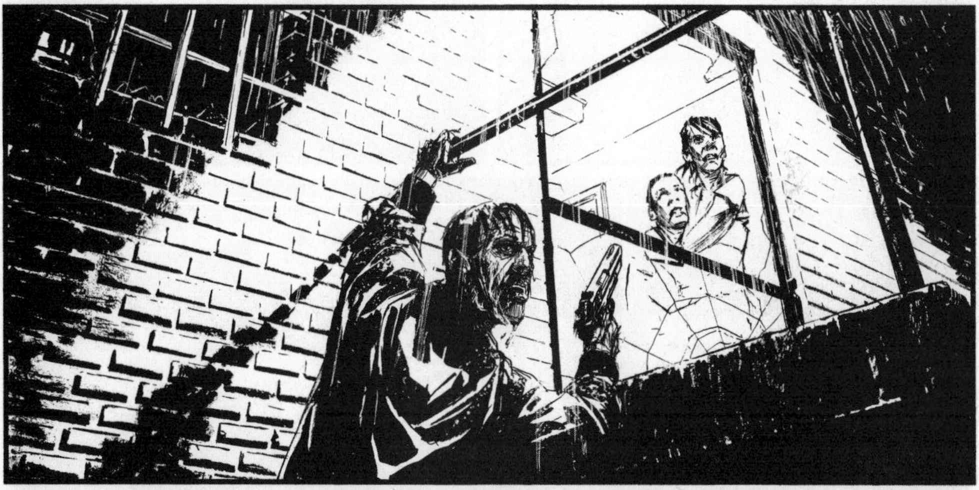

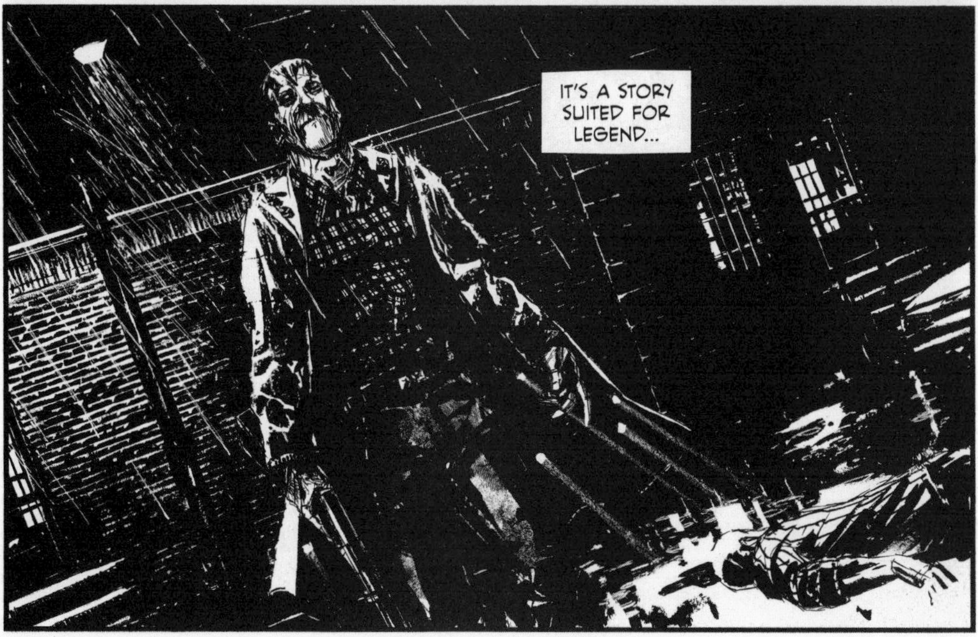
IT'S A STORY SUITED FOR LEGEND...

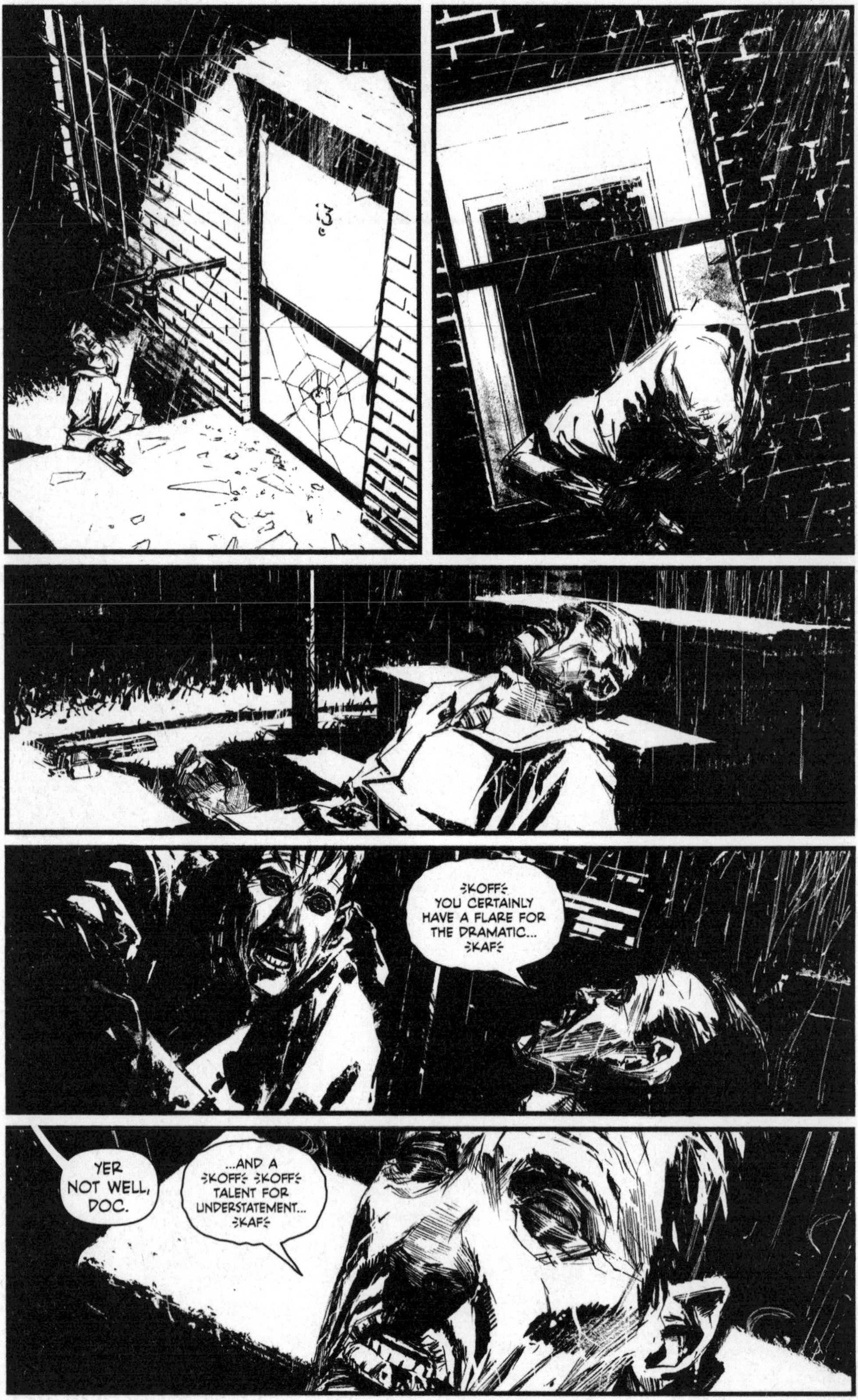
13
KOFF YOU CERTAINLY HAVE A FLARE FOR THE DRAMATIC... KAF
YER NOT WELL, DOC.
...AND A KOFF KOFF TALENT FOR UNDERSTATEMENT... KAF

Then.

EPILOGUE

Now.

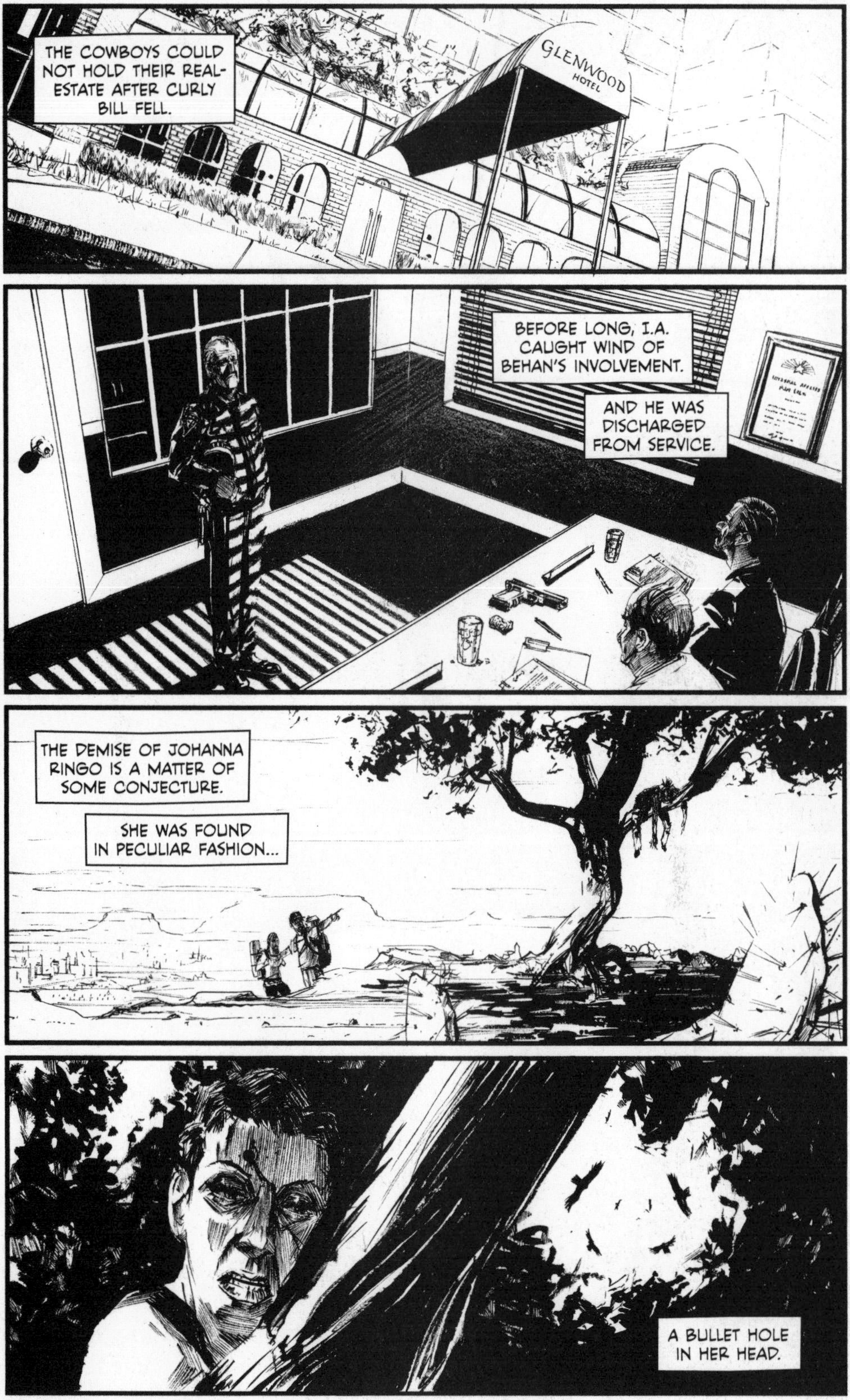
THE COWBOYS COULD NOT HOLD THEIR REAL-ESTATE AFTER CURLY BILL FELL.
GLENWOOD HOTEL
BEFORE LONG, I.A. CAUGHT WIND OF BEHAN'S INVOLVEMENT.
AND HE WAS DISCHARGED FROM SERVICE.
THE DEMISE OF JOHANNA RINGO IS A MATTER OF SOME CONJECTURE.
SHE WAS FOUND IN PECULIAR FASHION...
A BULLET HOLE IN HER HEAD.

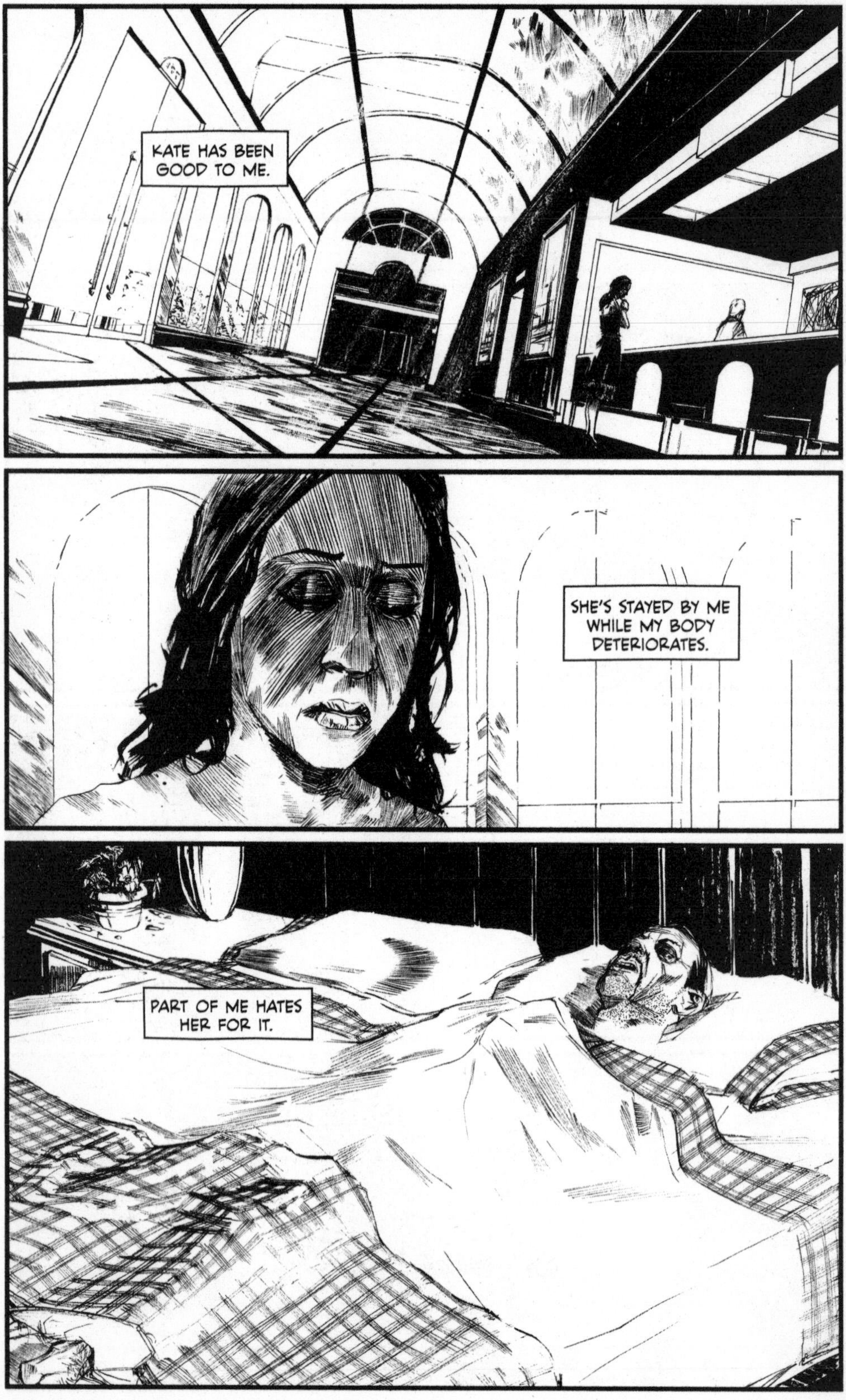
KATE HAS BEEN GOOD TO ME.
SHE'S STAYED BY ME WHILE MY BODY DETERIORATES.
PART OF ME HATES HER FOR IT.

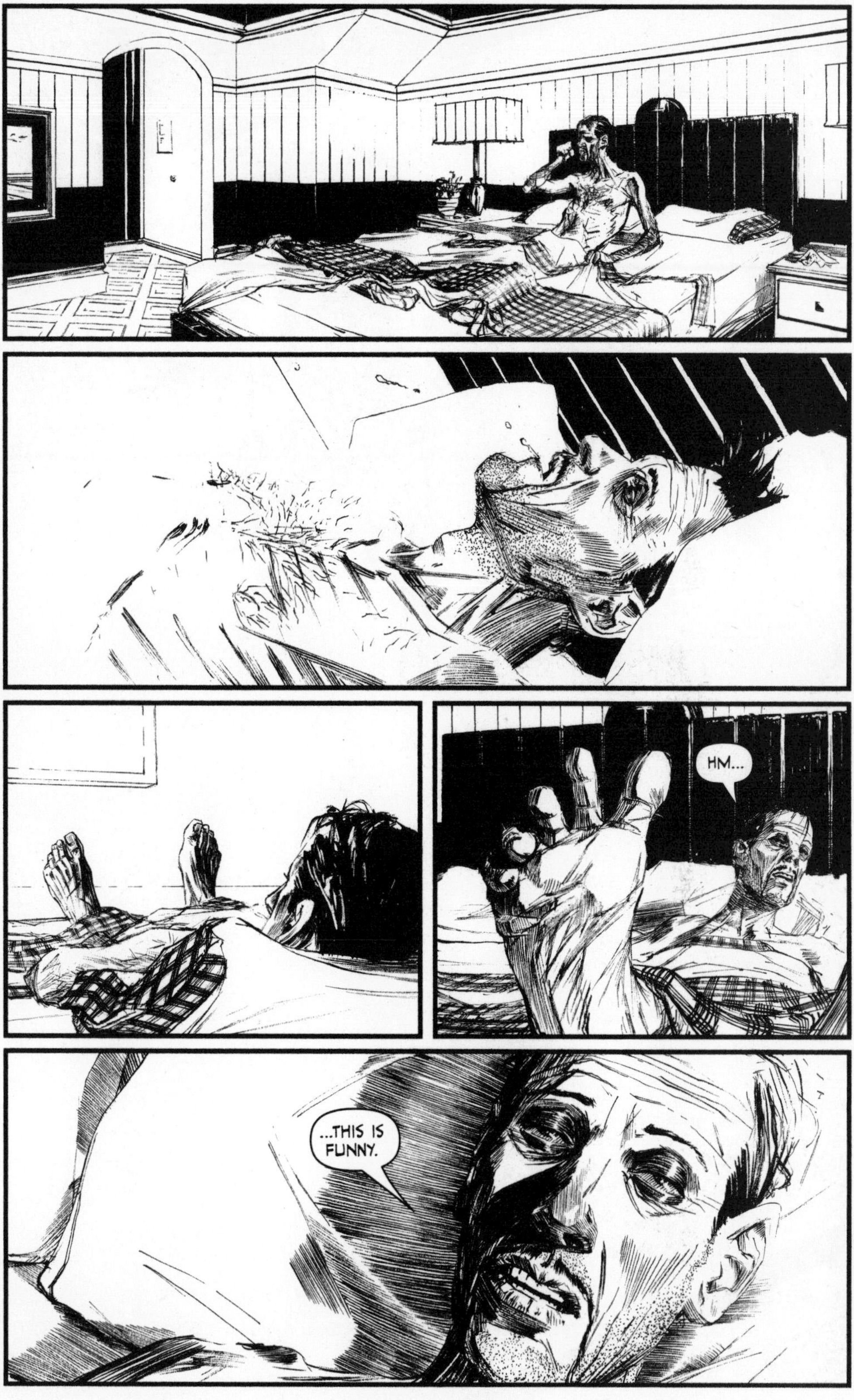
HM...
...THIS IS FUNNY.

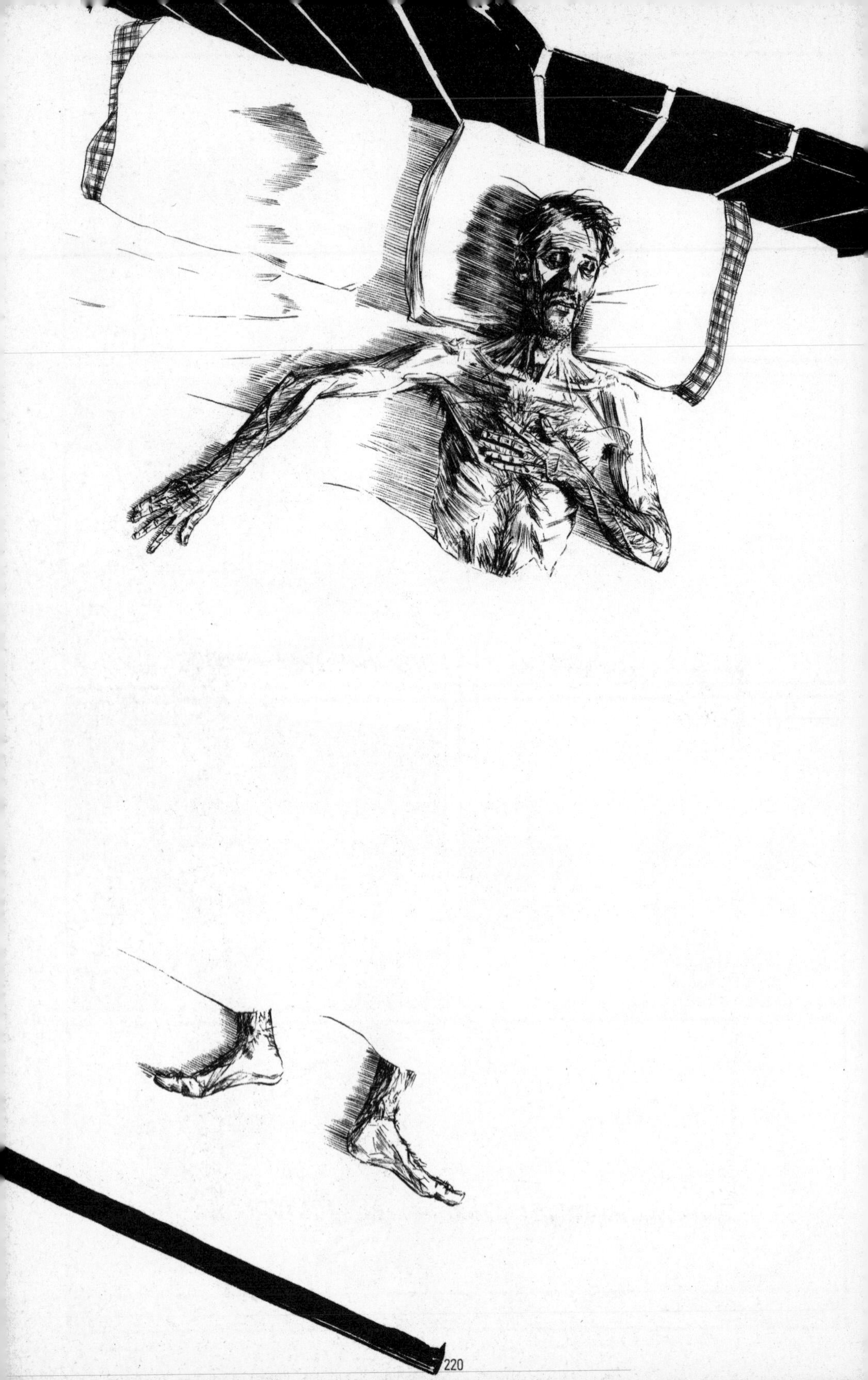

NATE BOWDEN

On the wall in Nate Bowden's tiny Savannah office hangs the quote: "The first draft of anything is shit." As Hemingway suggests, Nate works tirelessly at the art of story. He draws inspiration, if not influence, from great storytellers such as Gene Roddenberry, Jim Henson, David Simon and especially Aaron Sorkin.

After starting out self published under the label FishStick Comics, Nate contributed to a *Star Trek* anthology and produced two volumes of the graphic novel series *Riding Shotgun* for TokyoPop. Additionally, he has served as an editor and story consultant for several popular web-comics.

THANKS TO:
Many thanks go to Jill Beaton and James Lucas Jones for all their hard work.

Special thanks to Ross Campbell.

To my parents and family for encouraging a kid to draw funny-books and my wife, Jami Stone Bowden for her support, and who am I forgetting?… Oh!

Ryan, Steve, Ebeth, Brandon, Stuart, Jacob, Daniel, Lindsay, Tracy, Luis, Doug, Mimi and…

Doug Dabbs for his truly stunning artwork. Unbelievable.

DOUG DABBS

Doug Dabbs was born in Nashville where he was raised by his basset hound with the help of his parents. He is known for having a very dry sense of humor that usually causes looks of confusion. Doug Dabbs sometimes writes in third person to make it seem as though someone else is stating facts about him. He is the coolest guy on earth.

Doug currently lives in Atlanta with his beautiful and talented wife, Nicole, and is a full time professor at SCAD-Atlanta teaching sequential art and foundation studies. Doug solely survives on watching soccer, eating peanut butter and jelly, drinking coffee, and regular viewings of *The Wire*.

THANKS TO:
First of all, I would like to thank you, the reader, for purchasing *Holliday*. I hope you enjoy the book as much as I loved illustrating it. A lot of work, time, and emotion went into its creation and it definitely would not have been possible if it weren't for some extremely important people. Thank you to my talented and beautiful wife Nicole—the art of *Holliday* would not have been what it is without your support, feedback, patience, and belief in me. To my parents and sister, your continual encouragement and love means more than you know and I wouldn't be here without you. Thank you to Joe Spann and Ben Gooch, whose mutual childhood love of comics pushed me to pursue my dream of becoming a comic book artist. A special thank you to Shawn Crystal for teaching me everything I know and inspiring me to teach, and to Chris Schweizer for providing feedback and brainstorming sessions. I would also like to thank James Lucas Jones at Oni Press for believing in me and Jill Beaton for being an amazing editor.

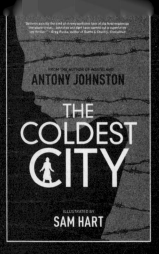

THE COLDEST CITY
Antony Johnston & Sam Hart
176 pages · 6"x9" · Hardcover
B&W · $19.99 US
ISBN 978-1-932664-87-4

DAMNED, VOL 1: THREE DAYS DEAD
Cullen Bunn & Brian Hurtt
160 pages · 6"x9" · TPB
B&W · $14.99 US
ISBN 978-1-932664-6-38

GHOST PROJEKT
Joe Harris & Steve Rolston
152 pages · Hardcover
Color · $19.99 US
ISBN 978-1-934964-42-2

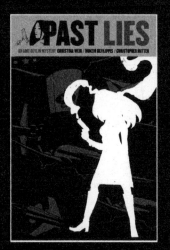

JULIUS
Antony Johnston & Brett Weldele
160 pages · Digest
B&W · $14.95 US
ISBN 978-1-929998-80-7

PAST LIES:
AN AMY DEVLIN MYSTERY, VOL. 1
Christina Weir, Nunzio DeFilippis,
& Christopher Mitten
160 pages · Hardcover
B&W · $19.99 US
ISBN 978-1-934964-39-2

WHITEOUT, VOL. 1:
THE DEFINITIVE EDITION
Greg Rucka & Steve Lieber
128 pages · 6"x9" · TPB
B&W · $13.95 US
ISBN 978-1-932664-70-6

For more information on these and other fine Oni Press comic books and graphic novels, visit www.onipress.com
To find a comic specialty store in your area, call 1-888-COMICBOOK or visit www.comicshops.us